FEEL THE FLOOR

FEEL THE FLOOR

RESTORING THE LIFE AND LEGACY OF JAZZ CHOREOGRAPHER BUDDY BRADLEY

MAUREEN FOOTER

BEACON PRESS, BOSTON

BEACON PRESS
24 Farnsworth Street
Boston, Massachusetts
www.beacon.org

Beacon Press books
are published under the auspices of
the Unitarian Universalist Association of Congregations.

Printed in the United States of America

29 28 27 26 8 7 6 5 4 3 2 1

This book is printed on acid-free paper that meets the uncoated paper ANSI/NISO specifications for permanence as revised in 1992.

Text design and composition by Kim Arney

Library of Congress Cataloguing-in-Publication
Data is available for this title.
Hardcover ISBN: 978-0-8070-4524-4
E-book ISBN: 978-0-8070-4525-1
Audiobook: 978-0-8070-2332-7

FOR

Thong Nguyen
My Thaddeus Drayton,
Billy Pierce, and
Charles B. Cochran
all in one.

If the secret is beat upon the drum,
the secret will be revealed in dance.

—YORUBA PROVERB

CONTENTS

INTRODUCTION

Listen to my feet and I will tell
you the story of my life.

—JOHN BUBBLES

In 1932, when Noël Coward approached Harlem dancer turned choreographer Buddy Bradley to stage his new revue, *Words and Music*, he had high expectations. Coward gravitated to the chic and cutting edge, so it was only natural he sought out the hottest choreographer in London. But he had no clear vision of the dances he wanted—and, frankly, it was just as well. Buddy Bradley's pinwheeling opening number for *Words and Music*, blending white Eton jackets and West End sophistication with Hoofers' Club traditions of male dance authority, low-down gestures of the Baltimore Buzz, and the arching stance of the Cakewalk, was unlike anything London had ever seen, or even imagined, dance could be. The first-night audience erupted in applause before even a single Coward witticism had been uttered. That night, Bradley once again redefined what dance could be.

In a career that began in the Harlem Renaissance and spanned decades on stages, film sets, and nightclubs on both sides of the Atlantic, Bradley pushed the boundaries of dance. He introduced jazz dance to theater, where he revitalized fusty mincing and parading with movement that aligned with the new jazz sound. He brought jazz-trained bodies to George Balanchine and Frederick Ashton, thereby assisting in the creation of neoclassical ballet. He was an early pioneer of dance on film, devising techniques that made dance seen in picture palaces more intimate and immediate, more akin to live dance onstage. Through his legendary dance school in the West End, he implanted American rhythm tap throughout the British Empire. In his nearly forty years overseas, he worked at the Folies Bergère in Paris; in nightclubs in Spain, Italy, and Germany; and, via the global reach of British film, telegraphed his aesthetic to all four corners of the Earth. Bradley was the international emissary of jazz dance.

But, even more than an ambassador, Bradley was an adventurer. Just as he resisted the predetermined expectations imposed on him as a Black man, he challenged preconceived categorizations of dance. He refused to pigeonhole his work, to adhere to others' notions of what Black dance, tap dance, or theatrical dance should be. (Like Martha Graham, he recognized only two kinds of dance: good and bad.) All the while, as he ushered African American dance into new spheres, he found new tools in his encounters with ballroom, ballet, folk dance, and mime to heighten his own choreographic expression. In doing so, he proved that tap dance could be romantic as well as percussive, that jazz dance could reveal character and tell stories, and that both could be integrated into book musicals. Alongside talents like Hermes Pan and Fred Astaire, Bradley blazed the trail in musical theater that Agnes de Mille and Jerome Robbins built into a road, one that Twyla Tharp, Camille Brown, and Justin Peck explore to this day. He had but one criterion for jazz dance: that it never be separated from jazz music.

Bradley, as his obituaries noted in 1972, was a visionary ahead of his time. Today, musical theater could hardly move if stripped of the grammar of African American dance that Bradley introduced nearly one hundred years ago. Yet archives, records, catalogues raisonnés, bodies of criticism, and books have somehow failed to document his achievements. Art, until recently, was what happened in conservatories, not on musical comedy stages, nor in film, nor—heaven forbid!—in nightclubs and on street corners. It didn't help that Bradley was soft spoken and reserved, just the type of gentle personality that would be mangled in our noisy age of soundbites and social media, or that he operated from London, outside the artistic cauldron of

New York and beyond the gaze of America's dance critics, the gatekeepers of dance history. Of course, being Black only made it easier for him to recede from view.

It was at a colloquium at the Fashion Institute of Technology that I first learned of Bradley. When Theresa Ruth Howard, founder of the Memoirs of Blacks in Ballet project, alluded to the revolutionary influence of someone named Buddy Bradley on the work of George Balanchine, I sat up a little straighter. As a lifetime balletomane, I had read extensively on Balanchine and could not recall a single word written about Buddy Bradley. Even when, a few years later, a magisterial biography of Balanchine appeared, it glossed over Bradley in a single phrase, as "the legendary tap and jazz man." How strange this all was to me; there are endless books on Balanchine, Martha Graham, and Frederick Ashton. Why was there no written history of this transformative creator?

I was immediately intrigued. Then, after months of preliminary digging and contextual research, I was impassioned and, yes, incensed. Yet, I asked myself if I had the right to tell this story. I flew down to consult with Dr. Thomas DeFrantz, then at Duke University, and came away realizing the urgency of the task: no one else was collecting Bradley's story. Not only did we all benefit from knowing Bradley's life and work, but if I did not find Bradley's remaining colleagues as soon as possible, so much of the story would be lost forever. With this support, and consulting many, including Bradley's family, who could help me sensitively access this story, I proceeded.

The fact that Buddy Bradley was a legend cloaked in mystery made him all the more enticing. Even the Jerome Robbins Dance Division of the New York Public Library—the largest dance library and archive in the world—had virtually nothing to offer as I began my journey. My search to understand this man and his talent next led me to the genealogical room at the New York Public Library, the Schomburg Center for Research in Black Culture (also at the NYPL), and the archives of the African American press. Slowly, I began to piece together an outline of Bradley's life, his story in New York, and the shows he had choreographed on Broadway.

In Britain I began a parallel search, scouring archives and periodicals in the British Library, delving as far as I could in the frustratingly closed-for-renovation dance collection at the Victoria and Albert Museum, running queries in *The Stage* and *The Call Boy* for actors and dancers who had worked with Bradley, and sifting through stacks of yellowing theater programs in the Westminster Archives. I traced every name of every dancer who appeared in any Bradley project, a search that often dead-ended with an obituary. As most nonagenarians (eighty-year-olds were mere striplings in my search for a man who had died in 1972) have little virtual presence, I had to hire private investigators to help recreate the trail. Rushing against the clock, aware that these stories could disappear forever in a blink of an eye, I flew back and forth between New York and London, anchoring myself in Bradley's neighborhoods in London, traveling to seaside towns to interview Bradley's former dancers, capturing stories that made Bradley come alive, making wonderful new friends, and sometimes triumphantly exiting with a new lead.

I walked to all of Bradley's flats, schools, and theaters, imagining the shops and squares, the sights and sounds that populated his experience. There were hours in the underground screening rooms of the British Film Institute with "Basement Steve" Tolevy, threading and scrutinizing reel after reel of undigitized Bradley movies, with former Bradley dancers and Ashton experts sometimes squeezed into the viewing room with me. There were lunches at the Ivy with a choreographer, a Bradley student from the 1950s; in a glow of red wine, we went to the former Bradley School of Dance on Denman Street and imagined it circa 1955. I dug deep into the Noël Coward Archive Trust and came up with some astonishing footage; parsed theater reviews for clues of Bradley's dancing; scrutinized photos in old theater magazines to analyze the poses, gestures, and patterns of Bradley's stagings; and froze-frame every Bradley dance sequence on YouTube. In a quest that led to actors' retirement homes and villas in Brixton, reaching as far as Arizona and South Africa, a man, three dimensional, living, and breathing—and very charming—slowly emerged and accompanied me on a five-year journey.

Again and again, I marveled not only at his huge talent but also his generous spirit. How did a thirteen-year-old orphan escape the confines of Jim Crow Birmingham and embark on a journey of such creativity, tenacity, and resilience? How did he find the poise, the acumen, the wherewithal to blossom despite the constant obstacles of race? How did he gather the strength to give up his community in New York to lead a life apart in London for nearly forty years? How did he remain, despite everything, so open and so kind? Bradley left no diaries, writings, or letters to reveal his soul. Instead, my clue to finding these answers came from James Baldwin, another Black expatriate, who reminded me in *Notes of a Native Son* that it is the past, our ancestors, that makes the present coherent. I looked beyond Bradley, the artist, and into his family to understand him.

Bradley's secrets were revealed to me in visits to the small town in the Blue Ridge Mountains, where he was born on property owned by his mother's family since before the Civil War. They were whispered among gravestones in cemeteries in Gainesville, Alabama, in documents found in a dusty courthouse in Sumter County, Alabama, in shotgun houses, flimsy schools, and urban decay in Birmingham, Alabama. In these distant corners, light years from Bradley's cosmopolitan existence in New York and London, Bradley's character was forged. I learned the resolve and pith of an extraordinary great-grandmother, a free person of color in Georgia, as well as the supple creativity of his paternal grandfather, a formerly enslaved man who took a tiny legacy from his enslaver (his father) and parlayed it into a wholesale trading business on a river that flowed down to Mobile, and the determination and dignity of Bradley's own parents, both of whom died at horribly young ages, overcome by hardship and injustice.

Bradley's invention and brilliance, his diplomacy and kindness, his discipline and his reserve, his creativity and talent, it turned out, were the heritage of elders who had steered through slavery and its aftermath in America. The path he explored through dance reveals not only his story but one of a family, of a legacy, and of African American history. Like his grandfather, Bradley took his birthright and shaped it to his dreams—dreams that shaped, indelibly, more than one country's cultural life and legacy.

Several years into this project, I found a letter written by Bradley to Marshall Stearns in 1963, buried in a metal file cabinet at the Institute of Jazz Studies at Rutgers University. Glancing at this seemingly banal document to notice only clarification on a few details for Stearns's magnum opus, *Jazz Dance*, I dutifully photocopied it and continued my research. Only months later, combing through my notes, I came upon the sentence that made my heart stand still: Bradley longed to tell his story. Would Stearns write it?

Three years after that letter, Stearns was gone; his own book unfinished. His wife, Jean, would shepherd *Jazz Dance* posthumously into production. Bradley's story remained untold. At that very moment, as I held the copy of his letter in my hand, Bradley and I came into alignment. It became my mission to tell his story, to piece his life back together, to bring his work, in all its vital impact and importance, back to the conversation where it belongs.

I'm hoping he is dancing in the firmament as you read this.

PART 1

SOUTHERN RHYTHMS, 1838–1920

CHAPTER 1

ANCESTRAL WHISPERS

And so our mothers and grandmothers have,
more often than not anonymously, handed on
the creative spark, the seed of the flower
they themselves never hoped to see.

—ALICE WALKER

Long before Buddy Bradley was born, in 1905, the die was cast. For nearly a century, his ancestors had defied the restrictions placed on Black peoples' lives, overcoming obstacles with invention and resilience, and establishing patterns of agency that Bradley, in turn, would inherit. In the early nineteenth century, Bradley's maternal great-grandmother, Harriet Allen, already exceptional in her status as a free Black woman in the antebellum South, embarked on foot along faint dirt paths from Pendleton (now Pickens) County, South Carolina, to acquire her own farm land in Habersham County, Georgia—a journey that would shape her family for generations.[1]

Three hundred miles away and a generation later, in the Black Belt of Alabama, Bradley's paternal grandfather, the formerly enslaved Robert Louis Epes, established a trading house in the late 1860s in Gainesville, Alabama, a key stop on the river route to Mobile. What traces we can reassemble of his life—a graceful carved tombstone, an enslaver's will, a wholesale liquor distribution license—testify to supple creativity that defied societal limitations and expectations.

If knowledge is power, knowing one's ancestry confers subconscious power. With his grandmother's status as a free person of color, and his grandfather's more complex status as the natural son of his enslaver, Bradley was unusual among African Americans: he could trace his family, name by name, to the early nineteenth century. In their claim to full rights of citizenship and individual expression, Harriet Allen and Robert Louis Epes bestowed an invaluable birthright.

From the very beginning, Buddy Bradley was swaddled in family legacy. He was born as Clarence Bradley Epps (the spelling of the last name varied over the years and also appears as Epes; by Bradley's father's generation, it was most frequently spelled as Epps) on July 24, 1905, in the very place Harriet Allen had set down roots, surrounded by cousins. Clarkesville in Habersham County, Georgia, had not been a random destination. When Harriet Allen set out on her walk from South Carolina, sometime in the late 1830s, accompanied by her sister, Polly, as well as a horse, cow, calf, and hogs, she had a distinct goal in mind. Twenty-one years before the California gold rush, the discovery of gold in northeast Georgia made this former region of the Cherokee—now banished via the infamous Trail of Tears to Indian Territory west of the Mississippi—glisten with opportunity. It also represented a frontier, one not yet rigid with established practices and social hierarchy, where a person of ambiguous legal and social status might construct a future.[2]

Most importantly, land was available. Like W. E. B. Du Bois, Allen grasped that land represented food, shelter, stability, and a key to autonomy. Unlike the fertile soil of Georgia's Piedmont region, which suited large-scale cotton cultivation, the rugged terrain of Appalachia lent itself to tenacious small farmers. The mountainous geography, with romantic scenery, waterfalls, and flora and fauna at every turn, also made Clarkesville a resort for those from southern and central Georgia seeking respite from summer heat, as well as residents of Savannah and Charleston escaping summer bouts of malaria in the low country, and provided opportunities for hotels, small enterprises, and skilled labor that catered to the seasonal visitors.[3]

Record-keeping in the rural South, spotty at best, was nearly nonexistent for people of color—a fact fully evident when assembling Harriet Allen's sketchy origin story. Before she left South Carolina, Harriet appeared in a census as a member of the household of Betsey Allen. Harriet, described as "mulatto," was light skinned, seemingly with Caucasian features, suggesting that Betsey and Harriet Allen may have been half-sisters, sharing the same father and surname. (Just as possibly, however, Harriet used the family name of her enslaver and the given name of a member of the white family—both common practices for African Americans at the time.)[4]

If Betsey and Harriet were half-sisters, was Harriet's mother enslaved or freed? To ensure the continuation of an enslaved population, children inherited the legal status of their mother. Whether Harriet's freedom was inherited or conferred, one thing, however, is crystal clear: "free" or not, Harriet did not have the same rights and privileges under the law as Betsey Allen.

Though it may have seemed a salvation, the legal status of free people of color was problematic: they were threats to societal conventions. Morally, their existence represented a reproach to slavery. Practically, it was feared that their freedom might inspire others to seek liberation. After free man of color Denmark Vesey led a rebellion of slaves in Charleston in 1822, and as antislavery arguments became more heated, the restrictions on free people of color increased. Harriet would have to surmount each of these barriers.

As always, taxes were more than a way to raise public funds; they were a means of control. Dauntingly high taxes were intended to discourage enslaved people from aspiring to free status, reenforcing the narrative that Black people were better off when they had room, board, and taxes assumed by white owners. Prior to the Civil War, in Georgia, where Harriet paid tax, the annual head tax for the average white male citizen was twenty-five cents, while free people of color paid a whopping twenty times that amount: five dollars, the sum paid by professionals like doctors and lawyers.[5]

Constantly hovering over Harriet's head, taxes also served as a mechanism to return free Black people to a state close to slavery. In Georgia, if a free person of color could not pay his or her tax, the state could place the individual into servitude, withholding wages until the debt was settled. Harriet's sister, Polly Allen, might very well have encountered this issue: by 1850 she had returned to Pendleton County and the relative safety of familiar terrain.[6]

Watching her sister retreat might have shaken Harriet Allen's confidence. After all, she was just as vulnerable, an outsider and a Black woman venturing into parts unknown and facing an intimidating tangle of laws and bureaucracy intended to daunt her. She had no family to rely on. She was most likely illiterate. The only resource she had to fall back on was her own labor and the handful of livestock she had brought to Habersham County. But Harriet, in adversity, proved resilient and determined.

Gaining a legitimate foothold in this new environment required not only cash but an oppressive level of compliance. Not having ready money, Harriet most likely had to work for others as she set about establishing herself. Further, she needed a court-approved guardian to represent her legally, which, predictably, imposed another annual fee. Even as she became a landowner and mother of ten, Harriet, as a free person of color, retained an inferior status. Effectively, she was a minor in the law's eyes, with no voice. She had to be represented in all transactions by a white man, who possibly neither understood nor particularly cared about her situation.[7]

But such was the reality, and Harriet was a realist. She marshaled her forces and did what she needed to do. For a few years, she appears to have lived "under the radar," without a guardian, her life an uneasy parallel with undocumented workers in America today. Five years after her arrival in Habersham, in July 1845, after saving the necessary funds, finding a potential guardian, and drawing up the requisite documents (this itself complicated for a woman who probably could not read or write), Harriet Allen petitioned for William B. Shelton to guarantee her and her children, with bond set at one hundred dollars. The Sheltons were a prominent family in Clarkesville. Whether by coincidence or an instinct for self-preservation,

Harriet Allen had aligned herself with influence while navigating the system.[8]

Despite the bureaucratic complications and the arduous business of simply getting by, Harriet never lost sight of her goal: acquiring land. As the Civil War raged, and six months before General Sherman marched into Georgia, Harriet Allen purchased sixty-one acres in Habersham County for $244 in cash. In an agrarian economy, property was the source of independence: if you could grow what you needed, barter for what you didn't have, and sell just enough to pay taxes, you could survive. As she could not own property outright, Harriet paid a second guardian, Andrew J. Nichols, to purchase land in his name, then place it in her hands for use. She had become, despite the odds and a deliberately convoluted legal structure, a Black landowner.[9]

Harriet had ten children—most, if not all, with Mat Ivie, a free man of color born in Virginia who (by inference, as the document trail again goes faint) arrived in Clarkesville at roughly the same time. After Harriet was baptized in the white Bethlehem Baptist Church, worshipping in the Baptist Church became part of the family's experience. After her death, sometime prior to 1880, Mat continued to farm the sixty-one acres, dispersing them to the next generation upon his death.

In addition to her land, Harriet's children inherited her pragmatism and intentionality. Some followed closely in her footsteps. Various sons helped work the farm. Daughters, too, tended to stay close to the land. Charlie Ivie, one of the youngest siblings and Buddy's great-uncle, began acquiring parcels of land in the late 1800s, amassed three hundred acres, and lived until 1928.

Harriet's eldest daughter, Lizzie, named after Betsey Allen in South Carolina, would become Buddy Bradley's grandmother. Lizzie had the acumen of her mother: over the years she accumulated thirty-eight acres and two houses, married twice, and sustained a large extended family. Her youngest child, Georgia, born in 1880, would be the mother of Buddy Bradley.

Like Harriet, Lizzie was a strong matriarch. When one daughter died, Lizzie, now fifty-nine, took the three youngest children into her care. When Robert M. Epps, the husband of her daughter, traveled out of state in search of work, Georgia and her two young children, Robert and Ernestine, joined Harriet's household. It was in this house in the hills of Georgia, teeming with life, resolution, and cousins—the material heritage of Harriet Allen—that Georgia's second son, Clarence Bradley Epps, the future Buddy Bradley, was born in 1905.

Grandchildren and future generations lived Harriet Allen Ivie's legacy, acquiring land, pursuing security, and participating in the life of the community, always in pursuit of bettering themselves and their lot. One of Charlie's daughters married a skilled craftsman, a plasterer who founded a thriving family business and lived lavishly in town. A granddaughter married an enterprising bricklayer, who established the rambling bathhouse just outside of town that catered to the moneyed summer folk. Others fanned out to Atlanta, Birmingham, and Columbus, Ohio, as the economy shifted from farming to industry. Great-grandson Buddy Bradley would migrate to Harlem, then cross oceans, revolutionize theatrical dance, and bring jazz movement, rooted in Black dance traditions, to twentieth-century ballet.

Great-great-granddaughters would attend Spelman College and the US Air Force Academy; *their* granddaughters would become state debate champions and attend law school, carrying the torch Harriet had ignited on her walk across state lines and into agency.

CHAPTER 2

FATHERS AND SONS IN THE BLACK BELT OF ALABAMA

We read the future by the past.

—REV. ALEXANDER CRUMMELL

Northern Sumter County in the Black Belt of Alabama—so called for the dark, rich soil that lent itself so amenably to cotton cultivation—was only three hundred miles from Habersham County, Georgia, yet a world apart. Though hardly older than Habersham County with its up-from-the-bootstraps opportunism, Sumter County's traditions were forged in seventeenth-century Virginia. Younger sons of the plantation aristocracy from Virginia, prohibited by laws of primogeniture from inheriting family land, flocked to the Black Belt for new opportunities, often bringing with them the enslaved individuals who would tame Sumter County's soft hills and forests and replicate the established mores of Virginia. This was the world that Buddy Bradley's grandfather, Robert M. Epes, was born to—one that was seemingly immutable and forbidding for a Black man.[1]

For the white man who was Bradley's biological great-grandfather, however, Sumter County was a godsend. A proverbial younger son of a Virginia tobacco-growing family, Richard Junius Epes, in his twenties, first tried his luck in Georgia but found the land already showing signs of decline, depleted from successive seasons of cotton growing. Infinitely more promising was Sumter County, Alabama, virgin agricultural territory that had recently opened for white settlement when the Choctaw signed the Treaty of Dancing Rabbit Creek in 1830 and mournfully departed their beautiful ancestral lands. The soil of Sumter County, too waxy to be tilled with the light tools of the small farmer, favored plantation practice, drawing on an abundance of manual labor—the apanage of an enslaver. The combination of climate, soil, and resources lent itself superbly to growing cotton, which dovetailed with the surge in demand from the recently industrialized mills in England.[2]

Despite such auspicious circumstances, Richard Junius Epes hovers on the margins of Sumter County history. Though related to the celebrated Randolphs of Virginia, Richard Junius Epes displayed a diffident lack of purpose. Perhaps he was conflicted; the Epes records are problematic.[3]

Unlike the enterprising first settlers who arrived in Sumter County around 1833 and snapped up the best tracts of land as soon as the Choctaw territory was available—initiating the first land boom in the United States—Epes languidly arrived somewhat later. He ended up purchasing land on the secondary market in Jones Bluff (now the town of Epes), and, while the deed of sale is lost, he may have acquired the property of the ill-fated James Jones, the half–Native American for whom the town was named, who had been deeded the land in the Dancing Rabbit Creek treaty but was swindled out of it, killed, then dumped unceremoniously in the Tombigbee River. Epes continued to accumulate land, and over time his holdings would stretch halfway across the county, from Jones Bluff to Sumterville.[4]

Despite his large tract (in 1850 he owned one thousand acres—one of the largest plantations in the vicinity) and a labor force of ninety, Richard Junius Epes's plantation was a lackluster performer. In what was arguably the most productive cotton-producing land in America, and where cotton was indisputably the money crop, Richard Junius Epes produced an abysmal five bales of cotton in 1850, in contrast with his neighbor, John W. Dial, who produced over ten times Epes's output on one-fifth the land. Perhaps Epes was an inept farmer or lacked business acumen. Eschewing cotton, for whatever reason, Epes devoted most of his arable land to raising livestock (cows, sheep, swine) and victuals (wheat, corn, oats, and sweet potatoes).[5]

Nearly every aspect of Richard Junius Epes is shadowy. In 1843, Epes was commissioned colonel of the Third Division, Sixth Brigade, in the state militia of Jones Bluff, then reelected to the same commission in the Confederate Army in 1861, but he does not appear to have served in the Civil War. From the showy Masonic square and compass carved on his obelisk marker in the neglected Old Side Cemetery, behind Bethany Baptist Church in Sumterville, we know Epes was a Mason—but this, too, is hardly distinguishing for a white American male of privilege in the eighteenth and nineteenth centuries. Not only are twenty-one signers of the Declaration of Independence believed to have been Masons (and George Washington incontestably one), but the fraternal creed of anti-royalty, freedom, free enterprise, and a limited role of state were fundamental to the framing of the Constitution and Bill of Rights. Somewhat mystifyingly, Epes was also a bachelor, a curious fact in a conventional environment, especially given the isolation of plantation life.

Only one fact about Richard Junius Epes is unambiguous: he was an enslaver on a significant scale. The 1850 US Census records him as the head of a household of two white males and seventy enslaved, including a five-year old boy. In 1860, he listed eighty-eight enslaved people in his household, including a fifteen-year-old male, whom we can reasonably assume is the same person as the five-year-old child listed ten years earlier. (The dates of this young man correspond exactly with those of Buddy Bradley's grandfather.) Some of his enslaved had accompanied him from Virginia. (Correspondence with his brother in Virginia, dated 1848, indicates that Richard Junius had brought with him Suky, his childhood nurse.) Others he purchased. At least five others he had sired, violently or not, with enslaved women.[6]

The day before he died, on December 24, 1865, Richard Junius signed a hastily drawn will. Perfunctory but explicit, the will begins with five specific bequests to young, formerly enslaved, mixed-race members of his household, all of whom he designates as "yellow." For two girls, presumably daughters, Epes designated money for two years of school. For three boys, he left animals and commodities.[7]

The attention Epes gives to these bequests is revealing. Though these gifts appear paltry, even degrading, they reflect poverty more than stinginess. By the time Lee surrendered at Appomattox, the South was decimated: fields neglected, crops negligible, infrastructure and roads destroyed, markets inaccessible, and Confederate money devalued—though bills and taxes were still owed. Richard Junius Epes was now close to destitute. His money was worthless, his acreage had plummeted in value, and he had sold half of his land. A cow, a bushel of corn, or even a saw was not only practical but infinitely more valuable than handfuls of worthless Confederate currency or taxable unyielding soil.[8]

Even more significant is that Epes, on his deathbed, singled out these five young people among the dozens of formerly enslaved people living on his plantation. Knowledge of plantation practices and convention, and the specific context of Richard Junius Epes, tells us that these mixed-race people are his children. Epes's second listed beneficiary, Bob, a "yellow boy of African descent who waited on me," is of particular interest. Bob received from Epes a yellow mule (also named Bob) and a cow. Notably, too, Bob is yellow and a house servant, a relatively preferential position customarily reserved for "favored" women and illegitimate children. Though much about Richard Junius Epes is opaque, his dotted connection to Buddy Bradley is transparent: he is Robert "Bob" Louis Epes's father and, therefore, Buddy Bradley's great- grandfather.

Though technically free since Emancipation in 1863, twenty-year-old Bob remained in the Epes household until Richard Junius's death in 1865. Did Robert Louis Epes stay because, in rural Alabama, there were no obvious alternatives for a young Black man, especially one who had never worked the land? Did he stay because the US government sent a federal officer shortly after surrender to read a proclamation to freedmen, gathered on the courthouse steps at the county seat of Livingston, encouraging them to stay with their former owners, even without wages, so that they would not become financial charges to the public? Or did he stay out of a sense of loyalty, or even some vague hope that he might be recognized as a son? Even without formal acknowledgment of his paternity, Robert Louis Epes seems plenty astute. Observant of the ways of plantation culture, aware of his lighter complexion, cognizant of his role within the household, perhaps apprised by his mother, he may well have known exactly who his father was. It was, at any rate, a highly ambivalent situation: on the one hand, he was privileged but materially dependent; on the other, humiliated and enslaved to his father.[9]

While the death of Richard Junius Epes signaled a new beginning for Robert Louis, how to create an independent life in Sumter County remained enigmatic. The year 1865 coincided with the beginning of Reconstruction, one of the most equivocal chapters in American history, when promise hovered in the air but the realities on the ground changed little, if at all, in the South.

The resistance to Reconstruction in the South was hardly surprising. Its very economy depended on its caste system, where cheap (preferably, free) Black labor fueled its profits. In Alabama, the hostility was literally incendiary. Several churches in Mobile had been burned down. There were continual threats to destroy Black property. There was no support for enfranchisement or education. (One wonders what happened to Robert Louis's two sisters and their bequests of two years of schooling.) In desperation, Blacks assembled in Mobile in 1866 and called upon Congress for concrete measures to make their freedom secure.[10]

Robert Louis Epes's recourse was to stand proud. Living in unsettled times, surrounded by uncertainty, and hampered by limitations, Robert, like Harriet Allen, chose his course. He prioritized exercising his civil rights as a freeman. He registered to vote in Precinct 14, the twenty-first election district, for Sumter County. At age twenty-three, in 1866, he married, availing himself of an institution long withheld from African Americans.

His twenty-one-year-old bride, from nearby Gainesville, bore the African name Satanna, suggesting that her family was but a few generations away from Africa. Married in Gainesville on November 14, 1866, by a Baptist minister from England, Robert Epes and

Sattie Scott had a son, Robert M., one year later. Walter G. followed in 1869, Willie J. in 1870. No record reveals where the Epes family lived in town—a fire destroyed much of Gainesville and its records in 1886—but town maps suggest they lived in the active center of town, where Blacks, whites, residences, and businesses coexisted.[11]

Unlike the vast plantation lands that characterized Sumter County, Gainesville, with its white clapboard houses, picket fences, and bank with a patent to print US money, looked like New England, albeit with groves of pecan trees. To this day, locals refer to Main Street as "Yankee Street," a reference to the flood of New Englanders whose mercantile instincts flared when Alabama opened to white settlement. A prime position on the Tombigbee River had made the town a busy commercial hub, which led to its development as the third largest city in the state and a regional seat of culture.[12]

Before the war, more cotton was said to load on steamboats in Gainesville than anywhere in the country, testifying to both the productivity of Alabama Black Belt soil and the enslaved people who cultivated it. Boats from Gainesville then made their way downstream to Mobile, transferred to ships heading to points east, and ultimately fed the textile mills of New England and England. On the return journey, the boats brought furniture, flour, sugar, molasses, coffee, textiles, French ribbons, English bone china, sheet music, and books from New York, Boston, and even London, offering glimpses of another universe to little Gainesville. As mercantile interest flourished, a hotel, a steam gin, a grist mill, trading houses, liveries, milliners, pharmacists, physicians, skilled craftsmen, and small tradespeople thrived, making Gainesville a tiny but buzzing empire unto itself.[13]

All his life, Robert Louis Epes had toggled between two worlds: that of the Big House, with its mores of Southern plantation culture and those of his people, removed from their culture and families. He was conversant in the received pronunciation of the ruling caste and fluent in the African-inflected English of the quarters. He could wait on a table, inventory silver, or maintain a gentleman's wardrobe just as easily as partake of a shout. He could neither read nor write, for these skills were prohibited for enslaved people, but he was adept at practical skills—interacting with a wide range of people, managing supplies, knowing how diverse people lived, and anticipating what they needed.[14]

Now Robert Louis marshaled his resources to build a business in Gainesville, his new home. Perhaps he drew support from the local Friendly Society, a group of Black and white men that invited local white attorneys, government officials, and even ex-Confederates to counsel freedmen on citizenship and opportunities. He certainly benefited from the practical Yankee origins of Gainesville, a town less inclined to wail about the Lost Cause and more disposed to get on with the pursuit of profit. Less interested in retaining the old two-tier society, and anxious to regain its old momentum, Gainesville was an inviting arena for someone with a keen instinct for transactions.

How did this young man, not yet thirty, limited in exposure, untutored, and only recently released from a rigid hierarchy (which effectively still existed in Sumter County), have the vision, courage, and wherewithal to undertake such an adventure? Did Robert barter his meager patrimony (the yellow mule named Bob and the cow) for capital to set up his business? Whether or not this was his father's intention, it was a natural thing to do for one with no experience of farming—to sell the livestock, move to a town, and partake of a business that matched local opportunities with one's talents. His undertaking is extraordinary in its intentionality.

Even more extraordinary is that he was successful. Although the 1870 US Census describes him as a merchant, it is misleading to think of Robert Louis eking out a living selling nails and penny candy. Instead, as he was awarded a wholesale, rather than retail, liquor license, the record suggests he operated a trading house, instead of a retail store. His business capitalized on the river trade in Gainesville, not the mundane needs of a small town.[15]

Robert Louis Epes's scantily documented life poses intriguing questions. He died at age twenty-seven on March 22, 1873. The cause is not known—Alabama did not systematize death certificates until 1908. Equally puzzling is the fact that he is the only African American buried in the white section of Gainesville's Old Cemetery, also known as the Confederate Cemetery.

Upon her young husband's death, Sattie ordered a graceful gravestone, with a sculpted pediment, extensive text, and a deeply carved flower. The elaborate workmanship suggests that Epes's life had been materially comfortable. The family's circumstances, however, had been dependent on the cash flow from Robert's business. Sattie, now a young widow with three little boys under the age of six, moved in with her mother, Dilla, a laundress in town. Yet, even without money, Robert Louis Epes had left a legacy that would shape both his son and grandson, just as his own father's legacy, material and immaterial, had propelled his own life forward. His son Robert would inherit his resourcefulness and tenacity. His grandson Buddy would not only inherit these gifts but also his grandfather's fluidity, creativity, and ability to cross borders.

CHAPTER 3

POST-RECONSTRUCTION: EXPLORATIONS BEYOND HOME

We build our temples for tomorrow.

—LANGSTON HUGHES

When the Tallulah Falls Railroad whistled into Clarkesville, Georgia, in the mid-1880s, it swept fundamental changes into the sleepy mountain town. News now traveled quickly via a daily US postal bag or the telegraph line that ran alongside the railroad tracks. Strangers, too, now filtered in and out of Habersham County, intermingling with local communities and offering glimpses of possibilities once unknown. One of the lives that would be transformed by the prospects, uncertainties, and urban challenges ushered in by the train was that of Georgia Walker, Lizzie Walker's youngest daughter and Buddy Bradley's mother, born in 1880. Her life, vaulting from the agricultural nineteenth century to the industrial twentieth century, would have been unrecognizable and unimaginable to her intrepid grandmother Harriet Allen.

While the train expanded Clarkesville, it sealed the fate of Gainesville. As trains now hurried cotton to ports, river trade in Gainesville withered, stunting commerce, plunging the population to a spectral 175 citizens, and strewing in its wake a handful of genteel white houses with magnolia trees and shuttered churches. Most dramatic of all the changes wrought by the railroad system latticing the South was human mobility: individuals now sought opportunity well beyond their place of birth. One of those individuals was Robert M. Epps, the eldest son of Robert Louis and Sattie Epps, and the future father of Buddy Bradley.

Young Epps was six when his father died and the relative security of his life evaporated. Growing up in Gainesville, Robert and his younger brothers, Willie and Walter, learned to read and write, but it is doubtful they received more than a perfunctory education. In 1868 the overextended and underfunded Freedmen Bureau had recommended a school for the town and its two hundred African American children, but it never materialized. Instead, in 1869, the county and state wrested control of schools, delivering a blow to education for children of color. Liberal teachers were run out of town (some in Sumter County were even murdered), and the school Robert attended was consequently understaffed and poorly equipped.[1]

By the early 1880s, as Gainesville's economy was fading, Sumter County's future remained tied to agriculture. Robert's options for earning a livelihood locally were to become a fieldhand, sharecropper, or laborer. Like his father, Robert had no experience—or evident interest—in farming. After all, with its attendant peonage, it was hardly different from slavery. Unlike his father, who had served in the household of a planter from Virginia, Robert had grown up in simpler circumstances and probably did not share his father's facility for bridging cultures. Yet young Robert had two tools at his disposal that his father had not: literacy and mobility. Somewhere, somehow, Robert sidestepped the conventional path allocated Black men in the nineteenth-century South and became a brick mason.

Robert's choice of bricklaying, which required agility, stamina, precision, mathematical skill, and aesthetic judgment (skills his son Buddy would inherit and employ in a different métier), suggests a character that was exacting and determined. His decision, too, may well have been prompted by the fact that, in 1865, the bricklayers' union was among the first to admit African Americans, of which Robert seems to have become a member. Besides advocating for safer conditions and better pay, the union provided an additional perk and sign of changing times: a union travel card, which vouched for the competence of the bearer, fostering the brick mason's ability to travel and find work in far-flung venues.[2]

Traveling, Robert's lifeline to work, was not easy or comfortable. When, in 1892, African American Homer Plessy refused to sit in a train car for Black people, the Supreme Court responded with the *Plessy v. Ferguson* ruling, constitutionally legalizing segregation in 1896. Despite the soot, heat, lack of hygienic amenities and luggage storage (suitcases had to be crammed at one's feet), humiliation, and perpetual reminder of second-class status, Robert was determined to work and took full advantage of his union travel card to do so. He turns up at various times in Alabama, Georgia, Tennessee, and Illinois, his persistent travels indicating his resolve.

In the 1890s, a major construction project was brewing in Clarkesville: the Habersham County courthouse on the town square, the most prestigious location in town. The courthouse, with its Victorian brick structure of three stories, gabled roof, and four corner turrets, was a plum project for a mason. Robert, now a capable craftsman in his late twenties, most likely learned of the opportunity from his union network and hopped on a train. Working in Clarkesville was a local brick mason, Joseph Parker, similarly ambitious and entrepreneurial, who also happened to be married to Sadie Thompson, Lizzie Walker's oldest daughter.

It is likely that the two men, engaged in the same trade and both of enterprising temperament, became friendly, and that, through Parker, Robert Epps met Sadie's half-sister, Georgia Walker. Georgia, like her ancestors, was grounded, hardworking, and, probably, pretty. Like Robert, she was also of the new generation, benefiting from the state's institution in 1870 of public education, and had learned to read and write in one of Habersham County's four schools for African American children. Both also shared a love for music. In 1898, the year the courthouse was completed, Robert Epps, an accomplished craftsman of thirty-one, married Georgia Walker, age eighteen.

The following year, in 1899, Georgia and Robert's first son, Robert Louis Jr. was born. While the 1910 US Census records his birth in Georgia, Robert Louis Jr.' s own marriage certificate in 1923 states Alton, Illinois, as his birthplace. Regardless of where baby Robert was born, the appearance of Alton on a family document is highly relevant, indicating his go-getter father was working there at the time of his son's birth. Alton, a bustling industrial town on the Mississippi River, at one time even larger than Chicago, was the home of several brick factories and extensive brick construction projects, a natural destination for a striving brick mason.

Traveling for work was a pattern that Georgia and Robert Epps would have to embrace. After the county courthouse, there were no projects of scale in Clarkesville and few opportunities for Epps. Robert could not afford to limit his practice to building a random wall or occasional foundation; by traveling, he proactively pursued projects. As an itinerant lifestyle was hardly compatible with the needs of a young family, Georgia remained with baby Robert in Clarkesville, wrapped in the security of her mother's house, extended family, and familiar rhythms. Traveling far and wide for work, Robert would return to Clarkesville between gigs. A daughter, Ernestine A., was born in 1902, followed by Clarence Bradley (known as Buddy), on July 25, 1905.

Surrounded by cousins and countryside, the three Epps children had a seemingly bucolic childhood. The two elder children, Robert and Ernestine, probably attended the one-room school for Black children from grades one to seven that had recently been set up next to the Clarkesville firehouse. Buddy was too young for school and tagged along with his mother as she managed the household, tended the vegetable garden and yard animals, and kept house. Though the family had historically been members of the local white Baptist church, the Walker–Epps family would on occasion attend services at Deas Chapel, the Colored Methodist Episcopal church near the town square in Clarkesville and participate in church social gatherings.

But the foundations of life in Clarkesville, as experienced by Harriet Allen and Lizzie Walker, were shifting. Family life changed dramatically when, in the fall of 1905, just months after Buddy was born, Georgia's mother, Lizzie Walker, died. Without Lizzie, and with only one sibling left, Georgia's ties to Clarkesville loosened. Raising three children, managing a household, and executing her mother's will, without the support of immediate family, was a large responsibility to undertake alone.

The economics of their life were changing, too. For Robert, the financial panic of 1907 impacted potential building projects. It was time to reconsider the hub-and-spoke existence that Georgia and Robert had set up in Clarkesville. Birmingham, Alabama, on the other hand, was booming, a symbol of the rise of the New South. Perhaps Georgia had a little money from her mother that could absorb the costs of a move. At any rate, it was time to reassess, reassemble, and relocate the family.

CHAPTER 4

AN OBSERVANT CHILD IN BIRMINGHAM

No man exists who is not made
by the child he once was.

—MARIA MONTESSORI

For three-year-old Buddy Bradley, Birmingham was an unfolding wonder. Train whistles lulled him to sleep instead of mountain breezes. Chatter from the house next door replaced the cackling of chickens in the yard. Boarders' children replaced cousins as playmates; pecan pie instead of peach pie appeared on special occasions; pine trees morphed into smokestacks. A new kind of dust alighted on porches, too: not the light filter rising from country earth that could be swept away with a flick of a broom, but an ashy soot that settled into the grain of wood, clung to clothes drying on the line, and seeped into lungs. Like Birmingham's invasive dust, there would be other discoveries, latent, subtle, and enduring, that Buddy would carry with him forever.

For adults Robert and Georgia Epps, Birmingham was a shiny promise. In 1909, it was the beckoning symbol of the New South. Once overlooked in favor of the Black Belt with its lush cotton producing soil, Birmingham exploded after the Civil War, when deposits of coal, lime, and iron ore, the key ingredients for making steel, were discovered in the vicinity. Given the mineral deposits, the proximity of railroads, and the aspiration to wean the economy from agriculture, a cabal of business interests willed a city into existence. As if on cue, Pratt Coke and Steel, Ensley Works, American Cast Iron Pipe, Continental Gin Company, Sloss Furnace, and Tennessee Coal, Iron, and Railroad came into being. The new city, incorporated in 1871, rose to become a powerhouse.[1]

Birmingham was the Ellis Island of the South. While most Southern cities had been exhausted, if not destroyed, by the Civil War, and spent years recouping, Birmingham, fresh and new, could direct all its energies into developing new industries. Perversely, Birmingham's surge forward was based, like cotton, on backward thinking: exploiting African American labor. Business managers, *Plessy v. Ferguson*, and Alabama's punitive 1901 state constitution, which disenfranchised Blacks and poor whites, collectively closed ranks to ensure that Black labor remained available, cheap, and compliant. As dehumanizing as working in Birmingham's heavy industries could be, however, it was preferable to sharecropping and its inevitable peonage. Consequently, freedmen throughout the South descended on Birmingham's foundries, pits, and railroads.[2]

If Atlanta, closer to Georgia's family, had been tempting, Robert Epps, with a growing family to support and no farm skills, needed to be realistic. The momentum of Birmingham was persuasive; it was even starting to rival the North. So, like many others, the Epps family left the security of an extended family and rural town rhythms and moved to an unknown industrial city. It was a decision that required not just pluck but reserves of self-sufficiency and a new vulnerability. Birmingham was the psychological prequel to the Great Migration. The next generation of Epps would all move North.

Of course, as a skilled craftsman, Robert was not planning to work in mines or iron furnaces. Soaring Birmingham was spawning new construction opportunities, inevitably requiring the skills of brick masons. And, if local jobs were ever hard to find, the nine railroads that speeded deliveries of pig iron and steel from Birmingham to all points north, south, east, and west could just as efficiently deliver a bricklayer with a union card to a welcoming jobsite.[3]

Though Robert hailed from Alabama, little in familial Sumter County could have prepared him for the hustle of Birmingham. Naturally, there were small adjustments to be made, but there were also fundamental disappointments, material and moral. For starters, work was not as plentiful as anticipated: Robert was employed only half the time during his first full year in Birmingham. For a seasoned craftsmen who had worked, traveled, and sacrificed to solidify a career and support his family, watching his autonomy compromised must have been bitter.

In one train ride, the Epps had become a nuclear family. Like Robert, Georgia also faced challenges. In Clarkesville, she had lived with her mother as she raised young Robert, Ernestine, and Buddy. In Birmingham, after giving birth to her fourth child, Aurelius Lanier Epps, in 1909, she was on her own, cut off from the support of extended family, caring for her brood single-handedly. Everything was different, too, in this new urban setting. No longer did she walk across family acres to obtain her food and gaze at a landscape of mountains; her new environment was a teeming neighborhood of city blocks populated with houses on small lots. In Georgia, her family went to church occasionally. In Birmingham, Black life congregated around churches, the fulcrum of social as well as religious life. Soral groups and women's auxiliaries, some with high-flying titles and elaborate protocol, replaced families in this community of newcomers. Homespun Georgia may not have slipped easily into place.[4]

Nevertheless, living in Birmingham began optimistically. From 1908 to 1912, Buddy's family lived at 622 Fifth Avenue in Smithfield, an area that a resident proudly described as the home of the "Number One Blacks" in Birmingham. Indeed, this is true, but by default: there were few other places where Black families could, or would wish to, live. Though the section of Smithfield where the Epps lived, south of Eighth Avenue, had been built specifically as Black housing, the overall area, former farmland on the outskirts of town that had been subdivided and developed in the nineteenth century, began as a mixed-race community. As African American labor flowed in, Birmingham's population became 43 percent Black by 1900, and white families began to leave Smithfield for more homogenous precincts. By the time the Epps family arrived in 1908, Smithfield was 83 percent Black—and well on its way to becoming an all-Black neighborhood.[5]

Given the lack of alternatives for African Americans, people from all walks of life lived together. On Buddy's street alone, neighbors' occupations ran the gamut from train and blast furnace laborers to a driver of a coal wagon, a barber, a contractor, a carpenter, a hotel porter, a laborer in a private home (presumably some sort of domestic service), an insurance agent, and a physician. A lucky few—the physician, insurance agent, and coal wagon driver—owned their homes. Perhaps because Robert Epps was a proficient craftsman, and his expectations hadn't yet been fully tempered by reality, the family's rented frame house was nearly twice as large as the more basic shotgun houses on the block. But, even with its relative space, it is likely the plumbing was primitive, with an outhouse in the back: though the city had established a building code, with regulations for plumbing, paved roads, and sidewalks, it wasn't much enforced in the Black neighborhoods.[6]

Smithfield was a distinct and cohesive community. In Smithfield's terms, as described by Dr. D. E. Bradford, Pullman porters, barbers, mail carriers, and skilled craftsmen were considered professionals, placing Robert Epps and his family squarely, for the moment, in the middle class. This was indeed fortunate for a family finding its way in a new community, for not-so-subtle social hierarchies existed. One Smithfield resident haughtily sniffed that she carefully avoided the poorer people who lived in the alleys ("We knew nothing about them"). Ellen Tarry, whose father was a successful barber, recalls the "unrefined" Blacks she saw in theaters whom she "refused to know socially."[7]

Whatever esteem one enjoyed within the Black community, however, had little currency in greater Birmingham. When Peter F. Clarke, a longtime city taxpayer, bank officer, and founding member of the Alabama Colored Land Company, took his young son to the Avondale Park Zoo, a police officer instructed him to leave the park immediately, even though his child had wandered away and could not be found. Against such restrictions, Birmingham's Black population created its own community, establishing benevolent associations, newspapers, fraternal organizations, and even a baseball team, the Black Barons, which later nurtured the talent of a young Willie Mays.[8]

Being surrounded by a vibrant Black community was a new experience for Buddy. Up to the age of three, Buddy had lived in Clarkesville, Georgia, where he, as part of the Allen–Thompson–Walker clan, was a rare dark face in a predominantly white rural community. Now, in his formative years, he was not only immersed in a Black community but a complex one, where African Americans came from various classes and employment, arrived from every corner of the South, and descended from ethnicities up and down the west coast of Africa. Here, he had full access to the games, humor, cadences, foods, traditions, words, songs, and dances representing the varieties and nuances of Black culture. Birmingham was Buddy's first window into African American diversity.

Playmates, carnivals, and marginalization augmented his child's worldview. Right inside his own house on Fifth Avenue, he had two built-in playmates, Lilliet and Marie Dial, the daughters of fellow brick mason John Dial, who boarded with the Epps family. Though Georgia and Robert may have been ambivalent about taking in boarders to make ends meet, Buddy, approaching five, had two boon companions, just about his age. While the three were not allowed to visit Miss Fancy, the much beloved elephant at Avondale Zoo, they discovered exotic animals when the circus rolled into town. On the day the circus arrived, Black children streamed to the field next to the railroad siding in Smithfield, where they could have the circus grounds to themselves, watch as the roustabouts hoisted the big tent, wander among the elephants, and observe the circus folk set up their makeshift living quarters, dispelling bespangled illusions of the performing life.[9]

If the world of performance first entered Buddy's awareness via the Smithfield circus camp, dance as performative art arrived right next door. Buddy's neighbor, whose uncle was a tap dancer, undertook to teach Buddy and the neighborhood gang a time step.

Ironically, the attempt was not a success, at least with Buddy, who quickly became frustrated because his left foot couldn't pick up the steps, and, then and there, renounced dancing.[10]

Further up the street lived three-year-old Walter Scott Brown, the son of physician Dr. Arthur M. Brown. Walter Scott's father was a founder of the Children's Home Hospital, the only hospital in Birmingham where African American doctors could practice, and president in 1914 of the National Medical Association, the national organization for Black doctors. Dr. Brown was also a veteran of the Spanish-American War, where he had served as surgeon for the Black Tenth Cavalry Regiment under Brigadier General Charles Young. Young had been close to W. E. B. Du Bois since their days together on the faculty of Wilberforce University. The Brown house was a congregating spot for Black Birmingham, a place where ideas percolated, plans took shape, and where Du Bois's *Crisis* pushed the cautious conservatives of Birmingham to contemplate inequities, rights, and activism. Several years later, the Browns commissioned Wallace Rayfield, the second formally trained African American architect in America, to build a new family home, a rambling Tudor-style bungalow on nearby Fourth Terrace North, but, for now, they lived at 519 Fifth Avenue, where Buddy, witnessing the social awareness and individual resolve of his neighbor, may have begun to formulate, however subliminally, notions for his own future.[11]

Downtown offered worldly wonders and more new experiences. After the turn of the century, Jim Crow laws authorizing the distinct separation of races were applied to most public facilities—parks, theaters, zoos, even elevators. (Black people could share elevators in department stores but in office buildings had to use freight elevators.) These restrictions forced the growing Black business community into an area along Third, Fourth and Fifth Avenue North from Fifteenth to Eighteenth Streets. Colloquially known as "the District," the area was the business, commercial, and cultural hub for Black citizens. The presence of barber and beauty shops, mortuaries, saloons, restaurants, theaters, photographic studios, cleaners, shoeshine parlors, Dr. Brown's office, and the towering six-story headquarters on Eighteenth Street North of the Penny Savings Bank, one of only three

Black-owned financial institutions in the nation, animated the area by day. At the New Queen Theatre, the Black vaudeville house on Eighteenth Street, Bessie Smith, Clara Smith, the Whitman Sisters and other visiting acts made the District crackle at night.[12]

Buddy was too young to partake in many Friday and Saturday revels, and it is unlikely that his hardworking and often cash-strapped parents did, either. At the Pantopia Theater, an adolescent dancer, Leonard Harper, a native of Birmingham, was beginning his professional career, but Buddy would not meet him until the two were in Harlem. Elsewhere, at the New Queen Theatre, Buddy saw the elegant Jack Wiggins, a dancer famous for his floating half-turn with heel and toe taps. On another occasion—although this possibly was at the Lyric, Birmingham's most lavish vaudeville theater, which had a separate "colored balcony"—he saw the eccentric dancer One-Eyed Dotson, one of the few entertainers who navigated between the Black and white vaudeville circuits and who would cross paths, like Buddy, with George Balanchine in London. Buddy, still put off dance by his recalcitrant left foot, did not try to imitate either dancer. But his acute visual memory implanted both, particularly the graceful Wiggins, on his brain.[13]

Other incidents didn't merely imprint themselves on Buddy; they seared to the core. Lack of access to knowledge for a bright, curious child was a most painful experience and certainly the least forgivable. Birmingham, run by business interests, was neither bookish nor generous; while it wished to compete with rivals Chicago, Pittsburgh, and Atlanta in prestige of civic amenities, it was philistine in its reverence for commerce over culture and notoriously tightfisted. At one point it ranked ninety-fourth of ninety-five American cities with populations over one hundred thousand in per capita public spending. While a private subscription library was inaugurated in 1886, it was not until 1909 that it had a public library funded by taxes—which, it goes without saying, was off-limits for people of color. The Black community of Birmingham, knowing that literacy and access to knowledge were the keys to a better future, fought back. They petitioned the Carnegie Corporation, pointing to the "separate but equal" doctrine of *Plessy v. Ferguson*, for matching funding for a Black library. They did not receive a response. After nearly a decade of fundraising entertainments, the determined community had accumulated enough money for their own library, the Booker T. Washington Library at the Masonic Temple. But, even with independent funding, the Booker T. Washington Library met with resistance: the funds had been placed in escrow with the library board, who then balked at releasing them to the rightful owners. It wasn't until 1918, when he was thirteen, that Buddy could borrow a book from a library.[14]

Not having access to a decent education was even more egregious than lack of a library. Naturally, a philistine town like Birmingham was not enthusiastic about paying for education. But, ironically, as Birmingham's industries flourished, and just when the flush city might have invested in schools, its prosperity attracted Northern investment. Companies such as US Steel, which purchased Ensley Works in 1907, poured in and further imperiled education: the new absentee owners had no interest in paying taxes for benefits they would not utilize. (Consequently, as late as 1937, Birmingham had the highest illiteracy rate of any city of its size.) City officials with progressive inclinations were anxious to do well for Birmingham but were helpless in fighting the financial powers. And, anyway, when Progressive politicians talked about education, they usually meant education for white children. When it came time to parse out monies, Black children were given short shrift.[15]

When the Epps family arrived in Birmingham, architect W. A. Rayfield was finishing construction of the Graymont School in Smithfield, the first public school for Black children. Ernestine and Robert, both of school age, would attend this school. As soon as Buddy was old enough, he would go to Graymont, too. A look into the investment for the building provides a snapshot of racial disparities in Birmingham: Rayfield's school cost $2,000 to build; the previous year, the white Graymont School had cost $12,500.[16]

Though the population was about evenly divided between the two races, the 1908 report of the superintendent of education shows that Black schools received only 12 percent of school fund allocations, compromising facilities, teacher ratios, and the number of teaching days per year. Such inequalities, and many others, were rationalized by the argument that Black residents contributed less tax. There were nine elementary schools for whites and three for Blacks. The white schools were made of brick, the Black schools of flimsy frame construction. There were forty students to one teacher in the white schools, and seventy-three students per teacher in the Black schools. White sessions averaged 151 days; sessions for Blacks, 96. In 1905, when Blacks petitioned for improved facilities, the board of education dismissed the petition as "ill advised" and "a practical insult." Buddy learned that getting an education, just like having indoor plumbing, going to the zoo, and borrowing books from the library, was not his right; if he received any of these amenities, even diluted, it was only as a conditional gift graciously bestowed on him by white powers.[17]

Just as the child Buddy realized he was considered insignificant in the world, he faced growing insecurity at home. In 1912, when he was six, his father slipped from the Birmingham city directory. Robert's omission was probably due to the fact that he was spending more and more time out of town to find work, but even this tactic of chasing far afield for projects didn't seem to provide enough for the family; the records now show Georgia working as a laundress, though baby Aurelius was only two. The following year, Robert's name returned to the city directory, but the family circumstances appear even more insecure: they now lived in a narrow shotgun house at 705 Fifth Avenue, ever more tightly surrounded by neighboring houses.

Sporadic as Robert Epps's ability to be at home with his family may have been, it was vastly preferable to what was to come. On May 10, 1913, Robert died alone in Nashville, age forty-six. The death was so gruesome it made the front page of the local newspaper. Robert was found on a porch, at 10 p.m. on a Friday night, so bloody that, at first, he was believed to have been murdered. In fact, he had hemorrhaged profusely from the lungs, the result of untreated tuberculosis. It is unknown if he had consulted a doctor or received a diagnosis, but, given the family's financial circumstances, it is likely this had not happened.[18]

Yet even if Robert knew he had tuberculosis—an environmentally caused disease for which Blacks were four times more susceptible, given their poverty and living conditions—he had no realistic options for a cure. In 1913, before antibiotics, the sole treatments were either surgery, or sunlight and fresh air. Surgery was expensive and out of the question. And while Birmingham had a tuberculosis sanitarium for white patients, supported by the local Red Cross and the Lady Managers of the Hillman Hospital, and intended to set up one for Black patients as well, it was chronically short of the necessary private funding. Robert's younger brother, Walter, now known as George, brought his brother's body back to Birmingham.[19]

The ramifications of Robert Epps's death—alone, untreated, suffocating on his own blood—were chilling. Throughout his life, he had strived: to acquire a skill, to determine his own narrative, and to provide so that his children would have a better life, even persisting in working away from home as his body failed him. Resolve, it turned out, had not been sufficient to succeed. Now, the family lost not only their primary earner but their compass, the one who had a vision of what he and his family could be. Buddy had lost his father, a stoic protector, and a beacon. He was not yet seven years old.

The following year, the Epps family disappeared from the 1914 Birmingham city directory, their invisibility an apt reflection of their vulnerability. They reappeared in 1915, having moved to an even smaller shotgun house, no wider than twelve feet, at 813 North Second Street. No longer was their neighborhood a mix of clerks, skilled laborers, and professionals. Except for Charles N. Tolbert, an electrician, all their neighbors were laborers, and Georgia herself worked as a maid. Who took care of Aurelius when she worked? Did an older child stay home from school so they could pay the rent? Despite a few family members in Birmingham—Robert's brother, George, a presser; Georgia's nephew from Clarkesville, Governor McDonald, a miner—Georgia couldn't much lean on them; they had their own hard lives to manage. Buddy was probably left to his own devices.[20]

After three years of anxiety—an eternity to a bewildered child—an illusion of stability appeared. Georgia remarried William Tartt, a railroad hand, on September 16, 1916. For the next two years, the family continued to live in the minuscule home on 813 North

Second Street. Now Georgia didn't work outside the home, possibly due to having another adult income in the household, possibly due to illness. But, despite the apparently easier circumstances, the marriage was on uneasy footing. Georgia never used her new husband's name, and one wonders how a man with a humble laborer's income could voluntarily take on the financial responsibility not simply for a wife but four children, too.

Perhaps Ernestine Epps, Buddy's fourteen-year-old sister, was an impulsive teenager, carried away by ideas of romance. Or perhaps Ernestine hoped to allay a burden on her mother by leaving the household. Two months after her mother's marriage, fudging her age and declaring herself eighteen, she married Leo Strong on December 28, 1916. The hasty marriage was of short duration; perhaps it was annulled due to the young age of the bride. Yet, only months later, in 1917, Ernestine—now just fifteen—married again, this time to Thomas Patterson of Birmingham. The young couple moved to Harrisburg, Pennsylvania, where their first child, a son, Thomas, was born on March 21, 1918. A suggestion of urgency, an air of desperation, clings to this whirlwind of activity.[21]

Nothing now seemed permanent. However valiantly Georgia worked, penury, bad luck, illness, and systemic inequities pulled her family into a downward spiral. Addresses changed in ever more rapid succession. Rent was a stretch. Jobs didn't last. Pandemics arrived. In 1918, Georgia once again moved her family and resumed work, once again as a laundress. The new house, at 217 Seventh Avenue, was a slight, if picturesque, frame house with a gabled roof and a porch. Ernestine and Thomas Patterson, with their seven-month-old son, returned to Birmingham and joined the household. Thomas, who worked as a waiter at the posh Hillman Hotel, probably helped with the rent. There is no evidence of William Tartt; he is no longer in the city directory. Possibly conscripted into military service, he never resurfaces in the Epps family's life again. He, like everything else in it, was impermanent.[22]

Just as the family's sense of agency crumbled, Birmingham grew more threatening. The 1915 release of *The Birth of a Nation,* when Buddy was ten, unleashed a revival of the Ku Klux Klan and a rise in lynchings. In 1916, Birmingham's Robert E. Lee Klavern (as KKK chapters were called) emerged as one of the strongest in the southeast and would dominate state and local politics. For years, African American men had been intimidated and controlled by Alabama's convict work system; now this job was taken on by the Klan. To the annoyance of W. E. B. Du Bois, the Birmingham chapter of the NAACP kept a low profile, eschewing activism for fear of alienating any sympathetic whites. Powerless to counteract the violence through legal means, African Americans now exercised greater caution, or, like Buddy's eighteen-year-old brother, simply left for the North. By 1918, Robert was employed as a butcher by Swift and Company in Cleveland, Ohio. At thirteen, approaching manhood and dealing with increasing uncertainty, Buddy found himself short another older, male presence.[23]

The next year there were more changes, as Ernestine and her family returned to Harrisburg and George Epps, Buddy's uncle, now working as a chauffeur, joined the household on Seventh Avenue. Watching as the world swirled about him, Buddy may have found in school a through line of stability, or at least a diversion from worries. He may even have seen school as an exit strategy, a path to self-reliance. But for Buddy this was not to be: the only public high school for Black students in Birmingham was Industrial High. Many Black families resolutely avoided it, scrimping and saving so that their teenagers could study anywhere else, perhaps at the high school at Miles College or the prep program at Talladega College, founded by three freedmen who met at the Freedmen's Bureau convention in 1866 at Mobile. Industrial High was so academically weak that when families moved north with the Great Migration, their children had to stay back a year in their new, substandard inner-city schools to catch up on the algebra, Latin, and French that they had missed in Birmingham.[24]

But Industrial High was in a delicate position, as were all people of color in Birmingham. Arthur Parker, the kindly principal, had to walk the fine line between making education accessible to Black children and making the concept of Black education palatable to white interests. His hook was that while white business and philanthropists in town did not believe Blacks were equal to whites, they wanted a stable work force. The school they envisioned and were willing to fund would produce trained, obliging workers. To keep the school alive, Parker played the game—which meant emphasizing practical skills such as laundering, cooking, nurse training, tailoring, gardening, typesetting, and printing that kept Black children in a second, subservient class. Graduation festivities of 1914 included graduate Jacob Cole explaining how he could patch a roof and Susie Davis demonstrating how sewing could make simple articles more serviceable and reduce a seamstress's bill.[25]

Principal Parker shared Booker T. Washington's belief that cooperation with white interests would overcome racism in the long run, but he was also cognizant of the value of an academic education. Tucked in among the courses on caning and woodwork *were* courses in literature, mathematics, history, and science—but it was music, which acceptably bridged the gap between entertainment and art, where the school excelled. Just before Buddy came to high school, a charismatic teacher, John Whatley, arrived to form a school band. While Parker boasted that every male student wanted to be in it, a vintage photo of a grim-faced high school band in 1917 either belies Parker's upbeat comment or reflects the simmering anger of being a young Black man in Birmingham.[26]

Like the scowling young men in the band, Buddy couldn't help but feel resentment. He deserved more than the limited horizons and clipped aspirations of Industrial High. In later years, he was so aware of its deficiencies that he often denied attending school, though the record attests he attended through the spring of 1920. To compensate, he became an avid and lifelong reader.

The fact that he attended school at all is nearly miraculous, a testament to Georgia's dedication to her children's future as well as to Buddy's own tenacity. For Black families living on a shoestring, school was a luxury. Children old enough to work could contribute significantly to the family livelihood, making the difference between having to choose between putting food on the table or paying the rent.[27] Scanning the US Federal Census for 1920 one finds uncountable numbers of young Black men in Birmingham, ages thirteen, fourteen, and fifteen—Buddy's cohorts—working in steel mills and mines as laborers. With Robert and Ernestine now in the North, most likely just getting by and not sending money home, Buddy attending high school was a sheer act of will.

Precarity was now compounded by illness. Georgia, stressed from working long hours, eating scantily, and living in substandard housing conditions, was a natural target for the epidemic of encephalitis lethargica of 1917–27. Its symptoms of continual fatigue, fever, double vision, delayed physical and mental responses, and lack of upper body strength might explain why Georgia's jobs as laundress, cook, and maid were often of short duration. In January 1920 she was a cook in a restaurant; in the spring she was a maid at a Woolworth's downtown. That year, the family housing situation became even more dubious. The address where they were living, 713 Smith Street, didn't even officially exist, suggesting they either boarded with others or even lived in irregular lodgings, such as a lean-to, shack, or garage on a property, for which the census enumerator had simply invented a number.

Georgia's life was one that fell between the cracks. Mortality for encephalitis was only 20 percent, but this assumes the disease was treated. Private medical care was prohibitive for a family that was living on the edge, with employment constantly in flux, having to move whenever they could not pay the rent. Birmingham did not have a city hospital, and Dr. Brown's hospital for Blacks at the children's home was no longer in operation. Only one private charity hospital, the Hillman Hospital, treated Blacks, where it was obliged to build a separate clinic for them so as not to discomfit white patients.[28]

Like her husband, Georgia died alone. She was forty when she arrived at Hillman Hospital on April 11, 1920, and died two days later, on April 13, at 4 a.m. No neighbors, no brother-in-law, no adult children were with her, only a doctor to whom she was little more than a statistic. As the informant on her death certificate, Dr. Douglas Lannon couldn't fill in any personal information. She was buried in Pratt's Cemetery, now so overcome with weeds that her gravesite cannot be found.[29]

Together, Buddy, fourteen, and his younger brother, Aurelius, eleven, observed it all: the fevers, the exhaustion, the dragging to work, the firings, the moves, the isolation, and the despair. Their shared experience cemented a lifelong bond between them. They also were firsthand witnesses to something even larger than the tragedy of their mother. Despite bravery, resolve, and sacrifice to secure a future and provide more opportunities for their children, the momentum of Harriet Allen and Robert Epps Sr. had, at least temporarily, evaporated.

There was no obvious solution for what to do with the two homeless boys. Their elder siblings, Robert and Ernestine, were both far away, Ernestine with her family in Harrisburg and Robert a bachelor in Cleveland. The Epps family didn't volunteer; perhaps they couldn't afford to feed two more mouths. As for Georgia's family, she only had one sibling left, Lewis, and it is likely Georgia's extended family in Clarkesville were not even aware of her death; as late as 1948, only three Black families in Clarkesville had telephones. With such sparse communication, it's possible that they had lost touch or become estranged. Even though he hadn't seen Buddy since he was three and had never set eyes on Aurelius, it is likely that Great-Uncle Charlie Ivie would have taken the two orphans, just as he had taken in another great-nephew—he was seemingly kindhearted, and, besides, a farmer could always use a few extra hands. But haste was imperative; two adolescents couldn't be left indefinitely to fend for themselves in Birmingham, at the mercy and kindness of neighbors. The most expedient solution, it was decided, was to send Buddy and Aurelius across the Mason-Dixon Line, to live with Ernestine and Thomas Patterson in Harrisburg.

Though he would soon be heading north, never to return to the South, Birmingham would forever be part of Buddy Bradley. Here, he had lived in the heart of a diverse Black community, seen many ways in which to exist in Blackness. Here, he discovered books, dance, and music, elements that would accompany him all his life. Here, he had also watched as his father and his mother, one after the other, succumbed to forces over which they had no control. Birmingham was, above all, a lesson in lost illusions, in learning that very little could be relied upon, that there was no one he could depend on, and that here he was destined to be molded into a second-class citizen. But, if Buddy Bradley had been taught diffidence in Birmingham, he held within him the aspirations that had directed his family for generations. He dared to dream and determine who he was.

CHAPTER 5

CROSSING THE MASON-DIXON LINE TO HARRISBURG

Every journey begins with a single step.

—MAYA ANGELOU

Harrisburg's Pennsylvania Station was the sober counterpart to the marble grandeur of Birmingham's Terminal Station. That summer of 1920, Buddy Bradley, age fourteen, alighted in its dim wood hall in a similarly subdued mood. No one had consulted him after his mother's death about his preferences for where or with whom he might like to live. In fact, there would have been no point. The only apparent option had been to bundle him off to his teenage sister.

It happened at a tender time. Bradley had to wrestle with the loss of his mother and the stark implications of her death, just as he was becoming more self-aware and asking more questions. Harrisburg, for what it did and did not provide, would help him shape his answers. But Buddy could not know this then. Bitter as his experience had been in Birmingham, leaving the familiarity of Smithfield, separating from friends, even departing his ramshackle house, was an uprooting. Birmingham was all he knew; he had no memory of his earliest years in Georgia, no conception of another life.

Together with Aurelius, who had just turned eleven, he must have approached his next chapter with apprehension.

His new living situation compounded his sense of displacement. Ernestine Patterson, his eighteen-year-old sister, had settled with her husband and two-year-old son at 343 Muench Street, in Harrisburg's Eleventh Ward, a neighborhood at some distance from the center of town. Like all young couples, the Pattersons probably dreamed of setting up their first household, but, with the costs of a recent move and the ongoing expenses of a young family, they currently boarded with Henry Valtine, a chauffeur, and his wife, Anna, as they established a foothold in their new city. The issue for Bradley wasn't the scruffy neighborhood, with an automotive paint shop across the street, the C. Day Rudy Glass Works and the Bible Truth Church just a bit farther away, or the rudimentary two-story house in which they lived—he had known not too dissimilar circumstances in Birmingham. The problem was he was so obviously in the way.[1]

The two adolescents were more than a financial strain on the Pattersons; they were a burden on an entire household. At 343 Muench Street, eighteen others, working as waiters, firemen, laborers in tin mills, and a "gas poker" in a steel mill, squeezed into a single-bath house that was 1,200 square feet.[2] Shoehorned in a situation never intended for him, Buddy literally had to make himself small. He had already been primed by Birmingham to *be* small. Now, in Harrisburg, geniality and adaptability, two qualities for which the adult Bradley would be renowned, were honed as he attempted to mitigate his intrusive presence.

If the feeling of being extraneous was uncomfortably familiar, Harrisburg was wonderfully novel. With its splendid new Capitol building, quality education, public transportation, streets swept twice a day, and riverside park designed by a protégé of Frederick Law Olmstead, Harrisburg reflected the values of the Progressive local burghers who unstintingly devoted their services to a city they loved. Their most recent initiative was a library in the leafy estate area by the river, by local architect Charles Lloyd, which housed more volumes than many college libraries. Yet this seeming haven of enlightened civility in the North was an ambiguous destination for people of color. No one can state with confidence today whether a curious Black teenager would have been welcome to browse among its stacks in the 1920s.[3]

Only twenty-six miles away from the Mason-Dixon Line, the city had established links with the African American community. Easily accessible by its canals, river, and railroad and close to Quaker strongholds, Harrisburg had been an important stop on the Underground Railroad during the Civil War. Fifty-five years later, as many of its steel and railroad workers went off to World War I, the city recruited African American laborers from the South, often paying their travel expenses north, to keep its core industries running. Though this manpower was often let go after the war, the experience had been an eye-opener. After experiencing the contrast with the South, many of these men sought new employment in Harrisburg, then brought their families north in search of a better and more dignified life. Thomas Patterson and his fellow boarders on Muench Street, all from the South, were part of this pattern.

Buddy must have looked longingly at Central High, at the intersection of Forster and Capitol Streets, with its curricula in the classics, sciences, and literature and reputation burnished by graduates who went on to liberal arts colleges. It was so different from the compromised education of Industrial High in Birmingham and, quite marvelously, available to him. In 1883, it had graduated its first two Black students, one the class salutatorian. Even more recently, Horace Payne, Class of 1912, after working as a chauffeur for two years postgraduation, had enrolled at Harvard. Per *The Harrisburg Telegraph*, Payne was the first Black graduate from Central High who had been accepted by Harvard "directly and unconditionally," implying that previous Black alums had also attended Harvard. Such stories squarely placed the stuff of dreams into the realm of possibility for Bradley.[4]

Buddy would have flourished at Central High, and, technically, he should have been there. School attendance in Harrisburg was compulsory until age sixteen, and he was fifteen at the beginning of the 1920 school year. Though Aurelius attended Thomas Edison Junior High—forward-thinking Harrisburg was one of the early adapters of the concept of junior high school—and tried out for the football team, Buddy, taller and four years older, might have escaped the eagle eyes of the truant officer. Education, even free, was a luxury he could not afford. Perceptive enough to realize his burden on his hardworking brother-in-law, Buddy went to work instead.

Though progressive in many aspects, Harrisburg's proximity to Maryland and Southern culture, coupled with a white, working-class population who viewed Black labor as competitors for jobs, meant that currents of Southern-style racism permeated town. Though high schools had long been mixed, grammar schools were segregated until the 1970s. The YMCA, with its columned porch and arched windows, boasting a swimming pool, bowling alley, gymnasium, 425-seat auditorium, game rooms, reading room, and classroom, was reserved for white railroad workers. Only after Bradley had left Harrisburg was a Black Y established on Forster Street, with a bequest from the Julius Rosenwald Fund. As late as 1937, the august Penn Harris Hotel, a popular rendezvous for dealmakers, political masterminds, and socialites, infamously refused to accommodate two African American educators. A painful nostalgia for the Old South also reigned in its formal restaurant, the Plantation Room, which promised "the leisure and charm of the Deep South" and employed a Black chef who expertly turned out oxtail, fried chicken, and a smattering of French dishes, all served in a dining room with an 85 percent Black waitstaff overseen by a legendary maître d', Morris Cowan.[5]

Coupled with the fact that Harrisburg, a state capital and major railroad hub, supported a thriving hospitality business, and that Bradley's brother-in-law was a waiter in a hotel, it was natural that Thomas Patterson would help his unskilled but willing young relative obtain a job as a busboy. Patterson, with his experience at the posh Hillman Hotel in Birmingham, had most likely landed a post at either the Penn Harris or the equally prestigious Harrisburger Hotel, which also had a celebrated African American chef and employed an all-Black waitstaff, so it is likely that Buddy was employed at one of these hotels, where Patterson could keep an eye on the youngster as he learned the ropes. Such work was at once prestigious and painful: employment was steady, and tips were plentiful, but these benefits were earned in an environment that romanticized Southern values, inflicting a daily dose of dehumanization on the staff.

It is possible that the diligent Buddy worked two jobs; a friend recalled years later that Bradley mentioned also operating an elevator in Harrisburg. But it is the busboy experience—though hardly an important waystation in his career—which was propitious. Busboys depend on tips, and tips depend on service. In granular terms, service means removing plates, pulling back chairs, and folding napkins at the proper moment. In broad terms, it means sharpening one's powers of observation, constantly anticipating needs, and connecting with individuals while simultaneously managing the dining room hierarchy. A good wait staff effectively executes a seamless ensemble performance while chaos lurks just beneath the surface and arbitrary whims of managers and chefs threaten out of earshot.

Something else happened in the dining room, too, and it piqued Bradley's inherent curiosity. Just as Pullman porters speak of how working the trains provided a window into a different existence, different practices, and different society, working in a hotel restaurant in Harrisburg provided such a window for Bradley. In Birmingham, he had grown up within an insular, albeit diverse, Black community; now he interacted with another community, the world of power brokers and social leaders, celebrities and racketeers, and observed its language and mores and learned to navigate within its unfamiliar structure.

As a major hub on the Keystone Line running east to Philadelphia, Harrisburg was a jazz town, frequently the first to hear the new music coming in from Chicago and up from the South. Though he probably didn't have an extra dime, Buddy's new connections in the hospitality world would have enabled him to slip into the back of a club to catch the latest syncopated rhythms and popular dances.

As Buddy explored outward, Aurelius represented a link to family and the past. When the older siblings had migrated north, the two younger brothers stayed behind in Birmingham, helplessly watching their mother decline. With only each other for support, they embarked as orphans on their journey and together adapted to new circumstances that stemmed from good intentions but were not particularly hospitable to their needs. Buddy, four years older, was always one step ahead in experience. In Harrisburg, their roles solidified: Buddy was the responsible caretaker, Aurelius the carefree ward. Buddy was the trailblazer, Aurelius the complaisant follower.

Buddy wasn't destined to stay long in Harrisburg, listening to the strains of Chicago jazz. Nevertheless, his months in Harrisburg were a powerful catalyst for bringing his ideas and temperament into focus. It was here he learned to be supple and self-reliant. It was here he first experienced the North, observing both its opportunities and obstacles. It was here he made his first self-determining decision: he was not going to be a waiter like his brother-in-law. He was going to experience the world.[6]

Musicians and busboys in town now talked about Harlem, a place with wide avenues, fine buildings, and a developing cachet as a Black enclave. Now that he worked, Buddy knew he could support himself. The trains that incessantly roared through Harrisburg's Penn Station could carry him within hours to this tempting mecca. A coworker had given him a tip about a lodging house on Seventh Avenue near West 133rd Street. There was nothing to hold him back from following his curiosity. Around 1921, Buddy left Aurelius, the cramped quarters on Muench Street, and the predictable routine, and set out for the unknown.

Prohibition had been enacted. All of New York was thronging to *Shuffle Along*, the landmark revue written, produced, and performed by Black artists. Opening on May 23, 1921, at the Sixty-Third Street Music Hall, the show is credited with launching the Harlem Renaissance. It could not have been a better moment to arrive in Harlem.

PART 2

NEW YORK JAZZ, 1921–1930

CHAPTER 6

HARLEM CHORUS BOY

There is no dancing in America.
Outside, of course, of Harlem.

—TAMARA TOUMANOVA

Sleeping in a dingy back room of a lodging house and operating an elevator, the teenage Bradley had no clear plan for his future. Restless inquisitiveness had brought him here, to Harlem, a thousand miles from Birmingham. Mile by mile, step by step, his journey had been fueled by a quest to replace a narrowly prescribed path with a wide horizon. Yet, without identifying his own traits and talents that could lead to a specific plan of action, such a vision was only a dream. Bradley's journey had just begun, and Harlem would be his classroom.[1]

Harlem, an elegant neighborhood of tree-lined streets just north of Central Park, was not only the antithesis of Birmingham but an anomaly in New York, a neighborhood that Eslanda Robeson, wife of Paul Robeson, described emphatically as a place where "Negroes *belong*," a community where intentional Black individuals engaged with life and pursued their objectives, seemingly unrestricted by prevailing societal norms. A building boom in the 1880s and 1890s, coupled with delays in constructing a subway to serve the area, had led to the collapse of the real estate market in a neighborhood intended for the upper middle class. When entrepreneur Philip Payton, founder of the Afro-American Realty Company, noted that the construction of Pennsylvania Station was pushing Black people out of their traditional midtown neighborhood, he realized he could fill the vacancies in Harlem with these displaced denizens of midtown, all the while charging a premium.[2]

Thanks to the resourcefulness of Philip Payton, Harlem became the "Negro Capital of the World." As World War I brought manpower north, Blacks from the South followed and also settled in the neighborhood. As New York was a service economy, based on finance, the professions, and the arts, ambitious new arrivals often entered the service professions, anything from catering to entertainment to medicine, and lived by their wits and talents, guided by their personal aspirations.

With a burgeoning Black population, libraries, theaters, clubs, fraternal organizations, newspapers, commerce, and churches were established. Intelligentsia and talent gathered. Arts, ideas, cultural exchanges, and artistic collaborations flourished. Bradley fortuitously arrived in the early 1920s, just as this momentum was coalescing into the Harlem Renaissance.[3]

The aftereffects of World War I dovetailed with the energy gathering in Harlem. The senseless carnage of the war called into question the old European powers and their values. Effete thinking and fusty institutions were now suspect, viewed as morally bankrupt, ineffectual, and irrelevant. Europe was the past; America was the future. The world now looked to vigorous, unsentimental America for economic, political, and intellectual leadership. Yet the substitution of America for Europe as cultural leader came with a glitch: though it could invent a light bulb, an assembly line, and a consumer economy, its artistic invention was largely Euro-derivative and, therefore, of little interest to Europeans—except for its Native American and African American cultures.

As America dictated to the world what was fashionable and fun, Prohibition turned the spotlight on Harlem. A quest for novelty and amusement, knowledge of non-Western cultures, and pastimes that could divert from moral hollowness and the pain of needlessly sacrificed young men supplanted old social codes. With Prohibition, liquor was outré and chic; cocktails (which masked the taste of inferior bootleg alcohol) became a culture, drinking a ritualistic pastime. In midtown, there were speakeasies, like Jack and Charlie's 21 Club, but uptown, in Harlem, where liquor was distributed by the Mafia, drinking did not have to be clandestine; it could be lavish, fantastic, and highly lucrative. Nightclubs began to pop up and, with them, showcases for jazz and dance. And as much as W. E. B. Du Bois and Alain Locke, philosophical architects of the New Negro and Talented Tenth, would have liked to frame the Harlem Renaissance as a literary and visual arts movement, it was, at its most visible, popular, and compelling, a jazz phenomenon.[4]

In 1921, *Shuffle Along* sent jazz into world orbit. Written by two Fisk graduates, Flournoy Miller and Aubrey Lyles, with a score by Eubie Blake and lyrics by Noble Sissle, the show packed an off-the-beaten-track theater, the Sixty-Third Street Music Hall, for two years, captivating New York's interest in Black theatricals and catapulting a cast of unknowns to stardom. Even members of the replacement cast (Florence Mills, Adelaide Hall, and Josephine Baker) shot to fame. Eubie Blake attributed the success of his show to its attunement to the time, how it reflected the rhythms and spirit of the age while other Broadway shows were mired in a past bound to European musical models, such as operetta. Langston Hughes ordained it "the scintillating send-off to that Negro vogue in Manhattan."[5]

Of course, Black music and dance had long influenced the white stage. In the Five Points neighborhood of New York, Black hoofers had intersected with Irish steppers and bequeathed a legacy to George Primrose and George M. ("Yankee Doodle Dandy") Cohan. Vernon and Irene Castle, coached by African American musician James Reese Europe and inspired by W. C. Handy's "Memphis Blues," had unleashed a craze for foxtrots to ragtime rhythms before the war. Will Vodery for years scored orchestral arrangements for the Florenz Ziegfeld productions. But, as Europe, Vodery, and other Afro-American musician composers became slicker and found work in the white entertainment world, the real jazz and the low-down blues were being fueled by the Southern invasion in Harlem. Uptown, things were happening. In 1920, the plush Happy Rhone's Radium Club, a hangout of Charlie Chaplin, the Barrymores, and Ethel Waters, on Lenox Avenue and 143rd Street, introduced the floor show.[6]

With the success of *Shuffle Along*, performers began to feel a sense of real possibility. The play not only legitimized the Black musical; it proved, to a country enamored of profit, the commercial power of Black talent on the performing stage. As the *Shuffle Along* effect, Happy Rhone's success, and Prohibition took hold, Small's Paradise, the Cotton Club, and Connie's Inn opened, attracting swells from Park Avenue looking for a good time. By the end of the decade, on 133rd Street alone (a.k.a. Swing Street or the Jungle), there were twenty clubs, including the Nest, Pod's and Jerry's, Covan's Morocco Club, the Clam House, and Mexico's. In real terms, it all translated, as described by Florence Mills's husband, U. S. Thompson, to a big demand for "colored" talent. It also meant tap dancing was hot.[7]

Harlem was not all glitter and glamour, especially for the uninitiated. Unlike Chicago with its stockyards, Pittsburgh with its steel mills, and Detroit with its car industry, New York was essentially a white-collar city with little opportunity for the unskilled. While many men of color struggled to find work, women often found employment more easily, albeit as laundresses and maids. Housing was a chronic challenge. Following policies established by Philip Payton, Harlem rents were expensive, capitalizing on cachet, Black identity, proximity to midtown, and few alternatives for Black people. Large apartments were subdivided, chopped into smaller and smaller units to reduce costs and meet demand. Even with these measures, apartments were so crowded that some resorted to sleeping in bathtubs, coal bins, and cellars, while others turned to taking in lodgers, sometimes by the week, day, or hour, even employing a "hot bed" policy, in which daytime and nighttime lodgers alternated use of the same bed. Under such conditions, health standards faltered, and the mortality rate increased, despite a predominantly young population. Deaths from tuberculosis were two and a half times the city rate. Heart disease, cancer, and pneumonia spiked similarly. Twice as many children died in Harlem as elsewhere in New York City.[8]

Sixteen-year-old Buddy Bradley was one of those at risk. As an orphan without connections, he was far removed from the glitz and merely intent on survival. And, while he surely sensed giddy promise in the smartly dressed Black denizens of Harlem, he must have passed many sleepless nights in his narrow room at the top of five flights of stairs, his mind filled with calculations, questions, and self-doubt. Thanks to his work experience in Harrisburg, he was able to find work as an elevator operator. Although this provided a scant income, it was hardly an advancement of his dream to experience the world. Given his lack of access, education, and limited skills, coupled with his love of movies, Buddy's most ambitious and attainable plan, circa 1921, was to become a film projectionist.[9]

Fate intervened in the guise of his lodging house on 133rd Street. Because of her proximity to Swing Street, Bradley's landlady, Mrs. Douglas, had actors, dancers, and vaudeville performers among her lodgers. One was George "Tosh" Hammond, a versatile performer who could play the violin with stride pianist James P. Johnson one night, then, on another, toss off spectacular acrobatic steps such as backflips on a phone book with a group called the Crackerjacks. Another was journeyman Richard Bell, an up-and-coming dancer and man-about-Harlem, who still had to work in a shoe store to cover expenses.[10]

Bell's younger brother, Eddie, also lodged with Mrs. Douglas and taught Bradley tap steps as a lark. In his off-hours, Buddy began to wander over to a blind alley near Connie's Inn on 131st Street, where ambitious young men, like Derby Wilson, practiced their tap steps. For Bradley, alone in Harlem without friends or family, the camaraderie of peers was an initial draw, then the dance began to engross him, too. Soon he had mastered a time step, even with his tricky left foot, as well as an expanded repertoire of buck and wing steps. Although none of the aspirants would have dared at the time to set foot in the Comedy Club—to be renamed the Hoofers' Club in 1925—some of the ally gang, like Derby Wilson, would soon go on to acclaim, appearing with Pete Nugent and George McGregor as one of the Dancing Dandies in *Runnin' Wild*, the show that popularized the Charleston. Wilson, by the way, was considered the only dancer with stage presence and charisma equal to Bill "Bojangles" Robinson.[11]

As for Buddy, the accumulated rhythms of the Deep South, fragments of Baptist and Colored Methodist Episcopal services, glimpses of Jack Wiggins and One-Eyed Dotson on the vaudeville stage, strains of Industrial High band concerts, and his mother's singing at home, converged with his own musical sensibility and application to create a gifted dancer. Soon he caught the appraising eye of Thaddeus Drayton, another lodger in Mrs. Douglas's house. The elegant Drayton had been polished by an apprenticeship touring Europe as a supporting act for Johnson and Dean, the sophisticated African American dance team who were the first to use steel taps on their dance shoes. Now Drayton and his dance partner, Rufus Greenlee, performed at top venues such as the Palace, wearing tailcoats, monocles, and top hats while suavely bantering in several languages. In 1921, Greenlee and Drayton were so successful that the producers of *Shuffle Along* wanted but couldn't afford to hire them. In 1923, Greenlee and Drayton was one of the celebrity acts to open the new Cotton Club. It was Drayton who fatefully brought Bradley to the attention of Leonard Harper during a rehearsal at the Hollywood Club at Forty-Ninth Street and Broadway.[12]

Leonard Harper, also from Birmingham, was shaking up 1920s entertainment. In 1921, he and his wife, Osceola Blank, performing as the Smart Set Couple, had integrated the all-white Shubert circuit. He was credited with virtually inventing the nightclub floor show, Harlem style, and was now bringing it down to Broadway. Within the commercial constraints with which he worked, Harper pushed against racial barriers, featuring acts with fashionable costumes, artistic sets, and romantic contexts to humanize his dancers.

Harper pushed gender boundaries, customarily slipping a transvestite into his female chorus lines, implicitly posing the question: If one can change sexual roles, why not do the same with racial stereotypes? The jazz he used for his shows could also be trendsetting. When he brought in his own lodger, a newcomer named Edward "Duke" Ellington, to lead the band at the Kentucky Club, Paul Whiteman was soon spotted in the audience, gleaning inspiration for his "symphonic jazz." Harper also introduced newcomer Louis Armstrong to Broadway, placing him in the pit orchestra for *Hot Chocolates*. In demand on Broadway, in Brooklyn, and in Harlem, Harper was currently juggling work at the Hollywood Club and Connie's Inn. He asked Drayton if he knew any good chorus boys.[13]

Drayton knew what Harper liked: quick, musical dancers. And, as he was confident the hardworking Bradley could succeed in the pressure-cooker environment of a Harper revue, he pushed his young friend forward. There was no question that Bradley, with his high cheekbones, brown eyes, and slender frame—albeit with strong shoulders—would look good on stage. But there was also something else, something distinctive, that caught Harper's eye. Bradley was affable but calm. The very way he held himself was graceful. He didn't seem to walk but to glide.[14]

With his years of practice, Harper sensed a winner. He quickly dispatched Bradley to John Dancer, his dance captain at Connie's Inn, to learn the routines. If Harper was a king in Harlem, Dancer was demi-royalty: he was the brother of Earl Dancer, Ethel Waters's manager, and a future Jungle nightclub owner, and he would later have the signal honor of serving as an usher at the funeral of Florence Mills.[15]

It was a pivotal introduction. Overnight Bradley transformed from elevator operator to professional dancer. Under the wings of Drayton, Harper, and Dancer, he had a key entrée to African American show business. Significantly, too, Buddy was dancing not at just any club but at the swank Connie's Inn. At its splashy opening in July 1923, featuring a thirty-one-member Harper revue and Wilbur Sweatman and His Acme Syncopators, it was rumored that the sold-out club turned away hundreds. Connie's Inn was arguably the best club in Harlem.[16]

Glamorously decorated, accommodating five hundred and serving a cosmopolitan mix of Chinese and American dishes washed down by plentiful Prohibition liquor, Connie's Inn was not only a society stop but an important musical destination. Leroy Smith, Fats Waller, Moms Mabley, Fletcher Henderson, Louis Armstrong, Eubie Blake, and Andy Razaf all contributed to the magic of Connie's Inn.

After closing for the night, the club became even more of a hotbed for jazz. As a teenager, Fats Waller had worked as a delivery man for the owners, Connie and George Immerman; now he brought fellow musicians in after closing to drink and jam until the wee hours.[17]

As good jazz dancing depended on great jazz music, the dancing at Connie's Inn, under Leonard Harper, was top notch. Harper choreographed on the premise that each dancer was an individual, and work had to be tailored to each body. As a result, his choreography fit dancers like a glove. Geraldine Lockart, a former Harper chorine, remembered how she and her chorus girl friends would laugh at the choreography in Hollywood films, comparing it to the steps they'd danced for Harper. They knew that if Harper had been white, he would have been swamped with work in Hollywood.[18]

Without a doubt, Harper knew what he was doing. He also had a specific point of view. For his chorus lines, Harper liked tall women with long legs. His routines were fast-paced, stately, with just a hint of sex. He demonstrated the movements himself, hired the best, ignored gradations of color, and focused on talent. He created his own versions of the Charleston (the Charleston Buzz) and the Black Bottom. He gave special emphasis to his chorus line, knowing that his chorus dancers, beating out the rhythm of the music with their feet while the principals took the spotlight, were the true heart of the show. In the year that Bradley danced in Harper's chorus line, he overlapped with Snakehips Tucker, Eddie Rector, Ralph Cooper, Willie Covan, and Leonard Ruffin. Harper also made sure his old pal, Bill "Bojangles" Robinson, knew he had—and accepted—an open invitation to perform at Connie's Inn whenever he wished. To the end of his career, Bradley revered the cleanliness of Bojangles's taps, his ability to connect to his audiences, and his spectacular exits.[19]

Harper was a stern taskmaster. He fully understood he was paid to produce a dazzling show on a deadline. Consequently, he fenced himself behind a wall of professionalism, was strictly business, and was hard to get to know. He docked pay if dancers were late for rehearsal. He fined lazy and inattentive dancers, anyone using foul language, and those he thought were threatening their graceful dancer's line by overeating. Further, if a chorus member, inspired by

Josephine Baker's attention-grabbing antics in *Shuffle Along*, ever tried to upstage a principal performer, he or she would be immediately out of work. Bradley observed and absorbed.[20]

If Harper's professionalism impressed, and Drayton's polish awed, it was Eddie Rector who most inspired Bradley stylistically. Decades later, Bradley would still speak of Rector with reverence, ranking his inventiveness above that of charismatic Bojangles Robinson or stylish John Bubbles, the father of rhythm tap. Bradley admired how Rector would work out new things, like tapping out time subtly, then reversing the rhythm, then alternating with his partner, the devastatingly handsome Ralph Cooper, as if they were two drums, then once again beating out the rhythm, but now in counterpoint together. With Rector, the sound of his feet was all-important; even in his spins and turns one always clearly heard his taps.[21]

In the great jazz tradition, Rector absorbed, then transformed, elements around him. His innovation added plurality to the Black dance experience. While others danced in small areas, or on purpose-built stairs, Rector carved out space, traveling across the stage and using his upper body for expression. He daringly used music that wasn't stop time and chose "pretty" music instead. While others wore tailcoats or spangles, Rector dressed in understated gray. A virtuoso of technique and musicality, he avoided ostentatious steps, flashy acrobatics, or witty gimmicks. His accent was visual, his dancing painted pictures.[22]

Above all, Rector was not about mere steps, but *dancing*, dovetailing those steps, smoothing the transitions, and moving in fluid arcs. *The New York Times* called him effortless. Cholly Atkins, of the great Coles and Atkins dance partnership, and later the choreographer for Motown groups, described Rector's dancing as floating. Perhaps influenced by white minstrel star George Primrose, Rector traveled across the stage with grace and elegance, a style that transcended stereotypes of the strutting or shuffling "darkie." He could waltz alone with an imaginary partner and hold a theater spellbound.[23]

For Bradley, Rector was both muse and morality tale. There was a haunting quality about the gifted Rector, a dreamer who could neither read nor write, who did not know his birthday, who at times arrived at the nightclub so drunk that he had to be dressed into his costume. Later, he would be institutionalized, losing valuable performing years at the height of his career. Bradley was moved by this man, so brilliant yet so fragile. Self-preservation, Bradley observed, required detachment. Without a safety net, one could not afford to fall prey to demons; one had to hold oneself in check.[24]

Meanwhile, Drayton's intuition proved correct: Buddy was a quick study and versatile dancer who snappily added wings, flips, knee drops, and other tap and acrobatic steps to his repertoire while dancing at Connie's Inn, then went on to dance in Lew Leslie's hit *Dixie to Broadway* with Florence Mills, Eddie Rector, Johnny Nit, and U. S. Thompson. *Dixie to Broadway* was the first Black show to have a mainstream Broadway production and, at $3.30 a ticket, was the most expensive all-Black show to date. Bradley was reputedly both the youngest and the highest-paid chorus dancer. But, when *Dixie to Broadway* closed in January 1925, Buddy was restless. Dancing multiple shows with identical choreography every week bored him. There had to be something more—but what?[25]

At nineteen, Buddy had learned to balance on the cusp, closely adjacent to the frolicking nightclub world while, as one who made his living from it, holding himself soberly apart. He made the connection between discipline and dance. Thaddeus Drayton had provided a new vista: that a Black man could venture outside America and enhance his performance, reputation, and aesthetics through travel. Leonard Harper, who worked as best he could within society's constraints, was a model of stoicism. In Eddie Rector, Buddy saw talent felled by forces greater than oneself and learned what was needed to persevere. Harlem had been an apt tutor.

As he succeeded as a dancer, developed a reputation, and made connections, Bradley acquired self-knowledge. He discovered he needed stimulation and a creative outlet that he didn't find in the repetitive modes of performance. Perhaps he even realized he was different, that he was calm rather than ebullient, medium height rather than imposing, slender rather than strapping—qualities that didn't always project from center stage.

With the surge of Black revues, there was a surge of Black dancers, all chasing the same goal: solo spots. They were beginning to differentiate themselves with special "hooks"—acrobatics, eccentric elements, legomania, humor. Bradley, with his preference for the subtle aesthetic of Eddie Rector, for incorporating the full body, carving space, and drawing on other movement vocabularies, may have felt disconnected. It was Leonard Harper, yet again, who would open a new door for Bradley.

CHAPTER 7

CELEBRITY DANCE INSTRUCTOR ON BROADWAY

Buddy Bradley is the greatest teacher of them all.

—PETE NUGENT

On May 20, 1925, the entertainment broadside *Variety* announced that Clarence Bradley, former specialty dancer with Florence Mills in *Dixie to Broadway*, would be teaching at Billy Pierce's dance studio. It was a very small ad, discreetly tucked in the lower left corner on a back page, and, judging from the news in *Variety* that day, there was not much room for a Black man on Broadway. Nearly one-third of the issue's sixty-four pages was dedicated to celebrating *Abie's Irish Rose*, a comedy about a young Irish woman and a Jewish man who marry despite their families' objections, that just the night before had broken the record for Broadway longevity with its 1,292nd performance. (To provide context, *Shuffle Along*, the African American hit of 1921–1922 had 504 performances.) Further, what little editorial ink was given to Black entertainment that day was discouraging: a young white dancer, Bee Jackson, had been tutored in the Charleston by no one less than by Elida Webb, whose staging of the Charleston in *Runnin' Wild* had propelled the dance to an international craze. Now Jackson, whose Charleston act was backed by Black musicians, was summarily informed that she would only be booked by Keith-Albee, one of vaudeville's most powerful producers, if she replaced her Black jazz band with white musicians.[1]

Exiting the IRT at Times Square, the walk from the subway to the dance studio on Forty-Sixth Street confirmed what Bradley already knew: he didn't really belong here, a brown face in a sea of white. Broadway, a canyon of theaters and commerce, congestion and commotion, was a foreign country after the leafy expanses, awninged windows, and familiar argot of uptown. The laughably small cubbyhole that masqueraded as a dance school only emphasized the absurdity of the situation.

It was also laughably intimidating. He, Buddy Bradley, who had only mastered a time step a few years ago, was now to teach others from a position of authority. He was nineteen, had never been an expert in anything, had only followed orders from maître d's and dance directors until now, had really become a dancer by accident, and now found himself in this unfamiliar realm. In entering this makeshift room, Bradley would step into his destiny.

Everyone knew that music needed new dance. Eubie Blake, Fats Waller, and Duke Ellington had changed everything. Their jazz had inspired George Gershwin and Richard Rodgers, whose music now supplanted European operetta on musical theater stages. The parading of showgirls in headdresses, the prancing of ingenues, and suave waltzes suddenly looked outdated, literally out of step with the music and the times. Of course, largely out of sight of Broadway entertainers, in jooks in the South, clubs in St. Louis, and blind alleys in Harlem, as well as posh watering holes uptown, bodies in motion already held the key to the future of dance.

But the reality was that no white person knew how to dance to jazz, let alone swing. This was obvious as far back as 1914, when showman Flo Ziegfeld purchased the rights to numbers from J. Leubrie Hill and Will Vodery's *Darktown Follies*, featuring dancers George Walker and Eddie Rector. In order to transpose the dances on his white Follies cast, Ziegfeld had to summon *Darktown* chorus dancer Ethel Williams to teach the routines. That day and now, ten years later, it rarely occurred to producers to put the Black talent on their stages.[2]

Teaching the uninitiated was an uphill battle. The reference points for jazz were Black insider events: family gatherings, church meetings, street and levee dancing, and the Theatre Owners' Bookings Association, colloquially known as "Tough on Black Asses" (TOBA), vaudeville circuit. Ethel Waters predicted that without these foundational experiences, white audiences would never be capable of understanding her blues music and would always be off the beat. Yet these white folks clamored to learn nonetheless. In fact, Langston Hughes recalled, they were annoyingly persistent, ogling dancers in clubs in Harlem, barging in on rent parties, hovering behind Black dancers in attempts to pick up the movements. For better or for worse, with a handful of exceptions, they just weren't getting it, either.[3]

Jazz dancing had expanded beyond jiving, for a specific technique was taking over entertainment stages. Ever since *Shuffle Along* had burst onto the scene, tap, jazz dancing's subspecialty, was the main event for both white and Black dancers. Former dancer Leonard Reed, inventor of the tap-dance anthem "The Shim Sham," remembers that in the 1920s, if you couldn't tap you couldn't even think of getting a job. Every chorus girl needed to pick up a pair of Capezio or Haney taps and bring her skills up to date.[4]

Of course, there had been Black dance teachers before. The ballroom sensations the Castles, whose music choices were informed by James Reese Europe, had been taught by Johnny Peters, dance partner of Ethel Williams, setting the stage for other Black teachers. (It was the Castles' dancing that had been so influential on Fred Astaire's own fluid style and perfectly timed ease.) More recently, "Old Bad Foot" Charlie Davis, a hardworking veteran of *Shuffle Along*, was having a go of it. Ditto Elida Webb, with her ill-fated Bee Jackson, as well as others. Annoyingly, once these pupils picked up the dance, assuming they did it well, it became theirs. As far as the press was concerned, it was now Gilda Gray's shimmy, not Ethel Williams's shimmy. While tacitly acknowledging that it was Black dances, not the Black *dancers*, that were in demand, Black dance teachers worked around this situation, creating agency by elevating teaching to professionalism and profiting from their esoteric skills.[5]

Leonard Harper took the idea one step further. He envisioned a physical school, an institution, then embellished it with daring: this dance school was to be in the heart of the white entertainment world, Broadway, exactly where it needed to be to pitch his dance skills to white dancers. The school itself was an assertion of financial independence; it was funded by Harper's profits from his own revue, *The Hollywood Follies*. Given the changing trends in musical theater, the grip of jazz, and the vogue for Black dance, the ambitious scheme of a Black-owned business on the Great White Way was an all but a guaranteed success. Plus, Harper's expertise as a teacher was renowned: his devoted showgirls laughed that he could teach even an elephant to dance.[6]

Harper's genius was supplemented by an astute business manager, Billy Pierce, a former salesperson for *The Chicago Defender*, the leading Black daily. Securing Suite 309 in the Navex Building, an industry nerve center housing songwriters, producers, overnight costume cleaners, and music publishers at 223 West Forty-Sixth Street, right next door to the National Vaudeville Association, the two opened the Leonard Harper Studio in May 1924.[7]

If Harper was the industry insider, Pierce was the brains. While he knew nothing about dance—he could barely lift a foot, scoffed hoofer Pete Nugent—he knew plenty about communication. His ads for the school, peppered with catchy buzz words, played up the star power of Harper ("Learn the Leonard Harper way!") and his team of "colored" (read: uniquely qualified) instructors, emphasized that their desirable offerings were taught via a proprietary curriculum ("The Leonard Harper System"), available only to a limited (subtext: *very* lucky) number of students. After listing instruction in the latest dances, including the Charleston, buck and wing, and tap, Pierce's ads then prudently switched to a decorous tone, probably intended to address any lingering qualms of the rare prude dancer or hovering stage mama, stating that a lady attendant would be on the premises at all times. It seems Pierce and Harper didn't limit their sights to Broadway either; they also placed an ad in *The Chicago Defender*.[8]

But no matter how strong the team, perfect the timing, or tight the plan, the Leonard Harper Studio was a risk. A glance at the glossy-paged magazine *The Dance* reveals exactly how far Harper and Pierce were operating outside the established dance world. Amid glamour shots of stars, articles included stories on Jean-Georges Noverre, the eighteenth-century French choreographer; Spanish dance and shawls; beauty routines; and dance world gossip. The rest of its pages are filled by ads for blue-chip schools De Fonteny Academie de Danse, the Albertina Rasch studio, Fred Le Quorne studio, Adolf Bolm school, and the Cansino studio at Carnegie Hall, run by Eduardo Cansino, a former Ziegfeld dancer and father of Rita Hayworth. Institutional dance meant many things in the 1920s but did not—yet—include Black dance.[9]

Despite the odds, Harper chalked up some early successes. Word got out that Adele Astaire, hot from her West End success in *Stop Flirting*, was now preparing her "Fascinating Rhythm" number in the Gershwins' *Lady Be Good* with Harper, although the show itself was conceived by choreographer Sammy Lee with input from Gershwin. Bee Palmer, a former Ziegfeld Girl, shimmied in the *Passing Show*, groomed by Harper. Principals appearing in the 1924 Broadway hits *Ziegfeld Follies*, *Innocent Eyes*, and *Best Show in Town* had also studied at the school. Harper the showman celebrated with Pierce that summer over dinner in his rambling apartment at 2067 Seventh Avenue in Harlem, graciously served by his maid.[10]

A couple of marquee hits doesn't mean momentum, however. Underneath the bravado, the Harper Studio wasn't finding enough traction. (Pierce, possibly exaggerating, later recalled that the school had no pupils at all.) As his dance studio wobbled, profitable outside commitments, including a new revue for Connie's Inn, diverted Harper's attention. By December 1924, Harper had abandoned the dance studio venture; he didn't need the hassle. And, while the versatile Harper had plenty of opportunities to choreograph and produce shows, Pierce, with fewer options, gamely soldiered on alone, downsizing the studio to a cupboard of a space, Suite 307, and working as the building's night janitor to cover the rent.[11]

In the midst of the uncertainty, Pierce had a brainstorm: If one could provide white dancers with Black dances, why not provide white stages with Black entertainers? Taking a page from James Reese Europe and his Clef Club, a clearinghouse for jazz musicians that provided talent for Broadway orchestra pits and society parties, Pierce set up a placement agency to connect his talented contacts with a keen audience that did not know how to access them. The old glad-hander began by dusting off his long-standing relationship with singer Alberta Hunter, then dispatched eight chorines to Paris for a show at the Moulin Rouge in 1924. (Later, Pierce loved to boast that he sent Black dancers to Paris before Josephine Baker went in 1925.) Pierce was even hired in the Black entertainment sector, where he put together a team for a TOBA revue in 1925, supplied talent for the touring company of *Runnin' Wild*, and reviewed a contract for Bert Williams. Ever resourceful, he began to write a column on Black entertainment for the *Chicago Defender*, naturally taking the opportunity to publicize his agency's successes. It was just as well: the sideline agency, alongside his nighttime mopping of the Navex Building corridors, was all that kept the school, now called the Billy Pierce Dance Studio, afloat.[12]

As for the school itself, it hobbled without a celebrity teacher. Pierce, the adept spinner, put on a brave façade, letting word get out that he had an extensive staff in place: Tim Brymm, a songwriter and hoofer, as his composer and musical conductor; former cabaret man Walter Brogsdale as music arranger; Daisy Small and Willie Covan as dance instructors; and Arthur Granville as office manager. But the bald reality was that Pierce had created his own Potemkin village. The illustrious Covan is never encountered again in connection with the school; Pierce had not the remotest need of an office manager; and the studio itself, as described by *The New York Tribune,* was barely the size of a luncheon cloth, with just a screen around a battered desk to serve as an office.[13]

Enter, stage right, teenaged Buddy Bradley, most likely sent by Leonard Harper as a sort of parting gift but possibly introduced to

Pierce by Willie Covan, with whom Bradley had danced at Connie's Inn. Perhaps, as a fellow son of Birmingham, Harper felt protective of this first-rate but restless chorus boy whose attention and talents seemed to be elsewhere. Perhaps he noted Buddy's poise, his ability to learn quickly, to negotiate the unfamiliar, and to adapt gracefully, and knew he was up to the task.

Clearly, Bradley thought otherwise. Rumor has it that when Pierce first ushered Bradley into the studio, he hesitated. He was self-taught and filled with doubt. Perhaps some of the students, there to learn tap dancing, already had studied ballet, Dalcroze, Delsarte, eurythmics, ballroom, and stage dancing and brought more formal knowledge to the studio than he did. He was born in the South, used to subordinate roles and Jim Crow laws; he had never been in a position of authority, except, of course, over himself. He reputedly whispered to Pierce that he couldn't possibly teach and bolted for the door, while Pierce, ever the optimist and master of spin, responded by pushing him into the studio and brushing off his doubts, saying it was all just a matter of perception. True or not, the story is prescient: while Pierce made Bradley possible, Bradley put the Billy Pierce Studio on the map.[14]

They were an odd couple, Bradley and Pierce. Their only commonality seemed to be a similar softspoken manner. While Bradley was a neophyte, Pierce was a seasoned showman. Bradley turned out to be a charmer in the studio, respected for his knowledge and artistry. Pierce was at heart a razzle-dazzle salesman—with an uncertain past. The entertainment press stated Pierce had a background performing in plantation and medicine shows, press agenting at Washington's Lincoln Theatre, and managing the Attucks Theater in Norfolk, Virginia; his biographer adds he fought with the much-decorated Harlem Hellfighters in France. In the case of Pierce, however, perception may not be reality: professional dancer Pete Nugent, as already noted, scoffed at his complete lack of dance skills. Herbert Harper, who later joined the Pierce Studio—and, it must be admitted, left with some acrimony—insists Pierce was nothing more than a former taxi driver from Chicago, a con artist, and a pimp.[15]

Bradley's diffidence, offset by his credentials and experience as a dancer, was compelling in the studio. While Harper had likely brought his stern style of rehearsal director to the studio, Bradley's soft voice and gentle corrections created a supportive learning environment. His lean body moved with fluid ease and impeccable rhythms in demonstration. He lit up when a student finally "got" the step. His New York students adored him and called him Buddy.[16]

If he felt frustrated with the slow learners, the arrogant, and the high handed, he never showed it. It was part of the legacy of racial inequality, not permitting oneself to say what one felt, for, as Langston Hughes remarked, "Negroes are practically never rude to white people." If he was pained, too, that white people had to learn what he and his fellow dark dancers had invented, then used their newfound skills to get cast in revues and shows that were off-limits to himself, he concealed it with encouragement. He was sensitive to his students' abilities, talent, and moods on any given day, crafting routines to suit individuals and making efforts to cheer them on. Yet, as he reached out so beguilingly, he held himself a bit aloof. He protected himself by not fully revealing himself, always remaining something of a mystery. Being an orphan since fourteen, aware of the precarity of life, and having observed the tragedy of Eddie Rector, he had learned to contain his feelings.[17]

As a teacher, Bradley wanted to see style, not steps. Breaking movement into discrete steps was anathema. What interested him, and what he transmitted to his dancers, were the rhythmic connections. He emphasized a relaxed, loose tap that chained steps together into musical phrases. While his ideal fused musicality, technique, and visual appeal, he was also attuned to individual musicality, marveling how differently dancers would respond to the same music. For women, dancing in the beribboned and heeled tap shoes of the 1920s, Bradley aimed to combine pliability and the connection to the floor with prettiness and grace.[18]

Music was central. Every rhythmic tune Bradley heard gave him ideas for new combinations of steps. At first, Bradley thought most piano accompaniments were slightly corny and preferred to work with rhythmic patterns from recordings, usually by Louis Armstrong or his friend Fletcher Henderson. Later, when the gifted pianist-dancer Frank Harrington joined the studio, Harrington transposed works by Bix Beiderbecke, Miff Mole, and Adrian Rollini for class, playing the low instrument solos with his left hand and the high instruments with the right.[19]

Just as Bradley had become bored with the predictability of show dancing, he sought unexpected dance tempos. At a time when much tap dancing was executed in tempo with the music, Bradley preferred jazzier patterns, typically finding inspiration when a musician played on top of a riff. Like John Bubbles, who was concurrently exploring the fast, musically complex dancing that became known as "rhythm tap," Bradley brought aural complexity to tap choreography and teaching to underscore his core belief: if you divorce jazz dance from its African American roots, it is no longer jazz.[20]

As no one uptown or downtown was working with music like Bradley at the time, U. S. Thompson, Florence Mills's husband, came to Bradley in search of something different. Drawing on the spatial compositions and graceful "picture dancing" of Rector, old African American dances, and the individual qualities of his students, Bradley's choreography was distinctive from the classic fare seen on the TOBA stage. While some might feel his departure was heresy, Bradley believed that tap, like any art form, was an evolving, porous art that reflected the tenor of the times and could be inspired by other forms of dance. He also took into account his dancer, breaking up standard tap steps to respond to the capabilities and natural style of the individual, then added jazz movement, effectively creating his own hybrid based on jazz dancing.[21]

With a well-known dancer now on his roster, Pierce looked up from his agenting to promote dance instruction at the Billy Pierce Studio. While he had kept a low profile when the school was in transition, once Bradley was in place Pierce resumed advertising in the spring of 1925. As Bradley's reputation grew, and the school picked up momentum, Pierce updated the ads accordingly and quickly stopped offering children's tap classes. Though Bradley was great with children, the school no longer needed basic tap classes for survival—professionals were increasingly packing the studio.

Two years after Bradley arrived at the school, Pierce's ads showily brandished the names of over fifty noted Bradley students who had passed through the portals of the Billy Pierce Studio, "The Best School of Tap Dancing in the World/A School of Perfect Syncopated Rhythm." The studio was now so successful that Bradley, after splitting his fees fifty-fifty with Pierce, was said to take home a staggering $1,000 a week. (Adjusted for inflation, this was roughly $18,000 in 2025.)[22]

In fact, Bradley was now setting new standards of dance. The reigning dean of theatrical dance was Ned Wayburn, the buttoned-up, pince-nez-wearing director of a five-story dance school across from the Lamb's Club. Wayburn, developer of the stately Ziegfeld Walk, was known for minimal motion and grooming homogeneity into his students with courses in makeup, diet, and studio etiquette. He focused on formulaic "framing"—that is, arranging a chorus line to set off a soloist—and "processionals," essentially fashion shows of splendid costumes and towering headdresses. His display, entrance, and exit steps were all performed with a fairly rigid upper torso, in contrast to the looser upper body movement seen in Harlem clubs and Black tap soloists. He had choreographed the lackluster "A Rainy Saturday" for the disastrous New York debut of a young adolescent act, Adele and Fred Astaire, who then hightailed it to Aurelio Coccia, who turned them into a sophisticated, streamlined act. He wrote prim books on dancing. He had been in the theater since the turn of the century.[23]

In contrast, Bradley invigorated Broadway dancers with movement attuned to the times: he focused on jazz music, fast uptown footwork, and the individuality of dancers. His dances challenged old, rigid standards and thrillingly echoed the speed in communications, in transportation, and in production that characterized the era. The very sound of the aluminum tap, in fact, echoed the mechanical sounds of industrial production. Individuality, central to how Bradley built dance on dancers, was also one of the last defenses in this fast, full-steam-ahead, consumerist age. As Bradley pursued his own aesthetic and shaped new dance, Wayburn, esteemed dance director of so many Ziegfeld shows, looked hopelessly square.[24]

Pierce's studio registry became a blue book of Broadway. Everyone who was anyone in theater seemed to pass through Bradley's hands in the 1920s. Top revue producers George White and Earl Carroll periodically stopped in to source new talent. When *The Dance* published its 1928 "Best of Year" list, three who received top honors, Ada May, Ann Pennington, and Tom Patricola, had been Bradley students. The following year, two more in the "Best of the Year" summary had been shaped by Bradley: best eccentric dancer Clifton Webb and best juvenile lead Jack Whiting. Before the Roaring Twenties came to an end, it was rumored that in one class alone (and there were only eight dancers to a class), the total of the weekly salaries of the women was $28,000.[25]

Accomplished dance stars came to Bradley for up-to-date polish. Adele Astaire, back in New York for *Funny Face*, returned to the studio in 1927, then again for *Smiles* in 1930, and would continue to dip in and out of the studio. Eleanor Powell squeezed in classes with Bradley between her shows at the Paramount, studying jazz and tap movement, but, as a trained ballet dancer, she was still reluctant to put taps on her shoes. (It was later, studying with Jack Donahue and John Boyle, that she famously hooked sandbags on a belt to keep her movement close to the floor.) Ballet dancers from the Metropolitan Opera Queenie Smith and Ada May bourréed six blocks uptown and reinvented themselves as musical comedy stars. Winsome teenager Ruby Keeler, whose tap Black Bottom in 1927's *Bye Bye Bonnie* "caused a riot," found Bradley not only a terrific coach but a sympathetic listener and friend. Others who made the pilgrimage to Bradley's studio were Constance Carpenter and Claire Luce, Fred Astaire's first dance partner post-Adele.[26]

Glamour girls transformed into contenders under Bradley's tutelage. Jazz babies Anita Loos and Louise Brooks stopped in on their way to Hollywood. Mae West jumped ship from Wayburn to study with Bradley—when she wasn't lounging in the Jungle in Harlem. Betty Compton, Ziegfeld Girl and gal pal of Jimmy Walker, New York's dashing "Nightclub Mayor," now won roles in *Funny Face* with the Astaires and Cole Porter's *Fifty Million Frenchmen*. Pretty boys like silent screen heartthrob Ramon Novarro, then dancing in revues, came too. And, as it was the Twenties, gangsters' girlfriends routinely showed up at the school, hoping Bradley could turn them into bona fide dancers. With their boyfriends' money, they were in demand on Broadway; casting them meant the boyfriends would invest in the show.[27]

Thespians and singers turned to Bradley for specific tasks. Actress Bessie Love, the first to dance the Charleston on film (in *The King of Main Street*), was applauded for her grace and agility, without a hint of vulgar wiggling. Zelma O'Neal, a mid-level West Coast vaudevillian, came to Bradley, then received strong notices in George White's *Scandals* and relaunched her career in London. In what must have been a painful undertaking, Bradley coached Ethel Barrymore for her blackface role in *Scarlet Sister Mary*, a situation that underlined the limitations society then placed on Blacks, withholding casting in even the most logical of roles.[28]

Above all, Buddy Bradley was the dedicated dancer's dance teacher. Choreographer Seymour Felix sent his children to Bradley for instruction. An adolescent Henry Le Tang came to Bradley when his Harlem tap teacher, Ella Gordon, realized his talents exceeded what she could offer. In Bradley's class, Le Tang met two other talented teenagers, Buddy Ebsen (who would tap with Shirley Temple in *Captain January* and was originally slated to dance as the Tin Woodman in *The Wizard of Oz*) and Hal LeRoy, one of the few white dancers to enter the Hoofers' Club and an inspiration for Sandman Sims. Paul Draper, of whom Bradley despaired (he had no more sense of rhythm than a flea, Bradley recalled) also sought out Bradley.[29]

In Philadelphia, nine-year-old Chuck Green met Bradley in the wings of the Hippodrome and was immediately attracted by Bradley's aura. Bradley, in turn charmed by Green's persona and talent, made time to teach the youngster a tap strut and a combination that began with a heel click and ended with the Tack Annie (a step Jack Wiggins had devised and named after his girlfriend), and encouraged him to study formally at the Pierce Studio.[30]

As white dancers streamed to Bradley, Black dances flowed out of the Pierce Studio. If the Black Bottom, Mess Around, and other dances were old news in the South, they were red-hot revelations to Broadway. Bradley's dissemination of these dances, assisted by some clever marketing by Pierce, made the Pierce Studio their local font. By adding the twist of a tap to the Charleston, the studio laid a unique claim on the dance that had ostensibly originated in a Charleston orphanage. And though *The Baltimore Afro-American* smugly pointed out that the Mess Around had already been kicking around Baltimore for six years, *Variety* breathlessly reported in 1926 that Bradley was introducing it to showgirls, who were avidly adding it to their bag of tricks. Similarly, though Alberta Hunter allegedly held the copyright for the Black Bottom (and its murky origins could be traced to either Atlanta or Tennessee, depending on the source), it became associated with Bradley, who posed in shirtsleeves and suspenders for thumbnail sketches in *The Dance* in 1927—illustrating how Bradley, the Billy Pierce Studio, and Black dance were slowly integrating the Eurocentric dance establishment.[31]

New jazz dances, conceived by Bradley, emerged from the studio, too. In 1927, Pierce advertised instruction in the Kinkajou, a dance Bradley had created for a Broadway play, *Rio Rita*, and something called the Devil's Dance. That same year, Bradley also unveiled the Sugar Foot Strut. Suspiciously reeking of publicist palaver (most likely that of Billy Pierce), *Variety* reported that Bradley had gone south to find an accurate version of the dance. In fact, Bradley's inspiration *had* come from the South, but via Fletcher Henderson, his dance class music standby, who had recently recorded "Sugar Foot Stomp" based on Joe "King" Oliver and his Creole Jazz Band's "Dippermouth Blues," written for Louis Armstrong.[32]

Dancers like Earl "Snakehips" Tucker never worried about people stealing his dances. He knew it would only serve to prove that there was only one inimitable Snakehips. The same could be said of Bradley and his dancers. Stella Doyle had come from England, intent on dance stardom. After performing a Charleston on stilts in an obscure film (which, not surprisingly, got her nowhere), she came to Bradley. But even working with the best teacher, Doyle's reviews were, at best, damned with faint praise. Nevertheless, the ungifted but ambitious Doyle was thrilled with what she achieved: a spot on the program at the Hippodrome. She gifted Bradley a French cigarette case embellished with rough-cut diamonds and rubies, the first of a prized collection that would adorn his apartments.[33]

In 1928, Fox Film recorded Marie Saxon performing Bradley's Sugar Foot Strut. Saxon, married to Syd Silverman, the publisher of *Variety*, offered up a dutiful rendition of the dance. In the recording she executes the rapid footwork, the inward turning of the legs and feet, the off-center balances, the thrust hips. She dances on the ball of her foot, like Bojangles. She even smiles appealingly. But, unlike Buddy, who even in still photographs conveys sinuous curves, dynamic grace, and musicality, Saxon, with her inexpressive upper body and mechanical arms, looks more like an energetic majorette than a rhythmic, fluid dancer. Yet, as the wife of a powerful man in the entertainment world, it is Saxon, not Bradley, who basked in the limelight with Bradley's dance while its creator remained, perhaps by choice, in the hidden role of teacher and choreographer.[34]

But, even behind the scenes, Bradley was now a towering presence. A foot injury at the age of twenty was newsworthy enough to be reported by *Variety*—after all, not having class with Bradley was a near-tragedy for a dancer anxious to rise in showbiz. The press even noted the death of Robert Epps, Bradley's nondancing older brother, in its obituaries. By 1927, Bradley was so well known in theatrical circles that the press occasionally referred to him simply as Buddy, no last name required. A captivated African American press began to follow his rise, too, with the influential *Pittsburgh Courier* leading the way in 1927 with a photo of the twenty-one-year-old and a caption noting he had received a diamond-encrusted cigarette case from a grateful dancer.[35]

Dramatic photographs of Bradley in 1927 and 1928 heightened his visibility and mystique. His friend Vera Caspary, the editor of *The Dance*, was a long-sighted champion of dance, who, along with dance critic John Martin of *The New York Times*, brought legitimacy to dance as an art form in America. Caspary, using the nom de plume Elise Marcus, showcased African American dances to her readers, using twenty-two-year-old Bradley to demonstrate in photos. While Bradley twists, sways, bends, and shuffles his way through the polyrhythms (simultaneous movements to different beats) and weight shifts of Ballin' the Jack, the Mooch, the Washington Johnny, the Baltimore Buzz, the Heebie-Jeebies, and the Breakdown, the pithy captions, with their emphasis on musicality and performance, hint Bradley contributed to the text, too. The caption for the Black Bottom, for example, notes that the success of the step is dependent on rhythm but also includes specific instructions for hands and, even, eyes.[36]

Inevitably, the news about the man transforming theatrical dance with jazz traveled across the Atlantic. Dancers and actors from the West End made a point of studying with Bradley when their shows transferred to New York—with striking results. *Variety* pointed out that when the English musical *By the Way* played Broadway, Cicely Courtneidge was the star, supported by her husband, Jack Hulbert, but, after twelve lessons with Bradley in New York, it was Hulbert who walked away with the show when it played Chicago.[37]

With Bradley filling its studios, the Pierce Studio became a hub for entertainment industry news. Dancers rushing in and out of the studios brought gossip; Pierce's agenting business provided leads and updates. Before the widespread use of the telephone, the Pierce Studio was an invaluable clearing house for work, placing both white and Black talent in diverse venues. Proffering instruction with Bradley as part of the enticement, Pierce engaged a group of "16 peppy brown girls" for a Ziegfeld revue—the franchise known for "Glorifying the American Girl" had extended, temporarily, its palette. (Significantly, too, dance directing the Ziegfeld revue had long been the fiefdom of Ned Wayburn.) In 1930, Pierce placed eight tap dancers trained in his studio in Ruth Selwyn's short-lived but highbrow *9:15 Revue* and leveraged his newfound stature to serve the Black entertainment community, hosting panels with composer Will Marion Cook; S. H. Dudley (manager for the TOBA and "dean of our group in present day theatricals"); Nahum Brascher, president of the Associated Negro Press; and Jacques Charles, general manager of the Moulin Rouge in Paris.[38]

Gone now was the shabby little room with a screen to demarcate an ad-hoc office that Bradley had first entered. By 1926, Bradley's resuscitation of the school had allowed Pierce to sign a new lease for 4,500 square feet, moving the school from an obscure upper room to two floors of the Navex Building, including the highly visible street level. With the last word in comfort and convenience, the facilities rivaled those of Wayburn. Bradley had two dedicated private studios, in which he would work from 10 a.m. to 10 p.m., starting out in one room showing a dancer a routine and leaving her to practice a little, then starting another dancer in the other and alternating back and forth.[39]

Specially padded floors minimized strain on dancers' limbs and joints. Classrooms featured barres, mirrors, and a ventilation system to prevent draughts and overheating. For rehearsing, two studios could be combined into one room wide enough for a chorus line of sixteen and deep enough to mimic the depth of a stage. There were showers, private dressing rooms for stars, and locker rooms for chorus dancers. Superefficient secretary Freda Jackson, described as a society girl from St. Paul, Minnesota, who decorated the wedding reception of Isabelle Washington and Adam Clayton Powell Jr., could even teach class in a pinch, having once had her own dance school in St. Paul. After suffering the ignominy of scrubbing offices, Pierce now complained ostentatiously about the cost of his $2,100 dance floor.[40]

The new school, with enrollment topping three hundred in 1929, was a hive of activity.[41] Classes drilling the Syncopated Buck, Eccentric Buck, Devil Dance, Jungle Stomp, Zulu Stomp, Dirty Dig, Flapper Stomp, Harlem Hips, Black Bottom, Black Bottom with Taps, and even a version of Bill "Bojangles" Robinson's jealously guarded Stair Dance, took place every day from noon to 7 p.m.

The interior design represented the DNA of the Pierce Studio: marketing savvy, racial pride, and Black dance. Walls were lined with autographed photographs of celebrities. The color scheme was red and green with a fresco of figures in brown, red, and orange dancing the Charleston, Black Bottom, and Sugar Foot Strut. For the painting, Pierce had turned to Helen Smith, who had recently participated in an art show of "race" artists at International House sponsored by the Harmon Foundation.[42]

Larger space also meant more staff. When the new school opened in 1927, Bradley held the title Master Instructor, overseeing dance teachers whose influence resonates to this day. His staff of all Black men included Frank Harrington, Ernest Carlos, Herbert Harper, former student Roland Holder, and his younger brother, Aurelius, who now used the name Arthur Bradley. Shortly afterward, Aaron Gates came on board while, later, Henry Le Tang rose from pupil to studio assistant and Eddie "Pee Wee" Williams was engaged to shadow Bradley in the studio. Each in their own way extended the Bradley vision and made significant contributions to theatrical dance. Often unsung and mostly forgotten, their careers and lives illustrate their uphill battle, usually waged with few contacts and little capital, to integrate themselves and their dance into the institutional world of entertainment.[43]

Chief instructor Frank Harrington might just as well have held the title musical director. A pianist admired by professional musicians and enamored of Adrian Rollini's saxophone solos, Harrington was central to the studio's musical identity and success. It was Harrington's transcriptions that laid out the exact rhythms Bradley wanted to imprint on his dancers' bodies and project onto the stage. Seemingly as talented a teacher as a musician, Harrington, years after the Pierce Studio folded, coached chorus boy Gene Kelly, infusing his low-down dance with upper body movement. (Later, Kelly, who also sought to integrate dance, character, and narrative, would turn to Bradley when casting *An American in Paris*.)[44]

If Harrington and Bradley were musical soulmates, Bradley and Ernest Carlos were temperamental opposites. While Bradley was patient, the fiery Carlos was known to walk out of class if his students weren't focused. Yet Carlos brought a nearly ethereal beauty to tap, echoing Bradley's use of the entire body and emphasizing grace and musicality over tricks and acrobatics. According to choreographer Karin Baker, a former student, sound was as important as steps in Carlos's universe: his tricky rhythms would all but sing, virtuosically creating color and shadow, tracing a musicality of hills and valleys, in quick small steps. After Bradley moved to London, Carlos and Bradley met up at least once, at a Congress of Dancing Masters in 1934 in New York, where, characteristically, their programs were aesthetic complements: Carlos demonstrated his new poetic rhythm tap, and Bradley introduced ballroom tap, a nod to his inspiration, Eddie Rector. Though Carlos was a legendary teacher in New York through the 1970s, his life and work were spent quietly outside the public eye. Today, reverential dancers, newly aware of his legacy, seek to recreate him and his rhythms.[45]

Herbert Harper took over where Bradley left off. At the Billy Pierce Studio, he became chief instructor when Bradley left, accepting a doleful salary of fifteen dollars a week (perhaps because Harper had not fully risen in Pierce's eyes from his origins as school errand boy and emptier of spittoons), as he so badly wanted the job. In the theater, he also continued what Bradley had begun, bringing African American tap and jazz into the mainstream. Vincente Minnelli, a friend, helped Harper swing a few key breaks. Rouben Mamoulian next hired him to infuse the proper rhythm into Gershwin's *Porgy and Bess*, featuring John Bubbles. In 1936, Harper signed on as assistant choreographer to George Balanchine for *On Your Toes*, one of the rare times he received program credit, coaching Ray Bolger personally for the lauded "Slaughter on 10th Avenue" tap ballet, which is still danced by New York City Ballet to this day.[46]

Roland Holder, an immaculate dancer, was a former student whom Bradley promoted to teacher and who unabashedly stole Bradley's steps. Dancer Pete Nugent recalls Holder as mysterious and a bit sly. He didn't mingle with the other hoofers, then would appear out of the blue at the Hoofers' Club and astound everyone with a brilliant routine. Laid-back Bradley knew exactly what was going on: when Holder saw him teaching a routine he liked, he'd ask Bradley to show it to him, then go uptown and show it off as his own. The ploy worked for a time: in 1929, teenage Holder joined the cast of *Hot Chocolates*, directed by Leonard Harper. In 1931, he danced a nightclub number in the Oscar Micheaux film *The Exile*. Leonard Harper staged the ensembles and dances. Nevertheless, as soloists at the time often brought in their own choreography, and with Holder's known record of emulating Bradley, it is safe to assume that watching Holder, barely twenty, in top hat and tails, is watching an elegant proxy for Bradley: he moves three dimensionally, leaning forward deeply, back-bending, traveling, and making use of the entire, if tiny, nightclub stage. His feet are quick and light, his arm movements natural but polished. Thanks to Holder and his ruses, we have a rare record of what Bradley's coaching and choreography looked like on an African American body.[47]

Unlike the guileless Herbert Harper, Aaron Gates negotiated a short lived if mutually beneficial arrangement with Pierce. While Gates picked up an important Broadway credential from his association with Pierce, he offered Pierce a toehold in Harlem as well as a bit of luster from his own shooting-star name. In the spring of 1927, Gates started a dance school on 135th Street in Harlem that featured the Billy Pierce (a.k.a. Buddy Bradley) method of teaching and was also listed as assistant instructor in ads for the Billy Pierce Studio. Simultaneously, he nurtured a career as a choreographer, working on the book musical *Bottomland*, which received lukewarm reviews. Then Gates struck luck and staged the chorus, uncredited, for *Show Boat*, contributing more prestige to the Pierce Studio. Unfortunately, Gates's work on *Show Boat* did not lead to other opportunities on Broadway. The following year, no longer associated with Pierce, Gates staged an indoor circus and another show on a skating rink.[48]

At nineteen, Aurelius entered the Pierce Studio with a devil-may-care swagger. Underneath the daredevil façade, however, was still the little brother who depended on his elder. After following in Bradley's footsteps and moving to New York, he picked up tap dancing, perhaps tutored by his brother, and assumed the professional name of Arthur Bradley, "Bradley" now a highly convenient name in the entertainment world. Aurelius's aptitude for dance was real, for he landed a job at the Pierce Studio, probably with some help from Bradley, where the brothers' fundamental differences were much in evidence. Unlike Bradley, who was soft-spoken and decorous, Aurelius (i.e., Arthur) was so boisterous and loud that the staff called him "Arthurphonic" (a pun on a record player brand at the time). Aurelius was also cheeky. Like Roland Holder, he was untoward with women students, something the conservative Pierce would not tolerate. When Freda Jackson informed Pierce about Aurelius's antics, Pierce fired him.[49]

With a Tony Award for *Black and Blue*, Henry Le Tang, the youngest Bradley assistant, had the most visible and enduring dance career. His story carries in it the lineage of tap. His Harlem tap teacher was Ella Gordon, who had studied with Grace Giles and Elida Webb, now as well known for her work at the Cotton Club as for the Charleston, who in turn had trained with the great Aida Overton Walker. After working as a "pick" for Sophie Tucker and studying with Gordon, the adolescent Le Tang—he was about thirteen or fourteen—was brought to Bradley in 1928 or 1929 to take his skills to the next level. Perhaps Bradley saw himself in the small, deft teenager and soon brought him on as his assistant. Besides helping students work through Bradley's swift steps, the job had menial aspects to it, but Le Tang was always proud of his association with Bradley, insisting to colleagues later in life that he would have done anything to observe and learn from his mentor. At about the time Bradley left for London, Le Tang opened his own dance studio.

More than any other, Le Tang perpetuated the Bradley style in America, emulating Bradley by teaching sequential routines, tailoring dance to individual bodies, and emphasizing grace. Hinton Battle pointed out that Le Tang, like Bradley, balanced upper body style with lower body technique. Dancer/choreographer and disciple of Le Tang, Dexter Jones recalled how Le Tang always closed his dances with a strong visual image. Former dance captain, Leah Bass-Baylis, remembered, too, how Le Tang took into account a dancer's individuality: "He could make *anybody* look like they could really, *really* tap," she recalled. Like Bradley, too, Le Tang presented women dancers with finesse and polish, preferring that they dance in heeled shoes until relatively late in his career. In 1982, Le Tang paid an artist's tribute to his mentor, choreographing *Shim Sham*, a play inspired by Bradley's life starring Hinton Battle, and weaving dance quotes from Bradley directly into his choreography. With students Gregory Hines, Hinton Battle (whom he converted from a ballet dancer to show dancer), Dormeshia Sumbry-Edwards, and Savion Glover, Le Tang's influence stretches to this day into the twenty-first century.

As Bradley's career evolved, so did his name and the parameters of his life. Since arriving in New York, his name had morphed from his given name, Clarence Bradley Epps, through several variations, finally settling into a groove as Buddy Bradley, the name he would use colloquially, professionally, and semi-officially for the rest of his life. There are many possible explanations for this, from the personal to the practical. Certainly, he may have felt antipathy for the name Epps, the surname of his ancestor's enslaver. Using his first and middle name were problematic, however, as there was a contemporary drummer named Clarence Bradley; two in the entertainment field with the same name could easily lead to confusion. Reverting to his childhood nickname, Buddy, and affixing his middle name, Bradley, was the enduring result: jazzy, alliterative, melodious, and memorable.[50]

Success now allowed him to make choices aligned with his taste and temperament, rather than dictated by what he could afford. Bradley first upgraded from his airless back room to a new lodging house at 2332 Seventh Avenue, still conveniently close to the Hoofers' Club at 2237 Seventh Avenue. By 1930, he had swapped communal living for private quarters, acquiring an apartment at 334 Edgecombe Avenue in sedate Sugar Hill, overlooking the lively flatlands of Harlem. His monthly rent was $68 (about $1,000 in 2025), neither a stretch nor an extravagance, given his rumored income.[51]

While pleasant, Bradley's apartment building was restrained when compared to the opulent 409 Edgecombe, just up the street, where W. E. B. Du Bois and his family lived, or 555 Edgecombe, where Paul Robeson and Duke Ellington resided. Bradley's choice of Sugar Hill was significant, however, in that it revealed his own preference for an understated life. Now that he was a dance teacher, and no longer a dancer, he didn't need to live in proximity to Harlem's clubs and action. Plus he had a newfound domesticity: at age twenty-five, he lived with a twenty-one-year old Austrian woman, a "Martha M." who gives her last name as Bradley, though there is no record of a marriage. Without knowing this woman's actual last name, nothing can be gleaned of this relationship except what appears on the census: Martha had arrived in the US in 1912, was not a US citizen, and had no listed occupation.[52]

Other perks accumulated. In 1928 Bradley gifted himself a sporty car, the newly introduced LaSalle Roadster, the younger, hipper version of a Cadillac. Baritone Jules Bledsoe, who had originated "Ol' Man River" in *Show Boat* the previous year, had gleefully tooled about in a sky-blue Packard, explaining to the delight of Harlem that he had a uniformed white chauffeur so that the public could distinguish between the chauffeur and the owner. Although it is nearly impossible to imagine the modest, soft-spoken Bradley drawing attention to himself or springing for the outlay of a driver, the press, enamored of such flamboyance, reported Bradley had a white chauffeur, too.[53]

Bradley had also picked up the lifetime habit of smoking and, like Henry Le Tang, who was legendarily oblivious to the growing tip of ashes threatening to tumble to the floor as he taught, would smoke in the studio. Life in the dance studio wasn't always rewarding, which may have encouraged the habit. For every gifted Roland Holder or Henry Le Tang, there was a conniving Marie Saxon or a hopeless Stella Doyle.

The smoking, the charming modesty, and the reticence were quite possibly more than habits; perhaps they indicated an internal discord. In five years, Bradley's life had advanced with such velocity that that the jeweled cigarette cases, the sought-after status as guru of dance, and the quiet inner self had not yet fused into equilibrium. Perhaps he needed time to adjust to his new role as a voice of authority in the dance studio. Perhaps there was even some fundamental ambivalence about teaching. When he began to teach for Pierce, after all, Bradley had also been trying to put together a double act with Ralph Cooper, who had recently been dancing with Eddie Rector. Plus, teaching on Broadway kept Bradley continually in that uneasy in-between space, constantly monitoring himself from the eyes of another, what Du Bois referred to as living behind a veil.

The dignified apartment, the luxury car, the jeweled accessories, and the live-in girlfriend were somewhat deceptive, too. Even enjoying his first heady flush of success, Bradley was well aware that as a Black man he was constantly vulnerable, and he was quick to recognize this vulnerability in others. He empathized when a friend was feeling blue, others were struggling to make a go of it, or particularly when children such as Chuck Green required special attention. With composer and bandleader Fletcher Henderson, he led the Black Bottom at a fundraiser at Smalls' Paradise, organized by Mrs. Baird (a Bradley student from Harlem who eventually moved to Paris to pursue a dance career) to support the Christmas Glee Club's holiday dinners for Harlem's poor. For two years running, he also opened a fashion show for the charitable Utopia Club with a soft-shoe routine. And while Bradley naturally operated on a personal level, he could also be drawn to the political. When Billy Pierce participated in an NAACP radio program with Walter White discussing his experiences investigating lynchings, Bradley would be part of the entertainment team.[54]

In fact, Pierce had become a sort of compass for Bradley. The son of two formerly enslaved people, educated first by a Quaker and then at Storer College (founded by the Freedmen's Bureau in Virginia), he was fifteen years older than Bradley and had a more expansive personality. He not only brought—perhaps dragged—Bradley into the studio but expanded Bradley's vision. He was a charming go-getter, genially hosting parties in Harlem attended by Adele Astaire, Jack Buchanan, Jack Stillman of the Stillman banking clan, and the artist Miguel Covarrubias. He was also deeply committed to civil rights; in 1931 he rallied support among New Yorkers for the defense of the Scottsboro Boys, the young men who had been falsely accused of rape in Alabama. With his creative schemes, continual striving, and consciousness of being a "race man," Pierce showed Bradley what was possible, both professionally and politically.[55]

Most of all, Pierce had faith in Bradley. While Thaddeus Drayton and Leonard Harper had spotted talent, it was Pierce who had believed in Bradley's untapped potential. It was Pierce who laid the groundwork for Bradley's professional evolution. For someone who had been alone since the age of fourteen, making his way without a buffer or a champion, Pierce's faith and camaraderie may have provided an emotional lifeline. After a day in the studio on Broadway, Pierce and Bradley would sometimes spend evenings together uptown in Harlem, occasionally with Pierce's pal, the future filmmaker John Huston. As Buddy made up dances. Pierce, unwell and walking with a cane, would critique from the sidelines. It was as if the orphan had found a guardian angel.[56]

But, even with a compass, Bradley's journey took courage. There was the issue of being the first, of trailblazing in an industry not made for him, venturing into an environment of the dominant majority. Only a year after Bradley began teaching jazz, young Martha Graham established her own dance studio, proclaiming her ambition to create a pure American dance, free from the influences of European culture. Bradley and his colleagues were also offering a new expression of American dance, but, in contrast to Graham, neither he nor even Pierce, with his flair for communication, made grand pronouncements. Instead, he quietly did the work. Perhaps he felt lucky to have been granted a place at the table and did not feel entitled to express himself, while Graham, the daughter of the intelligentsia and trained in the modern language of Denishawn, the dance school in Los Angeles founded by Ruth St. Denis and Ted Shawn, was thoroughly comfortable with her convictions and confident speaking as an oracle.

It was a lonely undertaking. And it would be more than understandable if Bradley felt precarious in his seat at the table. The dance environment had barely evolved since the moment Leonard Harper placed his first brave ad in *Variety*. While the names on the pages of *The Dance* might have changed slightly since 1924, the profile of the Europeanist dance establishment had altered little. There was an occasional nod to Sri Lankan dance, hula dance, or African American dance, but little effort to accommodate them.[57]

Yet, at that very moment, Bradley was transforming dance. In choosing to remain both artistically and personally accessible, porous, and empathetic, he had become a superb teacher. The stream of students running to the studio and, even more critically, the growing list of noted dancers he trained, attest to this.

All the while his impact in the studio shifted jazz dance from the margins to the mainstream, Bradley reshaped theatrical choreography. Dances with roots in African American culture were now danced by more bodies and on new stages. In increasing the awareness, access, and visibility of African American dance, Bradley was a driving force in recasting vernacular African American dance as America's dance.

CHAPTER 8

A BLACK CHOREOGRAPHER ON THE GREAT WHITE WAY

After Bradley did the *Greenwich Village Follies*,
nobody needed to teach Bradley anything.

—THADDEUS DRAYTON

The effect of Bradley reworking the *Greenwich Village Follies* in the spring of 1926 was seismic. A failing show extended its run by a year. Irene Delroy, a promising soubrette, became a star. Inspired by her ascent, showgirls streamed to Bradley for instruction, generating the means for the school's expansion into new quarters. Theater insiders beyond the Navex Building took note, too: Buddy Bradley, all of twenty years old, was emerging as an exciting, and different, choreographic talent. As America began to wake up to the treasure its African American culture had forged, Bradley was part of the vanguard. Now jazz movement was not only danced in the South, in Harlem, and on segregated stages but had been reconceived for the Broadway stage by a Black choreographer.

A little backstory. In 1919, John Murray Anderson single-handedly invented the urbane revue, the *Greenwich Village Follies,* a sassy downtown alternative to the tinselly *Ziegfeld Follies*. What it lacked in budget, it made up in naughty sophistication. Anderson also had a flair for modernity, hiring young Martha Graham as well as Bert Savoy, an over-the-top, hissy drag queen, whose line in the 1921 edition, "You must come over," was quickly appropriated by Mae West. Quick-witted and irreverent, the show so resonated with the Jazz Age that it transferred from a small downtown theater to the established Shubert Theater on Broadway. For five years, Anderson wrote and directed new editions of the revue, then moved on to direct Broadway plays, London revues, and Hollywood films.[1]

Without Anderson at the helm, the *Greenwich Village Follies* lost its sass. It was not for lack of trying. Producers A. L. Jones and Morris Green offered cash prizes for clever new ideas in set design and comic sketches. They hired Hassard Short, an innovative director who invented bridge lighting and the revolving stage. A raft of talent was signed, including Herman Mankiewicz (who later wrote the script for *Citizen Kane*) and costume designers Gilbert Adrian and Charles Le Maire. Seasoned dance director Larry Ceballos, who would later ghost for Busby Berkeley at Warner Brothers, was brought on board. But the *Follies* had lost its way: Anderson's light wit and bare-bones sets had been replaced by heavy dancing and opulent display.[2]

Early reviews from Boston sounded the first alarm. "Unleavened and unrehearsed," one critic said, adding that the chorus became lost in a maze of complicated steps. Another sneered that the extravagant show had every blessing but laughter. Some tinkering was done on the road, but the New York reviews were hardly better. There was one saving grace: Irene Delroy dancing "Go South," a Charleston number that brought the longest and loudest applause of the evening. As was the custom at the time, the dance director staged the dances for the ensemble, but featured dancers hired their own choreographers. Delroy had gone to Buddy Bradley.[3]

Bradley cast a professional eye on Delroy and quickly sized her up. She was fetching and had a little ballet training but lacked any sense of jazz movement.[4] Bradley, as one of the best young dancers in Harlem, could do just about anything: knee drops, splits, lots of wings, even some eccentric things, but shrewdly realized that the job of a choreographer is not about his or her own abilities, or even exploring dancing's possibilities, but a practical reality: making the dancer look good and captivating the audience. This, Bradley did. He tailored up-to-the-minute steps—the Charleston, in this case—with old-fashioned jive steps like the Tack Annie that Delroy could manage gracefully, then transformed with artistry what could have been simplistic into something theatrical and exciting. Mixing the Charleston strut steps and body movements with jive, Bradley created a routine of sixty-four bars (two choruses of thirty-two bars), coached Delroy from entrance to exit, sent her on stage, and stopped the show.[5]

Two stars, Bradley and Delroy, were born that night, but the show floundered. Director Hassard Short, hypersensitive to every spangle and spotlight but tone-deaf to rhythm and repartee, had run fifty thousand dollars over budget. Sinking under costs and anxious to repay their backers, the producers did the logical thing: they sacked the director and the choreographer then consulted the unknown who had created the hit "Go South" routine for Delroy. When Bradley suggested new ideas and new dances, Morris Green brought him on to rework the show.[6]

Alas, in the rush to bail out the sinking show, they did not discuss credits. Bradley, after all, was a neophyte, not yet sufficiently savvy or confident to demand proper recognition, and the producers were harried: Hassard was preparing to sue the producers, and the show was hemorrhaging money. It is likely, too, that Larry Ceballos's agreement required that his name stay on the production. That Bradley was inexperienced and a minority may have made it particularly easy for producers to gloss over the point, but the reality was that withholding credit was not uncommon. Young Agnes de Mille, despite promises from the producers, saw her work in *Flying Colors* not only distorted beyond recognition but also uncredited. Even an old pro like Ceballos found his contractual credit in *Footlight Parade* blatantly sacrificed to promote the career of Busby Berkeley.

No show on the commercial stage is easy; doctoring a show is even worse. Tensions were high, and tempers flared. The production and creative staffs were in turmoil, stars' reputations were on the line, backers' money was at risk, and the clock ticked loudly. Two weeks is very little time to reconceive or create a total of nine dance numbers, some quite complex, involving both chorus and soloists. Many of the preexisting elements had to be integrated into the new show, hamstringing creativity even more. Yet Buddy Bradley, an outsider who was neither part of the old team nor the Broadway clique, quietly set to work. Given the limitations, he felt he hadn't produced his best work. He was shocked by the response.[7]

"Venus de Milo after a blood transfusion!," the press roared after the reopening on March 15, 1926. "Wood nymphs as light, gay and carefree as on their day off!" The revue now began with a snappy number, quickly followed by Irene Delroy, who, incidentally, had been given much more to do. The big fifth scene was easily the standout on the bill: a brand-new piece called "Those Knowing Nurses," with Delroy wearing a nurse's uniform with a Red Cross insignia, partnered by Kendall Capps, a corking soft-shoe tapper, backed by four showgirls and an entire chorus. Overall, the transformations were smoother, the whole revue was lighter, and the arrangement of dances—still credited to Ceballos—better.

Bradley had converted an imperfect opportunity into an artistic triumph. It was not mere beginner's luck; what he created was more than an exuberant first-time romp, full of interesting but not fully realized ideas, showing youthful promise but not mature craftsmanship. Instead, he presented work that was adept and appropriate. His vision went beyond single steps for single dancers; he moved groups on stage. In two weeks, he had the dancers confident. He didn't dilly-dally and debate as he worked out new dances. He got the entrances and exits right. He finished with a graceful movement, leaving a satisfying visual in the audience's memory. He not only got the job done but also produced a winner: box office jumped a whopping 50 percent in its first week—and stayed there. By June, the show's tour was booked to the following March.[8]

Bradley's talent drew, of course, on his own experience as a professional dancer, of working in rehearsals, of watching Leonard Harper create and direct, and of observing the pros. He had seen how Eddie Rector could hold a room spellbound, how Bill Robinson reinterpreted Black dance into his own sleek, modern expression, and how Florence Mills, presenting herself simply and unapologetically, could put over a number more effectively than many a flamboyant diva. Teaching had made him sensitive to the capabilities, strengths, and weaknesses of individual dancers. He had learned not to forsake Black rhythmic patterns but to adapt them to new bodies. Perhaps, too, living with what W. E. B. Du Bois described as "double consciousness," the constant awareness of the external gaze, gave him an innate sense of the performative aspect of dance, of how a work on stage would be viewed by an audience. He now filtered these cumulative influences through his own sensibility.

Experience shaped Bradley professionally, but what had given him the fortitude to soar over tense, possibly hostile, circumstances on Broadway? It is quite likely that, aside from the desperate producers, there was little support from the creative team in the theater. As numbers were axed and talent dismissed, and Delroy got more dancing, other dancers had surely resented him. Further, few on Broadway had collaborated with a Black person before. Many did not think normal rules for behavior applied to their dealings with him; quite a few probably viewed him not as an individual but as a threatening Other whose talent and style could render them obsolete. Bradley's emotional armor included the DNA of his persevering family, his professional geniality, and his good manners. He also simply couldn't dwell on any animosity. As an orphan who had to rely on his own wits for survival, he had no choice but to make the situation work. Fortunately, he was fascinated by matching movement to music, and he was being paid to do so. He focused on making dances.

If Bradley needed the work, Broadway needed Bradley. The recent wave of jazzy, syncopated Black musicals, *Shuffle Along*, *Runnin' Wild*, and *Chocolate Dandies*, had made their mark; speakeasies like the Cotton Club and Connie's Inn drew crowds uptown to see dancing and hear music. Though the taste for jazz dance was now pervasive, there was little representation of this in-demand phenomenon on the Great White Way. That year, Lew Leslie was off to London with Florence Mills and his new *Blackbirds* revue. New musicals, *Africana*, with Ethel Waters, and Miller and Lyles's *Rang Tang*, would not open until 1927. Nevertheless, jazz, embedded in American culture, continued its groundswell, rippling outward in ever-broader circles. As Rodgers and Hart penned *Peggy Ann* and Gershwin *Oh, Kay!*, swishing and semaphoring became irrelevant. Dance needed a jazz emissary.[9]

Producer George White, of the *Scandals* revues, also had a keen ear for music and a sharp eye for dance. In 1920, he hired an unknown George Gershwin as his rehearsal pianist and occasional composer. In 1923, he produced *Runnin' Wild*, with Elida Webb's famous Charleston, launching the dance that symbolized the Jazz Age. As a former dancer, White understood that on the musical theater stage the audience is always looking at something—and, because of the way the senses work, they register what they are seeing before what they are hearing. Dance, he knew, conveyed the power of music as effectively as lyrics and lingered in the senses long after the words were sung. White often choreographed his own revues with some success. In contrast to Ned Wayburn, who posed lovelies in static tableaux for Ziegfeld, White filled his stage with movement—for example, working a Charleston number around sixty dancers and a soloist.[10]

But, as times evolved, White looked outward. In 1926, he planned a new revue at his Apollo Theatre featuring three songs, "The St. Louis Blues," "The Black Bottom," and "Rhapsody in Blue," and three stars, Ann Pennington, Tom Patricola, and Frances Williams. He was smart enough not to attempt the staging of these jazzy numbers, instead hiring the hot choreographer that producers were talking about, the one who had resuscitated the *Greenwich Village Follies*: Buddy Bradley. For White's *Scandals* of 1926, Bradley created three dance iterations of the Black Bottom, a dance that originated in African American culture, to accompany a sung version by lissome chanteuse Frances Williams (who would go on to introduce the ballad later associated with *Casablanca,* "As Time Goes By," in the 1931 musical *Everybody's Welcome)*, a zippy tap version for Tom Patricola, and a feminine version for Ann Pennington, gowned by Erté of Paris.[11]

The effect of Buddy's Black Bottom on George White's *Scandals* was as unmistakable as that of Elida Webb's Charleston on *Runnin'*

Wild. With 424 performances, the 1926 *Scandals* broke records for revues, leaving White's prime competitor, Flo Ziegfeld, smoldering. But one wonders where Pierce, with his business savvy and fondness for Bradley, was during contract negotiations. The program lists no dance director and only mentions staging by George White, even though Bradley, at a minimum, had created the three jazz numbers. Understandably, Bradley, facing another opportunity to work on Broadway and gain more professional exposure, may not have dared to ask, let alone insist, on the recognition routinely awarded to Sammy Lee, Seymour Felix, Albertina Rasch, and other contemporaneous dance directors. Yet even the brash Pierce seems to have been cowed, too, when dealing with the institutional powers of Broadway, an insular crew that consisted largely of scrappy first-generation Eastern Europeans and Irishmen.[12]

Meanwhile, Ann Pennington and Bradley's Black Bottom became synonymous. The fact that the red-haired dancer oozed plenty of Twenties' "It," inspired songwriters like Cole Porter and George Gershwin, and enjoyed such popularity that the two major revues, Ziegfeld's *Follies* and George White's *Scandals*, had to settle for alternating yearly engagements with her, only added to the buzz on the street about Bradley.

As an accomplished dancer, originally trained in ballet by Catherine Littlefield in Philadelphia, Pennington provided Bradley with an ideal canvas. Her understanding of movement liberated him from having to focus on the mechanics of dance, as he had with Delroy, and gave free rein to his aesthetics. In addition to working three-dimensionally and dovetailing steps, Bradley had a clear idea of how to present women—his intuitive sense of performance kicking in again—and leavened straight tap with eclectic movement, perhaps some jive, or, later, a touch of Afro-Cuban dance. He choreographed to highlight Pennington's individuality and musicality, circumventing his favored hip emphasis to draw attention to her famous knees as well as her diminutive satin-shod feet. [13]

Choreographers are only as good as the dancers who convey their vision. As such, Pennington was already important to Bradley, the next, after Irene Delroy, in a line of critical women interpreters who showcased his work; she would also become a friend. Underneath the silky surface was a generous and thoughtful Quaker, almost as well known for her charity work as her career. While other producers, directors, and stars might "inadvertently" neglect to invite Bradley to shows, Pennington would invite him to openings, most likely those for which he had created her choreography. She navigated a tricky situation. Though the New York State Penal Code forbade segregation, theater owners continued the practice on the grounds that white audiences would be uncomfortable. Even as distinguished a presence as James Weldon Johnson, first executive secretary of the NAACP, when arriving at a theater with orchestra tickets in hand, was directed upstairs to the balcony.[14]

That June, as Bradley staged dances for George White and Ann Pennington, a new rumor circulated in the Black press: Billy Pierce and Buddy Bradley were to stage numbers for a Broadway musical. The play would be the first white production to have a Black dance director. (The term "choreographer" did not come into use until 1936, when George Balanchine requested this as credit for *On Your Toes*.) The scoop, though intriguing, was slightly inaccurate: *Broadway* by Philip Dunning and George Abbott, a behind-the-scenes story of a hoofer and gangster in love with the same chorine, a member of a sort of Floradora sextette, was a play, not a musical, so it wasn't technically a dancing show.[15]

Nevertheless, the news was significant and an important development for Bradley. First, it was a good connection. The producer was the enfant terrible of Broadway, a twenty-six-year-old Yale dropout ("I'm neither rich enough nor dull-witted enough to endure this awful place") and Austrian-born Jew named Jed Harris, who by the time he was twenty-eight had produced four back-to-back hits on Broadway and would later produce Broadway's first play alluding to homosexuality, *The Green Bay Tree* (1933), with Laurence Olivier. Second, working on a play, musical or legitimate, was a big opportunity, giving Bradley an important new credential on Broadway.[16]

Like John Murray Anderson and George White, producer Jed Harris had a knack for the sure thing. It was he who insisted that Dunning's original script be doctored by playwright and director

George Abbott, turning a clever idea into a major hit that would run nearly two years, an eternity for a play in the 1920s. And, just as he had the unerring instinct to bring in Abbott, he had the genius to seek out Buddy Bradley. There was an innovative twist to the production, too: Dunning, a former vaudevillian, intimately knew the milieu of which he wrote and invested it with nuance and color. Harris, therefore, insisted on actresses rather than chorines for the dancer roles because he wanted each to have credible individuality. He also wanted an actor for the hoofer role, the male romantic lead. The dance director then, would not only use movement to convey personality—a fairly novel idea at the time; he would also have to get the actors to move, gesticulate, and behave like dancers as well as pick up a little musical comedy technique. Bradley had already proven adept at teaching as well as creating compelling choreography that less skilled dancers could manage, and he was ready for the challenge. By September, the male lead, Lee Tracy, was deftly rotating his hips and riff walking. Together, *Broadway* and Bradley were laying new ground for theater.[17]

What we can reconstruct about Bradley's role in *Broadway* poses questions, however. After the play received rave reviews and was an assured hit, Dunning took out a full-page ad in *Variety* to thank the individuals who contributed their talent to his success. Dunning was generous with his acknowledgments, although, oddly, he directed his gratitude to Billy Pierce, not Bradley, "for limbering up the legs of the chorines," and to John Boyle, for instructing the cast in the Black Bottom. It's not hard to fathom how Pierce overshadowed Bradley and monopolized the recognition. However fond he may have been of Bradley, Pierce's objective was to foster an ongoing business, not the reputation of an individual highflyer, particularly a young and rapidly rising one who might very easily fly the coop. On at least two other important junctures—both in which Bradley was on the ascent—Pierce would subordinate Bradley's name to his own business interests.[18]

But the fact that John Boyle, a technically capable dancer devoid of style and personality, receives credit for instructing the Black Bottom—Bradley's dance—is harder to explain. The mystery becomes

Thaddeus Drayton (left, with dance partner, Rufus Greenlee) discovered adolescent Bradley tap dancing in an alley in Harlem. Their elegant Class Act, including repartee in multiple languages, inspired Bradley's own style as well as his desire to see the world.

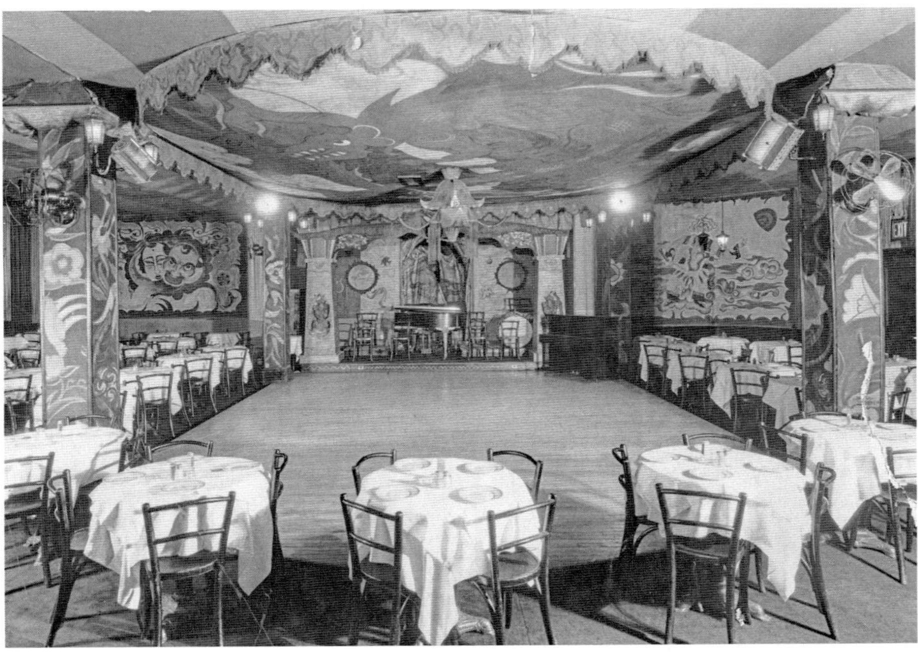

Bradley debuted in the chorus line at Connie's Inn, a luxurious Harlem Renaissance–era nightclub. The club was not only a destination for high society but also a hotbed of jazz artists: Fats Waller, Fletcher Henderson, and Louis Armstrong all played there.

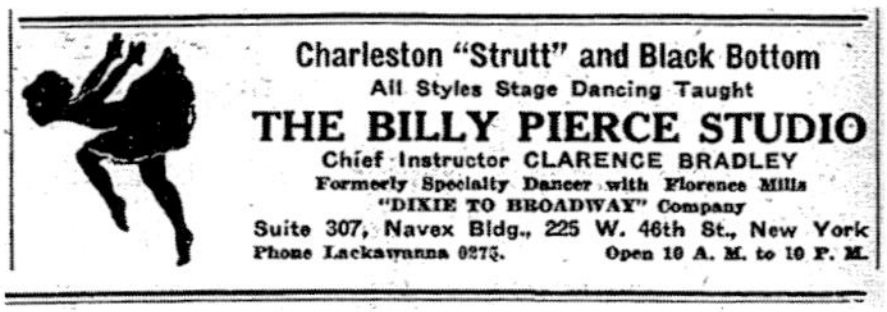

(TOP) The advertisement in *Variety* on May 20, 1925, that heralded the arrival of Bradley as head dance instructor at the Billy Pierce Studio.

(RIGHT) Dancer U. S. Thompson, Florence Mills's husband, one of the rare Black dancers who ventured to Pierce's Broadway studio, sought out Bradley for his unique routines.

Tony Award–winning choreographer Henry Le Tang studied tap and assisted Bradley at the Pierce Studio, and often spoke of his mentor with esteem and affection. Here, Le Tang is with his student, the tap great Gregory Hines.

Ziegfeld Girl Betty Compton studied tap with Bradley at the Billy Pierce Studio, then won roles in Astaire shows on Broadway and danced for Bradley in the English production of Cole Porter's *Fifty Million Frenchmen*.

The Dance Magazine   September, 1927

Low Down Dancing

The Low Down on the Real Negro Steps

By ELISE MARCUS

BOOKS and books have been written about Negro music, from the haunting spirituals to those maddening, marvelous blues. Lecture upon lecture has been delivered on African sculpture, but, to my knowledge, the only people who know anything about real Negro dancing are the professional hoofers. By low down dancing I don't mean the prehistoric dances of the savages, but those rhythms we indulge in now in the best places, those rhythms that are seen in every musical show and on every vaudeville stage in the country, rhythms that had their origin down on plantations and levees.

You have seen them often enough; you know all their amusing characteristics—the bent knees, the humorous hips, the raised hands, the angular arm. You may even do a very comic camel walk yourself without knowing just which animal your strut is named after. This simple glossary will help you recognize these steps when you see them on the stage. It will also teach you to do them yourself. The easiest way to practice is to stand in front of a long mirror with the magazine open before you. It really won't matter if you look silly—you are supposed to.

I want to acknowledge my thanks to Buddy Bradley, of the Billy Pierce Studio. Without his help it would have been impossible to gather this information.

Buddy Bradley, you know, is the fast-footed young teacher to whom so many of the Broadway stars—really famous folk like Ada May, Joyce White, Marie Saxon and Pert Kelton among others—have gone for their eccentric steps based on Negro rhythms.

By the time you have mastered these steps, the October issue of The Dance Magazine will be on its way with another chapter of the low down primer. You will want the rest of the basic Negro steps, the Camel Walk, the Charleston, the Sugar Foot Strut, the Texas Tommy, the Washington Johnny and a few more with equally enticing names.

Ballin' the Jack

Hands placed on bent knees. The knees move in a crescent path, going from side to side, in a mere suggestion of a curve.

Baltimore Buzz

Step with one foot, and slide the other foot up to it. This is done on toes with knees bent. Hips sway in direction of stepping foot.

Black Bottom (dance)

This, as with all other dances, is a mixture of "low-down" steps. The basic step, however, is one dependent entirely on rhythm. This step is 2 long stamps, first right and then left, followed by 4 short ones; they are done off the regular beat of the music. Accompanying this, the index finger on both hands is pointing up, and the eyes are rolling. Any other steps may be done to lengthen the dance.

Breakdown (Birmingham or Cincinnati)

Feet spread. Hop up and come down with one knee bent. Come up with short jerks. It is optional as to whether one or both knees are bent on coming down.

Photographs of Buddy Bradley by Nasib

BALLIN' THE JACK

THE BALTIMORE BUZZ

THE BREAKDOWN

38

In the vanguard of disseminating African American dances to new audiences, Bradley demonstrated low-down Black dances in the September 1927 issue of *The Dance Magazine*.

Pete, Peaches, and Duke, one of the great Class Acts: Pete Nugent (r), Irving "Peaches" Berman (l), and Duke Miller (center). Nugent, a friend of Bradley's since their Hoofers' Club days, guest-taught at Bradley's London school and would be a lifelong friend.

Bradley's incendiary Snake Hips routine for Clifton Webb was a tour de force that translated a dance from the Congo, via Harlem, to Broadway. Described by the *New York Times* as a milestone for jazz dance, it was Bradley's swan song on Broadway.

Dancer Eddie Rector's artistry forever inspired Bradley. He was not about mere steps but about *dancing*, dovetailing those steps, smoothing the transitions, and moving in fluid arcs.

Bradley auditions dancers with producer Charles B. Cochran (in hat). Noting the excitement that Bradley created on Broadway, the mega-producer brought him to London in 1930 to choreograph *Ever Green*. Bradley became the go-to choreographer in the West End.

(TOP LEFT) Choreographer Frederick Ashton was fascinated by the way Bradley moved. He studied jazz at Bradley's London studio, then invited him to choreograph the world's first jazz ballet, *High Yellow*. Later, Ashton based the role of The Lover in his own ballet, *Les Masques*, on Bradley.

(TOP RIGHT) Bradley taught ballerina Alicia Markova the Snake Hips en pointe for *High Yellow* and spent late nights with her and Ashton, discussing jazz, art, and dance. The tragic quality of Markova reminded Bradley of Florence Mills.

(LEFT) It was inevitable that Noël Coward, the thirty-three-year-old wunderkind of the West End, would want Bradley to choreograph *Words and Music*. Bradley was the last word in London theater chic.

Bradley's all-male opening number for *Words and Music* drew on African American dances from the Cakewalk to the Baltimore Buzz and drew thunderous applause from an enraptured British audience. London—and New York, for that matter—had never seen such dance before.

In *Words and Music*'s "Club Ballet" number, Bradley displayed sophisticated spatial distribution, dance characterization, and groupings, all the while spoofing Diaghilev's Ballets Russes.

Guianan Ken "Snakehips" Johnson skipped university classes in London to study tap with Bradley, who cast him in a cameo in *Oh, Daddy!*, which summarized the Bradley style. Johnson died in the Blitz at the age of twenty-seven while leading the band at the Café de Paris.

George Balanchine's momentous first studio encounter with jazz dance took place when he choreographed *Cochran's 1931 Revue* with Bradley. The bent knees, asymmetry, and turned-in stance of Bradley's dance quickly translated into the hallmarks of Balanchine's neoclassical ballet. Here, Balanchine applies these cornerstones of jazz dance as he rehearses Arthur Mitchell, the future founder of the Dance Theatre of Harlem.

When Bradley found the rare male dancer who could match Jessie Matthews in musicality and technique, he could create eloquent—and supremely sexy—pas de deux, as he did with Cyril Wells in *It's Love Again*.

threefold: Did the perennial press-agenting of Pierce, a slick operator, exaggerate the role of Pierce and Bradley in the play; did the African American press enthusiastically overstate their involvement; or was Boyle given credit for Bradley's work? Whatever the circumstances, *Broadway* was another case in which Bradley saw his own work claimed by another. As Thaddeus Drayton bitterly observed about Broadway: they let Bradley rehearse, and then he was out.[19]

That winter of 1926, as Bradley pursued nightclub work, and Keeler rose through the ranks, Jerome Kern and Oscar Hammerstein were developing a milestone show, *Show Boat*, that obliterated in one stroke three Broadway norms. Musically, it was a front-runner, a cross-fertilization of European operetta and African American song, typified by "Ol' Man River," a blend of spiritual and Broadway that compressed suffering, resignation, and bitterness into twenty-four taut lines. Dramatically, Kern and Hammerstein used song for the first time on Broadway to advance a narrative: when the songs started, the story didn't stop, but forged on, illuminating and enlarging. Culturally, it was a racial tipping point: Black singers and dancers now appeared alongside whites onstage. Further, it portrayed African Americans as complex human beings, not the pickaninnies or carefree jocular types of vaudeville. Even casting broke barriers: the show deliberately sought, with mixed effect, to hire dark women rather than typically light-skinned dancers (who passed the infamous "paper bag" test) seen at places like the Cotton Club.[20]

Effectively, there were two *Show Boat*s: the speaking and singing show and, equally important, the dancing show. No longer were dances interpolated numbers, with little connection to the narrative, intended to entertain audiences while sets were changed. Dance now worked in concert with music and narrative for dramatic purposes. Dance director Sammy Lee (né Levy), who had recently provided the dances for *No, No Nanette!*, *Lady Be Good*, and *Oh, Kay!*, was brought onto the team. Oscar Hammerstein, however, wanted more African American input and hired Aaron Gates, then affiliated with the Pierce Studio, to stage the corps for the "Hey, Feller!" number (and possibly other numbers). Bradley was involved, too, hired by actress Elizabeth Hines to coach her in African American dances for her role as the ingenue Magnolia. Bradley would have been directly compensated by Hines. Production books reveal that Gate's role was either limited or inequitably compensated: Sammy Lee received $2,500 for the show, Gates received $118.50.[21]

Broadway had provided Bradley with the opportunity to employ movement to reveal character. Now this experience dovetailed with *Show Boat*'s ambition to synthesize dance, music, and storyline. Two specific numbers for Magnolia with foundations in Black dance, the "Mammy" dance, performed with Julie in scene 2, and a thigh-slapping number for "Can't Help Loving That Man of Mine," were most certainly coached and choreographed by him. Yet, because he had come to the production through a "side door" as the personal choreographer of the actress, as he had with Irene Delroy for the *Greenwich Village Follies*, it was Sammy Lee, dance director of record, who received overall credit for dances that, in part due to Bradley's contribution, were heralded as exciting and authentic Black dances. It must be noted, too, that when *Show Boat*'s production was delayed, Elizabeth Hines left the show for personal reasons, and Norma Terris took over the part. Bradley worked closely with Terris, too: by the time *Show Boat* finally opened on December 27, 1927, *The New York Times* acclaimed Terris's dancing a revelation.[22]

Show Boat signaled a first attempt to switch from the saucy revue to the character-and-narrative-driven book musical. This was not a coincidence. As Hollywood gathered force and promoted storytelling, Broadway writers and producers now realized that their only hope of competing with the movies was to focus on character and plot development. Pasting disparate scenarios, songs, and dances into revues was on its way out; by 1928, George White's *Scandals* was the only revue that attained hit status. Theatrical dance would follow suit. Bradley and Broadway would increasingly veer to book musicals; only the wittiest, most novel, or most renowned revues would survive the shift in New York.[23]

Flo Ziegfeld didn't miss a beat as Broadway transitioned to book musicals. With his *Follies* franchise under siege, he mounted *Rio Rita*, with book by Guy Bolton, about the love of a Texas Ranger for a tempestuous Mexican beauty, the plot complication being that he's hunting for a bandit known as the Kinkajou, who may be her brother. It was a lavish 1920s production, suitable for the inauguration of the producer's flagship Ziegfeld Theater. Joseph Urban had designed both the theater and the production so that the gold, cream, and rose sets blended with the auditorium, decorated with elegant, muted gold murals. Sammy Lee was again the choreographer, now seconded by newcomer Albertina Rasch, whose own troupe of dancers would perform two modernistic ballets and participate in four other dances. Anachronistically, Lee marshaled one hundred Ziegfeld dancers into formations that moved like seamless machines.[24]

Probably at the eleventh hour, Bradley was brought in to doctor *Rio Rita*. Once again, he came aboard, calmly producing amid chaos and under pressure, and did what he could under imperfect creative conditions. His knockout contribution was the Kinkajou, danced by the supporting actress Ada May and described as a stylish variation on the Charleston. In fact, it was more than merely stylish: it brough the performance to a halt.[25]

The critics raved. The show was a smash, running for 494 performances, and it was Ada May, clad in green satin trousers, orange blouse, and enormous black turned-up hat, dancing the Kinkajou, who was consistently described as the life of the party. By April of that year, Ada May, though technically in a supporting role, was the acknowledged star of the show.[26]

Bradley's Kinkajou then went, in modern parlance, viral. Slightly reworked as a social dance with a foxtrot beat, the Kinkajou won first prize at the convention of Dancing Masters of America, Inc., at the Waldorf Astoria Hotel in August 1927, where the convention also named it the dance of the year, the one that instructors would promote throughout the coming season. (For the record, it was described in its ballroom form as a strut step, little side steps, a twinkle step, a heel point in a half-open position, a right pivot turn in strut position, and a left turn.) The Kinkajou was talked about in Boston, danced in Southampton, showcased at Junior League entertainments, and taught in Baltimore, Los Angeles, and London.

There was a racehorse named Kinkajou, and even a sailing sloop. But something was amiss in its apotheosis. Bradley's name was not connected to the dance.[27]

Did Lee's contract, perhaps, protect him from acknowledging any other dance directors in his show? Perhaps he already felt threatened by Rasch and her new ideas and had put his foot down at credit for yet another interloper. But, whatever the case, it was becoming increasingly hard to rationalize the crediting oversights and slights dealt to Bradley. At first, not receiving program credit, as well as future recognition for a dance craze he had engendered, might have been ascribed to Bradley being an unsuspecting novice, or coming to a project at the eleventh hour, or working on a legitimate play rather than a musical, or creating discrete numbers for a star, or even just bad luck. But, happening consistently, it became clear he was facing systemic headwinds. After all, others who provided special dances got listed in theater programs. The cold fact was that he was sidelined time and time again as his work was lauded yet credited to others.

Buddy's artistic throughline and lifeline was his connection with his women dancers. Following Irene Delroy and Ann Pennington, Ada May was the next in the line of Bradley's important female interpreters and catalysts for his career. After *Rio Rita*, Ada May continued to work with Bradley. A former ballet dancer at the Metropolitan Opera, Ada May handled all dance forms with the same aplomb as the Kinkajou. While one reviewer would admire her grace and thistledown lightness, another acclaimed the spontaneity of her dancing, and yet another celebrated her introduction of a modern Juba to Broadway.[28] An African American critic declared her the greatest exponent of Black dancing. (Presumably, the critic meant *white* exponent.) Unlike others, Ada May would speak Bradley's name—"I owe so much to him," she explained to the press; "He's quiet and unassuming. His name's Bradley."—while also calling attention to Frank Harrington, the gifted pianist, and the Pierce Studio at large.[29]

Compared to the pyrotechnics of the Kinkajou in *Rio Rita*, *Half a Widow*, with book and lyrics by Frank Dupree and Harry B.

Smith, music by Shep Camp, at the Waldorf Theatre, was an anticlimax. It was a sweet-humored show, and it received warm reviews but, dealing with World War I as its subject matter, it was out of step with the amusement-seeking 1920s and quietly closed after sixteen performances. The most notable aspect of the now-forgotten play is that it was the first to give program credit to a Black dance director: Billy Pierce.

As Pierce was dance challenged, his name could only have served as an umbrella reference to the Pierce Studio—most likely the experienced Buddy Bradley. (At the time neither Frank Harrington nor Ernest Carlos, the more senior teachers at the school, had much experience as choreographers, while Roland Holder and Henry Le Tang were too young, Herbert Harper was still running errands, and Arthur Bradley, if still on Pierce's payroll at all, was too untested to be considered.) Bradley's name was once again willfully erased—ironically, this time, subjugated to a Black man's interests. Such is human nature. With such a short run, there were few reviews for *Half a Widow*, so little can be gleaned about its choreography. What we do know is that lead Benny Rubin, as the American officer in love with a French woman, was lauded for the freshness he brought to the dance, while the chorus, though noted for its beauty, was a little ragged.[30]

Far more impactful was 1927's cheeky *A Connecticut Yankee*, a new Rodgers and Hart collaboration with book by Herbert Fields, direction by Lew Fields, dances by Busby Berkeley, and a corps of twenty-four dancers. The female lead was played by Constance Carpenter, an English comedienne who had arrived in New York via *Charlot's Revue*, then landed a featured role in Gershwin's *Oh, Kay!* with Gertrude Lawrence, and had teamed up the previous fall with Bradley protégée Betty Compton for a well-received engagement at the Fifth Avenue Club. As was the custom, Carpenter hired her own choreographer for her new show—in this case, Bradley.[31]

An extant photo of a rehearsal is revealing. On the stage, Carpenter rehearses with leading man William Gaxton at the Vanderbilt Theatre. She is elegant in her Chanel-like ensemble and silk-stockinged legs. The artistic crew has clustered in the orchestra, surrounding director Lew Fields. Fields, who is smiling and gesturing energetically at the stage, evidently liked what he was seeing. Far in the back of the auditorium, deep under the mezzanine overhead, sitting apart, one sees what appears to be a dark face, carefully observing his work. It appears to be Buddy Bradley.[32]

A Connecticut Yankee was Busby Berkeley's third Broadway project as a dance director. He had strong visual instincts that he'd honed as a military parade director, and that in the future would literally make cameras dance in Hollywood. But, in technical dance skills, he was on par with Billy Pierce, with little dance background. He did not come into a rehearsal with any steps planned, because he had no steps, and looked to his dancers for cues, wrapping his ignorance in false bravado. With good reason, Lew Fields had never been convinced about Berkeley. He wanted a dependable Broadway dance man—say, Sammy Lee, Bobby Connolly, or Seymour Felix—for *A Connecticut Yankee*, but, when all turned out to be otherwise engaged, he reluctantly signed Berkeley. One asks why he hadn't thought of Bradley, who had so notably produced the sizzle for the *Greenwich Village Follies*, George White's *Scandals*, and *Rio Rita*.[33]

Three weeks into rehearsals, Field's reservations about Berkeley were confirmed. He called on Bradley, quietly producing interesting dances for Carpenter in the background, to fix the show. Bradley took on the task, under what was now the familiar duress of working on a struggling production with an opening night looming on the near horizon. Once again, he was frustrated with the lack of time and dissatisfied with his work. Once again, he underestimated his talents. The quick-study chorus boy was now a quick-study dance maker, who had acquired a lot of experience during two years of working on Broadway. The reviewers went wild.[34]

"It is a rushing, twirling affair with a tom-tom beat leaving the chorus breathless and the audience applauding," wrote *The Herald Tribune* of the first number, an amalgamation of classic, jazz, buck, acrobatic, and pageant dance unfolding on the stage. The unexpected combination of jazz, individuality, and Charleston with acrobatic leaps was an early crystallization of Bradley's interest in gathering disparate dance forms into exciting, innovative, modern dance.[35]

But, as the theater erupted, it was Busby Berkeley, not Buddy Bradley, who basked in the praise. There was no public acknowledgment of Bradley because, once again, he had no program credit: only the creative team and cast knew he had re-created all the dances. Although Berkeley seemed properly embarrassed by the attention, it apparently didn't occur to him to mention Bradley. Worse, as the laudatory reviews came out, the offers flew in. Immediately after the opening, producer Russell Janney signed Berkeley for his new operetta, *The White Eagle*. Bradley, meanwhile, looked for his next job.[36]

As the injuries mounted, there was no time to heal; instead, they fused into an open wound. The night before *A Connecticut Yankee* opened, the rehearsal ran late as dances were calibrated to costumes, exits fine-tuned, and tempos approved. Depleted and hungry, Bradley packed up with some of the pit musicians—an illustrious crew of Benny Goodman, Ray Bauduc, Jack Teagarden, and Jimmy McPartland, the then-backbone of Ben Pollack's band—and set off to grab some ham and eggs around the corner. Like Paul Robeson, even surrounded with a crew of white men, Bradley was refused service at the restaurant. Trombonist Teagarden was so outraged he was nearly violent, but, Bradley, resigned and weary of rehearsing, of sitting apart, of making things work, of cleaning up other people's problems, of working with dancers selected by others, of fixing and not conceiving a show, of being overlooked, and of Broadway, was too tired to fight. Exhausted and disillusioned, Bradley insisted on leaving. He was twenty-three.[37]

If *A Connecticut Yankee* was fatiguing, Bradley's next show was exhausting. After producing *Yankee*, Lew Fields launched into a new project, *Hello, Daddy!*, with book by Herbert Fields, music and lyrics by Dorothy Fields and Jimmy McHugh, the team who had provided the songs for the *Blackbirds*' 1928 revue. Carryovers from *A Connecticut Yankee* included Bradley's allies, Constance Carpenter, now heralded by *The New Yorker* as the new Gertrude Lawrence, in the ingenue lead, and Ben Pollack and his orchestra playing the musical numbers as well as jazz during the entr'acte. The director was John Murray Anderson, founder of the *Greenwich Village Follies*, not yet en route to Hollywood. Though Bradley was outside the Broadway clique, he had become essential to its infrastructure.[38]

Lew Fields had learned from his experience on *A Connecticut Yankee*. He now had the good sense to hire Bradley from the get-go. Bradley and Pierce, too, had also been around the block and understood their worth to Broadway. When *Variety* announced on November 14, 1928, that Buddy Bradley, "the colored dance stager," would have full charge of the dances in *Hello, Daddy!*, it also reported that Bradley and Pierce would have billing credit. Just a month later, however, their euphoria was dashed: Busby Berkeley had inexplicably been added to the team.[39]

The division of duties seemed to play to each man's strengths: Bradley would focus on the tapping and dance numbers, Berkeley on spectacular staging. Although the program doesn't indicate specifically which choreographer produced which dances, it's highly likely that, of the twelve musical numbers, the two grand finales were staged by Berkeley, while the six numbers that showcased the stars and soloists would have been given to Bradley. Of these, four numbers, including the show hit "Let's Talk About You," featured Constance Carpenter, and, therefore, would have logically been assigned to Bradley. The five remaining numbers involved either stars or soloists backed by an ensemble and were also likely the work of Bradley, especially if they involved tap dancing.[40]

Casting was a merry-go-round. Carpenter, who had been Bradley's ally and entrée into the Fields empire, was an early announced but elusive lead. As the show rehearsed in Philadelphia, she was still on the road with *A Connecticut Yankee*. She also had accepted the lead in *Serena Blandish*, a new Jed Harris production scheduled to open that winter. By December, she was out of the cast, replaced by Mary Lawlor, a nineteen-year-old protégée of Sammy Lee, inclined to pretentious pronouncements about dance ("The dancer has nothing but her body. That must be given over completely and impersonally to her art"). Perhaps the entire cast and crew found Lawlor insufferable—just a few weeks after opening, having received excellent reviews for her dancing, she was replaced by Shirley Vernon.

By April 1929, there was still another change: Constance Carpenter was now back in the cast.[41]

Funding was a rollercoaster as the show was forever chasing backers. That winter, Broadway hinted that Morris Green and A.L. Jones—the team that had hired Bradley to fix the *Greenwich Village Follies*—were to take over production responsibilities from Lew Fields. Unfortunately, they didn't come on board. By March, however, the financial situation was resolved: Joe Le Blang, known for discounting tickets, was now in the role of producer and looking to cut costs. In the new regime, both Bradley and Berkeley were out. A new dance director, Russell Markert, who would later bring the Rockettes to Rockefeller Center, arrived and hired a less expensive crew of dancers. Le Blang had shrewdly retained two dancers from the original chorus to help Markert drill Bradley's dances into the new team.[42]

It goes without saying that anyone who wants to be part of the rough-and-tumble world of theater must have nerves of steel. The push-and-pull of creativity, egos, budgets, time, and commercial interests inevitably leads to tensions. Choreographers, dependent on dancers, musicians, lighting designers, costumers, and stage designers for the success of their work are particularly susceptible. Bradley, who could rise above these tensions, ignore chaos, adapt to change, and retain his cool while creating and coaching, was well suited to his métier. But he could not be indifferent to those elements that weren't inherent to the theatrical process: the half-truths, mistruths, breached contracts, and willful disregard that surrounded his experience in *Hello, Daddy!*

From the beginning, agreements were ignored—most importantly, that of receiving credit. Of course, producers and press agents cannot control the press, but it is revealing that Brooks Atkinson of *The New York Times*, the most important theater reviewer of the day, carefully enumerated the cast and production credits without a nod to Bradley. He was not the only critic to do so. More egregious is that the producer not only violated his agreement with Buddy Bradley when he brought in a second dance stager, Busby Berkeley, for the ensembles but that Berkeley alone received credit in the *Hello, Daddy!* program.[43]

While having the two complementary dance directors may have had artistic merit, it was Bradley's dances that received great notices. Reviewers lauded their originality and predicted that dance directors would soon be plagiarizing Bradley's ideas. One did not need to look far: the *Hello, Daddy!* producers were doing exactly that already.[44]

Bradley stopped shows, made stars, and created work that stemmed from his unique sensibility. He had only been given imperfect opportunities, late fixes, interpolated dances, outside coaching contracts, and shared responsibilities. He was also working twelve-hour days, eating catch as catch can, and diplomatically defusing tensions, all to further his career. Piecemeal breaks and hard work were, of course, a given for any unknown aspirant. But, once Bradley had proved his talent, he remained in the role of a postulant, called in when the producers were desperate, working unobtrusively, careful not to fluff sensitive feathers, make a fuss, or appear threatening, and was never invited to see his shows.[45]

James Baldwin wrote that the only difference between the North and the South is that the North promises more. Broadway in the 1920s, for Bradley, proved not so very different from Birmingham, in the end. This was not a mere personal impression, gleaned from individual experience: historians point out that between 1910 and 1930, the quadrupling of New York's African American population led to a hyper-racialized society, informal and formal segregation practices, and a resistance to Blacks advancing beyond menial labor. As Florence Mills had pointed out, withholding credit was a way to suppress name recognition and the development of a professional career. At twenty-four, Bradley could clearly see the exact limits of his agency in New York.[46]

There was one more watershed, and heartbreak, awaiting Bradley on Broadway: his staging of "Moanin' Low" in Schwartz and Dietz's intimate 1929 revue, *The Little Show*. Reviewers once again raved. Standees jammed the aisles of the sold-out theater when word got out about the provocative dance. The number sent Clifton Webb on a sparkly career in Hollywood and bequeathed torch singer Libby Holman her signature song. Bradley's choreography was heralded as nothing less than a milestone for jazz dance. It turned out to be Bradley's Broadway swan song.[47]

In the course of the 1920s, Clifton Webb transitioned from a career as a ballroom dancer and solidified a reputation as a suave musical comedy type. He had just come off a successful turn alongside Gertrude Lawrence and Bradley protégée Peggy O'Neill in *Treasure Girl*, yet he knew he was capable of more and seized on *The Little Show* to showcase his breadth. He joined forces with the guttural-voiced Libby Holman, then went to Bradley hunting for ideas.[48]

It was the era when, according to Langston Hughes, "the Negro was in vogue." Webb had recently read Carl Van Vechten's runaway bestseller *Nigger Heaven*, which had furnished him with a vague notion of what he wanted. Bradley took the prompt, glanced at Dietz's lyrics, then imagined an interaction in a shabby hotel room between a pimp and his prostitute. While the sultry Holman, knocked violently to the floor by Webb, crooned "Moanin' Low" in the background, Webb counted his girl's take, then began a grinding Snake Hips routine, swinging his pelvis in erotic figure eights. It was a dance few people expected a white man to attempt, least of all the usually dapper Webb, who, wrote a critic, never scintillated like this before. It was exactly the review Webb wanted.[49]

For inspiration, Bradley had only to recall his time dancing at Connie's Inn where Earl "Snakehips" Tucker had mesmerized audiences with a suggestively undulating dance, believed to have origins in the Congo via Trinidad and said to charm poisonous snakes into death trances. Bradley dipped into his dance memory, reconfigured the steps, played up the drama, visualized the decor, fitted it to the slinky Webb, and coached it in secrecy—in point of fact, in the toilet of the Music Box Theater. Both men suspected they were on to something and wanted to protect the shock element of the dance for opening night. They didn't anticipate, however, the magnitude of the reaction.[50]

The audience alternated between shock and fascination. *Variety* described the response as hysteria. *The Telegraph* called it execution assailed by panic. *The Telegram* reported an uproar. *The Billboard* said it was the dramatic highlight of the evening. But it had more than shock value, it had dance significance. *The Dance* grasped the importance, carefully deciphering its cross stepping, pigeon-toed mincing, knock knees, and pelvis twisting with photos of Webb.[51]

The New York Times spoke of high art.

John Martin, the *Times*'s tireless critic and promoter of modern dance, was transfixed. He had never seen jazz dance at this level; dance that could be so expressive; dance that conveyed tragic overtones, mournful implications; dance that so perfectly mirrored the music, the mood, the drama on the stage. The dance, wrote Martin, "pointed the acting, lingered in the memory as few bits from musical shows have a habit of doing." Martin was not given to gratuitous praise. Martha Graham, Agnes de Mille, and Doris Humphrey had all felt the sting of his pen. Martin's words were meaningful. These were words that could anoint a career.[52]

But there was one problem: Martin had no idea he was writing about Bradley.

By now, the situation was disturbingly predictable. Webb's career had been ignited, while Bradley was ignored. Webb reaped the benefit of Bradley's choreography, a dance with Black roots and a scenario that the actor could not have otherwise accessed. He not only didn't see what was wrong with not sharing credit—he'd compensated Bradley for his choreography, after all—but he also felt entitled to Bradley's services. While it was standard practice then that a performer's personal choreographer was not listed in the program, Clifton Webb's lack of recognition revealed a prevailing attitude, the assumption that Black and Brown people should naturally support all white objectives while disregarding their own aspirations. Webb was even personally affronted when Bradley considered an important project in London that would have made the choreographer unavailable for Webb's future dance needs. (The actor first tried to block Bradley's plans; failing that, he refused henceforth to take Bradley's calls.)[53] In spite of Bradley's creativity and contributions, Webb and directors viewed Bradley as a sidekick, not a visionary creative.

The glamorous Libby Holman, known for her guttural voice, her strapless dresses, and dangling earrings, behaved much better: she joined Billy Pierce, Buddy Bradley and NAACP secretary Walter

White for a NAACP broadcast that winter. A few weeks later, she participated—with Webb, probably goaded by her—in a NAACP benefit alongside Alberta Hunter, Duke Ellington, and Rosamund Johnson at the Forrest Theater. A lifelong civil rights activist, she funded Martin Luther King Jr.'s trip to India.[54]

As Thaddeus Drayton observed, the artistry was always Bradley's own: he had nothing of substance to learn from others. As he evolved as a choreographer, he would naturally find inspiration in other aesthetics and polish his professionalism, but he would not need an artistic mentor. He had a personal vision of dance: graceful, musical, eclectic, spatial, and visually arresting. In his four years choreographing on Broadway, Bradley had learned to tailor dances to showcase a dancer to best advantage in the *Greenwich Village Follies*, to elevate a star in George White's *Scandals*, to shade character in *Broadway*, to integrate dance with drama in *Show Boat*, to craft a dance fad in *Rio Rita*, to convert lackluster to glittering in *A Connecticut Yankee*, to press Black dance into white dancers to stop a show. He could visualize groups, exits, and entrances, and he knew how to settle a disparate group of dancers into a corps and create dances that served the show, neither indulgent nor flat. He may even have learned a thing or two watching Busby Berkeley's over-the-top stagings. He had become an experienced choreographer.

By the end of the decade, Bradley's influence could be seen in virtually every show on Broadway, be it through his direct involvement, routines he created for dancers in his studio, or imitation.[55] Broadway needed Bradley's talent but ensured his invisibility.

All he needed was a platform.

PART 3

LONDON CALLING, 1931–1932

CHAPTER 9

EVER GREEN AND AFFIRMATION

The Negro artists went to Europe because we were recognized and given a chance.

—ALBERTA HUNTER

It was inevitable that Bradley, now a proven talent and versatile dance director, would come to London in 1930. For a decade, energy from Broadway had poured into the West End. In the 1920s, twenty-five musicals, including *Show Boat*, *Rio Rita*, *A Connecticut Yankee*, *Lady, Be Good*, and *No, No Nanette*, transferred from Broadway to London; only one English musical, Noël Coward's operetta *Bitter Sweet*, traveled west. Dance, as always, took its cues from music, and, as it was, theatrical dance was not much of an English tradition. Operettas, which predominated on the West End stage before the arrivals of musicals like Gershwin's *Funny Face* and Rodgers and Hart's *One Damn Thing After Another*, had focused on song, not dance.[1]

At the time, dance on the West End stage was still a patched-together affair: a stage manager like Frank Collins would set a piece or two; dancer Max Rivers might contribute a troupe of dancers and choreography for a number; the precision dancers, the Tiller

Girls, might add a kick line; stars like Tilly Losch brought her own choreography; and even Noël Coward, a word man, not a dancer, grabbed a few tips from Fred Astaire and staged a few songs. The idea of a dance director assuring a cohesive through line of dance was novel—another one of those radical ideas from America. Further, jazz dancing, ingrained in America, had no indigenous roots in England. Mysterious and of the moment, it needed an African American translator.

One saw the signs. British actor Frank E. Franks ran ads in *The Stage* seeking a first-class dance producer with knowledge of all dances from America. Others went straight to the source: three London dance directors regularly visited Harlem clubs for ideas, then rushed downtown to Bradley for instruction. When English shows transferred to New York, the stars also flocked to the Pierce Studio, among them the elegant Jack Buchanan, who transformed under Bradley from mechanical puppet to seductive dancer, and Jack Hulbert, who, after several classes with Bradley, outshone his sparkly stage partner, Cicely Courtneidge, and monopolized the limelight.[2]

Megaproducer Charles B. Cochran had consistently sought out the new and noteworthy; it was he who introduced England to Ibsen, Eleanora Duse, Les Ballets Russes, and rodeos. Now he trained his eye on Buddy Bradley. He noted the rising dance man's impact on Buchanan, watched his former chorus girl Constance Carpenter soar as she danced Bradley's choreography in *A Connecticut Yankee*, and heard Bradley's name on the lips of the Astaires. Meeting Ada May tipped the scales.

Following her success in *Rio Rita*, Ada May arrived in London with *Follow Through* and captivated Cochran, who engaged her for his *1930 Revue*, choreographed by Ralph Reader and George Balanchine, the former maître de ballet of the Ballets Russes. Smitten by her quicksilver dancing, and perhaps in love with her, Cochran toyed with having her replace leading lady Jessie Matthews in the upcoming Rodgers and Hart musical *Ever Green*. (To Matthews's annoyance, Cochran even invited Ada May to attend preliminary rehearsals.) When Ada May announced that she owed all her success to Bradley, Cochran kicked into gear. As *Ever Green*, spiced with a breezy score and jazzy attitude, did not yet have a dance director, he made an offer to Bradley via Billy Pierce.[3]

Sniffing out opportunity, Pierce inserted himself into the conversation, explaining, disingenuously, that it was he who organized the ensembles and kept the young Bradley focused, obsequiously offering to forgo a salary for the honor of working with Cochran.[4] Pierce may have hoped to split a commission with Bradley or, at least, solidify a valuable new overseas contact, but the reality was that Pierce, who had once been Bradley's sole champion, allaying his qualms and promoting his talent, was now expendable. Bradley was twenty-five, more confident, and—as the very situation testified—a sought-after professional in his own right.

Even a bout with pneumonia did not dissuade Pierce from tagging along. That summer, Bradley and the recuperating Pierce crossed the Atlantic second class on the Cunard *Aquitania*, then checked into rooms at the Piccadilly Hotel. Meanwhile, the news of the Black team getting the nod from Cochran circulated on Broadway and was greeted with patronizing envy. *Variety* crassly announced, "Cochran Wants Colored Stagers from New York, and Likely Getting 'Em."[5]

London, in contrast, was hospitable. The arrival on British shores of a jazz choreographer, one who could incorporate jazz and street elements into dance and fulfill London society's insatiable need for the novel, the "amusing," and the culturally fluid, was widely welcomed. For the first time, Bradley was afforded circumstances that supported his creativity: Rodgers and Hart arrived the following week, giving Bradley an opportunity to familiarize himself with the book, the music, and its creators, map out initial choreographic ideas, and attend preproduction meetings before rehearsals began in mid- September.[6]

In a moment of clairvoyance, Cochran passed on Ada May and placed his bet on twenty-four-year-old Jessie Matthews. Like Bradley, Jessie Matthews was a young outsider with outsize talent. Their temperaments were yin and yang: she was susceptible and high-strung, he was calm and reassuring. Their talents were complementary, too:

she had trained with a disciple of ballerina Adeline Genée, while he was a font of syncopation, polyrhythm, and invention. Together, they fused ballroom, ballet, and jazz into the memorable "Dancing on the Ceiling," the show's big song-and-dance number that had audience members leaving the theater half-humming and half-dancing, and other choreographers agog. *Ever Green* was a triumph, in no small part due to the chemistry of Matthews and Bradley.[7]

The show was ambitious. Cochran intended *Ever Green*, premiering in London, to compete directly with the trendy musicals of Broadway. As such, he assembled a cast, headed by appealing up-and-comers Jessie Matthews, Joyce Barbour, Albert Burdon, and Sonnie Hale, with extraordinary skill. All the dancers could sing, all the singers could dance, and everyone could act. It also trailed Cochran's customary lavish production values and complex mechanisms. There was a glitzy team of not one, but four, designers: professor Ernst Stern, famous for his staging of *The Miracle*, which had shot Lady Diana Cooper to celebrity; poetic artist Rex Whistler; society painter Doris Zinkeisen; and Gladys Calthrop, a pillar of Noël Coward's production team and erstwhile lover of Mercedes de Acosta. *Ever Green* even signaled a fashion moment: bodice-hugging costumes, some by young Norman Hartnell, heralded the end of the straight-waist garçon style of the 1920s and the return to feminine glamour. Bradley was a full partner in the effort.[8]

Cochran hired the best, gravitating toward cool, self-assured professionals whom he could trust, then removed himself from the fray so that their talent could flourish. Whereas he lost confidence in young Agnes de Mille when she appeared unkempt and insecure at rehearsals, tidy and self-contained Bradley was just his style. With a negligible storyline—a young woman in the theater masquerades as her mother, then, of course, for love, reveals her true identity—designed to showcase dance and talent rather than ideas, *Ever Green* balanced on the cusp of a revue and book musical. With its success largely dependent on its choreography, it was a high-powered, high-stakes opportunity for Bradley.[9]

It was also exhilarating. Bradley now had unprecedented responsibility: sixty-four dancers—sixteen regular dancers, sixteen Tiller girls, sixteen showgirls, sixteen chorus boys—and sixteen numbers to stage spanning three countries, casinos, traveling fairs, Paris music halls, boardinghouses, boudoirs, streets, and a revue within a play. Dance numbers ranged from the English ("Doing a Little Clog Dance"), to the je ne sais quoi ("Je m'en fiche du sex-appeal"), to the familiar ("Harlemania," whose lyrics about "shaking what nobody mentions" were rumored to be inspired by Bradley's choreography). For all of this, Bradley summoned jazz, tap chorus lines, ballroom adagios, character, and acrobatic dancing. Some of these dance styles were longtime staples from his days as a chorus dancer; others he had picked up more recently working on Broadway; some were fresh fodder for his creativity.[10]

Bradley's artistic crossover, the height of chic in 1930s London, was consequential. Dance historian and critic Alastair Macaulay points out that an arm gesture devised by Bradley in "Dancing on the Ceiling," a languorous pushing away against air while bending backward, influenced two young ballet choreographers, resurfacing in both George Balanchine's *Serenade* and Frederick Ashton's *Façade*.[11]

The jazz-ballet exchanges traveled in two directions, equally enrichening Bradley. Ballerina Alexandra Danilova, at loose ends after the collapse of the Ballets Russes, had a cameo in *Ever Green*. Though she would have brought her own choreography, Bradley as dance director oversaw her staging, putting him in immediate proximity to the gestures and line of Mariinsky ballet technique.[12] Long an admirer of Eddie Rector and his graceful "picture dancing," Bradley now had, in his direct work with Matthews and in his adjacency to Danilova, access to new ideas and tools that would shape his own dances throughout the 1930s.

Bradley made even simple dances visually exciting. Communicating via steps and sign language with Joan Matas, a dancer from Spain who did not speak English, Bradley incorporated the sardana, a circle dance with precise footwork and rhythm, for a festival scene in a Catalan village. As authentic folk dances, particularly one so elementary that villagers of all ages could dance together, may be a satisfying community experience but not necessarily compelling to watch, Bradley reinterpreted it as a performative dance, seeding contrast and variation in its rolling dips and repetitive rhythms, all the while refraining from gross caricature, winning the admiration of *The Times* of London, which noted the maturity of his work. The sardana, like ballet, provided Bradley with new dance inspiration: as he staged it for London, he simultaneously considered how he could adapt it for future New York projects, perhaps injecting more dramatic movement in the body.[13]

Inspired by German impresario Max Reinhardt, Cochran decided to equip the Adelphi Theatre with a revolving stage, the only one of its kind in the country. Bradley needed to get his dancers comfortable on a stage that rotated under their feet, but this was a minor technical hurdle. The real challenge was strategic. As the turning stage allowed one scene to revolve seamlessly into the next but didn't permit any time for costume changes, Bradley had to plan his numbers and cast with the dexterity of a chess grandmaster, making sure no dancer was scheduled for back-to-back numbers, all the while taking into account everyone's abilities, height, and training. Further, while the stage was installed in the Adelphi Theatre, the cast had to be ferried by motor-charabancs to rehearsals at the remote Alexandra Palace, where they remained confined all day, then were returned to central London at the end of a long day. The artistic stimulation, technical challenges, and responsibility evidently energized Bradley, despite the grueling hours: he found time to take on a side gig, the buffing up of the chorus of *Cochran's 1930 Revue* with a little jazz technique.[14]

It has been said that Charles Cochran was a dance director's nightmare, for he insisted on choosing his celebrated chorus dancers himself. Fortunately, there were plenty of dancers to choose from (nearly every young woman in Britain dreamed of becoming one of "Mr. Cochran's Young Ladies"), and Cochran's eye was close to infallible. Like Bradley, he looked not just for dancing acumen but indefinable star quality. Eventually Bradley would partner with Cochran in the audition process, but, for *Ever Green*, the dancers were certainly assigned to him.[15]

Who chose the chorus line made little difference; Bradley knew how to handle dancers. He was comfortable directing people and establishing an environment in which he could work productively. His no-nonsense, no-drama approach instilled confidence. He gave instructions with a smile, always demonstrated his choreography, his voice never rising above a conversational tone. After making sure his dancers had the segment, he would methodically proceed to the next, stopping to adjust the ideas to suit the individuals.[16]

His challenge was that English dancers had little, if any, exposure to jazz dance. Though this limited Bradley's possibilities, it was not insurmountable. Many of the numbers in *Ever Green* drew on dance forms other than jazz and tap, and Bradley, since his early days of working with Irene Delroy, was adept at creating dances that corresponded to a dancer's abilities. He was not a choreographer with a rigid style. Like Albertina Rasch, he understood that the primary job of a theatrical choreographer was to deliver dances that kept the objectives of the show in mind and looked good on the dancers, not to showcase sophisticated theories of dance that eclipsed emotion or narrative. Working with George Abbott, the director and playwright who had turned Philip Dunning's clever idea into the long-term hit *Broadway,* Bradley had learned to ask at every juncture (as his artistic heir twice removed, Bob Fosse): forget art—does it *work?*

Though he worked incessantly, often putting in ten hours in one day on one dance to get it right, *Ever Green* was so complex, packed with so many and such varied dances, that after the company boarded trains to Glasgow for previews, the production wasn't ready. Bradley, with Pierce's help, divided the dancers into groups and continued rehearsals in the aisles. The last-minute polishing of dances did the trick—reviews from Glasgow were glowing, consistently noting that, beyond the spectacular beauty, dazzling settings, and catchy songs, it was the innovative, eclectic, cosmopolitan, musical, *and* well-rehearsed dancing that was the star attraction. As Cochran well knew, good dance made for excellent box office: ten thousand pounds worth of tickets—an out-of-town record—had been sold in advance, and, thanks to the adulatory reviews, *Ever Green* was sold out for the entire run.[17]

Bradley could only have smiled his famous twisted smile, which conveyed simultaneously amusement and reserve, when he saw the

Ever Green program on opening night: his name, in capital letters, was on the title page. That evening, December 10, 1930, expectant show biz personalities including Beatrice Lillie, the Dolly Sisters, director Hassard Short, and producer Max Gordon of the Erlanger outfit in New York packed the newly renovated art deco Adelphi Theatre. Ada May, still appearing in *Cochran's 1930 Revue*, came directly from the London Pavilion to lend moral support. With its revolving stage and elaborate sets—especially that of Neuilly fair, with its lights, booths, side shows, merry-go-rounds, barkers, and pulsating crowd—*Ever Green* couldn't fail to captivate, but it was the dancing, in all its forms, rhythmic, eccentric, muscular, and linear, that astonished. The gifted Jessie Matthews, radiating confidence in every dance Bradley created for her, was rising as his next muse.[18]

It was a heady debut. Deemed by *Country Life* the loveliest of Cochran's productions, *Ever Green* was the succès fou of the season. By spring there was talk about transferring *Ever Green* to New York, bringing with it the giddy prospect of unmasking Bradley's talents and name on Broadway in a prestigious international show. (Ultimately, the deal fizzled, in part due to the prohibitive expense of mounting a production with a cast of two hundred, twelve elaborate scenes, countless costumes, and the necessity of installing a revolving stage.) The show, however, did cross to the Continent, where it played at Max Reinhardt's Kurfürstendamm Theater in Berlin.[19] On July 9, 1931, *Ever Green* marked its 250th performance and would continue its run through the late fall.

After a few weeks of fine-tuning and giving notes to his dancers, Bradley returned with Pierce to New York on the *Paris*. Noble Sissle, the lyricist for *Shuffle Along*, and his band, fresh from an engagement at the night spot Ciro's, were also on board. In the unlikely event that the musicians and dancers did not know each other beforehand, the extroverted Pierce could be counted on to finesse an introduction, ensuring a jolly, jazzy voyage home.[20]

There was reason to celebrate. For once, Bradley was proud of his choreography, for he had finally been given working conditions in which his talent could soar. Most wondrously, too, he was credited on the title page of the program and recognized by the press.

Even with the production anxieties, the atmosphere of *Ever Green* had been so convivial that ten cast marriages had taken place, and stories of romance between Bradley and one of Mr. Cochran's Young Ladies were in the air, causing the Austrian girlfriend on Sugar Hill to fade from the picture.[21]

On the surface, London was eminently civilized and attractive. After first billeting at the Piccadilly Hotel, Bradley had settled into a quiet routine at 25 Old Burlington Road, behind Savile Row, a stone's throw from both Cochran's office on Old Bond Street and the bustle of the theaters. Without a wholesale heritage of slavery on its own soil, and a small percentage of people of color in its population, Britain viewed Bradley differently from America.[22] In London, he was not a marginalized statistic but a coveted ambassador for jazz culture. Provided one had the right entrée—and Bradley did, thanks to the aegis of all-powerful Charles B. Cochran—London offered social and professional access and opportunities for eclectic experimentation.

Yet, while the increasing fascination of London society with "everything Black" opened doors for artists, it was also problematic. Black people might be lionized in London, but they could also be as objectified as in the Deep South. Evelyn Waugh was known to issue invitations for cocktails with a drawling caveat: "It's not a *party*. There won't be any Black men." As dance director, Bradley rehearsed onstage with his dancers but knew very well that his presence there was exceptional; Jessie Matthews recalled that when Leslie Hutchinson, a glamorous cabaret artist from Grenada, worked as a rehearsal pianist, he had to accompany her in the orchestra pit, barred from occupying a stage with a white woman.[23]

Nevertheless, opportunity as well as acknowledgment came to Bradley in London that did not come in New York. Worldly London softened the demarcations between classical, concert, theatrical, and popular dance, providing Bradley, the known jazz and tap maestro, with carte blanche to experiment with Spanish dance, can-can, and even aspects of ballet. Key relationships materialized, too. In Jessie Matthews, Bradley found a graceful dancer to embody his vision and a colleague whose career would often parallel his own. In

Charles B. Cochran, the producer who shrank from nothing but the safe and boring, he found an anchor. Even after forty years of collaborating with renowned international producers, Bradley would hold Cochran above all others, not only for his sense of theater but for his keen understanding of men.[24]

How could it be otherwise? Cochran had given Bradley hope in a moment of despair, seeking the choreographer out from afar and entrusting him with a groundbreaking show that provided the showcase New York denied him. Cochran's gesture was life-changing. In London, in 1930, Bradley proved his worth. What is more, he found the path, and optimism, that would shape his future.

CHAPTER 10

APPRAISING LONDON

What Europe still gives an American is
the sanction to become oneself. No artist
can survive without this acceptance.

—JAMES BALDWIN

Returning to New York three days before Christmas, Bradley barely had time to check in on his brother Aurelius, get a decent haircut, and pack his winter clothes. *Ever Green* had detonated a chain reaction. Cochran now wanted him to choreograph his *1931 Revue* as well as *Creation*, the latest edition of his Trocadero Grill cabaret. Two shows to conceive, choreograph, and rehearse, with back-to-back openings, meant intensive work on a short runway. Right after the New Year, Bradley made a quick turnaround, Pierce once again in tow, and headed back to London. Before the year was over, two more book musicals in England would also come his way.[1]

While New York retained some of its brisk optimism throughout the Depression, London emanated disillusion. One felt it everywhere, in the extremist politics of Oswald Mosley, the crumbling of core industries, even in the January days that vanished into night by 4 p.m. Yet, despite the gloom, Bradley stepped lightly off the Cunard *Mauretania* on January 10, 1931. New York squeezed his talent into a predetermined cubbyhole. London saw broad possibilities and offered him a future. Just days earlier, *Variety* had underplayed Bradley's involvement in *Ever Green*, sniping he had worked on a "special" contract to create only the low-down and hot numbers.[2]

But Bradley lightly dismissed the slights from New York; his thoughts were focused on London, on his next Cochran project. In the early twentieth century, Cochran had imported the concept of the French revue to England, a formula that balanced clever scripts with lightness, color, variety, and pace. By the 1920s, Cochran revues, presented annually at his elegant neoclassical Pavilion Theatre, had become an intrinsic part of the London social ritual, handily filling the gap between final theater curtain and late soirées. Attended by royals, aesthetes, and members of the bourgeoisie alike, they were vital to Cochran's ongoing enterprise, as their revenues made possible the intellectually and artistically adventurous undertakings that Cochran adored. As such, Cochran took his revues seriously and never entrusted their choreography to just anybody.[3]

Cochran revues were also essential to many a dancer's survival. With the collapse of the Ballets Russes in 1929 and before the advent of institutionalized ballet in England, gainful employment for concert dancers in the 1930s was almost nonexistent. Working in Cochran revues helped make ends meet, and conveniently so, as their late-night timing allowed a dancer to perform in a West End show, then dash down Shaftesbury Avenue to partake in a midnight revue, picking up two paychecks in one evening. The system benefited choreographers, too: revues enlarged their pool of available dancers and range of skills, brought them face-to-face with new talent, and increased choreographic possibilities.[4]

Cochran designed his *1931 Revue* around his jazzy young choreographer from America, investing it with themes of modernity and Americana and casting Ada May as his headliner, supported by two Midwestern comics, Clark and McCullough, and Texan Phil Baxter, who supplied a fast-moving upbeat dance tune, "Ding Dong Daddy." There was also a good dash of Harlem aesthetics. During his split-second week in New York, Bradley had engaged his former studio assistant, Eddie "Pee Wee" Williams, and his performing partner, Joey Shields, for the show. Williams and Shields would introduce the Lindy Hop, with music by Andy Razaf and Eubie Blake, and a tap dance, "Harlem," with Ada May and West End newcomer John Mills, who would also become a student of Bradley.[5]

Thanks to Bradley, the music got a jazz spin, too. When Cochran proposed his usual music director, Bradley was appalled. Movement and music, for Bradley, were inextricably linked; dance was a direct response to music, and an orchestra had to support the onstage choreography. He pushed for a good symphonic dance band, one that produced a jazzier, faster sound for his choreography. He got Percival Mackey, the original pianist for Jack Hylton's band who had led the house band at the Kit Kat Club, watering hole of the style-setting Prince of Wales and recent conductor of the London productions of American musicals *No, No, Nanette* and *Follow Through*. Prophetically, in the pit with Mackey for the *1931 Revue* was jazz bassist Spike Hughes.[6]

Surprise and contrast were bywords for Cochran revues. Bright Young Thing Oliver Messel and Ada Peacock produced cutting-edge, even daring, costumes for the *1931 Revue*, but, when actual dresses were called for, Cochran turned to Reville, the ultraconservative dressmaker to royalty for elegance. Similarly, the fatuous "Ding Dong Daddy" was offset by the worldly-wise songs of Noël Coward and the double entendres of cross-dressing Douglas Byng. Contortionist Isabel MacMurray, performing under the name of "Eve," dispelled with refinement any preconceived associations with circus sideshows. And, while Bradley had overall responsibility for the show, Georges Balanchine (then Balanchin), of the late Ballets Russes, was brought on board to choreograph the act 1 finale, a commedia dell'arte scene with music by Pergolesi, and "Stealing Through," a number by Byng.

Cochran's pairing of Balanchine, a twenty-seven-year-old ballet choreographer, with Bradley, a twenty-six-year-old jazz choreographer, is a landmark in the history of dance. Despite evidence of their creative synergies, there is no written documentation on whether Balanchine and Bradley—two reserved orphans who did not leave trails of diaries and letters to reveal themselves—discussed dance, commiserated about the challenges of working on the minuscule stage of the Pavilion Theatre with only a sole entrance, or even smoked a cigarette together.[7] Yet their similarities explain why they were keen observers of each other's work. Clean, quick footwork, musical phrasing instead of isolated steps, and elegance were common hallmarks of both. What is more, both envisioned extending the boundaries of their respective dance genres.

Until that moment, Balanchine, the nascent architect of neoclassical ballet, had been fascinated with jazz dance but had never worked with it firsthand.[8] Now, through Bradley, he not only had an opportunity to observe the American's combination of simplified rhythms and Black vernacular steps but, even more crucially, to experiment with jazz-savvy bodies in the studio.

Though jazz was not native to England, Bradley had already made inroads on English soil. *Ever Green* had given the West End a first glimpse of his aesthetic. On a more pragmatic level, he had coached Mr. Cochran's Young Ladies for *Cochran's 1930 Revue*. Now, eight of those Young Ladies were returning to work with him on *Cochran's 1931 Revue*: Sepha Treble, Sheila Wilson, Peggy Willoughby, Dorothy Dobson, Gladys Lincoln, Peggy Beatty, Aimee Gillespie, and Kathleen Gibson.[9] Flitting between rehearsals, consciously and unconsciously introducing the gestures, postures, and steps of Bradley, these eight fed Balanchine a primer on jazz.

Ada May, Eddie Williams, and Joey Shields, Bradley's dancers from the United States, offered Balanchine an advanced-level seminar in jazz dance. Of these, Ada May, trained at the Metropolitan Opera in Balanchine's language of ballet, fluent in jazz after years with Bradley, and already known to Balanchine via her casting in *Cochran's 1930 Revue*, was Balanchine's most capable translator. Featherlight and musical, she could move in two dance languages, transitioning from deeply bent knees to relevé, parallel legs to turned-out pirouette, syncopated rhythm to flowing adagio, adding off-center balances, cocked hips, and broken wrists. Given her versatility and technique, Balanchine singled out Ada May for the lead roles in "Scaramouche," the harlequin act 1 finale, and the jazzier "Stealing Through." To this day, the saucy grands battements with forward-thrust hips in *Symphony in C* (1947), the most regal of all Balanchine neoclassical ballets, bear witness to Balanchine's practical exploration of the crossovers of jazz and ballet that began with *Cochran's 1931 Revue*.

Through Eddie Williams and Joey Shields, Balanchine had a ringside seat to analyze African American bodies executing jazz dance. Balanchine observed not just the moves but the downward thrust and cadences of real jazz dance. What is more, Bradley's dancers peeled back the surface of theatrical tap dance to expose its percussive heart and underlying musicality. Employing these tenets and casting Williams, Shields, and Ada May in "Scaramouche," Balanchine turned a potential frothy divertissement into an intersection of ballet, jazz, and Baroque music, a precursor to his 1941 *Concerto Barocco* with its en pointe references to the Charleston.

Williams's and Shields's rhythmic tap inspired Balanchine to predict a merging of tap and ballet, an idea he would test a few years later in the 1936 musical *On Your Toes*, a segment of which is still danced, in tap and jazz shoes, not pointe shoes, by his New York City Ballet. Nor was it coincidence that Balanchine would even attach taps to his own jazz shoes and work with Herbert Harper, Bradley's successor at the Pierce Studio, as his assistant choreographer for *On Your Toes*. Their modus operandi was that Balanchine would create the sequence; Harper would translate it into tap. As late as 1967, Balanchine was still invoking tap in *Rubies*, choreographed to Igor Stravinsky's *Capriccio for Piano and Orchestra*. Ballerina Patricia McBride recalls Balanchine specifically wanted the frappé to sound like an explosion when it hit the floor, effectively mimicking the percussive footwork of Williams and Shields.[10]

While it is not known if the two choreographers directly collaborated, Bradley had been an astute observer all his life and selectively drew inspiration from Balanchine. Now he would watch Balanchine's construction of the harlequin jazz-ballet finale, noting the configuration of dancers, and the way dance filled and flowed through space. Perhaps he even smiled as he glimpsed his Russian-trained colleague develop a foxtrot for "Stealing Through."[11] In his own studio, his sharp eye would have picked up any balletic mannerism that a dancer may have unconsciously adapted to his own choreography or noted a chorine in a corner marking out Balanchine choreography before he began a rehearsal. Before the year was out, he was inserting balletically inspired choreography, with dancers in soft ballet slippers, in the musical *Hold My Hand* and an arty black-and-white "ballet" in Cole Porter's *Fifty Million Frenchmen.*

Despite its significance in the annals of dance, *Cochran's 1931 Revue* met an unhappy fate. Opening night weather was lethal, followed up by sledgehammer notices the next morning. The slapstick American humor of Clark and McCullough was antithetical to the British, who revered dry understatement. The numbers were too loosely held together, and the show desperately lacked a good writer. The sketches of suburban life, courtroom antics, and small-time theater were labeled dreary. *Cochran's 1931 Revue* closed after three and a half weeks.[12]

Notably, the dancing survived the salvos. Critics singled out Eddie Williams and Joey Shields for their snappy clean taps. *The Daily Telegraph* gushed that Ada May could "shake and shimmy with the best," while *The Stage* marveled at her delicacy and lightness of foot in Balanchine's "Stealing Through" and "Scaramouche." For his part, Bradley expertly displayed her customary insouciance in a boot black dance in "Harlem," and the quality of crazy abandon that had so captured New Yorkers in "Ding, Dong, Daddy." But he plumbed new depths in Ada May, too. His foxtrot to Noël Coward's "Half-Caste Woman" elicited a new pathos from her that stirred one critic to shivers.[13]

Cochran well knew the dancing was worth a second, maybe even a third, look. He dropped the leaden humor and sketches, and even the Balanchine ballet (which *The Tatler* had dismissed as "arty smarty"), then cleverly repackaged his revue as a show within a show, and placed it at the imposing Palladium, site of the annual royal variety performance. Eddie Williams, Joey Shields, and Ada May—the Bradley nucleus—supported by Mr. Cochran's Young Ladies were the core of the revamped show. Then Cochran topped it off with his best showman's flourish: Buddy Bradley, the sensational choreographer from America, would also dance.[14]

By coincidence, baritone Jules Bledsoe (of the white-chauffeured Packard) was also performing at the Palladium. The fact that African Americans Bradley, Williams, Shields, and Bledsoe were all abroad and performing in a legendary London theater called for celebration. Just behind the Palladium lay Soho, with its visceral cosmopolitanism, labyrinthine streets, and burgeoning Black jazz scene.[15]

Ten days after *Cochran's 1931 Revue* opened, Bradley showcased Broadway, Harlem, and African American influences for a smart new cabaret show, *Creation*, at the Trocadero Grill. It was an immediate hit, described by critics as concentrating nonstop interest into fifty minutes, with more verve and brilliance than most full-blown revues. Ivan Patrick Gore, the nightlife columnist at *The Stage,* deemed *Creation*, treated with all the care of a big show, as one of the best London had ever seen. Given the convivial, late-night atmosphere of cabaret—a concept, incidentally, imported from Jazz Age America—guests were disinclined to listen to monologists and comics and more responsive to dance and visual entertainment. Again, Cochran turned to Bradley for something new and exciting. By now, Bradley had yet a few more London dancers with whom he had previous experience. Their bodies, increasingly familiar with his cues and technique, allowed him ever more latitude in creating his dances.[16]

If being able to coax the dance he envisioned out of English bodies was becoming easier, the physical space became more difficult. The Trocadero stage was not only small, like that of the Pavilion, but shallow, suited for a lineup of Mr. Cochran's Young Ladies but incompatible with the expansive choreography that increasingly interested Bradley. To gain space, Bradley could, and did, take advantage of the steep stairs descending from the stage to send dancers into the cozy dining room, but this was only a partial solution. Besides the obvious tripping hazard for a dancer balancing a cumbersome costume, there was a landmine of tight tables to negotiate. One reviewer quipped that he feared that the dainty toe of a Young Lady might whisk a cutlet airborne.[17]

Fortunately, Cochran productions, whether Shakespeare or cabaret, were never small-budget affairs. Bradley had the support of a savvy stage manager, Maurice Edmonds, who could look after the logistics, including the spacing of tables, and leave Bradley to focus on creating dances. An able orchestra was conducted by Ernest Annereau, with splendid costumes by Ada Peacock, and the cast included, in addition to many now-familiar Mr. Cochran's Young Ladies, a handful of Tiller Girls, Eddie Williams, Joey Shields, as well as Eve, the slinky contortionist, to round out the show. Bradley's choreography was the anchor, while interpolated specialty acts, such as acrobats and illusionists, would be changed periodically, encouraging repeat attendance in the course of the run.[18]

The opening number of *Creation* was pure visual theater. In keeping with the theme of creation, Bradley depicted darkness driven away by light, followed by a procession of sun, moon, stars, fish, fowl, animals, and flowers. When the story reached the Garden of Eden, Bradley felicitously cast the sinuous Eve as the Snake who tempted a scantily clad Young Lady with an apple. (He wisely omitted Adam from the story, since his male cast members, with the exception of Williams and Shields, were the weak link in the show.) Photos show one of Mr. Cochran's Young Ladies, Margaret Neeson, as a flower, with a basket headdress filled with posies, garlands draped from her shoulders, and panniers. This was Bradley channeling Ziegfeld, and he, a dance chameleon, could do this well.[19]

With these ritual preliminaries out of the way, Bradley shifted into a livelier tempo, bringing American vaudeville to the West End. In record time, the Tiller Girls shed their elaborate plumage and donned black tights, top hats, and gilt-rimmed eyeglasses in an homage to the sartorially impeccable African American Class Acts that Bradley admired.[20]

A South Seas number with Mr. Cochran's Young Ladies, "Let's Go Native," was described as a compelling advertisement for a trip to the Pacific. No eyebrows were raised when Williams and Shields appeared as King and Queen of the savages—such caricature reflected norms so universally accepted that those within the system had difficulty seeing them objectively. But one wonders about Bradley. Was he so swept along by the cultural values of the time, so preoccupied staging two shows simultaneously, so grateful for the association with the great Charles B. Cochran—or simply so happy to be working somewhere other than Broadway—that he didn't allow himself to register the relegation of Black individuals, two friends, to the debased status of Others? Perhaps for similar reasons, Williams and Shields didn't register discomfort, either. As ambitious young entertainers determined to make the most of the entrée Bradley had given them to London, they turned in sharp, praiseworthy performances.[21]

Spirituals had been sung in London before, but rarely, if ever, supported by dancing. Now Joey Shields, gifted with the face of an Apollo and the voice of an angel, sang "Roll Jordan" through a megaphone, accompanied by Mr. Cochran's Young Ladies, gowned in black by Ada Peacock and gently swaying in waving formation. Envisioning dress materials that conveyed the impression of a murky, rolling river, Cochran had sent his agents on a hunt to commission black velvet that would specifically glisten in the limelight like "the color of a wet seal's back." Scarlet gloves accessorized the streamlined gowns, dressing the liquid undulations of Bradley's choreography with drama. "Roll Jordan," like a gospel refrain, lingered long in memory.[22]

Showcasing dance, divertissement, and visual drama, Cochran's annual Trocadero cabarets served Bradley as a well-funded laboratory to experiment with novel dance ideas. As Bradley's association with Cochran blossomed, his commonalities and relationship with Pierce slowly faded. After the opening of *Creation*, the last show with which Pierce would be nominally associated, Pierce left Buddy tap dancing (unchaperoned!) at the Palladium and took off for a prolonged visit to Paris, where he attended the races at Longchamps, hobnobbed with nightclub owner Ada "Bricktop" Smith, and caught Josephine Baker at the Casino de Paris. By the time Pierce returned to New York, he was larding his conversation with such anglicisms as "Topping, old chap!" Meanwhile, once his Palladium engagement ended, Bradley hastened back to New York and quietly resumed his role as dance director at the Pierce Studio.[23]

With his visibility rising via three high-profile commissions for Cochran, it was inevitable that other English producers would approach Bradley, too. Ironically, he next crossed the Atlantic to choreograph the London transfer of an American show, Cole Porter's *Fifty Million Frenchmen*, a spoof of Prohibition-era Americans in laissez-faire Paris.[24] Though Bradley knew of Porter's work from Broadway, the street-taught choreographer and the French-polished composer, at a glance, seemed poles apart. Nevertheless, an invisible thread bound their sensibilities close together.

Despite its ebullient veneer, *Fifty Million Frenchmen* signaled an emotional advance in book musical songwriting. Porter, a gay man in international high society, knew of alienation, masks, and subterfuge sex. His brooding, twisting melodies warmed and deepened his nonchalant lyrics. Unlike the brittle chic of Noël Coward or nonchalance of Richard Rodgers, Porter's music reflected melancholy, dropping in and out of minor keys, ranging over octaves, and weeping, its pain protectively camouflaged in smartness. In short, Porter's music found its expression in jazz and brought Bradley one step closer to connecting musical comedy dance with emotion.[25]

From the very beginning, *Fifty Million Frenchmen* reveals the duality of Porter—and offers a choreographer a vast range of mood and music in one score. After the clever opening number, "Step Right up to the Bar," with Americans jubilantly quaffing cocktails in Paris, the second number, "You Do Something to Me," slips into a wailing jazz horn solo, then drops into a minor key and the perennial Porter theme, longing ("I thought my life was through / Until I gazed at you"). Bradley naturally drew on his accumulated professional experience—the jazz dancing at Connie's Inn, the character development in *Broadway*, the bravado dancing of *A Connecticut Yankee*—but now he also had to dig within, to find that sense of displacement, of sadness, of sexiness, that echoes under Porter's jazzy jauntiness, and added new depth to his choreography.[26]

Fifty Million Frenchmen desperately needed the Bradley touch. When the Broadway production opened the previous year, the New York critics barely mentioned Larry Ceballos's choreography, though one critic politely commented that it showed off the costumes to full advantage and made good exits. Now Bradley's solo and ensemble numbers shook the critics out of their lethargy, surprising them with an inventive hurdle-jumping dance, a black-and-white "ballet" with a trick lighting system—perhaps a response to his collaboration with Balanchine—and a fast tap number for American actress-dancer Mary Cecil as Hildegarde Violet, a New York fur buyer looking to be shocked, which meant looking for sex, in Paris. For act 1's "Happy Heaven of Harlem," with Porter's references to gender fluidity uptown, Bradley produced a jive specialty spot for the character of Boule de Neige, a Black jockey at Longchamps. He brought the house down in "You've Got That Thing," Porter's ode to sex appeal, with the syncopated tapping he created for his New York protégée Betty Compton, who had transferred from Broadway with the production. Frances Day, in the role of cabaret singer May de Vere, also earned critical praise.[27]

Bradley's noted coaching skills came in handy when the ailing Compton had to withdraw from the cast. In the sliver of time between the Edinburgh and Manchester tryouts, he had Annette Mills, sister of John Mills, putting over Compton's number with audacity. Joyce Barbour, an English dancer-actress with whom Bradley had worked on *Ever Green*, would shortly take over the quick hoofing dance of Mary Cecil with equal aplomb. Dancing the lead of Billy Baxter was American actor-aviator Hal Skelly, whom critics declared had the same loose-limbed ease of Jack Buchanan, another Bradley disciple. (Today, the dashing Skelly is largely forgotten, as he died only three years later in a train accident.)[28]

The London transfer, however, faced some fundamental issues. Racy, edgy material would not pass muster with the Lord Chamberlain's censorship, so the very English Arthur Wimperis (who won an Oscar for his film script for the very proper *Mrs. Miniver*) anglicized the book by Herbert Fields, author of *A Connecticut Yankee* and *Hello, Daddy!*, dampening some of its flip allure. But the biggest issue was the producer's inability to secure a West End theater. Until recently, the Daniel Mayer Company had managed artists such as pianists Arthur Rubinstein and Ignacy Paderewski and ballerina Anna Pavlova. Now, Mayer's son, who had taken over the business, aimed to be a theatrical producer, not a high-art impresario. But, without the pull or know-how of Cochran, he sloppily arranged the transfer of a show with a cast of over one hundred (and a dancing and singing chorus of sixty) without securing an appropriate theater in London, such as the Palace, that could accommodate a large musical. While *Fifty Million Frenchmen* played to rave reviews in Glasgow, Edinburgh, and Manchester, and notices indicated it was to move to the West End, no theater materialized. An expensive beginner's mistake. And another example of the vagaries of show business.[29]

After setting *Fifty Million Frenchmen,* Bradley returned to America that fall and resumed his old life. He taught class. He coached Adele Astaire, who left the studio rhapsodizing about Buddy's "dirty steps" to Cecil Beaton. He received a visit from Zelia Raye, an English dance entrepreneur, who was conducting a survey of American tap and methods. Though Raye methodically recorded steps, she missed the inherent swing of jazz dance. Later, she would distill her findings, focusing on definitions and discrete steps, rather than musical phrasing, into the teaching syllabus adopted by the Royal Academy of Dance for accredited tap-dance instruction in England.[30]

But, amid the day-to-day activity, Bradley wrestled with an existential decision. Seymour Felix had gone out to Hollywood to stage musicals for Fox and wanted Bradley to join him. Movies had not only been Bradley's first dream; Hollywood, with its captive American market, immense soundstages, and adventurous directors, represented the future, its resources and visibility dwarfing the power of the theater. Tinseltown, however, was potentially (and proved to be with time) as risky a proposition as Broadway for a Black creative. Bradley sensed he would once again be consigned the role of faceless talent behind a white man. How could he direct his own story if he remained nameless?[31]

By November 1931, Bradley had declined the allure of Hollywood and was back in London, perching in temporary quarters and receiving his mail via *The Stage*'s letterbox—a sort of post restante for nomadic entertainers—all the while drilling a chorus of twenty-four youthful dancers (megaproductions on the lines of *Fifty Million Frenchmen,* it seems, were the exclusive province of

Americans and Cochran) for a new show called *Hold My Hand*. If *Fifty Million Frenchmen* had been a foray into Americana, *Hold My Hand*, replete with earls, butlers, and lawn tennis parties, was Bradley's baptism into all things British. Its score had been composed by a young Yorkshireman, Noël Gay, who would go on to fame with *Me and My Girl*. As evidenced by many recordings—for dance music was what sold records in those days—the *Hold My Hand* score was highly danceable, if not jazzy. Stanley Lupino, Sonnie Hale, and Jessie Matthews led the dance-savvy cast. Inventive dances for giddy maids, sassy ingenues, and dissolute rakes, successors to the clever hurdle-jumping dance in *Fifty Million Frenchmen*, were Bradley's clever contribution to the show.[32]

The plot was sheer lunacy: a millionaire, a failing newspaper, its editor, and the mistaken identity of a supposed ward who turns out to be a saucy lass. There was a wedding scene, a garden scene, even a spanking scene (unthinkable now), all, of course, staged by Bradley. Both Lupino and Hale, reared on musical comedy, seized any opportunity for song and dance. (As Lupino was conveniently the producer, this was quite easy to implement.) "Never has an editor danced with such versatility," observed one reviewer, while another acerbically noted it was hardly surprising the newspaper was going under, as the editor spent all his time dancing.[33]

By the time the show opened on December 23, 1932, Bradley had the dancers in neat and well-trained order, toggling from graceful to grotesque. Most of his ensemble choreography, alive, full of gaiety, and pointed with fun, was performed in heeled dance shoes, but there was one notable departure. Again, recalling Balanchine, Bradley created a sort of balletic jazz rite of spring for three cavorting housemaids and a butler. The maids, in the skimpiest poufs of tutus, their frilly maids' caps dizzily askew, execute an acrobatic jazz ballet in soft ballet slippers. It was one of the most talked-about numbers in the show.[34]

There was another reason for buzz. Twenty-five-year-old Jessie Matthews, coached by Bradley, was emerging as the show's acknowledged star, despite Lupino's and Hale's top billing status. Everything she did, *The Tatler* exclaimed, was more artful and more artless than ever before. Always promising, she now looked comfortable on a stage. And if, perchance, in youthful eagerness, she may have overacted a bit, nothing detracted from her ever more impressive dancing.[35]

The secret was that Bradley understood Jessie Matthews and her abilities as a dancer—and probably the psychological makeup of Matthews—almost as well as she did herself. With a near-intuitive sense of his dancers, he created work for Matthews that felt completely natural on her body. They had already forged a successful working relationship in *Ever Green*, a breakout vehicle for both. Now every movement, from a hip kick to a heel-tap to a cartwheel to a tippy-toe solo as a bride, was lyrical and harmonious, in a style that exactly suited her. Even deceptively simple dances, like the foxtrot number "Hold My Hand" with juvenile lead Harry Milton, were not throwaway but cause for critical admiration.[36]

As Paula Bond, the unruly ward tuned high-style bride, Matthews posed effortlessly in fifth position, fingers elegantly elongated, head turned gracefully to one side, wearing gauntlet gloves and feathers cascading down her back. This is Matthews, cockney gamine aspiring to poised princess. Bradley's choreography often drew on her balletic grace, employing effortless sidekicks, plush waltz steps, and high carriage that Eddie Rector would have admired.[37]

But there is another side to their collaboration. A photo shows Matthews, surrounded by those wayward maids, with arms stretched high overhead. She is not in a ballet position, or even a stock musical comedy pose. Instead, she's adopted a Bradley pose, one that traces its lineage right back to African dance: her wrists are flexed, her hands pull back, her back is swayed, and her feet are firmly planted on the floor.[38] Bradley had steered Matthews onto his own dance territory and, in doing so, made her exciting. Her confidence in the dances he created for her translated into charisma onstage. As such, *Hold My Hand* launched Jessie Matthews's film career.[39]

London reached out to Bradley for the same reason as Broadway: his choreography came smartly packaged and temptingly tied with a bow of Harlem jazz. Yet London offered in return something far more important than mere program credit. Producers entrusted entire shows to Bradley, deferred to his judgment, and gave oxygen to his ideas. He could segue from revue to book musical, from Cole Porter to Noël Gay, from staging spirituals in *Creation* to church weddings in *Hold My Hand*. He could observe ballet through George Balanchine and experiment with Jessie Matthews. Not everything was perfect—stages could be awkward, some shows flopped, not all producers were created equal—but what it offered was essential for an artist. In exploration, latitude, and agency, Bradley could define himself and his art. In return, his art redefined the West End stage. *Variety* noted that by 1932 his dancing ideas were conspicuous in practically every West End production.[40]

CHAPTER 11

EXPATRIATION

I have discovered in life that there
are ways of getting almost anywhere you
want to go, if you really want to go.

—LANGSTON HUGHES

By the time young dancer Chuck Green made it to New York, hoping to study with Buddy Bradley at the Pierce Studio, Bradley had taken off again for London. A new book musical, a Cochran cabaret, and a booking at Ciro's nightclub were awaiting him that spring of 1932. A Noël Coward show was in the offing for the fall. After eighteen months of crisscrossing the Atlantic, camping in temporary quarters, and receiving correspondence at the offices of *The Stage*, it was time to assess Broadway and its string of broken promises. Bradley's acquisition in London of a wire-haired terrier signaled a decision: London would henceforth be his home.

With its seductive stream of opportunities, breadth, and visibility, moving to London may have seemed an obvious decision. It was not. Even though the Depression had sent choreographers like Albertina Rasch scurrying to Hollywood, New York was the epicenter of dance and would remain so throughout the twentieth century.[1] In working on Broadway, Bradley had already largely given up choreographing on Black dancers. If he were living in London, he would be one step further removed from his jazz roots, unable to keep his eye on the dances emanating from Harlem nightclubs, let alone Broadway stages. English dancers could be diligent, unique, and even supremely talented, but only American dancers, nurtured in jazz from the cradle, could truly understand and interpret his choreography.

The dilemma was personal as well as professional. The Scottsboro trial, revealing the depth of racism in America, provided Black men with plenty of incentive to leave the country. Yet, for an orphan with little moral support, London was as much deracination as defense. Leaving New York meant giving up the guidance of African American elders Thaddeus Drayton, Leonard Harper, and Billy Pierce; the collegial network forged with Fletcher Henderson, Herbert Harper, Ralph Cooper, Pete Nugent, and Henry Le Tang; and even what remained of his family, with Ernestine now living in Chicago, and Aurelius in perpetual motion. Bradley would be alone, more isolated than ever, and, once again, a "first" uncomfortably charting unknown waters. It would mean traveling without a road map, learning by constant observation, code-switching when necessary, and advancing via trial and error—and painfully accepting that, despite talent, despite will, despite dedication, his choices were circumscribed in America.

Buddy Bradley chose exploration.

Bradley's first show in London that spring was *The Cat and the Fiddle,* a moody love story by composer Jerome Kern of *Show Boat* and lyricist Otto "Tea for Two" Harbach. Kern wove his music so deeply into the texture of the play that when the characters broke into song, it seemed inevitable that they should sing rather than talk. Such expressive music sent Bradley into new dramatic and dance terrain, demanding similarly character-revealing dances. Charm, charm, and still more charm, raved *The Sphere,* noting with relief (or condescension?) that *The Cat and the Fiddle* was atypical of the usual musical from America. High-energy razzmatazz and trendy gimmicks were nowhere to be seen.[2]

Instead, the play was sophisticated and "European": set alongside Brussels quays, in music conservatories, artist's lodgings, and an opera house, populated by a brooding Romanian composer, a cultured American, and various French and Belgian characters, all speaking a polyglot of languages. The acting was so restrained as to be nearly imperceptible. The Marchioness of Queensberry designed the costumes. Critics spoke of the Pirandello touch: more than once, Kern's melodies didn't match Harbach's text but illustrated the moods of characters, and the plot blurred the line between truth and perception. It was just the sort of innovative property Charles B. Cochran adored—as did London.[3]

On Broadway, such highbrow shows were routinely given to someone like Viennese Opera–trained Albertina Rasch (who in fact choreographed the Broadway production of *The Cat and the Fiddle*), not to Buddy Bradley, a former elevator operator. The selection of Bradley not only justified his move to London but had internal logic: the story of a classical composer and jazz musician wrestling to forge an aesthetic (and romantic) synthesis mirrored Bradley's own quest to blur conventional distinctions of dance. The intimate tone required dances that explored, with a chorus of only a dozen or so dancers, yearnings, disillusion, hope, jealousy, and romance. Other dances, still carefully worked into character and story, showcased Bradley's New York aesthetic: a bit of jazz in four gesticulating figures before a dark curtain and sheer tap electricity from American Gina Malo, with legs "simply to be looked at," crosstalk, and jazzy footwork.[4]

Prodded by Margot Asquith, widow of the late prime minister, Cochran invited up-and-coming ballet choreographer Frederick Ashton to help with the act 1 finale, a commedia dell'arte operetta-within-a-play. Ashton, the future Sir Frederick Ashton and principal choreographer of the Royal Ballet, then twenty-six and still struggling to patch together a livelihood from movie house stints and occasional commissions, quickly agreed. While Pierrot and Harlequin (evidently quite the vogue in the early 1930s) animated the stage, the serendipitous encounter of Bradley and Ashton sparked a stream of experiments, introductions, and collaborations of jazz dance and ballet.[5]

Between *The Cat and the Fiddle* rehearsals, Bradley slipped off to Ciro's, the debutante-circuit club with underlit glass dance floor behind the National Gallery, where he staged a cabaret show of six English girls and "two slim Negro youths" who galloped, squirmed, and twisted in a Lindy Hop and a tap Snake Hips. If it were unusual to see Black men and white women dance together, Bradley's more astonishing feat was that he pulled off the dances, with their origins in African American culture, with English dancers. Without a doubt, the two unnamed male dancers (most likely Bradley's New York imports, Eddie Williams and Joey Shields) carried the show. Nevertheless, the very fact that he could stage something like a tap Snake Hips with its bewildering variety of quick taps, jumps, and slides with English dancers was visible proof of the Bradley effect permeating London. With credits now on four book musicals, a major revue, and a cabaret in the West End, Buddy had a mounting list of English dancers on whom he could increasingly rely to realize his vision.[6]

Spring in London also meant the annual unveiling of a new Cochran cabaret at the Trocadero. For the 1932 edition, *Magic Nights*, Buddy Bradley and Ernest Annereau returned as dance director and musical director, respectively, while Frederick Ashton contributed a ballet. There was the usual glamorous opener, a procession of fantastically clad dancers personifying radio towers throughout the world (New York was represented by a radiating headdress of skyscrapers, London by a three-foot-high sequined and diamante Big Ben), all very mindfully descending the stairs to the rhythm of a foxtrot. Adding to the luster was live filming, projecting audience and dancers onto newsreels seen throughout the world.[7]

Once the obligatory parade was dispensed with, Bradley moved on to themes that reflected his current choreographic interests and the capabilities of his dancers. As if eulogizing his past life in New York, Bradley peppered the program with references to New York: Eddie Rector, the *Blackbirds* revues, Harlem colleagues, and strenuous all-out hoofing. Half of Mr. Cochran's Young Ladies in *Magic Nights* had danced with Bradley in previous shows; two, Bunty Pain and Eileen Clifton, even stretched back to *Ever Green*. All were beginning to understand the way he accented dance and to anticipate his admonitions to "feel the floor."

"Valve Girls," a tap number described by British Pathé as an ultramodern technical work, incorporated shimmy arms, emphatic stamps, shoulders and legs moving in polyrhythm. In "Syncopation," Bradley brought out a line of swaying dancers executing swiveling hips, twisting shoulders, dragging steps, and deep forward-bending in rhythmic time. For "Magic," the de rigueur titular number, Bradley had each Young Lady execute a different conjuring trick while dancing, reminiscent of Tosh Hammond, his old lodging-house mate in Harlem, who produced tricks and backflips while landing on a telephone book. For the ever-game Ashton and ubiquitous Eve, dressed in identical uniforms, Bradley created "The Bell Boys Stampede," in the lineage of U. S. Thompson and Johnny Nit dancing as Pullman porters in the *Blackbirds* revue and Pete Nugent and Derby Wilson as the Dancing Red Caps in *Runnin' Wild*. Among the guest specialty acts during the cabaret's run were an equilibrist, a cigarette wizard, a golliwog (yet another example of systemic English racism in the 1930s) and—reflective of Bradley's growing influence on Cochran—the Condos Brothers, the tapping duo from Philadelphia with the staccato energy of pneumatic drills.[8]

Bradley and Ashton continued the classical-jazz dance dialogue they had begun in *The Cat and the Fiddle*. For "An '1805' Impression," Ashton cast the Garbo-like ballerina Pearl Argyle as Madame Recamier but used Mr. Cochran's Young Ladies for his corps. As it was a given that theatrical dancers in England had some ballet training, Ashton was not greatly disadvantaged working with the Young Ladies.[9] Nevertheless, given the different levels of proficiency, Ashton, like Bradley when he imposed jazz dance on white dancers, resorted to choreography that was elegant but simplified.[10]

What was novel for Bradley was the fluidity and scale of Ashton's work. While Bradley was crafting "Moanin' Low" for Clifton Webb in 1929, Ashton had been performing in Paris for Bronislava Nijinska, absorbing her theory of movement, where even the simplest footwork was accompanied by graceful epaulement (the angled relationship between head, shoulders, and hips). And though he had danced on the small stage of Connie's Inn at the beginning of his career, most of Bradley's choreography had been created for

Broadway stages, where dance had to communicate to the farthest reaches of the theater. Ashton, on the other hand, was accustomed to working in Marie Rambert's tiny Mercury Theatre, with an audience so close to the stage that they could see the color of the dancers' eyes. The smallest details, everything from eye direction, finger placement, and hints of humor, had enormous audience impact in an intimate setting. Now Ashton's work for *Magic Nights*, filled with close observation, interlaced fingers, aligned arms, bending torsos, and harmonious groupings, provided Bradley with new ideas for creating dance.[11]

Bradley's blazing finale, "The Changing of the Guard," was the complement to Ashton's delicate gesturing, a panoply of color, movement, and sound. With dancers costumed in Grenadier Guards jackets (minus the buttons, as it was forbidden to wear the exact uniforms), the finale paid tribute to the military pageantry of England, Bradley's new home, and Eddie Rector's tap "March of the Wooden Soldiers," infamously appropriated by *Blackbirds* producer Lew Leslie for Florence Mills.[12]

Requiring military precision, alternating steps as if playing the drums, then tapping in counterpoint, Bradley streamlined Rector's original dance for his neophyte team. As Ashton was doubling as a dancer in the cabaret, Bradley had to teach him (as well as future ballet director Walter Gore and dancer/costume designer William Chappell, also picking up extra quid in *Magic Nights*) how to tap. By opening night, Ashton was jauntily leading the regiment, but he confessed he had to "fake" tapping. Piqued but perplexed by Bradley's world of dance, Ashton realized Bradley had a lot to offer him.[13]

All the while Bradley fascinated Ashton, London astonished Bradley. When "The Changing of the Guard" closed the cabaret in a flourish of tattoos and crimson, the opening night audience burst into applause and Cochran came out, per custom, to thank his audience, impulsively pulling a dazed Bradley and Ashton to the stage with him.[14] Theatrical choreography was acquiring stature in London, due to game-changers like Bradley. Choreographers now had faces; they were even applauded. Jazz dance was approaching parity with ballet.

As Buddy Bradley racked up one credit after another, it was clear he would not lack work in the West End. What he would lack were enough dancers to cast his shows, and, what is more, dancers who could execute the dances he envisioned. There were only sixteen Mr. Cochran's Young Ladies per show, and if he depended on this channel, he would be forever short of capable dancers and limited in what he could achieve. That winter, the Home Office became increasingly protective of its entertainers, stringently issuing work permits only to foreign artists deemed absolutely necessary and only for limited periods. Even Ben Welden, an American actor who came over to perform in *Broadway* in 1926 and married an English woman, had his permit withdrawn. Bradley's former pupil Peggy O'Neill was bracing to lose her permit, too. Bringing over dancers, like Williams and Shields, was at best a stopgap solution.[15]

Now that he was settled in London, living in a small flat near Leicester Square and working steadily, it was high time to address the issue of sourcing dancers. Borrowing a page from Billy Pierce, Bradley applied in June 1932 for a license for a dance school and employment agency. Practically, the school created a pipeline of dancers trained in Bradley's methods and aesthetic. Culturally, it was another powerful conduit for disseminating American jazz dance across an ocean. Bradley-trained dancers would not only share his vision on stage but also go on to work in the provinces, where they would teach, choreograph, and transmit Bradley's legacy.[16]

The Buddy Bradley School of Stage Dancing, at 25a Old Compton Street, was a well-conceived plan from every angle. The employment agency would allow Bradley to assemble and hire out teams of dancers with choreographed routines ready to drop into a show or nightclub act. Teaching could be a lifeline if there were ever a downturn in the West End or his own fortunes. Partnering with Coleman "Coley" Goodman, an Englishman and a former musical hall proprietor, would sidestep the thorny issue of an American "overtaking" the West End. Plus, Coley's administrative experience in the English entertainment world made him a savvy manager of the school, while Buddy Bradley, the acknowledged rainmaker and life force behind the school, would be the sole name on the business and would concentrate on what he did best—choreography and teaching.[17]

Soon, Coley and Bradley hired a secretary, the competent Miss Tanner, to coordinate Bradley's rehearsal and teaching schedules as well as the steady stream of advertisements that ran in London's entertainment newspapers, *The Stage* and *The Era*, prominently promising that Bradley himself would attend the tap and rhythm classes, given daily at 12 and 2 p.m. Later, as his theater commitments multiplied, the wording was amended to state that private classes were by appointment, while the group classes were taught by people like Harold Eden, Bradley's right-hand man at the school in the 1930s. Custom choreography was offered, of course, with costs for routines beginning at twenty-five guineas and soaring skyward from there. By the mid-1930s, as the Nicholas Brothers were coming into prominence, and as a nod to the diversity of tap styles, Frank Duncan, an American, taught acrobatics and limbering several times a week.[18]

Proximate to all the great theaters of London, buried in what had been the center of coffeehouse culture in Georgian London, Soho radiated bohemian romance, which suited Bradley. His school at the southwest corner of Old Compton and Frith Streets overlooked, from second-floor windows emblazoned with Buddy Bradley's name in diagonal script, the nineteenth-century Algerian Coffee Store, with its bags of coffee beans and litter of brass cafetières. Up and down the street were the shops and offices of costumers, Italian hairdressers, suppliers of musical accessories, a scenic contractor, a French news agent, purveyors of foreign provisions, oyster dealers, tobacconists, and, of course, restaurants, cafés, and clubs. With its mélange of sophisticates, left-wing intellectuals, Jewish musicians, theater people, socialists, homosexuals, and transsexuals, Soho was a crossroads of ideas and cultures.[19]

By the 1930s, Soho was also an affirming sanctuary for Blacks, particularly musicians from far-flung British colonies, marginalized from the mainstream music profession. Soho's little clubs—there were easily hundreds in the "Belt" alone—offered employment, if meager compensation, and a platform for creative expression, where lyrics, melodies, and instrumentation from Africa to the Caribbean, as well as some jazz from America, were reworked, rewired, and fused, redefining, like Bradley, the boundaries of their art. As a dance man (and a successful one) and not a musician, Bradley was more an observer than a full-fledged member of this confraternity. Nevertheless, as music was the driving impulse of his own work, and, as all these artists had come to London seeking cultural riches and opportunities unavailable at home, there was a tacit bonhomie.[20]

Lovely as it was to be in Soho—as easy to run off to a theater rehearsal as to stand in his doorway nursing a cigarette and observe the local rhythms—the raison d'être of 25a Old Compton Street was creating dancers. If students had already studied tap dance in England, it was invariably of the hippity-hoppity school, the marionette kind of dance Jack Buchanan had been dancing when he first came to Bradley in New York. But Bradley was unfazed unteaching one technique and replacing it with another. Provided that a student had a decent sense of rhythm (a big prerequisite) and dedication, Bradley was confident he could teach him or her to understand gravity and weight, bend his or her knees, press into the ground, and move with swing, then eventually speed up these basics to be musically responsive, and, in short, create a jazz dancer. This, however, was not an end point for Bradley.[21]

Bradley was on the lookout for dancers he could mold into stars, those with personality that telegraphed from the stage to the very top of the house. Identifying and evolving these individuals became a passion, a life's work. When students like Sepha Treble, a Mr. Cochran Young Lady in the 1930 and 1931 revues, starred in *Mother of Pearl*; when Aimée Gillespie replaced ballerina Pearl Argyle as the lead in Ashton's "An '1805' Impression"; or when Nancy Burne rose from a small part to a much-applauded leading role in *Ballyhoo* and became a pillar of the theatrical dance community, it was a personal point of pride for Bradley.[22]

Of course, there were already plenty of full-blown stars at the school. Besides Mr. Cochran's Young Ladies, and any other dancer eager to acquire facility in the dance style taking over the West End, early pillars of the school were the stars who had discovered Bradley in New York. Jack Buchanan, Evelyn Laye, Jack Hulbert, and Cicely Courtneidge continued to come to Old Compton Street to acquire another coat of polish and new ideas for their dancing, as well as unique routines that looked like no other dancer's (or dance director's). Jessie Matthews was now a dedicated disciple. John Mills and Elsie Randolph would shortly follow, as well as aspiring bandleader, Ken "Snakehips" Johnson, the son of the minister of health in British Guyana, who played hooky from his university coursework to study with Bradley.[23]

In 1932, Bradley's career in London was in steep ascent. He was working on innovative highbrow plays, forging partnerships with ballet, jazz, and tap, and choreographing to music that ranged from the romantic Jerome Kern to the naughty Douglas Byng. Charles B. Cochran now looked to him for the selection and training of his prized Young Ladies. He had a business with a staff and his name in letters on the windows. Via British Pathé film, such as the newsreel footage taken at the Trocadero cabaret, his dances were seen and influential throughout the world. London was providing exactly the opportunities he should have had in New York.[24]

But the seemingly endless possibilities were tempered by wistfulness. America's rejection of him, a Black man, was a heartbreak. To friends he vowed that he could never return, the pain of rejection cut so deep. London for Bradley was both balm and banishment. Exploration came at the price of exile.

PART 4

THE EXPANSIVE YEARS, 1932–1938

CHAPTER 12

ON POINTE WITH FREDERICK ASHTON AND NOËL COWARD

I never knew who got more fun out of it: Ashton, seeing his choreography influenced by typical Negro movements or Buddy seeing his routines performed by classical dancers.

—SPIKE HUGHES

Charles Cochran's shepherding of Bradley and Ashton onstage for a curtain call at *Magic Nights* was high-level recognition of an on-the-ground reality. Since working in London, Bradley had been layering elements from soft ballet slippers to imaginative jockey dances on his core jazz vocabulary while ballet choreographers like Balanchine and Ashton looked to jazz cadences and movement, often through the intermediary of Bradley, to revolutionize their own art form. Concert and theatrical dance were converging.

Frederick Ashton was so fascinated with jazz dance that he made a beeline to Bradley's school the moment it opened. It wasn't that Ashton was particularly keen on tap—he thought it rather boring, actually—it was the *quality* of Bradley's movement, the twisting shoulders, torso, and hips, the rolling walk, the confident placement of foot to floor, that he was so keen to understand. Accompanying him to the Bradley studio were two other ballet dancers, Alicia Markova and Frederic Franklin. Franklin, who had danced at the

Casino de Paris with Josephine Baker and would become a mainstay of the revived Ballets Russes, expressed the mysteries and exhilaration of studying jazz dance with Bradley. "We simply couldn't *find* a way to do it. You know, all that skimming, one thing moving against the other, shoulders going one way, hands another—but, *finally*, we got it!"[1]

Realizing he could learn much from Bradley, Ashton invited him to see his work at the Ballet Club, Marie Rambert's breeding ground for ballet dancers and dance ideas. Equally curious about ballet, Bradley found he had an easy rapport with Ashton—they were both young, relative outsiders, and latecomers to dance who brought curiosity, openness, and natural grace to their work—and accepted the invitation. Finding Bradley enthusiastic about his work at the Mercury Theatre, dance that was big even on a minuscule stage, Ashton was emboldened to propose blending their styles in a collaboration.

There were so many reasons to say yes. Two years ago in New York, Bradley could only have fantasized about such an experimental partnership and an entrée into the rarefied world of concert dance. The venue was reason alone: the commission was not for a West End revue or the bohemian, albeit highly respected, Ballet Club but for the highbrow Camargo Society, the forerunner of the Royal Ballet. Most importantly, the result would be a milepost: *High Yellow*, a story of a departing island man and his two jilted girlfriends "set somewhere off the coast of Florida," was the world's first jazz ballet and the first ballet ever choreographed by an African American.[2]

Whenever Ashton was at Bradley's studio, "Six Bells Stampede" seemed to be turning on the turntable. During the run of *Cochran's 1931 Revue*, Bradley had met its composer, Spike Hughes, who had played the bass in the pit orchestra. They had cemented a friendship during late-night listening sessions of Bradley's coveted Duke Ellington records in Bradley's hotel room during the Manchester tryouts.[3] (Hughes considered these sessions with Bradley a major contributor to the development of jazz in Britain, as the records weren't available in the UK.)[4] As Ashton was equally taken with "Six Bells Stampede," the two approached Hughes for a ballet score. Surprisingly, Hughes, who had swerved from classical music to jazz after seeing

Blackbirds with Florence Mills in 1923, was reticent, only agreeing to the project when it was suggested—probably by the exuberant Ashton—that their three-way collaboration would give birth to A New Art Form.[5]

Perhaps they should have taken Hughes's apprehension more seriously, for it nearly sabotaged their success. The three began by conferring, and Hughes drinking, late at night in Bradley's small flat off Leicester Square, Bradley dancing on a tap board that nearly filled the small sitting room, requiring Hughes to creep around the periphery to reach the window-sill bar.[6] As the choreographers brainstormed about their upcoming ballet, Hughes was hesitant; it seems he composed only under the last-minute pressure of a Decca recording session. Failing to compose a single note for The New Art Form, Hughes finally proposed reusing "Six Bells Stampede," supplemented with the finale from his "Harlem Requiem" and a few random pieces. Liking the elegiac opening of "Stampede" and finding that the "Harlem Requiem" made an upbeat closer, Bradley and Ashton agreed—they really had no choice, after all—then settled down to choreograph.[7]

If Spike Hughes caused anxiety, Alicia Markova, their ballerina, instilled confidence. Tutored in music by Igor Stravinsky, schooled in modern art by Diaghilev, Picasso, and Matisse, and shaped by Balanchine in her years at the Ballets Russes, Markova was a sophisticated vehicle for transposing jazz and ballet. For six weeks, in his flat, Bradley tutored her in the Snake Hips, syncopated rhythms, and African American dances. Twenty years later, the Snake Hips was still so deeply embedded in her body that she danced it, impromptu, on television. Abetted by Bradley's proficiency in the kitchen, a skill he had likely acquired in his restaurant apprenticeship in Harrisburg, with his dutiful terrier, Mose, at his feet, the coaching sessions of Bradley, Ashton, and Markova often ended in collegial evenings discussing dance, music, and the arts.[8]

Bradley bonded with his ballerina, whose tragic aura reminded him of Florence Mills. Both she and Bradley were renowned for their composure, whether facing chaos before or behind the footlights, a trait with origins in similar life experiences. Markova had been thrust into premature adulthood by the heartrending death (rumored suicide) of her beloved father and, as a Jew, had suffered prejudice firsthand. (Joey Shields, whom Bradley had brought to London for *Cochran's 1931 Revue*, had been shocked to see how much the English despised Jews, calling them "Yids" and shunning them, while he, a person of color, never encountered overt prejudice.) When the Ballets Russes collapsed and dancers scrambled to salvage their careers, a powerful and seemingly anti-Semitic hierarchy at the Camargo Society had effectively barred her participation—she, the foremost English dancer of the era—until Ashton and Bradley produced her as a fait accompli in the casting of *High Yellow*.

Though Spike Hughes recalled that the dancers took to Bradley's typical smoothness and languid hand movements with remarkable ease and skill, rehearsals were far from easy. Dancer Elisabeth Schooling remembered Bradley could only laugh—with resignation?—after going along the line to see who had grasped a movement he had demonstrated. Some dancers struggled to piece it together, while others had incorporated the movement but lost the swing, but, in the end, Bradley pulled it off. Reviewers remarked on Markova's sense of rhythm, found Maud Lloyd and Nadina Newhouse excellent in their mastery of the choreography, and marveled at Doris Sonne, in the role of a discarded sweetheart, who captured, more than any previous European dancer, the very essence of jazz.[9]

If Bradley's name on the program of *Ever Green* had been reason to smile, his credit line in *High Yellow* burnished his reputation. At the ballet premiere at the elegant Savoy Theatre on June 6, 1932, Bradley was listed as choreographer, while Ashton was relegated to a supporting role, as responsible for the groupings. Such a delineation of credits, not to mention *High Yellow*'s inclusion by the Camargo Society, speaks to the acceptance of jazz dance in British culture, triggered by Bradley (and supported by Ashton's large-heartedness). The Camargo Society was institutional ballet at its highest level. Its directors included Arnold Haskell and former Ballets Russes ballerina Lydia Lopokova, the dance committee Ninette de Valois, Tamara Karsavina, Princess Astafieva, Margaret Craske, Anton Dolin, and Anna Ludmila. Its patrons were the leaders of fashionable and intellectual interwar London: Lord Berners, Samuel Courtauld, Lady Cunard, Edward Marsh, John Maynard Keynes, Lady Ottoline Morrell, Anthony Powell, Vita Sackville-West, Siegfried Sassoon, Lytton Strachey, Rebecca West, H. G. Wells, and Leonard and Virginia Woolf.[10] *High Yellow*'s premiere audience included Prince George, ex-King Manual of Portugal, and Serge Lifar. Its opening night party, which Bradley surely attended, took place at a grand Georgian house in Mayfair.[11]

While the *Sunday Referee* praised the ballet as "a lovely, feverish thing," not everyone was ready to embrace the fact that new ideas strengthened old art forms. Lady Cunard and her friends were shocked at the mere thought of a jazz ballet, and Russian ballerina Olga Spessivtseva was so upset she did not want to dance *Swan Lake* on the same program. Spessivtseva's qualms, it turned out, were well founded: as the London *Times* praised *High Yellow*, it criticized *Swan Lake*, nominating it for the banality stakes, along with Anton Dolin's Satan in Ninette de Valois's *Job*. The landmine turned out to be a lifeline. With its jazz, syncopation, whirling color, quick action, humor, feeling, and excitement, *High Yellow* breathed new life into ballet.[12]

"Ballet Is Coming Back!" rejoiced *The Era*. Dance was now relevant and exciting, neither music-hall nor ballet, wrote *The New English Weekly*, due to *High Yellow*'s synthesis of "entirely negro" inspiration and movement with European structure and groupings. *The Guardian* acclaimed it the perfect accord of music and choreography—hardly surprising, given that the score was played by Sir Thomas Beecham's London Symphony Orchestra, augmented by nine of Hughes's own jazz-band musicians with Hughes himself on the podium. (It was said that Beecham, Lady Cunard's lover, had declined to conduct.) Colorful Caribbean sets by Vanessa Bell and costumes by dancer/designer William Chappell, praised as artistic translation rather than pastiche (and captured on the pages of *Harper's Bazaar*), affirmed the Camargo Society's ambition to continue the artistic collaborations of the Ballets Russes.[13]

High Yellow erased boundaries and boldly asked that dance not be subjected to categorization but simply evaluated as dance.[14] It was not a desultory excursion into modernity, accomplished simply because Markova was a direct link to Diaghilev, or because the choreographers sprinkled Bronislava Nijinska's aesthetic on a new movement vocabulary. It was a fundamental working-through of new ways to move. Bradley had already brought jazz up from the feet to the shoulders and arms; now he considered gestures, the pose of a head, even the extension of a finger, and how such ideas might support and extend his own jazz aesthetic. Collaborating with Ashton, he expanded his resources, exploring how to structure a dance, group dancers, and exploit every coordinate on the stage to magnify the impact of dance.

It was also a turning point for Ashton. The characteristics of Ashton's ballets—a plasticity of the upper body, the centering of weight in the pelvis area, and the apparently relaxed approach to movement—derive from his work with Bradley. The year after *High Yellow,* Ashton paid homage to Bradley in *Les Masques*, basing the role of the Lover, danced by Walter Gore, with its jazzy and sinuous movement, supple rippling back, deep knee bends, and poised confidence, on Bradley himself. From watching Bradley create a Snake Hips en pointe for Markova, he had also learned how to "balleticize" vernacular movement, something he would do with increasing finesse as he wove clog dancing, bouncing balls, and pecking chickens into his repertory.[15]

Experimentation, by definition, is a risk. What potentially was a triumph could just as well be a disaster. There was the vulnerability of depending on others—would Hughes ever deliver a commission, and would Bradley and Ashton like it? Would the dancers ever be able to express the movement Bradley had in his mind? For Bradley, there was also the uncertainty of being exposed and, yet, not fully seen. Markova and Ashton were the most sympathetic of collaborators but sometimes oblivious to Bradley's reality. Ashton's libretto was filled with ethnic stereotypes, and the dancers had performed in blackface. Even the title, *High Yellow*, not only referenced the paper-bag prejudice of the Cotton Club (to which dark-skinned Bradley may have been particularly sensitive) but also alluded to the horror of the droit-de-seigneur practices of the antebellum South.

A member of the press described the ballet as "a nigger fantasia."[16] These were the prices Bradley paid to experiment, adhere to his own vision, and honor his individuality.

Perhaps Bradley let the intoxicating exchange of ideas override any discomfort. Ashton's infectious enthusiasm, the excitement of experimentation, the artistic satisfaction of working with a dancer of the caliber of Markova, and the stimulus of creation—learning, advancing, chiseling his individuality and artistry—might have also dampened any personal distress. Or perhaps not. That summer, Maurice Dancer, brother of John Dancer, who had rehearsed Buddy for his debut at Connie's Inn, reported in *The Pittsburgh Courier* that Bradley and his white chorine wife, a Mr. Cochran Young Lady, had parted.[17] While Dancer may well have been parroting unfounded transatlantic gossip, for neither a record of a marriage nor a divorce exist, two things are certain: the African American press was keen on following Bradley's glamorous trajectory overseas, and new dance ideas were spiraling out of Bradley.

Bradley's next project, Noël Coward's *Words and Music*, was the perfect canvas to work his new ideas into a cohesive vision. If Bradley ever permitted himself to be excited, this would have been the occasion. Coward, the loftiest star in the Cochran constellation, had shot to fame at the age of twenty-four with his shocking 1924 play, *The Vortex*, and effortlessly occupied the vanguard ever since. Known in the industry as "The Master," Coward was fastidious and protective of his productions, dictating everything from cast, sets, and costumes and refusing to make changes, even when suggested by Cochran. He had a sure instinct for novelty and never copied current modes. At thirty-two, as he penned *Words and Music*, the revue that gave the world "Mad Dogs and Englishmen" and "Mad About the Boy," however, he had little knowledge of dance, so he turned to Bradley.

Bradley had been well aware of Coward since the 1920s in New York, when *The Vortex*, *Hay Fever*, and *Fallen Angels* mesmerized Broadway. Once, Bradley may have had trepidation about working with such an imposing figure, but now, girded by a resume that included a West End hit and collaborations with emerging ballet giants, Bradley came to the project as an established professional. As soon as Coward finished writing the revue, a discreetly poisonous punch of sparkling wit and social commentary, the two convened at Coward's Belgravia studio to plot out exits, pauses, scene and costume changes and to plan the final production together. By August, planning sessions had given way to nonstop rehearsals at the Adelphi Theatre, ending with three days of final polishing in a heatwave, the dancers wearing bathing suits and furrowed brows as they followed Bradley's intricate steps.[18]

Inspired by his work with Ashton at the Camargo Society and stirred by the high-flying Coward, Bradley ventured further into audacious dance territory. Though a few cast members—Joyce Barbour, Margaret Braithwaite, Peggy Willoughby, and Gladys Lincoln—had worked with Bradley before, previous experience only guaranteed familiarity with Bradley's jazz and tap choreography. Dancing in *Words and Music* required not only speed, musicality, and complex stagings but, astonishingly, ballet technique. If Bradley retained his customary aplomb, it was nevertheless a vertiginous wager from a jazz choreographer with no ballet training. Bradley, however, had three elements working in his favor: talented dancers, a gift for observing and assimilating dance, and the prevalence of ballet in London.

In keeping with *Words and Music*'s theme of youth and the future, the show had bypassed name stars for promising talent. Steffi Duna, an accomplished dancer/actress from Hungary, was just beginning to be compared to the esteemed Tilly Losch. Other up-and-comers included John Mills, an alum of the *1931 Revue* and a promising new student at Bradley's studio; Romney Brent, a newcomer from America, with whom Bradley would later work on films; Pearl Rivers, the daughter of choreographer Max Rivers, an early English proponent of American tap; Graham Payn, a cash-strapped South African who would earn extra cash by covertly selling Bradley routines to dance professionals in Durban and Johannesburg; and a graceful dancer from Ireland, Cyril Wells. Bradley also had a musical ally in the wings: Spike Hughes, bouncing back from *High Yellow*, was the orchestrator. When the amateur Coward took to the podium—and conducting, it turned out, was one of the few things the polymath genius did *not* excel in—Hughes would slip into the pit and take over the dance numbers.[19]

Coward's personal filming of the revue shows Bradley in full command of his talent. The revolutionary opener—a swirling all-male dance number that had the audience applauding before a single Coward witticism was uttered—exploded, in minutes, age-old notions of theatrical dance. A chorus of men, not women, monopolized the stage. Eighteen dancers in suave white jackets burst from the wings, twisting, leaping, and glissading, their shadows swinging and shrinking on a backdrop that magnified their every movement. Lines turned in pinwheel formations, bodies leaned back in a Cakewalk stance, arms outstretched to infinity, then swung loose and easy. Upward went the arms in a gesture lifted from the Baltimore Buzz, in perfect imitation of Bradley's pose for *The Dance*. Downward leaned the bodies in a crouch. Backward brushed their feet along the floor. *The Observer* interpreted this as chasing their own lime-cast shadows, but, in fact, they were male dancers finally emerging from longtime obscurity to occupy center stage. Notably, they were not acrobats, specialty acts, or eccentric dancers, but that relatively rare entity, a male chorus (disconcertingly called the Dancing Boys), lifted to newfound prominence by Bradley's choreography. London—and New York, for that matter—had never seen such dance before.[20]

Bradley's choreography for "The Club" sustained the brilliance. He continued to focus on an all-male cast of dancers, suggesting with gentle mockery the effects of Diaghilev (and Ashton) on an ultraconservative London club. Photos show how Buddy worked every corner, angle, and elevation, developing an explosive dynamic onstage, and sent his thirteen dancers airborne. He loosened the stranglehold of tight formations and synchronized movement. He grouped his dancers, shaped them into curves, posed some symmetrically to give structure to the sprawl, and provided each of them with individualized movement—card players seated in a corner, politicians standing in debate, effete aesthetes poised in tendu back, arms raised in fifth position, two men leaping and reaching into the distance. Bradley supplemented the patterned groupings with close observations and gestures: a porter stands at attention, gloved hands clenched at his sides. The barman balances a tray on his right hand, his left arm aloft in a balletic fourth position. The conversation group arches into Botticelli's Three Graces. One club man has his finger to his chin in question, another raises a hand in admonition, while still another assumes an attitude of studied reflection.[21]

With epaulement, pointe shoes, and fluid arms, Steffi Duna, dancing the role of the Matron in "Crèche," soars across the stage, shifting the dance focus back to the feminine. Falling into back bends, kneeling in a pretty pose worthy of Taglioni, wrists and fingers swirling, Duna is the cynosure of the ballet, supported by a corps de ballet of Mr. Cochran's Young Ladies, as dancing nursemaids.

Reminiscent of a Petipa staging, the nursemaids frame Duna in a half-circle as they cradle infant dolls in their arms. They use their head and shoulders in the manner of Bronislava Nijinska, shifting and sloping shoulders as they rock their charges rhythmically, dropping them precariously, then raising them aloft, their blankets swirling like streamers in the air. Romney Brent, as the doctor, is reduced to a mere auxiliary, obligingly lifting Duna and executing an occasional (and indifferent) arabesque. Cool in its porcelain blue-and-white setting, charming in its femininity, and sly in its humor, "Crèche" could be described as a modern *Les Sylphides*.

But how was it possible that Bradley could make a pointe shoe ballet? How would he have come to quote, however cheekily, Michel Fokine's *Les Sylphides*? After working alongside George Balanchine, Alexandra Danilova, Alicia Markova, and Frederick Ashton, Bradley's eye had ingested ballet. His dancer's body may even have absorbed a modicum of its movement. After co-choreographing *Cochran's 1931 Revue* with Balanchine, Bradley had transposed some of his new ballet observations into his maids-celebrating-spring number in *Hold My Hand*. Now, in *Words and Music*, he had Steffi Duna, an exceptional dancer, with whom to experiment more fully. While Duna was no Markova, she was a standout among theatrical dancers. (*The Tatler* wrote she said much without actually speaking.) She could take Bradley's ideas and process them on her body into ballet movement. She may very well have been the interpreter of Bradley's movement into ballet steps (as Herbert Harper had been Balanchine's tap translator for *On Your Toes*), acting as the choreographic assistant to Bradley for "Crèche."[22]

A photo of the Young Ladies, all in pointe shoes, baby bundles in crooked arms, each with a foot in *tendu en arrière*, backs cambered, and with reasonably good turnout (though three could have used some coaching), provides another clue. London was an established ballet town. Since George Jacobi's nineteenth-century residency at the Alhambra Theatre, "toe dancing," was frequently seen in London theater and music halls. In the twentieth century, the relay was picked up by Oswald Stoll at his Empire and Coliseum Theatres, and Nigel Playfair at the Lyric Theatre. Nearly half of the performances of Diaghilev's Ballets Russes had taken place in London, acclimating the London eye to sophisticated dance collaborations and forward-looking ballet choreography. George Balanchine and a small troupe of Russian émigré dancers performed a two-week run at the Empire in 1924. Teachers like Serafina Astafieva, Tamara Karsavina, Anna Pavlova, and Lydia Lopokova kept ballet visible and its training accessible. Even the daughter of a cockney greengrocer, Jessie Matthews, could access solid ballet instruction. In the interwar years, it was essential that a theater dancer have ballet training. The Young Ladies would have been no exception.[23]

Throughout *Words and Music*, Bradley experimented with gleanings from his recent collaboration with Ashton. He elevated male dancing; layered African American dance, English theater, and ballet; thought in new spatial volumes; choreographed with increasing complexity; and, in the process, advanced theatrical dance. In "Something to Do with Spring," he created a tidy tap sequence for Joyce Barbour and John Mills, backed by the full lineup of Mr. Cochran's Young Ladies and the Dancing Boys, then tilts their bodies forward in a sway, hands on knees, perfectly mirroring his Ballin' the Jack stance in *The Dance*.[24] In "Children of the Ritz," Bradley sent a frieze of debutantes dressed by Molyneux slinking along the front of the curtain, one hand on hip, pelvis thrust forward. For "Housemaids' Knees," Bradley drew dance out of feather dusters, with the Young Ladies tracing stylized gestures of housekeeping, eventually flourishing the dusters as canes, then switched from domestic to African American vernacular for "Children's Hour," where John Mills, Doris Hare, and Steffi Duna, as precocious children, imitated their parents with a polyrhythmic Charleston. For "Journey's End," Bradley's energy could barely be contained onstage as Tyrolean lads, Spanish dancers, military personnel, and chorus cavorted, jigged, and jumped over obstacles, posed, spun, kicked up their heels, and raced across the stage at breakneck speed and in all directions, lampooning Erik Charell's dizzy overcrowded staging in the current hit *The White Horse Inn*.

Bradley's choreography in *Words and Music* gave John Mills a dancing diploma to supplement his credentials as an actor, solidified Joyce Barbour's career and hung her portrait in the National Portrait Gallery, sent Steffi Duna to a career in Hollywood, and handed a powerful assist to Romney Brent, who would direct *Nymph Errant* for Cochran the following year. It also conferred cachet on Bradley: the dancing was revolutionary, and working with Noël Coward was tantamount to a royal warrant in show business. Coward and Bradley evidently considered their partnership a success: they would next collaborate on the film version of Coward's *Bitter Sweet*.[25]

But *Words and Music* mattered on a scale beyond the individual, too. In the show's finale, "The Party's Over Now," Steffi Duna's arms reach forward, as if resisting air, her back bends opulently, and her legs execute ronds de jambe en l'air. Weaving jazz and ballet, fantasy and dancer into a narrative foreshadows not only Bradley's work on film—a refinement of the Duna sequence famously appears in the movie version of *Ever Green* and would inspire other choreographers—but the future of theatrical dance. It was not that Bradley wished to be a ballet choreographer any more than Ashton dreamt of becoming a jazz dancer. It was a question of augmenting the tools for expressivity, refashioning dance to bring it to its fullest expression. It was certainly not coincidence that, after Bradley wove ballet into *Words and Music*, Cochran would hire the fledgling Agnes de Mille as choreographer for *Nymph Errant* the next year. Bradley had opened new territory, not simply for himself, but for dance.

CHAPTER 13

BALLYHOO TO THE FOLIES BERGÈRE

Every revue *had* to have
a Buddy Bradley dance in it.

—FREDERIC FRANKLIN

Words and Music launched Bradley into the stratosphere. Cochran, Bradley's early champion, nabbed him for a sophisticated musical, *Mother of Pearl*, and an upcoming revue with the glamorous Nina Mae McKinney. New producers and directors came rushing, too, attracted by Bradley's combination of jazz, versatility, and discernment. Time-honored players like Leslie Henson and chic up-and-comers like Herbert Farjeon also entered Bradley's orbit and, like Ashton, forged ongoing partnerships. That year, too, by consulting on the stage dance curriculum for the Imperial Society of Teachers of Dancing (ISTD), Bradley joined the ranks of the English dance establishment. His fellow contributors included Zelia Raye, an English proselytizer of tap dance, and Italia Conti, whose acting school had produced Gertrude Lawrence and Noël Coward.[1]

Indeed, Bradley seemed ubiquitous in 1933, caroming between the West End, Elstree, Scotland, and Paris as he juggled nine projects and a busy dance school, layering influence upon influence to craft a ziggurat of dance with jazz at its base. *Cinderella* was his

Bradley was the go-to choreographer for British musical films in the 1930s. In *Evergreen,* he stylishly evoked the passage of time in an Art Deco number for Jessie Matthews and made a cameo appearance as a street tap dancer.

In hurtling Phyllis Stanley out of a bookcase in "Book Worms" in *Lucky Break,* Bradley demonstrated his flair for showmanship. By 1934, Bradley's choreography influenced musical theater throughout the West End.

When Nina Mae McKinney, MGM's glamorous Black star, and Bradley teamed up on Cochran's *Revels in Rhythm*, the two tacitly understood each other's challenges, from growing up in the South to barriers in the entertainment industry.

JENI LE GON

(LEFT) In *Blackbirds of 1936*, Bradley gave charismatic tap dancer Jeni Le Gon a key assist at a difficult time. Her raggedy costume in *Blackbirds* emulated that of Florence Mills. Later, she emulated Bradley in pursuing a career of dance teaching and choreography.

(FAR LEFT) Florence Mills, in a street-urchin costume for 1924's *Dixie to Broadway*. Bradley, who had performed in the revue, admired the simplicity and authenticity of Mills's style.

(RIGHT) It took acclaimed dance teacher Bradley just six months to bring the tap-dancing skills of Jessie Matthews to camera-ready proficiency for *It's Love Again*.

Bradley transformed British matinee idol Jack Buchanan from mechanical puppet to jazzy, supple dancer. They began their partnership with lessons in New York, then continued in London.

Bradley lived for nearly thirty years in a book-lined flat in Radnor Lodge in the Tyburnia neighborhood of London's Paddington area. Here, his girlfriend, actress Patricia Burke, exits the building with household metal for salvage during World War II.

After collaborating with choreographer Frederic Ashton, Bradley wove aspects of ballet into jazz dance. Here, the esteemed ballet mistress Mary Skeaping teaches at Bradley's studio in London. (Turbans and trousers were standard garb for women in London during the Blitz.)

Bradley rehearses Patricia Burke for her role in the pantomime *Mother Goose*. Their eye contact, smiles, and body language reveal the pleasure they took in each other's company.

Bop routine is favorite with British students at Bradley's highly-rated school. Pennsylvania-born one time chorus boy keeps pace with dance developments in America through phonograph records, is an ardent devotee of bop music.

BUDDY BRADLEY

Nimble ex-Harlemite runs most successful dance school in England with 500 students

THE FRED ASTAIRE of England is a nimble, fast-stepping little Negro dance tutor and arranger in London with fame as a hot hoofer on two continents. He is 5-foot-9, 160-pound Buddy Bradley, an American-born, ex-Broadway chorus boy, who learned most of his dance tricks as a kid on the streets of Harlem some 30 years ago.

Now sole operator of the British Empire's top dancing school (named for him), the fortyish Bradley is no longer active on the stage in the cunning dance roles, which endeared him with Londoners for more than 15 years. He currently devotes most of his time to teaching novice dancers every type of intricate dance step and rhythm from ballet to bop. His students number about 500, almost all white.

…rring on musical script with actors or producers is frequent job for dance teacher …ly Bradley, seen here with British movie and stage star Graham Payne, who stars in …new Noel Coward movie, *The Astonished Heart.*

…n dance leap is demonstrated by white student instructor under Bradley's eye. …ourse includes ballet, tap, character and rhythm dancing. Among notables who have …ed at his school are movie actresses Merle Oberon and Eleanor Powell.

Comedy routine for current popular British musical, *Sauce Tartare*, is worked out by Bradley with popular English comic Joan Heal. Show highlights former *Carmen Jones* star Muriel Smith singing lyrics by Langston Hughes.

Continued on Next Page 61

Ebony celebrated Bradley in 1950 as a London dance institution, showing him in his various roles as teacher, choreographer, coach, and theatrical consultant.

African and tom-tom rhythms are important features in dancing course at Brad school. He learned teaching technique in New York at Billy Pierce dance sch before trekking to England in 1931 to score dances for Sir Charles Cochran.

Rhythm tap is worked out by Bradley and his white assistant, night club dan Elizabeth Shelley. She is only other full-time instructor at his school, often he him work out new dance routines. Bradley first gained fame as tap dancer.

Beginning class in tap step goes through paces under alert Bradley. His list illustrious pupils is long, includes American movie stars Clifton Webb, Irene Du Eleanor Powell and Jack Oakey. He once was partner of Adele Astaire.

(LEFT) *Ebony*'s camera caught Bradley teaching, drumming, and leading a riff walk. After World War II, with the rise of bebop jazz, Bradley increasingly reverted to the tap-dance style he had learned on the streets of Harlem.

(TOP) In London, Baby Laurence dropped by daily to visit Bradley. When they talked and traded steps, age differences fell away.

(TOP LEFT) Kansas City tap dancer Carnell Lyons brought Bradley the latest bebop tap steps from America. Bradley in turn lent Lyons his studio to practice the tap-and-tray-spinning dance he would perform with John Bubbles.

(TOP RIGHT) Bradley, known for his own elegant and eloquent hands, famously taught singer Shirley Bassey to use her hands and entire body to communicate a song.

(LEFT) Glory Van Scott, the star of Bradley's last play, recalls Bradley's distinctive walk, smooth and deliberate, as if he were thinking as he moved. When Bradley walked down the studio during a barre, it was clear that music was playing in his head and that he was thinking of the next step.

initial foray into pantomime, England's raucous answer to commedia dell'arte. *Mother of Pearl*, on the other hand, was so cool and stylish that even his dances spoke in a classical whisper. He staged "Slow Water Blues" to a syncopated score by Raie da Costa for ballet dancers Anton Dolin and Vera Zorina. Within this whirlwind of activity, his experimental piece for Marie Rambert's Ballet Club, an adventurous revue, a dance-forward play, and—the pièce de résistance—an engagement at the Folies Bergère were among his most consequential undertakings.[2]

Immersed in discovery, acquiring new dance vocabulary, and conquering new challenges, Bradley's creativity thrived as his career, if not his psyche, detached from America. So many memories hurt, from his family's painful journey to his childhood in Birmingham, that he shrouded them in silence. The 1933 death of Billy Pierce, age forty-two, was also a blow. Of all the elders who had taken Bradley under their wing, it was Pierce, who had literally pushed him into the dance studio, who was the most instrumental to his career. Visionary, resourceful, exasperating, and controlling, Pierce had given Bradley the platform, and the confidence, to reach beyond his grasp.

As with much of Pierce's life, it is hard to distinguish fact from legend. *The Amsterdam News* said he had died of complications of diabetes, meningitis, and mastoiditis. Herbert Harper insisted it was syphilis of the brain. *The Chicago Defender*, Pierce's former employer, eulogized Pierce as "the most influential Race man in Broadway." But the reality was that, in spite of his imagination, foresight, and dedication to jazz dance and the African American community, Pierce was quickly forgotten.

Bradley wrestled with the implications of Pierce's disappearance. Despite his own dizzying activity, introduction of jazz dance to prestigious stages on both sides of the Atlantic, mounting theater credits and celebrity students, would he be as ephemeral as Pierce? Would he, too, vanish without a trace? Would his life have any enduring impact? The question would haunt him to the end.[3]

Already, Bradley's life was a delicate balance, teetering between inner and outer realities, rushing from one challenge to the next, meeting one bar higher than the last, all driven by a need to assure himself of his individuality. Now, he sustained another loss, a by-product of his overcharged life: Mose, his unwavering companion as he adjusted to the unfamiliarities of London, was lost. It seems to have occurred when Bradley had left the terrier in the care of others to attend a dance conference in America. Upon discovery, Bradley ran a lost-and-found ad in *The Evening Standard,* offering a substantial reward, but Mose never returned. Bradley had lost another unconditional friend.[4]

Work, as always, was the palliative.

When Marie Rambert invited Bradley to choreograph at the Ballet Club, he leapt at the opportunity. Marie Rambert, renowned for assisting Vaslav Nijinsky with *Le Sacre du printemps* and *L'Après-midi d'un faune* at the Ballets Russes, now nurtured the talents of Frederick Ashton, Agnes de Mille, Antony Tudor, and Hugh Laing. Interest from Rambert was a prestigious vote of confidence for any choreographer.

The Ballet Club, where Bradley had first seen Ashton's work, was ground zero for ballet and experimental dance in England. Perhaps to calm any jitters about working on such hallowed territory, Bradley assembled known collaborators for the project. He selected William Chappell, the art student turned dancer who had performed in *Magic Nights* and designed the costumes for *High Yellow,* as his soloist. For music, he turned to Jerome Kern, the American composer with whom he had worked on two shows, *Show Boat* and *The Cat and the Fiddle.* Instead of working with one of Kern's melodic scores, however, he chose something closer to his own sensibility, *Desperate Blues*, a now-lost jazz piece.

Desperate Blues premiered on Sunday, November 27, 1932, at the Mercury Theatre alongside works by Balanchine, Ashton, and Massine, with William Cook (the future Antony Tudor) acting as stage manager in a sort of work-study arrangement. Like many artistic experiments, *Desperate Blues* appears to have been a mixed success—it had but one performance. But, for Bradley, after years of choreographing anonymously in the shadows of Broadway theaters, it was a triumph. That he would be known and solicited for concert dance choreography had once been unimaginable. Creating a jazz ballet was a hard-earned luxury.

In these years, Bradley experimented with tap choreography, too. Before the widespread use of microphones, projecting tap sound in the theater could be tricky. In rehearsal in an empty theater, taps might sound fantastic, but as soon as an audience entered the house, their presence deadened the sound. The thrilling click of aluminum against wood simply didn't travel, negating the excitement of tap, whose language was time and tempo. To compensate, orchestrators often built breaks into the music, creating moments when tap dancing did not have to compete with the band.

Still, Bradley the perfectionist looked for new work-arounds. Strength in numbers helped—if Bradley had the luck to have a skilled chorus tapping cleanly in unison (as he would as the decade progressed and his tap teachings took hold), taps could be heard; it was the solos and partnered sequences that suffered. Using wood platforms, especially if raised a little off the floor, could help, but posed a tripping hazard for the rest of the cast. Worse, dancing on platforms limited the ability for dance to move across stage, a quality Bradley prized. (Some theorize Bojangles Robinson incorporated his famous stairs in his act so that he could both dance on a raised platform *and* travel; some even say he concealed microphones under the structure.) Jingle taps, producing a muddied sound, were not ideal, either. Buddy's partial solution was either to use tap dancing for his big production numbers, or to feature it judiciously, as a novelty, as he did with a dependable tap dancer like John Mills in *Words and Music*.

He also leaned into his new dance vocabulary, blending aspects of ballet and vernacular dance picked up in London with his own mix of jive, jazz, and tap, to break new tap ground. For solos and pas de deux, typically more expressive and romantic dances, he compensated for the inaudibility of tap by emphasizing the visual qualities he so loved: eloquent upper bodies, elegant lines of dancers, individualized and character-driven movement, and choreography working on multiple planes.

Bradley slipped some of his new ideas into *Ballyhoo*, a revue with the unity and strength of a dry martini. While Robert Nesbitt, William Walker, and Herbert Farjeon, a posse of well-connected up-and-comers, had conceived of the show, it was the inventive choreography by Bradley (and Ashton) that provided the twist. *Ballyhoo*, according to *The Manchester Guardian*, was full of sophisticated dance and less sophisticated fun.[5]

If the young writers' work was still a bit uneven, Bradley's work was precise and confident. It was his smartly trained Ballyhoo Girls, dancing both "straight" and "rhythm" dances, who received the lion's share of applause from the audience and the press. He had them swinging in "Black Magic," accompanied by blues singer Zaidee Jackson, the darling of tastemakers Elsa Maxwell, the Duke of Kent, and the Countess of Carnarvon, then stylishly closed the first act with "Mediterranean Madness," with dancing as pared down as the minimalist Billy Chappell costumes, punctuated by outrageously large hats.[6]

Despite such creative advances, Bradley remained clear-eyed about his role as choreographer. His dances coupled novelty with functionality and longevity. William Walker found that when *Ballyhoo* closed, he could conveniently repackage extracts, key performers, and the Ballyhoo Girls (now rechristened the Mayfair Girls) for a cabaret at the Mayfair Hotel on Berkeley Square—and increase the show's profits. Back home in the United States, Ivan H. Browning at *The Chicago Defender* gleefully crowed to his African American readership about Bradley's involvement in *Ballyhoo*, the latest and most intimate show in town.[7]

Then there was the Bradley effect on the box office. One project, *Yours Sincerely*, was negligible, its sketches so weak that Bradley's dances were deemed the sole reason to buy a ticket. This was far from mere coincidence: savvy producers now realized that hiring Bradley guaranteed success for even a mediocre show.[8]

Soon the creatives behind *Ballyhoo* regrouped for *After Dark*, a revue so fanciful and effervescent that some of the skits had no easily discoverable point at all. The revue's irreverence was typified by Farjeon's sendup of the Brontë sisters ("We used to dwell in a parsonage / But now we've gone upon the stage / If you are gay and feeling glad / Just count on us to make you sad"). Yet, even with such delectable treats, Bradley's dances once again eclipsed the text.[9]

Cynical and lofty, with unusually wide appeal, *After Dark* allowed Bradley, coming off his many successes, plenty of creative latitude. One of his advancements was using the chorus as a through line for the show, an idea he had begun to explore in *Words and Music*. (Now, instead of Molyneux, the dancers wore sassy petals that recalled Josephine Baker's banana skirt.) He also staged a takeoff of a rumba for four repressed, self-doubting men and choreographed "Deuce," an absurdist tennis ballet. Though the music was not particularly jazzish, Bradley's exits—what Freddie Franklin called those marvelous Bradley exits—were flamboyant, with exaggerated jazz dance postures. Caricatures in *The Bystander* show Roy Royston and Louise Brown "making a typical Buddy Bradley exit," faces thrust to the light, backs swayed, fannies out, feet flexed, with dancer Betty Frankiss exiting as "Miss Muffett" while leaning precipitously in a Cakewalk back bend, hands on hips, knee raised high.[10]

It was frustrating to be lauded in London while still ignored in New York. At *After Dark*'s opening-night party, Ashton met Virgil Thomson. Soon the ballet choreographer was off to New York to choreograph Thomson's new opera, *Four Saints in Three Acts*, with book by Gertrude Stein, armed with advice to scout dancers at the Savoy Ballroom and revealing to the fascinated press that his choreography would be a "combination of snake hips and Gothic." Ashton's Black-vernacular tinged choreography, inspired by Bradley, galvanized New York's press, cocktail parties, and cartoons for months; Macy's even named its fall collection Four Suits in Three Acts. Bradley must have been happy for Ashton, who had been a consistently generous colleague, but quizzical, too. Why had his own work, so intrinsic to Ashton's success, not been similarly received on Broadway? Was it simply a matter of timing, that jazz dance in 1934 had more deeply permeated American culture than when Bradley had been working on Broadway in the late 1920s, in the vanguard of the rapprochement of jazz and theatrical dance?

Or could it be a question of the platforms given to white and Black choreographers? Increasingly, it seemed right to be in London.[11]

Ensconced and appreciated in England, surrounded by Oxford and public-school types who spoofed Brontë for amusement, referenced Freud and homosexuality in code, and mingled among art dealers and impresarios, Bradley easily connected with his new coworkers via the creative process. He was anyone's equal, if not their superior, in artistry, as his contributions to the success of *Ballyhoo* and *After Dark* proved. His affability allowed him to cross borders; his inherent elegance and intellectual curiosity established commonality.

While Bradley swapped his casual shirtsleeves and suspenders for tidy English suits, he protected himself with a mantle of reserve. He was still finding his footing on unfamiliar—albeit exciting—territory. Solitude was where he was most comfortable and relaxed. His cherished end-of-day ritual was to sit alone in a pub, sipping a pint of Guinness and perusing the paper. When he learned that he would work with African American Nina Mae McKinney on *Revels in Rhythm*, his third Trocadero cabaret for Cochran, he must have exhaled with relief. He would neither have to explain nor conceal himself.

If *Revels in Rhythm* was all about glamour, its subtext was Bradley's connection with McKinney and his dancers. With her unusual lingering voice and lithe beauty, McKinney, MGM's first (light-skinned) Black star, was much anticipated in London. Nicknamed "the Black Garbo," she was increasingly temperamental, beleaguered by a grueling schedule, a complicated marriage, and disillusion with Hollywood.

Bradley could soothe a challenging diva. He, too, knew the frustrations of a childhood in the South, the early disappearance of a father, what it was to fend for oneself as a youngster in New York, and the daunting barriers that faced even Blacks of exceptional talent and ambition. He gently coaxed performances from his complicated star. He could afford to be indulgent of his mercurial leading lady—after all, he had known since his days with Leonard Harper at Connie's Inn that it really was the chorus dancers, beating out the rhythm with their feet, who were the heart of a jazz show.[12]

As such, the success of *Revels in Rhythm* depended as much on Mr. Cochran's Young Ladies as on its alluring headliner. While there had only been a few weeks of rehearsal to whittle the classical references out of English dancers and replace them with energy, attack, and swing, by opening night Bradley had all the Young Ladies tap dancing a speedy, close-to-the-floor Charleston, displaying polyrhythm in their shimmying shoulders, waving arms, and bobbing heads, and hitting rhythmic accents with their feet in a performance that would have made Leonard Harper smile. It was an unlikely result in 1933. True, some of the Young Ladies had studied at Bradley's on Old Compton Street, and eleven of the sixteen had worked with him previously and were beginning to ingest his style, but Bradley's trump card, as always, was the way he assessed the individual skills of his dancers and communicated movement at a level they could understand.[13]

Dancing a medley of Black Bottom, Varsity Drag, Rumba, and the Charleston, the Young Ladies prime the stage for the entrance of McKinney, dressed in fetching mirrored shorts. As she dances the Charleston, her expressive hands and insouciant toss of head remind us that Buddy, renowned for his own elegant hands, had been coaching singers since *Show Boat*. Yet her purred opening lines, written by former Bradley dancer Annette Mills (it was she Bradley had coached to take over Betty Compton's role in *Fifty Million Frenchmen*), must have grated. It apparently occurred to no one (except the star and the dance director) how belittling it was for a Black woman to coo seductively, "When them darkies do it . . . " But Bradley and McKinney, comrades in arms and staunch professionals, had dealt with these issues many times before. McKinney delivered the lyrics with panache.

Welcoming as London was for Bradley, another number in *Revels in Rhythm* suggests that his new home was both mirage and oasis. The "Mooshli-Mooshli" number, a loose interpretation of a West African dance, elicits another shudder: Oliver Messel, designer of *Mr. Cochran's 1931 Revue* and *Mother of Pearl*, blithely zipped the Young Ladies, dressed in black tailcoats, into full head and neck masks with curly hair, turning the Young Ladies into blackface minstrels. In the context of the 1930s, the masks were surely considered a clever innovation, but they speak of the casualness with which people of color were seen as faceless Others—even in the cosmopolitan reaches of London.[14]

Mixing British production values with low-down dancing, *Revels in Rhythm* was an odd show. Annette Mills, sister of John Mills, was hardly Andy Razaf, but her brassy music and lyrics suffice. William Chappell's frothy party frocks (he seems to have followed Bradley from show to show that year) for the Charleston number seem incongruous. And while Bradley must have adored staging for McKinney, who registered personality with the ease of a born beauty, a mid-performance cough gives weight to the rumors of her health and substance issues. By June, McKinney had retired from the show and was replaced by the white Eda Peel.[15]

Elsewhere, Bradley continued to explode the chorus line. For the opening of *Nice Goings On*, he distributed two principals and the thirteen Buddy Bradley Rhythm Girls about the stage and on multiple planes. Different choreographies emerge simultaneously. Some dancers lean forward; others lean back. Hips thrust forward; others pull back. Arms draw overhead; other arms sway. Some faces are raised upward; others address the audience. In Bradley's hands, the chorus ceased to be a line and became three-dimensional.[16]

By giving his chorus dancers specific characters and speaking lines, Bradley further integrated dance into the plot of the book musical. Reviewing *Nice Goings On* for *The Sunday Mirror*, critic Herbert Farjeon (and a writer of *Ballyhoo* and *After Dark*) noted that the dancers rose to the new dramatic challenge and entered the spirit of the comedy with gusto. Some of the energy was due to the return to the stage of Leslie Henson, a witty and highly subtle comedian. But, in addition to the beloved antihero, it was the dance, in all its forms, tap, acrobatic, and farcical, that made *Nice Goings On*—generally considered Americanized drivel—an important production.[17]

Throughout, Bradley retained his signature cool. The theater, after all, was where he felt most secure. As *Nice Goings On* raced to its opening night at the Strand Theatre, he made time to lend a hand to newcomer Agnes de Mille, showing up late at night to help

Gertrude Lawrence rehearse her Harlem tap number in *Nymph Errant*. As always, Bradley also found time to support efforts that addressed the needs of children. He participated with his Rhythm Girls in a ball and cabaret at the Royal Opera House in aid of the Infants' Hospital, Westminster; sent eight of his Rhythm Girls to the Kit Kat Club for a fundraiser for the Victoria Hospital for Children; and choreographed an amateur cabaret at the Savoy for debutantes raising funds for an orphanage.[18]

The year closed out spectacularly, with a dash to Paris, where twenty-eight-year-old Bradley decked a Christmas tree with dancers wearing little more than rhinestones. Arguably, Bradley was simply working within the rhinestone-and-feather conventions of the Folies Bergère, the Paris institution where revue was born, but he was also inciting a minor revolution. Like any time-honored institution, the Folies Bergère took its traditions seriously and made changes reluctantly. (Paul Derval, its director, maintained feathers were a weighty responsibility that mustn't be taken lightly.) When Mistinguett, the reigning queen of French revue, had insisted on engaging the choreographer who was all the rage in London for the upcoming *Folies en Folie* revue, Bradley had no intention of working with petite dancers executing the precision kicks to which the Folies Bergère was accustomed. Like his early mentor Leonard Harper, he liked long-limbed dancers and dance that moved: he personally selected sixteen dancers in London, then crossed the Channel.[19]

Paris idolized Black culture, which had certainly been a factor in Mistinguett's jettisoning the house dancers, the Blue Bell Girls, in favor of Bradley. But the French view of Black people was encapsulated in négritude, a fetishized and generalized interpretation of Black culture. (In point of fact, it was the Folies Bergère that had costumed Baker in her infamous exotic-erotic banana skirt.) It played fast and loose with the facts, as whim and commerce dictated. It now placed Bradley, not yet thirty and credited as the maître de ballet, and a young African American dancer, Henri Wessels, in its flattening glare.[20]

That summer, Henri Wessels, a light-skinned dancer from the Cotton Club, had danced in a revue staged by Clarence Robinson at the Leicester Square Theatre in London. Lithe and elegant, he was just the kind of dancer Bradley favored, and he was hired for *Folies en Folie*. Working with Wessels was anything but ordinary for Bradley. He was one of the very few African American men (Florence Mills's husband, U. S. Thompson, and Roland Holder the others) to dance Bradley's choreography, and the opportunities this proposed were extraordinary. In "A Little Jazz," Wessels sang and danced with Bradley's chorus line, now christened the Sixteen Miami Vamps. For the "Hydrangea Conservatory" number, Bradley created for Wessels the incongruous-sounding role of a double hydrangea, while the Vamps danced as blue hydrangeas. He also created a sailor dance for Wessels in the "The Boys from the Navy." Noticeably, the gorgeous Wessels, who had posed for homoerotic photographer George Platt Lynes, was *not* cast for the Casanova ballet. It would have been too incendiary.[21]

Working on the stage that bore the legacy of Josephine Baker was fraught with ambiguous messaging and a minefield for the dancer of color. For "Black and White," a number designed by Erté, the father of art deco, the Sixteen Miami Vamps, wearing masks by Oliver Messel, creator of the full-head blackface masks for *Revels in Rhythm*, danced as the Coloured Boys, a fantastical approximation of Black men.[22] Wessels, on the other hand, couldn't dance as a Black man—he was cast in the role of the White Boy.

The incident communicated how easily a Black man could have his identity bent by white authority. Even men with the level of accomplishment of Bradley or the connections of Henri Wessels, the stepson of Henry Creamer—of the Creamer and Layton songwriting team—were not immune. It conferred a hierarchy of color, too, assuming that a light Black man would prefer to pass as a white man. Wessels, for whatever reason, soon stopped performing and is now remembered more for his work with the flash act the Berry Brothers than his dancing. The practical Bradley pressed on.[23]

In replacing the precision kick lines with jazz and tap, substituting uniformity with individuality, and exchanging petite chorines for elongated dancers—all the better to see the lines of his choreography and show off the costumes, or lack of them—Bradley made a lasting imprint on the Folies Bergère. The following year, Margaret Kelly and her expelled Bluebell Girls were reinstated. While banished, Kelly had made a point to watch what Bradley was doing in *Folies in Folie* and embraced his changes. Following suit, she broke up the chorus kick line, gave her dancers more interesting choreography, encouraged them to transmit their personalities, and immediately raised the minimum height of her dancers to 5' 9" (over time it would creep up to 5' 11").[24] As the Folies Bergère set the standard for international cabaret, Bradley's aesthetics now became universal. Dancers—except for Black men—were emerging as individuals.

Despite the contretemps at the Folies Bergère, 1933 was a milestone year for Bradley. The broadening recognition of his talent, wide-reaching influence of his choreography, and continuous flow of work meant more opportunities to experiment, evolve, and refine his artistry. In expressing his unique vision, Bradley would achieve what he long sought. He would have tangible evidence of his individuality.

CHAPTER 14

SEDUCTION AND THE CAMERA'S EYE

Is there, we ask, some secret language
which we feel and see, but never speak, and,
if so, could this be made visible to the eye?

—VIRGINIA WOOLF, *The Cinema*

There was another reason that 1933 was a seismic year for Bradley: he ventured into film. Seeing dance through a camera's eye changed everything. There was a newfound intimacy. One might hear a slipper squeak as it spun turns on the floor (as one did in the film *Evergreen*); catch a feather-arrayed dancer correct her knee position to line up with her fellow dancers (thank you, center-screen chorus dancer in *Oh, Daddy!*); or see dancers lock eyes. But there was more, unspoken. Buddy Bradley, partnering with the camera, could share *his* experience of dance, the mesmerizing sensuality of a hip synchronized to music, the tentative elation of just-discovered love, the mysterious power when word, image, movement, and music converged and transported one to an unseen reality.

Bradley grasped these possibilities from the moment he stepped onto a soundstage.

When *The Jazz Singer* swept sound into film in 1927, tap dance, with its thrilling sound, became the cinematic dance form par excellence. Yet, in 1933, the potential of tap dance on film was hardly explored and tap awaited a visionary to free it from its Sleeping Beauty slumber. Fred Astaire, whom RKO had been reluctant to sign ("Can't sing, ears stick out, can dance a little"), was just gaining momentum in supporting roles in *Dancing Lady* and *Flying Down to Rio*. Fox would not release their first Shirley Temple movie, *Stand Up and Cheer*, until the following year. There was still so little relationship between dance and drama that Albertina Rasch recalled what she choreographed for one movie was often dropped into another film instead. When Sam Goldwyn released his first musical, *Whoopee!*, in 1930, his "choreographer," the dance-deficient Busby Berkeley, concentrated on the maneuvering of the camera and neglected any opportunity to express character or emotion in dance.[1]

Film directors, like stage directors, didn't know much about music or dance. Because cameras didn't move much in those days, it was tempting to focus on a stationary singer and overlook dancing altogether. Cinematographers, just mastering the rapidly evolving technology of cameras, light, and angles, were perplexed. It fell to the dance director to explain the potential of dance, to suggest how it should be shot, and to advocate for the angles he or she wanted—and this spelled opportunity for those who could articulate what was possible, collaborate diplomatically, and create dances that communicated. In Hollywood, Busby Berkeley approached this with bold formations of dancers and clever camerawork while Fred Astaire and Hermes Pan fine-tuned a dance persona and romantic scenarios. In London, Buddy Bradley explored how dance could tell a story and capitalized on film's potential to draw a moviegoer into the dance experience. He, whose loftiest dream had once been to become a film projectionist, innately understood the power of film.

Above all, Bradley understood that dance was subliminal, not cerebral. He appealed to the screen audience via sound and movement, then infused his dance sequences with humanity and intimacy, the inherent qualities of film. In this medium, he did not have to shy away from tap dancing and its compelling sound, provided he could find adequate dancers. Microphones on a soundstage were possible, and studios were beginning to experiment with post-recorded dance tracks (which Bradley disliked, as they disconnected tap from its essential sound). Bar by bar, step by step, films choreographed by Bradley inched their way toward integrated dancing.

Bradley's first two films were Herbert Wilcox's *The Little Damozel* and Noël Coward's operetta *Bitter Sweet*, both shot in 1933. Dance-wise, they were child's play for Bradley—both mainly involved staging dancing scenes in nightclub settings—but career-wise they were invaluable stepping stones. They offered a key connection with Wilcox, a powerhouse in the British film industry, and a primer in how the camera captures dance, and they led to a continuous stream of British film projects over the next five years.[2]

While Bradley's films for Jessie Matthews, a bankable international star, are luminous, and those with Jack Buchanan benefited from lavish budgets and a seductive personality, Bradley's lesser-known films, mostly undertaken before he was subsumed in a maelstrom of Matthews and Buchanan projects, are subtle exercises in wit, inventiveness, and charm. Often shot on tighter schedules and lesser budgets than Hollywood films, their success derives from clever writing and Bradley's originality.

Among these twelve films, *Radio Parade of 1935* was the first to sparkle. Produced by British International Pictures (BIP), a trailblazer in musical films, *Radio Parade* sports high production values, quintessential art deco sets of double staircases and fluted pilasters, and a well-knit story that marries song, dance, and satire at the expense of the BBC bureaucracy. The director, Arthur Woods, just a year older than Bradley, was England's youngest film director.[3]

Throughout the filming, the producer and choreographer seem to compete in sleights of invention and irony. Bradley mirrors the irreverence of Woods, devising synchronized head swiveling for company yes-men in a boardroom, causing doors in a circular hallway to shut in rhythm, and injecting obsequious hand pumping ("I was at Oxford, you know") of an aspiring songwriter, Ronald Frankau, as he introduces himself down a line of pompous directors.

But, of course, it is the geometric dancing, book-matched to the modernist interiors, where Bradley triumphs hands down over Woods. The opening number, "Good Morning," brings a cast of smart-looking secretaries up a swirling staircase, hands coolly trailing on the metal handrail, followed by the grand arrival of the top brass through swinging glass doors, led by a top-coated lackey, cheekily brandishing his Jermyn Street cane like an American drum major. With multitiered choreography and swift changes of camera angle, the number is dizzyingly ambitious, if a touch disappointing in execution. The dancers' placement of hands on the banister is inconsistent and messy, and their arm movements are not always synchronized. Surely Bradley, a perfectionist, saw this, but shrugged his shoulders and moved on. There was always a dancer or two he had to use. ("It was like the Russian aristocracy, where every estate had a ballet company," explained one of Bradley's colleagues. "In London, every producer had a girlfriend.") And there was a systemic reason, too: time for rehearsals, polishing, and retakes was limited on British film sets. *Radio Parade of 1935* was made in a breathless six weeks—production began in October 1934 before the script was fully written, and filming was completed in late November—then released in December for the holiday season.[4]

There is lots of clever dancing and equally crafty camerawork in the film. When the young executive/romantic hero of *Radio Parade* falls out with his manager, he rallies by staging an outdoor public performance. The numbers include Fred Conyngham, who had danced in *The Cat and the Fiddle* and *Nice Goings On*, now blithely tapping up and down a flight of stairs in a silver lamé jacket. Dozens of chorines dressed as bellhops join him, executing the time-honored dance simplifications that Bradley had first conceived in New York for novice dancers like Irene Delroy. Distributed among the not-too-difficult shuffles are the telltale signs of Bradley, the neat twisting and shifting of hips, the well-bent and inward-turned knees, and the highlighting of the beat with emphatic stamps, as well as further reminders that film, like theater, was both business proposition and art: the lines can be a bit ragged, arms are noticeably not in time. The camera, meanwhile, brings the moviegoer to those privileged vantage points that no theatergoer can access, shooting from above, showing geometries of dance formations, and stirring the eye.

But it is the emotional heart of the movie, the "Black Shadows" number with Alberta Hunter, smoldering with dignity and indignation, that takes one's breath away. Hunter, accompanied by John Payne's legendary Black choir, sings a compelling, if ersatz, spiritual written by John Bunting, an Englishman who had contributed to the film script. The singers, dressed in the white robes of a Baptist choir, assume a kneeling posture of weeping, then stand and sway with raised arms, as in a revival meeting. The lyrics, describing the pain of being Black in a racist society, are affecting and straightforward.[5]

Bradley and Hunter, at the time a celebrated chanteuse at the Hotel Dorchester on Park Lane, had a mutual connection with Billy Pierce, who had managed her. They may have joined forces to advocate for this number. The studio got behind the effort, even electing to film it in expensive color (most of the film is shot in black and white), yet there is a discordant unease. Tempting as it was to present this Black reality with an exceptional African American singer, the number *is* a stretch in a lighthearted satire. Woods clearly worried that the audience could not sustain such emotional intensity within the witty froth of *Radio Parade of 1935*. After two minutes, the camera switches back to familiar ground, the world of entertainment.

Suddenly, the screen is overwhelmed by dancers in leopard print, heeled shoes, and feathers dancing to a tom-tom beat on a pyramid of oversized drums. Though rumors circulated that the Black Garbo, Nina Mae McKinney, would be the featured dancer, she did not appear, possibly beset by personal problems. Instead, Joyce Richardson was Bradley's lead dancer, and the late casting was felicitous. McKinney was an all-around crowd-pleaser; the obscure Richardson was a knockout dancer. Described as a "coloured specialty dancer" and billed the previous year as "pep and personality" in *Paris Fantasie* at the Prince of Wales Theatre, Richardson now traded ebullience for authority.[6]

Richardson owns the number. Dancing on the apex of stacked drums, reminiscent of Eddie Rector's dance on kettle drums when he refused (or Bill Robinson forbid him) to dance on stairs when he substituted for Robinson in *Blackbirds*, Richardson runs through a series of isolations, swirling her hips to one rhythm, shoulders and arms to another, dipping asymmetrically, emphatically leaping with high-raised knees, and arching into plush back bends. The dancers on the lower tiers, all white, lean backward in Cakewalk stances, swaying their hips, skewing their knees, and pushing rhythmically against the air—a gesture that becomes a leitmotif for Bradley. Some move expansively and rhythmically, and a few are off the beat, but it hardly matters; it is Richardson's feline grace that magnetizes the eye.[7]

The camera brackets the dance closely, heightening its moody spectacularity. But, in 1934, British filmmakers still had much to learn. The switching back and forth between heartfelt lament and 1930s go-go girls on drums is disorienting. Frustrating, too, for any lover of dance is that Richardson's feet are rarely in the camera's frame, leaving the spectator in ungrounded limbo. Nevertheless, this is Bradley's first significant contribution to dance on film—and an important one. His creativity is intact, his staging is photogenic, his truth is present, and the dancing must have been an eye-opener for those in the empire who had not had access to Bradley's work in the West End.

Like British humor, British musicals were circumspect. They favored wit over emotional stirrings and dramatic content. *Oh, Daddy!*, a 1935 adaptation of a German play (this, too, was a British trend, as Continental transfers often carried a whiff of exoticism and racier content than the Office of the Lord Chamberlain would allow in a native British production), fit neatly in this box. Written by Michael Powell, who would go on to direct *The Red Shoes* and *The Tales of Hoffman* after the war, *Oh, Daddy!* is a high-speed farce that cavorts through the cabaret adventures of Purity Leaguers off the leash who fall under the spell of Champagne and an alluring cabaret singer. Rising brilliantly from this Pandora's box are Ken "Snakehips" Johnson, Frances Day, and Leslie Henson, all dancing under the direction of Bradley.[8]

Oh, Daddy!'s first dance scene is a dazzler: long-legged Johnson deftly executes a series of wings and trenches, then exits with a precursor of a moonwalk. Everything about this turn spells Bradley, from the relaxed attitude to the occasional forward lean. Watching the sequence in the 1990s, Bradley's widow, Dorothy Bradley, remarked on Johnson's elegant posture, reminiscent of her husband. A Bradley-trained choreographer recalled Bradley's love of trenches; another noted the relaxed stance, the feather-light footwork, and the clean sound that he drilled in his classes.[9]

Not surprisingly, the Guyana-born Johnson was a student of Bradley and, like another Bradley protégé, Roland Holder, was born to hold the spotlight. The fleeting footage of a buoyant Johnson is a powerful record of the Bradley style freed from the undertow of dancers who weren't innately conversant in tap's roots. Thanks to Bradley's predilection of peppering his films and revues with turns by West Indians in London, it is also the only moving image of Johnson, who died tragically in the Blitz at the age of twenty-six, while conducting the band at the Café de Paris.[10]

In "The Savage in Me," Bradley gives a master class in visual seduction, proving that he knew just as much about dance openings as exits. To the insistent beat of a drum, the camera focuses on silk and rhinestone-draped twisting knees, gradually raises its gaze to undulating hips, then slides upward along a sinuous torso, and, finally, as the dancer arches into a lateral curve and opens two enormous feather fans to reveal her face, focuses on Frances Day herself. Now in full camera frame, Day proceeds to gives *her* own master class in polyrhythmic head bobbles, shoulder shimmies, isolations, and eloquent hands. A critic described the bewitching Day as an entire Cochran revue in herself.[11]

Day had previously caused a stir in 1931, when she played cabaret singer May de Vere in the British production of *Fifty Million Frenchmen*, choreographed by Bradley. With her distinctive mischievous smile (the wattage Bradley loved that "reached the back row of the house") and sensuous response to music, her casting was a boon not only to *Oh, Daddy!* but to the choreographer—and, by extension, to dance. As Bradley gifted Day with Afrocentric dance movement, and as she avidly embraced it, he solidified his template for theatrical jazz dancing. Several steps removed from its origins in Black communities in the Deep South, it draws, like Bradley, from a broad spectrum of sources to create a distinctive dance vocabulary.

Twenty years later, choreographer Jack Cole used a similar template to adapt exotic dance references for Marilyn Monroe's "Diamonds Are a Girl's Best Friend" number in *Gentleman Prefer Blondes*.

The ensemble in "The Savage in Me," dancing a variation on the Charleston, hands on knees, torsos forward, legs splayed to the side, demonstrates the headwinds Bradley faced daily: dancers who are not quite capable, lyrics dense with gross caricature and colonial tropes, and costumes that include fright wigs and feathered skirts. Once again, Bradley was in the no-man's-land of *Revels in Rhythm* and the Folies Bergère with the zip-on minstrelsy masks. It's unlikely that a producer, director, or costume designer intended this assault; it stemmed from something more pervasive, a collective expression of empire. But, if the impetus was impersonal, its consequence was personal: choreography was not only Bradley's mission, but the element that defined him. It was also his livelihood. He *had* to choreograph, and he had to choreograph *that* number, which meant that he had, once again, to accept silently the discomfort, the diminishment, and the indignity.

As Bradley's stress level climbed, so did his creativity. He ventured into uncharted dance territory, creating the first dream ballet in a musical film. (Balanchine would follow in 1937 with *Babes in Arms*.) With wood sprites in *very* transparent drapery, film-set glades, and garlands, Bradley explored the psyche of a middle-aged man with thinning hair and thickening torso (Leslie Henson) who transforms miraculously into the son of Pan after a chance detour at the Fountain of Youth. Bradley drew on many dance forms to express these latent desires, combining the intertwined arms and sculptural poses of Frederick Ashton; the Cakewalk back bends, struts, and rolling shoulders of African American dance; and the languid arm pushes he and Jessie Matthews turned into a signature. In accord with the British reticence of *Oh, Daddy!*, Bradley's choreography is light and suggestive instead of probing. He hints, rather than shouts, at how dance can express unarticulated thoughts and enter the realm of surreal fantasy.

As in theatrical dance, Bradley was game to work in every genre of film—the question was not if a film was highbrow or popular but whether there would be opportunities for interesting dances. When he pivoted from the polished *Oh, Daddy!* to the madcap *A Fire Has Been Arranged*, he made his point—the reviewer for *The Observer* dismissed the film in two succinct sentences but praised Bradley's choreography. She was not wrong. As a showcase for popular variety comedians Flanagan and Allen, the film was little more than an exercise in inspired tomfoolery. As a platform for dance, it was superb, sending Bradley's creativity into sweeping formations, fire drills, and grand store openings. Bradley recognized a good opportunity and seized it.[12]

Dance was still a relative rarity inBritish film in 1935. It was time consuming, and therefore expensive, to capture; it increased the cast head count; and, as it was still considered entertainment rather than a way to advance narrative or drama, it was hard to justify. Given the broad draw of Flanagan and Allen, however, the film, which centered on an arson in a department store, had a budget that allowed for some stylish sets and the talent of a top choreographer.

From the very beginning, Bradley unleashes catnip for the eye. The opening dance deploys twenty dancing shopgirls, several store executives, a few mannequins, and, naturally, an art deco calyx staircase. The dancers, featured as the "Buddy Bradley Girls," move with loose hips, pliable knees, bobbling heads, and deep forward bends. Marching up and down the staircases, they move with easy bouncing steps, adding a skipping jump here, a shoulder shimmy there, a variation, in fact, on a riff walk. Despite the limited production time, the women are reasonably well rehearsed, but they are not precision dancers. They give the impression of individuals, not machines. If the dancing is reasonably straightforward, the staging is complex. As Bradley sweeps the dancers through formations, kaleidoscopes them into circles that condense into a "v," then pulls them up into strict lines, he and the filmgoer explore together the optics of dance.[13]

His other striking number, a fire drill for the shop staff, is an exercise in smart parading in backless dresses and heels. The team neatly pulls a fire truck, then rests at ease, each posed naturalistically, one with a foot propped on a fender, another with hands clasped behind her back, another shifting her weight to one side. After the arson attack, they return to complicate the plot, which *The Era* summed up quite neatly, writing that the Buddy Bradley Girls were as dainty a group of amateur firemen as ever poured oil on a troubled fire.[14] It is all rather silly but satisfyingly effervescent—it's a Flanagan and Allen film, after all.

Other films kept Bradley commuting out to film lots in Elstree, Shepherd's Bush, and Twickenham in the 1930s, including Cary Grant's only British film, *The Amazing Quest of Ernest Bliss*, and a film with Lupe Velez, *Stardust*, in which Larry Ceballos is the choreographer of record. Soon the success of Astaire's *Gay Divorcee* and Bradley's *Evergreen*, both released in 1934, unleashed a groundswell of ever more lavish dance films. But, as dance on film gathered momentum, Buddy Bradley's choreography on film—whether inventing dream ballets, creating striking numbers that justified color film, or seducing the eye with a camera view of dance—retained the same qualities that distinguished his work onstage. Bradley linked steps to music, worked on the individual body, considered always the viewer's experience, and absorbed new dance influences, all to heighten the expressive power of dance.

Film spread Bradley's aesthetic beyond the West End, to every corner of the British Empire, across the Channel to the Continent, and even America. Did a teenage Jerome Robbins see these films? Or burlesque baby Bob Fosse? The answer is almost irrelevant: Bradley had shone the light on their future.

CHAPTER 15

THE GAUGUIN OF THE DANCE

Buddy Bradley is a sort of Gauguin of the dance,
and his use of time and pattern is significant.

—*MANCHESTER GUARDIAN*

By 1934–35, with twenty projects claiming his attention, Buddy Bradley was in full ascent. Running between rehearsals, out-of-town tryouts, openings in the West End, classes on Old Compton Street, and film lots, Bradley was in continual motion and under constant pressure. The Crash had brought a new wrinkle to the theater, just as musical comedy inched toward the integrated book musical. As more affordable movies cut into market share, big musical comedies, with their long lines of chorines loosely connected to plot, became rarer in the West End.

Bradley now used his opportunities with smaller productions to experiment and sculpt his choreography to diamond brilliance. He brought dancers off the stage and into the auditorium aisles in *Tulip Time*. He imaginatively enacted a speed chase with a steering wheel—minus a chassis—in *Happy Weekend*. He created a balletic pas de deux for pal Frederic Franklin.[1]

Having known penury firsthand, Bradley valued work and treated every project with respect. While he invested every commission with invention and creativity, three specific projects from these years stand out: *Why Not Tonight?* pushed musical boundaries. *Lucky Break* startled with boldness. *Anything Goes*, by Cole Porter, magnificently proved what America had lost: a choreographer who had jazz under his skin.

Success took its toll. The rituals that replenished Bradley and stoked his creativity—the pint taken in solitary splendor in a pub, the happy puttering in the kitchen, the quiet nights at home with a book—often fell victim to his peripatetic schedule. Relationships with women, a near-constant in the life of this sexy, gentle bachelor with the good shoulders and graceful gait, may not have been on hold but suffered from a want of time; no individuals lingered long enough for their names to be recorded. Ads for the school, flaunting his latest credits and star pupils, delicately sidestep the fact that he wasn't frequently teaching class, either, while still giving hope to chorines looking to be cast in his next show. Fortunately, there was steadfast Coley—Coleman Goodman, Bradley's business partner—to keep the school humming.[2]

For what was really important in these years was not what Bradley taught, but what he brought to dance, exemplified by the tang in his "Modern Rhythm" number in *Why Not Tonight?* Bradley's switching-up of rhythm, flattening of perspective, experiments with lighting, and intermarrying of vernacular and established dance conventions earned him nothing less than the sobriquet "the Gauguin of the dance." Bradley, schooled in the theater, had to look up "Gauguin" and discovered a kindred artist who defied convention.[3]

"Modern Rhythm" was daring, even in an iconoclastic revue that skewered such sacrosanct institutions as modern mating and Mickey Mouse. Described by *The Manchester Guardian* as subtle, with deliberately shaken blues rhythms worked out in time and gesture, the number drew on tap's African origins, polished and transformed for the present. But, as the *Guardian* explained, this was not the buck dancing tradition of yore: the new rhythms of Bradley were neither simple nor secure. Playing with the possibilities of time and tempo, Bradley anticipated the bebop rhythms of the next decade.

Layering visual drama on aural audacity, "Modern Rhythm" assaulted the senses. Bradley matched complex tap tempos with ethereal shadows, projected on a backcloth by his front-lit dancers. As terrestrial and spectral united, Bradley, concluded *The Era*, was the secret sauce of *Why Not Tonight?*

While the accolades for Bradley unfurled easily and continuously—"conspicuous in all the most important and imaginative sketches and dances," "a supremely effective chorus," "the chorus, trained by Mr. Buddy Bradley, is a delight to watch"—they underscore a reality of Bradley's career. Anyone who has ever entered a dance studio knows such consistent reviews are not gratuitous; they are earned through hard work and eagle-eyed attention to detail. Bradley was far from inhabiting an ivory tower of dance, luxuriously contemplating changes of rhythm that anticipated bebop. He was showing up on time at rehearsals day after day, producing a show.[4]

That Bradley could freely explore complex dance ideas in "Modern Rhythm," liberated from his usual worries about clean and audible taps, owed much to the presence of Gina Malo, the American dancer who had commanded the stage in *The Cat and the Fiddle.* He was also supported by a known crew of creative comrades. Herbert Farjeon, who had scored big with his send-up of the Brontë sisters in *After Dark*, wrote the book. Romney Brent, the breakout star of *Words and Music*, directed. Composer Ord Hamilton wrote the smoky-sultry score. Only Agnes de Mille, contributing two little-remarked dances, was a neophyte still finding her footing (the year before, Cochran had summarily replaced her in *Nymph Errant* at the last minute, and *Oklahoma!* was nine long years away).[5]

In contrast to the high-concept *Why Not Tonight?*, *Lucky Break*, with its skeleton plot of Mayfair bachelors hocking counterfeit antiques, was fantastic balderdash. But the absurdity was deceptive; Bradley packed innovation into *Lucky Break* that would propel the book musical forward. The previous year, in *Nice Goings On*, he had integrated dancers into the book with speaking lines; now he further differentiated the chorus, with each dancer so distinctive she was listed on the casting page as a separate character with a specific name, rather than lumped into a chorus. After five years of implanting his style in London, Bradley could now demand more technique and variety from his dancers, and he upped the ante, requiring seamless transitions between acrobatics, jazz, tap, and *poses plastiques*.[6]

Hurtling Phyllis Stanley out of a bookcase in "Bookworms," Bradley shatters all notions of librarians in pince-nez. Stanley bursts triumphantly from a wall of books, followed by eight tapping maids in sequined sarongs and strappy halter tops. (How many bodies can a bookcase contain? Do bookworms really wear sarongs? Bradley begs we suspend reality.) Then Stanley poses sculpturally—she looks like the Oscar statue—framed by dancers, two flanking Stanley with raised arms, two kneeling with backbends in front center, two dancers on the corners, shoulders open, in a pyramidal grouping, all expertly arranged to draw the eye to center stage. In another scene, Richard Hearne (of *Nice Goings On*), a natural tumbler for whom stairs and ladders were irresistible, threw himself with abandon down stairs and off ladders, looking for all the world as if he might easily kill himself twice nightly. For transatlantic zip, Bradley had American June Clyde snap very neatly.[7]

More moxie arrived from America when Bradley's brother, Aurelius, who had briefly taught at the Pierce Studio, came to London. After a trip to New York in late 1934 during which Bradley attended the International Congress of Dance Masters, where he demonstrated ballroom tap and caught up with former colleague Ernest Carlos, he returned to London in a first-class stateroom on the *Paris*, with Aurelius trailing in tourist class. Aurelius (a.k.a. Arthur Bradley) had been working as a dancer, but now he listed his profession as "teacher" on the ship manifest. Trained by his brother and steeped in the impetus of African American dances, Aurelius was slated to teach at the studio. Potentially, he might become a quasi-partner in the school.[8]

After five years alone in London without a safe harbor, Bradley welcomed Aurelius's presence. Despite kindly West End champions such as Cochran and Ashton, Bradley was perforce self-protective, the one who listened quietly and revealed little while larger personalities worked the room. But having his closest sibling in town was more than a reassuring familial connection—Aurelius was an au courant link to the tap scene in America and reinforced Bradley's stature as an authority on African American dance. Bradley introduced Aurelius to the dance community with a presentation of the latest dances from America at the Drill Hall on Chenies Street (now studios for the Royal Academy of Dramatic Art) on Friday, January 25, 1935.[9]

Aurelius's timing was excellent: the spring of 1935 was particularly hectic, with three shows opening in one month. To celebrate King George V's silver jubilee, Cochran pulled out all the stops for his 1935 Trocadero cabaret, *Jubilation*, and, naturally, expected Bradley to choreograph. Bradley was not only keen to keep his enviable position as Cochran's go-to choreographer but also grateful to the man who had engineered his transformation from behind-the-scenes Broadway dance maker to international celebrity choreographer. He could hardly say no. He also couldn't resist contributing to *Char-a-Bang*, the final revue of André Charlot, Cochran's legendary rival. And, finally, there was *Let's Go Gay*, a jaunty revue that pointed to the future.[10]

Fortunately, an easy familiarity in *Let's Go Gay* counteracted the intense schedule. (Most projects were fairly chummy, for Bradley now knew virtually everyone in the West End.) His musical collaborator of choice, Percival Mackey, orchestrated the music; Ord Hamilton, of *Why Not Tonight?*, led the band. Actor-turned-writer Cecil Landeau, who would return to Bradley for future hits, cowrote the book. In such an environment, Bradley's creativity flowed freely. He opened the show with the slinky "Oozing with Oomph"; indulged in silliness with "Piccadilly's Gone Cuckoo-Racha," a zany fantasy of Piccadilly Circus gone rumba mad; and worked in some American syncopated dancing in "Rhythm of Wheels," with scenarios that evoked New York's Park Avenue, Harlem, and Chinatown.[11]

If *Let's Go Gay* was the classic West End revue with a veneer of American jazz, *Anything Goes* was the quintessentially American show with blues in its soul. *Anything Goes*—a landmark in the evolution of the musical—was Bradley's birthright, the type of show he should have been doing on Broadway. Author and composer

Cole Porter supplied Bradley with gutsiness that only an American could provide. Unlike Noël Coward, who crafted chiseled musical gems, Porter reveled in the swing of the American language and the dead-on pow! of its singing style. He had grown up hearing African American music; he favored pulse and rhythm, foxtrots and swing, syncopated piano and brass to accompany his lyrics. Drawing on the American jazz tradition, Porter spun out one hit tune after another, using bluesy undertones for "I Get a Kick Out of You," a refrain of unrequited love, and descending chromatic melody and jaggedly syncopated phrases for the title song, "Anything Goes."[12]

Bradley intuitively understood the closeted Porter and his underlying melancholy; he, too, in a sense, was "passing" and paying the emotional price. As a Black man, he grasped Porter's music, exactly why it was so lilting and longing, bluesy and brassy. Unlike its Broadway choreographer, Robert Alton, who ran speedy no-nonsense rehearsals with a whistle between his teeth, Bradley brought nuance and complexity to the West End transfer, seamlessly working dances into its fabric, investing the erotic ballad "All Through the Night" with sensuality, "Where Are the Men?" with tap rhythms, and "The Gypsy in Me" with flamenco overtones.[13]

After his five years in the West End and a stint in Paris, Bradley had what Robert Alton did not: a sure handle on jazz and a talent for showy dances that stood up to a vigorous score. For "Public Enemy Number One," the opener for act 2, Bradley distributed eighteen chorus girls, six sailors, eight actors, each invested with appropriate character and dance, on the deck of a ship that traverses the entire stage. He snatched American soubrette Betty Kean from *Jubilation* and built the tap extravaganza "Where Are the Men?" to showcase her easy open shoulders, swinging arms, and adept weight shifts. Jack Whiting, a former Bradley student, prophetically arrived from New York when talks with Leslie Henson for the role of Billy Crocker fell through. With a rare spontaneity on stage, an American intuition about jazz, pliable knees, and a forward thrust of shoulders, Whiting bewitched in "You're the Top" and "I Get a Kick Out of You." His ability to interpret character in dance would be critical to Bradley's future success in integrating the book musical.[14]

With its punchy dances that caught the mood of each song, and its dazzling music and lyrics, with a hint of social commentary, *Anything Goes* brought musical theater one giant step closer to the modern book musical. Though it still had its share of songs that came out of nowhere, it daringly opened with a book scene and, only then, was followed by a musical number, "I Get a Kick Out of You." The fact that a midwestern Yale-educated, Paris Schola Cantorum–trained composer could write such music was yet another sign of how jazz, once the sole realm of Black musicians, now permeated and shaped culture at large.[15]

Working on Cole Porter's flashy American hit was another coup for Bradley, but it also posed questions: If Bradley was capable of such a show in London, why not in New York? (For that matter, why weren't there big jazzy shows written by, say, Duke Ellington or Noble Sissle for him to choreograph?) But London was the platform he had been given, and Bradley, resigned and realistic, made the most of his opportunities. The frenetic pace of the past years, capped by *Anything Goes*, solidified his skills, taught him the art of balancing multiple demands, and matured him as a choreographer. At thirty, Bradley had gathered all the tools and confidence he would need to make the glossy book musical films that, in parallel with Hollywood, would integrate the book musical.

CHAPTER 16

DANCING ON THE CEILING

No praise is too great for Buddy,
he's a genius of dance.

—JESSIE MATTHEWS

From the outset, the chemistry between Buddy Bradley and Jessie Matthews was right. He provided the vision, she, the visibility. They first came together in 1930 for *Ever Green*, two outsiders brimming with talent who would share a dance destiny. Early in their careers, exposed and tentative, they blossomed together, proceeding to make six art deco musical films from 1934 to 1938 that elevated their craft and cemented a bond. In parallel with Hermes Pan and Fred Astaire in Hollywood, Bradley, with Matthews, brought theatrical dance to new levels of expression. And, while the release of every Jessie Matthews film was a major event, it is in three of her films where dance reaches a dizzying height: *Evergreen*, a fantasy of imagination and invention; *It's Love Again,* oozing sexuality and suggestion; and *Sailing Along*, melding dance, narrative, and emotion.

Bradley and Matthews were a mutual admiration society. He praised her charm and sense of rhythm. She paid homage to his genius. Bradley had no use for the mechanically proficient. (He was quick to dismiss Hal LeRoy, reeling off ever more intricate tap steps, in favor of Fred Astaire, who invested dance with personality.) Neither a classic beauty nor a conventional theatrical dancer (she didn't know how to tap until their third movie), Matthews delivered what Bradley most wanted: musicality, narrative thread, and emotional undercurrent. She radiated grace, susceptibility, and personal charm. She had ballet technique and gorgeous feet, her moves stretched into infinity, and she had an exceptional sense for music and rhythm. Matthews, said director Victor Saville, had a heart, and it photographed.[1]

One understands Matthews's adoration, too. Bradley intuitively understood her body and how she moved. He found a way to fuse her ballet training with his touchstone, jazz dance, making everything he created look lyrical and natural on her body. In Bradley's choreography, Matthews floated and charmed to international stardom. In fact, if it hadn't been for his sensitivity, she may well have missed stardom, for Matthews was a notoriously fragile artist, alternating brilliance with nervous breakdowns.[2]

Bradley understood fragility and knew how to manage demons—he had the cautionary tale of Eddie Rector to thank for that. While every artist reveals his soul, filming dance creates unusual vulnerabilities. Not only is a dancer laid bare, but a mere few minutes of footage requires infinite fortitude, different camera angles, and special effects, and it may take days to capture. Between takes, dancers second-guess themselves and lose connection with a partner, and the momentum that first animated the piece often evaporates. Many Matthews projects came to a halt, with Jessie retreating to a rest home, wrestling with urticaria, hallucinations, or other torments. Bradley became Matthews's steadying force, and the two made landmark dances happen.

The pattern of fear alternating with luminosity began with *Evergreen* (unlike the play, the title of the 1934 film is written as one word). Matthews had grown up humbly, above a stable in Berwick Street, Soho, and suffered from what we might today call "imposter syndrome"—Bradley understood that, too. On the initial day of filming, Matthews collapsed, throwing off the schedule of the first big-budget British musical. For weeks she cowered in a corner of her bed looking frightened, threatening the production calendar and budget, and causing widespread anxiety on the set. It was Bradley, with director Saville, who eventually coaxed her out of bed and into performing "Dancing on the Ceiling," the camera trailing to capture the sequence in one take; he knew all too well how quickly the winds could change with her. With her pliant backbends and expansive arms, and her piquant face flattered by the camera of Glen MacWilliams, that single take of "Dancing on the Ceiling" made Matthews internationally famous.[3]

It was Bradley, reading Matthews, that made the difference. Even during the traumatic filming, Matthews looks relaxed as she fan-kicks in a gossamer peignoir and heels, skips upstairs in a dance quotation of Bill Robinson, and sways in Buddy's now-famous "Jessie Matthews backbend," an eloquent bending back as she rhythmically pushes an outstretched arm with flexed wrist against air. The lushly dipping shoulders, lilting jumps, and spinning turns of Bradley's choreography for "Dancing on the Ceiling" convey the elation of youthful love while they oh-so-tantalizingly anticipate the future of the book musical, where song and dance integrate into the storyline.

Accustomed to the relatively limited budgets of British films, Bradley savored *Evergreen*'s deep production pockets. His stylized robotic dance sequence for "When You've Got a Little Springtime in Your Heart" looks as if some reels of Fritz Lang's *Metropolis* got mixed up with the footage. Anecdotal details are not overlooked, either: a bartender shakes cocktails to the jazz rhythm. Elsewhere, like Alfred Hitchcock, Bradley inserts himself in a fleeting cameo to display the deeply bent knees and rapid tap footwork he had mastered in the alley behind Connie's Inn. It's a vital reminder of the force behind his genius, completely irrelevant to the story, and our only footage of Bradley dancing. In the lavish finale, "Over My Shoulder," Bradley places Matthews—in a bias-cut slip dress that reveals a modernist dancer's figure—on top of a revolving tiered set with sixty-plus chorus dancers. The big production number ends with an engagement: Matthews and romantic hero Barry MacKay effectively becoming the celluloid bride and groom atop a wedding cake. The camera closes in on Matthews's hand, but the engagement ring has swiveled sideways so that the stone cannot be seen. Did no one request a retake? Even the grandest British musicals, it seems, had budgetary constraints.

Hollywood script writer Frances Marion reported that *Evergreen* caused the American film industry to sit up and notice how exciting "real" dance—unlike Busby Berkeley's clever camera manipulations—could be on screen. Bradley's choreography, which drew on real steps, *was* arresting not only because it was based on African American suppleness and executed by an agile muse but also because Bradley, too, was baring his soul as an artist. He made his work personal, not formulaic. He connected with his dancers. His idiosyncratic choices, such as including dance sequences without a dubbed sound track (the sound of Matthews's shoes squeaking as she pirouettes across the palatial floor in "Dancing on the Ceiling" draws the viewer into a charming intimacy with the dancer), were endearing and distinctive. It was in *Evergreen*, too, that Bradley introduced the extendable stage to British films, in which performers are first seen on a realistic stage that then proceeds to lose its proscenium arch and expands at will—a recurring device in his films.[4]

Like Fred Astaire and Hermes Pan, or Bob Fosse and Gwen Verdon, Bradley and Matthews gained trust and momentum as their collaboration evolved. At times, Matthews's musicality so deeply mirrored Bradley's that she not only reflected him; she embodied the music itself, anticipating the next movement. Their artistic partnership thrived on reciprocity. As Bradley gifted Matthews with rich weight shifts, rhythm changes, polyrhythmic head, shoulder, and feet movement, and the pliancy of jazz dance, she gave him access to the extensions, line, and balances of her classical ballet training, complementing the ideas of upper-body grace, fluid arms, and poses Bradley had acquired when working with Ashton. The amplitude of Matthews's dancing, her open postures, smoothly connected movements, and upward lift of ballet technique suited Bradley's vision for theatrical jazz dance.[5]

It's Love Again, their third film, was a triple breakthrough. For the first time, Bradley was called in for preproduction meetings. He could suggest script modifications to better integrate dance, scheme the choreography before the script was finished, create dances to dovetail with the story, and experiment with floor materials to obtain the best sound effects. It was also the first film in which he could create tap routines for Matthews. (In the break after her previous film, he had taught her how to tap dance.)

Wonderfully, too, the acoustic challenges that live performance posed for tap dancing were erased by the technical capacities of the soundstage. And, just as wonderfully, his choreography could now take flight into romantic realms. Barry Mackay and other previous romantic leads had been but affable dance tag-alongs. Now he had long-legged, mournful-faced dancer Cyril Wells, a standout Dancing Boy in *Words and Music*, and one of the most apt to pass through Bradley's Old Compton Street studio, who could match Matthews in intensity and skill. Bradley's creativity—and tap dance—could now annex new territory.[6]

The film, another big-budget extravaganza—for Matthews is now proven box office bait—is full of eye candy: Hindu-inspired headdresses that required twenty weeks' labor to bejewel; gossamer yashmaks that played up Matthews's eyes; camels trotting on Rotten Row; an art deco nightclub with real-life sommeliers, carvers, and maître d's borrowed from a posh West End carvery. Yet even such riches don't distract from Bradley's dances. An early scene has Matthews encounter Robert Young (imported from Hollywood to lure American audiences) on a landing. After her mere six months of tap instruction with Bradley, she literally dances circles around the future Dr. Marcus Welby. Her dimensional dancing carves the air as she sways her back, dips her shoulders, and affects the polyrhythmic head, shoulders, hips, and feet of Bradley. The sequence ends, movie-fashion, with a butler confessing he can dance a Shuffle Off to Buffalo as he serves cocktails from a tray.[7]

But Bradley isn't content with simply celebrating a gamine. He next dives into the sphere of the senses, taking Matthews with him. Girlish desire gives way to seduction when Matthews and the inexplicably uncredited Cyril Wells take over the dance floor. Every long languorous step is deliberate. He leans into her with insistence. Hip for hip, step for step, eye for eye, Matthews and Wells ignite an electrical current that charges the entire dance. Hands graze along bodies. Martha Graham contractions are traced. Matthews's swooping back bends as she succumbs to the power of the dance empty the dance floor and leave the audience breathless. By the time the number climaxes, the stage has elevated, and Wells and Matthews dance alone, oblivious to all.

The big tap numbers revel in their new dance domain. In "I Nearly Let Love Go Slipping Through My Fingers," Matthews, now masquerading as a glamorous world traveler, appears in a bodysuit and tap shoes shimmering in seven pounds of mirrors and sequins, followed by a male chorus in white dinner jackets. The men look terrific, with their sauntering riffs and syncopated hops. Then Cyril Wells emerges to dance with Matthews. He leans into her, hands on hips, to engage her in dance. Nothing is labored, everything is quick, light, and American-easy. Matthews is radiant as she and Wells dance a tap tango, hold hands, and fuse steps with music. They cease to be two individuals dancing on a stage: they fuse into a single entity, connected by their movement, the music, and the dance.

Then it's back to sheer, spectacular dance for dance's sake. To frame Matthews's debut as a tap soloist, Bradley created a jazzy "temple dance" laden with sinuous hands, angled arms, isolations, and rhythm tap. Dressed in a jeweled hip wrap and Hindu-inspired crown, combining swinging hips with low-down stances, emphatic taps with uplifted skips, temple dancer arms, and head bobbles, all the while flirting offstage and with the camera, Matthews gives a bravura performance.

On his way to the final big production number, Bradley casually tosses off random treats. There's a flirtatious little number for Matthews and Young that gently riffs on Johnny Nit's famous chair-tapping. He again opts to record dances live, so steps and music are seamlessly synchronized, and has dances filmed from a tricky "staircase complex," an unpopular device with cameramen, in which a cramped rostrum holds a camera and crew ten to twenty feet above the studio floor.[8]

For the finale, "Dance My Way to Heaven," Bradley has Matthews open with soft ballet focus—the now-familiar penchés and pirouettes—then surprise-switches to sand dancing, complete with the audible and syncopated shuffles that hearken back to dancers like Eddie Rector. Matthews alternates low slides with an upward buoyancy, dipping shoulders with expansive arms, fan kicks, and Cakewalk stances, then winds up with a hot tap number. She leans forward slightly, moving her feet quickly and subtly, close to the ground, not stepping high as an English tap dancer. Those who studied tap dance with Bradley find in her relaxed arm movements, easy fast beats, soft rib cage, close-to-the-floor footwork, interspersed occasionally with an air step, the signatures Bradley would advocate until the very end.

It is interesting to think about Bradley's integration of dance into the film musical relative to the work of Fred Astaire. In Hollywood, Astaire was also looking for ways to weave dance, and, notably, tap dance, whose primary expression is time and tempo, into a storyline. Were Bradley and Astaire aware of each other's efforts and spurring each other onward—as Braque and Picasso jointly created Cubism—or operating in separate universes? *Evergreen* preceded Astaire's *The Gay Divorcee* by a few scant months. Astaire's *Top Hat* was released in September 1936, just two months before Bradley's *It's Love Again*. For "No Strings" in *Top Hat*, Astaire, too, uses tap to develop character (Astaire delivers a parting salvo of taps as he departs a stuffy London men's club). Was it coincidence that, in the next scene, Ginger Rogers is awakened by Fred tapping in the room above her? This is the very premise of 1934's *Evergreen*'s "Dancing on the Ceiling." History has hidden the answers to these questions, yet it is clear that film, in the guise of Bradley and Astaire, was enamored of tap dance and searching for ways in which it could serve a story.[9]

With the Gaumont-British studio in increasing disarray, and the sensitive Victor Saville moving into new film genres (and eventually to Hollywood), the next two Jessie Matthews films, *Head over Heels* and *Gangway*, fell short of the high bar of *Evergreen* and *It's Love Again*. Matthews's husband, Sonnie Hale, who had come to an impasse in his acting career, now decided that he would direct his wife's films. Hale had neither directing experience nor the emotional sensitivity of Saville, adding tension to an already strained marriage. Matthews seems to mirror the angst with unflattering coiffures and mounting pounds. The films suffered, too.

Frustration with both films coincided with a professional disappointment in America. Following the brio of *Evergreen* and *It's Love Again*, Twentieth Century-Fox approached Bradley to choreograph *Alexander's Ragtime Band* (1938) with Tyrone Power. For Bradley, Hollywood was the pinnacle. Supported by the vast studio system, endless resources, and wide distribution, American films were the gold standard. Bradley had nevertheless passed on Broadway choreographer Seymour Felix's invitation to join him in Hollywood in 1931, fearing he would be relegated to a ghost choreographer. Now he was approached, not as a handy subordinate, but in his own right as a recognized dance director. Per Bradley's recall, *Alexander*'s shooting schedule was delayed; when rescheduled, it bumped up against a previous commitment for a Jessie Matthews film. Returning to London, he found the unnamed Matthews project canceled, presumably due to another health crisis. In the interim, Seymour Felix replaced him on *Alexander's Ragtime Band*, dashing Bradley's dreams. He would have been the first person of color to choreograph a Hollywood film.[10]

After the disappointment, *Sailing Along* was a joyous renaissance. Everything the last two Matthews films had lacked—spontaneity, original story material, and the freshness and charm of the star's personality—came roaring back to life. Matthews was now back in dance form, well coiffed, and wearing winsome clothes by Norman Hartnell, future couturier to Queen Elizabeth II. As Sonnie Hale had finally figured out how to direct, the film was swift, gay, and witty. Most wondrous of all was that, with Jack Whiting, the romantic lead in *Anything Goes*, now partnering with Jessie Matthews, Bradley could now explore the possibilities of the tap pas de deux and introduced another theatrical innovation: a "tap ballet."[11]

Whiting didn't merely interpret a dance; he inhabited it and, in doing so, even elevated Matthews. In "Souvenir for Love," a top-hat-and-tails routine, Whiting segues from animated to smooth to energetic, his legs extending in endless lines, his pliés so plush they suggest they might last forever, and his turns start from a beguiling swing of his hips. If Whiting's pleasure in dance is infectious, Matthew's pleasure in dancing with *him* is irresistible. It registers in the vibrance of her face and the fullness of her moves. Both dancers arch elegantly in a few steps of a waltz and turn a few measures of call-and-response into a playful challenge dance. When Matthews leans deeply into him, Whiting emits a spontaneous "Ooh!," which, disarmingly, remains on the soundtrack.

For all its charm, "Souvenir for Love," it turns out, is just a prelude. A flirtation masquerading as a rehearsal session, "When Your Heart Skips a Beat" reveals a new tender side of tap, the capacity to express human relationships, that tap—the perennially perky, "happy dance"—had never previously displayed. Bradley has now added elements to his rapid footwork, mobile upper bodies, and a musical response to music that make the dance linger in the mind. Matthews and Whiting interact with each other throughout, united by the music, connected by their eyes. They hold hands. Their shoulders touch as they come forward. Whiting puts an arm around her neck, then lightly on her back. Matthews jumps impulsively into Whiting's personal space. There are teasing moments and minor contretemps. Whiting even matches Matthews in a few fan kicks and penchés—a dance indication of true love, if there ever was one. Bradley brings tap into the regions of the heart.

While "When Your Heart Skips a Beat" is intimist, the finale, "My River," is narrative sweep. Vast in set as well as storytelling reach, its filming put Bradley's invention, the extendable stage, to magnificent use. A half-ton camera on a custom-built truck followed Matthews and Whiting for nearly a mile of filming, on a set so large that it had to be built across two film studios. With its tricky tap, mime sequences, dream ballet, and dancing off into the proverbial sunset (in this case, a sailboat), Matthews estimated that "My River" required twenty miles of dancing, including rehearsal time, to produce seven minutes of footage. "My River" is striking, however, not because of its statistics and technical challenges but for its impact on musical theater: Bradley mapped out new ground in "My River" by binding dance, pantomime, characterization, and music to tell a complete story, a parable-within-a-film that recounts the transformation of a saucy ingenue into a romantic heroine.[12]

Matthews opens the number wearing a trim skirt and blouse, sauntering nonchalantly, skimming tap steps up and down a flight of stairs, an insouciant free spirit. During the dance, she encounters streetwise toughs and spikes of testosterone (premonitions of Jerome Robbins's *Fancy Free*) on the lower docks, scuffles and swoons, at-risk heroes and forbidding bobbies, misunderstandings and resolution. There are dashes of color—indifferent workmen, a sylvan picnic reminiscent of *Dejeuner sur l'herbe*, dockhands rolling barrels, clever posturing—as Matthews and Whiting dance through the picaresque events and landscape, then pass through a gate into a dreamscape of the bucolic upper Thames, discover their shared fate in a tap pas de deux, and ultimately embark on the future together. The *Monthly Film Bulletin* immediately recognized its importance, describing the number as a "tap ballet." With smart taps and a keen sense of theater, Bradley's work foreshadows that of Agnes de Mille, Jerome Robbins, and Gene Kelly.[13]

Sailing Along marked the apotheosis of Matthews and Bradley. Over four years, two plays, and six films, their artistic synergy had flourished. Their partnership gave birth to a new dance vocabulary, one that combined the specifics of Matthew's natural movement with the jazz vision of Bradley, telegraphed the Bradley aesthetic around the world, and explored the far horizon of theatrical dance. Time, taste, finances, an upheaval in the British film industry, and a world war would take its toll on musical films in both America and England. There were no more film collaborations after *Sailing Along*, though Bradley and Matthews would once again come together in the West End for *Come Out to Play*, and, after the war, Bradley would cast Matthews in a revue, *Sauce Tartare*, with a young Audrey Hepburn.

More than twenty years later, for the BBC program *This Is Your Life*, Matthews gasps with pleasure, and her voice drops to a purr, when she learns Bradley will be a guest on the show. Bradley saunters onto the set with his high-wattage smile and settles into his chair, voicing his admiration for the earnest waif from Soho who soared on her own talent, dedication, and vision, without the benefit of birthright, money, or connections. He might have been speaking of himself. Her fragility was part of their intimacy; he remembers that Matthews could "let her hair down" with him. They had been partners on a journey, quietening their fears, discovering their potential, and raising their art. Bradley had made Matthews Britain's cherished "Dancing Divinity." Matthews had made Bradley's vision leap beyond the confines of the West End and into consciousness worldwide.[14]

CHAPTER 17

TOP HAT AND TAILS

Part of show business is magic.
You don't know how it happens.

—SAMMY DAVIS JR.

A bit of Rex Harrison with the nose of Toulouse-Lautrec's Aristide Bruant, Jack Buchanan was the English revue idol par excellence between the wars, deemed, along with Gertrude Lawrence and Beatrice Lillie, the shining future of musical theater. Fred Astaire envied his stylish saunter, Noël Coward the ease with which he could put over a song. The Prince of Wales learnt tap steps from Jack at post-performance suppers at Rules. In his bespoke Hawes and Curtis tailcoat, with top hat and cane, no dancer could have been more British—or more Bradley.[1]

When starring in the 1929 New York transfer of Cochran's *Wake Up and Dream*, Buchanan dipped into the Pierce Studio to pick up some lessons from Buddy Bradley, the dance coach insiders were talking about. At the time, Buchanan's dancing best suited English drawing-room comedies, but Bradley glimpsed possibilities underneath the bobbing and bowing. Buchanan had lazy charm, light feet, and a suggestion of swing; in his top hat and tails, he also bore a passing resemblance to a Class Act dancer. It was then that Bradley began the revamp of Buchanan from docile marionette to supple dancer.

Banished were the inexpressive back and inflexible knees captured in a 1925 Pathé film clip, replaced by suggestive drawling movements that recalled the rolling rhythmic cadence of Bradley and his fabled walk. The transformation of Buchanan from matinee prince to sexy hoofer was key in Cochran's decision to invite Bradley to choreograph *Evergreen*. What is more, it produced a string of collaborations that solidified Bradley's standing as a choreographer in England.[2]

If Henri Wessels, Cyril Wells, or Jack Whiting were possibly better dancers, Buchanan matched them in his ability to magnetize audiences and surpassed them in celebrity. This was critical. Though Bradley had shaped great women dancers from Ada May to Jessie Matthews, he had not worked with a high-visibility male dancer. And, in the 1930s, despite the towering accomplishments of Jeni Le Gon and Alice "Baby" Whitman, male hoofers still set the standard. From Bojangles to Bubbles, they were seen as the repositories for the tap tradition; it was men who carried the tap genes, so to speak, like Jewish lineage in reverse, and it was male dancing by which a choreographer was often measured. Whether we agree or not with such elevation of the male dancer, working with Buchanan conferred a certain gravitas.

As soon as Bradley established his school in London, Buchanan and Bradley picked up where they had left off in New York. They matched each other, step for step, trait for trait. If Bradley was the gentlest of men, Buchanan was the most decent. In the bitchy world of theater, one never heard stories about Buchanan; there were simply no stories to tell. If Bradley drove himself relentlessly, Buchanan did, too: his "throwaway" style disguised hours of dedication. If Bradley was cool, Buchanan was nonchalant: like Eddie Rector, he never courted an audience—he let it come to him.

Inevitably, Bradley became Buchanan's choreographer of choice. Their seven projects included West End plays and revues (one, naturally, entitled *Top Hat and Tails*) and an over-the-top musical, *The Flying Trapeze*. While footage of their stage collaborations does not exist, two films convey the quirky humor and languorous dancing that typifies their partnership and display Bradley's facility on film: *Brewster's Millions* and *This'll Make You Whistle*.[3]

Whereas Hollywood was a continent away from Broadway, the British film studios in Elstree, Shepherds Bush, and the like were in easy proximity to the writing and acting talent in the West End. Exploiting this advantage, Buchanan, with producer Herbert Wilcox, set out to harness West End talent to create a musical that competed head-to-head with Hollywood. Though money was the perennial Achilles heel of British film, Wilcox amassed sufficient backing for *Brewster's Millions* to import director Thornton Freeland, who had recently completed *Flying Down to Rio* (which introduced the dance team of Fred Astaire and Ginger Rogers); editor Merrill White, a longtime associate of Ernst Lubitsch's; and, for a little international glamour, French bombshell Lili Damita (Mrs. Errol Flynn). He'd planned on hiring Busby Berkeley, but, after seeing the choreography in the film, *Evergreen*, he switched gears and hired Buddy Bradley.[4]

Though he was too seasoned, too elegant, and, perhaps, too jaded to indulge in vindictive glee, Bradley could only have been chuffed by this unexpected turn of events, recalling how Berkeley had monopolized credit for his own choreography in *A Connecticut Yankee*. Bradley's high spirits are evident throughout the film: in a cabaret rehearsal in the film's opening scene, to a private party full of fox-trotting swells, to a glimpse of Lili Damita rehearsing in tiny shorts and a spangled belt. In "One Good Tune Deserves Another," Buchanan shows off his Bradley coaching as he dances with quick feet and a clean sound, nimbly bending his body to front and side, executing an occasional little kick, while Bradley's sly humor surfaces with a pool of rhythmic typists.

A yacht conveying a nightclub act to Monte Carlo provides an oh-so-natural opportunity for the first production number: a line of chorus girls in white split skirts and halter tops with anchors—by Schiaparelli, the Surrealist couturière—tap dancing while neatly semaphoring, a polyrhythmic take on "Hail Britannia."[5] Even within the limited confines of a ship's deck, Bradley creates big dances, thanks to his experiences working in the elbow-tight spaces of Marie Rambert's Mercury Theatre and the Trocadero. Though restricted in surface space, the dancers move through three dimensions, reaching upward, stretching sideways, and bending low at the waist, conquering space with epaulement, easy swinging hips, and somersaults.

For Bradley, who liked to experiment with innovation, be it in dance, music, lighting, or disappearing stages, *Brewster's Millions* was a delectable playground. Its highlight was a vast production number set in a Corsican market square crawling with eighty electricians snaking one thousand feet of cable, shot from a camera crane elevated sixty feet. With one thousand supernumeraries and two hundred dancers, it was the biggest and most expensive set in British film history to date and a splashy stage to introduce a new dance: the Caranga. Dancers cascade down a flight of stairs to a plaza, then execute a sand-sweeping step as they progress through the square with dipping shoulders and twisting hips, shifting their weight and flexing their knees, occasionally incorporating arm gestures that recall Jessie Matthews pushing against air. The self-effacing Buchanan dances as a dragon puppet, pauses mid-dance in a tired collapse, then crosses his legs languidly and exits with a hornpipe down an alley.[6]

The Caranga caused buzz. The *Daily Mirror* mused that it was a folk dance that Bradley had discovered and filmed on a preproduction trip to Corsica. *The New York Times* traced its origins to the Jota, Zapateador, Fandango, and Passacaille. Bradley laughed off such highfalutin nonsense—it was his own creation, his response to the Carioca in *Flying Down to Rio*, made while fooling around in his dance studio and hitting on a couple of steps he liked. He also pointedly noted that all modern dances of the past fifteen years, including his new Caranga, had roots in African dance. Like Bradley's 1927 Kinkajou in *Rio Rita*, it spawned a ballroom dance craze.[7]

If collective dance was the star of *Brewster's Millions*, individual dancers were the stars of *This'll Make You Whistle*. In "I'm in a Dancing Mood," Buchanan effortlessly swivels his hips, dips and twists his torso, and sculpts space three-dimensionally. He holds his arms distinctively, like upside-down goal posts. With a spinal cord injury that would lead to spinal arthritis, Buchanan's upper body would never attain the suppleness of Matthews's, but Bradley turns this potential drawback into a charming idiosyncrasy. The rapport Buchanan establishes with his partner, Elsie Randolph, is sexy, natural, and disarming. He leans easily into Randolph, sways his pelvis in subtle but perfect unison with her, expertly guides her in a foxtrot, then leads her off to the unknown. The low-down stance, thigh patting, Cakewalk arch, and hand on hip, all of which suit the laid-back Buchanan to a "T," came from Bradley.

A photo of Bradley rehearsing Buchanan in *It's Time to Dance* illustrates their dynamic. Both men, in well-draped suits, adopt a stance of relaxed knees and eloquent gesture. (Of interest, too, are Bradley's snappy two-tone shoes; Bradley, we are told, had a weakness for elegant dance shoes.) Bradley, smiling and confident, is clearly in charge; Buchanan peers intently at Bradley for cues. The choreographer's delicately arched hand contrasts with Buchanan's flat palm, and whereas Bradley is erect, Buchanan is slightly round shouldered. Yet such differences were immaterial to Bradley, who capitalized on individualistic charm, then infused it with the riches of African African dance. Capturing the two men at the very moment of a weight transition, the photo trembles with movement, as if ready to lift off the page. Just as engaging is its portrayal of bonhomie: Buchanan's respect for Bradley is obvious; Bradley's fondness for Buchanan is evident.

Bradley gifted Buchanan with a tour de force—British aplomb overlaid with Bradley sinuosity. It is, however, as much a gift to British dance as it is to any individual. Bradley proved through Buchanan the versatility of African American style to dancers and stages who never knew quite *what* was missing from their conscientious, hardworking dances. Was it the essential cool of Bradley, the languor of Buchanan, the discreet elegance of the two, or, perhaps, specific elements, such as pliant knees, mobile hips, and distinctive back, that made Buchanan's dancing so seductive? It is impossible to separate one from the other. As Sammy Davis Jr. stated, "Part of show business is magic. You don't know how it happens."

CHAPTER 18

FOLLOW THE SUN TO HAPPY RETURNS

There are years that ask
questions and years that answer.

—ZORA NEALE HURSTON

Park Crescent, a demilune of cream-colored terraced houses designed by Regency architect John Nash, forms a semicircle around a Crown Estate communal garden. Part of Nash's sweeping vision of a Roman-inspired West End for London, Park Crescent presents a uniform façade of Ionic columns, filleted overlights, black doors, and highly polished brass hardware. An elegant feat of urban planning, serene and slightly removed from the fray, it was here, at Number 12, that Bradley lived in 1936. He was at the height of his career.

So much had changed for Bradley over the years. The hardscrabble experience of Birmingham and sleepless nights in boardinghouses in Harlem were far away. Even the despair he had felt on Broadway was receding into memory. Now, as he stepped each morning onto his marble porch, Bradley was greeted by the scent of a weeping silver lime and the sight of two splendid plane trees planted in 1817 to mark the victory at Waterloo. In the afternoons there would be nannies pushing prams in the Nursemaid's Tunnel that connected the Crescent to Park Square, the prelude to Regent's Park. It was an idyllic walk to the studio at Old Compton Street, and just a bit further into the heart of the West End and its theaters.

The charisma that young Chuck Green experienced in Philadelphia had crystallized in London: Bradley was not only universally beloved and respected but now indispensable. He was in constant demand. Grateful dancers and directors continued to shower him with gifts and praise. The Buddy Bradley School of Stage Dancing had become an institution, one of only two professional dance schools that *The Era* endorsed. The reliable Coley Goodman continued to build up the dance agency, booking the Buddy Bradley Rhythm Girls at smart spots like the Kit Kat club for its 2 a.m. cabaret. (The jeunesse dorée apparently didn't have to show up in offices in the morning.)

Though circumstances had changed, Bradley hadn't changed a jot. His most severe reproof to a straggling chorus was still a gentle "We'll try that again." He still didn't like to hobnob (fortunately, success dispensed with the necessity), and he jealously guarded his privacy. He still supported charities, calmed anxious stars, and connected effortlessly with children. When eleven-year-old Johnny Brandon arrived at the school, Bradley stripped him of the cloying "teeth and eyes" mannerisms of the stagey child performer, replaced his Tiller Girl training with hip Berry Brothers struts, and befriended him, opening the child's eyes to a new world through the works of Richard Wright, Zora Neale Hurston, James Weldon Johnson, *The Chicago Defender*, *The Crisis*, and an indie music newspaper, *Harlem Jazz*.[1]

Perhaps Bradley hadn't changed because he knew from experience that nothing lasts forever. Even now, despite the seeming immutability of London, a vague unease hovered. Developments on the Continent troubled Whitehall. A monarchical crisis loomed. A mining disaster called powers and values into question. Even Aurelius didn't stay long in London, having run into labor permit issues. (He then went off to Paris with vague ideas about opening a dance school, but was back in New York in 1939, performing as Arthur Bradley and closing out a show for Buck and Bubbles at the Apollo Theater.)[2]

Now in his early thirties and internationally acclaimed, Bradley reconnected with his roots. Of the twenty-odd projects he choreographed between 1936 and 1938, *Follow the Sun*, *Blackbirds of 1936*, and *Burnt Sepia* featured African American dancers. The intersection of Bradley's dance origins and London style reinvigorated him and led to dance exchanges that crisscrossed the Atlantic.

If Bradley mourned the departure of Aurelius, he had little time to brood: Charles Cochran's *Follow the Sun* beckoned, luring him with opportunities to experiment and innovate tap dancing. With great dancers like Jeni Le Gon and Claire Luce in the cast, the revue was a delicate undertaking. Both stars, in different ways, required special handling.

Bradley knew he had a cutting-edge number in "The Lady with the Tap," a dance about a spy who communicates via tempos and taps as she runs up and down flights of stairs. For the first, thrilling time, the percussive sounds of tap drove a story, elevating rhythm and sound to a leading role in dance. He also had a problem. Claire Luce, a former student of the Pierce Studio with a languid, sensual style, had famously conferred sex appeal on Fred Astaire before the advent of Ginger Rogers. Now she was recuperating from a career-threatening injury (ironically caused by Astaire, who had fallen on her during a prop mishap, fracturing her hip and tearing a knee). Doctors had told Luce her dancing career was over, but, at thirty-three and at heart a dancer, she leapt at the chance when Cochran offered her a big dance role in *Follow the Sun*.

Eager to rebound, Luce had neglected to mention she didn't know how to tap (found in Luce's archive is a desperate note-to-self on Rockefeller Center letterhead: "Have never tapped in my LIFE—speak to Eleanor [Powell]!!") In record time, Bradley had to turn the slinky Luce into a sophisticated tap dancer, one who could communicate subtle gradations of sound. With an unprepared dancer and a dance that required an expensive, multilevel set, Cochran debated cutting the number. Luce convinced him the dance was too exciting to eliminate.[3]

Luce and Bradley were right to advocate for the dance. "The Lady with the Tap" told a narrative as no other dance form could.

Raves came in for Bradley's unprecedented "all tap-dancing ballet" and for the cleanly tap-dancing Luce. Consistent with her doctor's warning, however, dancing "The Lady with the Tap" definitively, if gloriously, ended Luce's dancing career. Luce, who had a habit of dropping into Cartier for cigarette cases for special men of her acquaintance—both Winston and Randolph Churchill were recipients of her largesse—now expressed her gratitude to Bradley with a glamorous cigarette case. With its happy associations, Bradley gave it pride of place in his ever-expanding collection.[4]

Jeni Le Gon, Bradley's other star, was also feeling blue. After fetchingly dancing in trousers with Bill "Bojangles" Robinson in *Hooray for Love*, she had been cast in *Broadway Melody of 1936*, as was Eleanor Powell. Neither Le Gon nor Powell were pliant feminine dancers, happily dancing backward in heels like Ginger Rogers. Le Gon could do flips, splits, double spins, and toe stands to rival the Nicholas Brothers, and Powell favored intricate routines she choreographed herself. There was little room in Hollywood for any woman who challenged sexual typecasting, let alone two in one movie. Having second thoughts, Metro-Goldwyn-Mayer kept the white hoofer with the Black sound and, in a bruising blow to Le Gon, bought the actual Black tap dancer out of her contract.

Agent-manager Earl Dancer (one of the three ubiquitous Dancer brothers—it was his brother, John, who had prepped Bradley for his debut at Connie's Inn) now tactfully whisked Le Gon out of sight and into the hands of Bradley in London. Bradley was sympathetic. Le Gon, young, vital, and made for the spotlight, had encountered the realities he had tiptoed around for years. He took her under his wing, as he had Henry Le Tang and Eddie Williams. Soon Le Gon was in the cast of *Follow the Sun* and had a British film contract.[5]

Le Gon and Bradley continued their mirror experiences in *Follow the Sun*, when issues arising in Le Gon's two dances affected both dancer and choreographer. In "The Steam Boat Whistle," the problem was clothes. Set on a quay as a Mississippi steamboat unloads its cargo and shot out of a barrel, Le Gon portrays a sunny gamine dressed in a raggedy pair of shorts and a polka-dot shirt. The pickaninny costume, besides falling into racial stereotype, referred to Florence Mills, who had donned similar togs in 1924's *Dixie to Broadway*, and reinforced the idea of Le Gon as the new Mills. This was not only demeaning but unfair. Le Gon was a superlative dancer with a charismatic presence and style all her own—why did she have to be slotted into someone else's success? Couldn't there be multiple ways to be a successful Black dancer? The question touched Bradley every bit as much as Le Gon; his own work bucked preconceived norms of Black dance, too.

The question posed by "A Brand New Suit," was a variation on the same theme—expressing individuality despite predetermined expectations—but the issue was dance itself. In the Broadway version of the show (titled *At Home Abroad* in New York), "A Brand New Suit" had been sung by Ethel Waters and danced by Eleanor Powell. Le Gon could handle the singing; she was a veteran of the Whitman Sisters troupe and had been coached in singing by Fats Waller, after all. But dancing in the literal footsteps of Powell, her very recent rival, stung. Bradley understood and deftly rechoreographed the dance to showcase Le Gon's spritely style, earning her accolades for charm, speed, and originality. Years later, Le Gon spoke about Bradley's choreography with admiration and fondly recalled how he supported her at a difficult juncture. Coincidentally, she took career cues from him, too. After a frustrating Hollywood career, she, too, turned her talents to behind-the-scenes teaching, coaching, and choreography.[6]

Blackbirds of 1936 was a homecoming for Bradley—the timely reconnect, at the apex of his career, with American jazz dance. His friends were back. Ditto the dances and the sounds that were his touchstones. Jules Bledsoe (of the baby blue Packard) was starring. The J. Rosamond Johnson Chorus, a mainstay of the Harlem Renaissance, supplied music. The Blackbirds Beauty Chorus, assembled from the best chorus dancers in Harlem, brought speed, dash, and precision. It was also exciting. Top-notch African American talent, including Fayard and Harold Nicholas, arguably the most explosive tap dancers of the twentieth century, now came face-to-face with the aesthetic Bradley had developed in London. Inspired by his style, they returned to America and studied ballet and acrobatics.

(The flawless results can be seen to this day in their "Jumpin' Jive" number in *Stormy Weather*.)[7]

The show annointed Bradley, the darling of the West End, a choreographer of Black dances for Black dancers. Once again, if not for Cochran, it may not have happened. Lew Leslie, the impresario whose all-Black revues had catapulted Florence Mills and Bill Robinson to international fame, never used a choreographer. He merely instructed his dancers in each *Blackbirds* revue to repeat their past successes, then improvised the staging. But Cochran refused to present the 1936 West End show with Leslie's usual disjointed rehash of dances and insisted that Bradley choreograph, making him the only choreographer, Black or white, to ever work on a *Blackbirds* revue.[8]

At a moment when his exploration lifted him to new levels of invention, *Blackbirds* grounded Bradley in his dance foundations. The opener, "Negro Cavalcade," with program notes by James Weldon Johnson, spanned from the landing of slaves at Jamestown, cotton fields, folklore, ragtime, and syncopation, to the birth of the blues, America's folk music. Intended to place jazz dance in historical context for an English audience, the introduction was also a timely review course for Bradley. As *Blackbirds* overlapped with the preproduction for *It's Love Again*, it's interesting to consider how Bradley's artistic refresher in *Blackbirds* translated into dances in his upcoming film.[9]

Influences fly back and forth within *Blackbirds of 1936*. In "Professional Night at the Ubangi Club," Bradley ends with a snappy Harlem-style walkaround finale, blending the polyrhythms he had performed in speakeasies with the complex formations and graceful upper body he developed in England. As the men moved forward on a four-four beat, simultaneously doffing their hats in slow, sustained time and bobbing their heads in double time, they weave patterns with the women, who, stepping back on the beat, wave their arms in slow, sustained time and twist their torsos. (He then reinterprets all into the sauntering riff walk in *It's Love Again*.) Bradley's loose, fluid choreography, punctuated with pulses of the head, wrists, and knees, also made the Blackbirds Beauty Chorus vibrate with rhythm in "Keep a Twinkle in Your Eye." The smooth-twisting motion of the torso working with and against the shimmying shoulders anticipates Bradley's tap solo for Matthews in *It's Love Again*, with its blend of African polyrhythms and Frederick Ashton's epaulement.[10]

Ever the intrepid pioneer, Bradley next ventured into a new medium: television. Taking on the choreography for *Burnt Sepia*, a BBC cabaret show focusing on talent of color, was a stimulating new challenge that involved climbing over cables, working in the restricted space of a television set, and understanding the new technology. Successful televised dances, he discovered, had to be arranged so that there was never a vacant spot in the center. A small group was more successful than a large one, as it allowed individual faces to be seen. Big ensembles could only be satisfactory if there was an overhead camera. It was an apprenticeship that would serve him well as he worked in television on and off through the 1960s.[11]

As *Burnt Sepia* also coincided with the closing of the precariously financed *Blackbirds of 1936*, Bradley conveniently had his pick among the unemployed Blackbirds Beauty Chorus for his Sepia Chorines. This not only prolonged his work with top American jazz dancers; it gave the Blackbirds Beauty Chorus dancers yet another chance to absorb the Bradley style before returning to American stages and studios.[12]

In the West End, the theater reflected the confusion of an abdication crisis that had turned a nation upside down. Revues and musicals of varying significance and success came and went, some of which had silver linings for Bradley. On the disastrous *Floodlight*, Bradley solidified his relationship with orchestrator Benjamin Frankel, who would collaborate with him to write dance music "note by step" and develop the BBC program *Swing Song*. On *Take It Easy*, he met ingenue Patricia Burke, who was the daughter of operatic tenor Thomas Burke and actress Marie Burke, and who would become his lover. In Blackpool, a dance extravaganza called *All the Best* reunited him with premier danseur Anton Dolin, African American singer Elisabeth Welch, and music hall legend Stanley Holloway. It was here, too, that Bradley created the North's answer to Noël Gay's Lambeth Walk, the Blackpool Walk, a dance that swept the North and headed toward London that summer.[13]

After choreographing these indifferent shows, all of which required just as much effort as a smash, it was a relief to turn to a sure-fire Charles Cochran project, *Happy Returns*, a revue that celebrated Beatrice Lillie's return to the London stage. Bradley choreographed a Viennese waltz set to Gershwin, a Highland fling set to jazz, tap dance numbers, and the introduction of a new social dance, "The Piccadilly." If the revue summarized the breadth of Bradley's work in London, the cast encapsulated Bradley's career. There was Constance Carpenter—it was Bradley's dances for her in *A Connecticut Yankee* in New York that had catapulted him to visibility—as well as relative newcomer Patricia Burke and tried-and-true Bradley chorus dancers, praised by *The Observer* as never better selected nor in better form. Phyllis Stanley, whom Bradley had once tumbled out of a bookcase in *Lucky Break*, had honed her style, lighting up the stage with her confident attack. In keeping with the uncertain moment, the show also looked back, resurrecting old Cochran hits: Constance Carpenter performed "Dancing on the Ceiling" from *Evergreen*, and there was even a nod to Florence Mills with "I'm a Little Blackbird."[14]

Happy Returns closed an era. The following fall, the Munich Pact, allowing Nazi Germany to annex Czechoslovakia, was signed, and with it the taste for expensive, worldly entertainments vanished. Bradley was changing, too. His refocus in "The Lady with the Tap" on the pure sound of tap and his reconnection with African American dancers in *Blackbirds* had sown new ideas about dance. The changing environment would encourage Bradley's pursuit of these ideas. As the world changed, so would Bradley's dance.

PART 5

SHIFTS IN RHYTHM, 1939–1960

CHAPTER 19

DANCING IN THE BLITZ

Dance is a reflection of the human spirit,
a testament to our resilience and strength.

—KATHERINE DUNHAM

Bradley was at the Coliseum Theatre on the morning of September 3, 1939, preparing for the opening of a new play for Jessie Matthews, *I Can Take It*, when Prime Minister Neville Chamberlain declared Britain at war. The country that had offered Bradley a lifeline was now facing its own peril. By the time Matthews arrived at the theater, Bradley had fully registered the news and was in tears.[1]

Bradley was not indulging in histrionics. An army would be flung into the sea. London would burn; cities would be destroyed. The English people would live in a constant state of anxiety for six years, subject to shortages of petrol and food, sleepless nights and air raids, displaced children, and missing loved ones. Once the ordeal was over, Britain found that its social fabric had unraveled, its culture had evolved, and its position on the world stage was ambiguous—revered for standing up to the Third Reich and economically tottering. Nothing would be the same again.

Though he experienced the war profoundly—his flat was bombed and no aspect of his life could now be taken for granted—Bradley, like Britian, carried on. Contemporaneous reviews show that his work—two dozen plays and films—remained consistent in quality and imagination. What stands out in his work during this time are three themes: a deepening commitment to rhythm, percussion, and tap dancing; relationships with creatives that facilitated his own creativity; and a slow pivot to ever more youthful dancers.

At first, producing any work seemed unlikely. After declaring war, the government closed all theaters, with *The Daily Express* sanctimoniously explaining that there was no place for culture in wartime. (Even television transmission was suspended, with Mickey Mouse unceremoniously interrupted halfway through a cartoon.) Twelve days later, the decree was reversed: theater, it was determined, raised morale and was an act of resistance. Despite the droning planes overhead, the whine of falling bombs, the deafening crashes as buildings were hit and crumbled, the theater thrived during the war—after all, if you are going to meet your fate, why not do so while having fun?

That did not mean, however, that theater continued as before. With the imposed blackout rendering London dark and impossible to navigate at night, most plays switched to an afternoon schedule. Treatments shifted from reflective to raucous; one needed to laugh more and ponder less. Rationing meant simplified costumes, sets, and effects while content and choreography, to compensate, had to be stronger. When the supply line of Scandinavian wood pulp was cut, paper became scarce and glossy programs were replaced by single-page newsprint foldouts. With an existential threat always hovering overhead, programs spelled out instructions to keep calm and remain in the theater in the case of an air raid—if one had to leave, to do so quietly and without excitement.

Films were affected even more drastically. Much of the British film industry repurposed its resources and personnel for the war, reducing film production. When films continued to be made, they were often menaced: Bradley's final war-era film was *Flight from Folly*, a lavish musical frolic with one hundred dancers presented in the form of a page from a psychiatrist's notebook. Two days before completion, a direct hit destroyed the studios at Teddington, resulting in a six-month delay in the film's release.[2]

Wartime required a new dexterity, an ability to reimagine, reconfigure, and refashion. *I Can Take It*, the play with Matthews, was rolled up and repackaged as a revue and toured the provinces. Bradley's revue with Beatrice Lillie, *All Clear*, was the first West End production to be transported in its entirety to an army camp, the garrison at Aldershot. Bradley also sent a string of Buddy Bradley Girls off with Jack Buchanan on an ENSA (Entertainments National Service Association) tour in France. Even his nightclub gigs reflected the war: when Italy joined the Axis powers, Italian maître d's who had reigned over Monseigneur, Quaglino's, the Embassy Club, and other nighteries were summarily dismissed. (If a catering establishment name closed in a vowel, so did the joint, quipped a journalist.) When the Embassy Club reopened under new management, Bradley staged the floor show. With so many men at war, Bradley himself returned to the boards, dancing in 1943's *Magic Carpet* and accepting a featured role in Jack Buchanan's *It's Time to Dance*. Bradley's role was not a cameo—he appeared throughout the show and in the process revealed inherent skills as an actor, which led to later work. Meanwhile, excerpts from *It's Time to Dance* were performed for the armed forces on the BBC on Monday, September 27, 1943.[3]

Bradley's dances registered war in subject and sensibility. *Light's Up!* opened with a cheeky number that incorporated gas masks in its choreography; elsewhere, Bradley's dances referenced the Royal Air Force (RAF), air raid shelters, and coupon rationing. War also permeated the studio. Bradley now anxiously counted noses at rehearsals. Some dancers didn't survive the previous night's raid, casting a pall over the ensemble and requiring a flurry of choreographic adjustments and recasting. Those dancers who did survive now became anonymous to the public—there was no longer room to print their individual names in the diminished programs.

Whether responding to the waning cosmopolitanism of London or feeling he had gone full circle with his experiments of the 1930s, Bradley's work increasingly embraced rhythm, percussion, and American tap. In "Rhythmic Echoes," in *Come Out to Play*, he staged three sets of dancers, each group performing different steps in counterpoint to the same music. In the title number for

La-Di-Da-Di-Da, the whole company broke out in rhythmic exercises. In *Full Swing*, Bradley had four dancers execute a drum routine. A year later, in a natural follow-up to the drum exercise, three Bradley veterans produced a rhythm exercise with xylophones in *Something in the Air*. In the film *King Arthur Was a Gentleman*, Bradley choreographed with flamboyant African American percussionist Freddie Crump a drumming routine that played off eyeglasses, officers' shoulder boards, and, even, teeth.[4]

Bradley now spoke directly about his own jazz heritage, hosting *Black Magic*, a BBC radio program for the armed forces in which he reminisced about the Black musicians with whom he had worked on Broadway and in Harlem. *Variety* reported that he followed up *Black Magic* with a five-part BBC series on how a tap dancer was made, though records of this program are unavailable.[5]

Amid wartime adjustments and accommodations, Cochran, increasingly frail, remained a constant for Bradley. A photo of the two conspiratorially huddling during auditions in 1940 for *Lights Up!* indicates the continued closeness of their relationship. Typical of Cochran's largesse, the producer showed his support for De Gaulle and the Free French by instructing the orchestra to open *Light's Up!* with "La Marseillaise," before playing "God Save the King." Bradley, too, rose to wartime gallantry: in contrast to co-choreographer Antony Tudor's studied historic dances, Bradley's routines offered sassy takes on battle dress, wartime dinner parties, and the desirability of dashing RAF pilots (a.k.a. the "Brylcreem Boys") over soldiers and sailors. Most notable of all was his transformation of dancer Robert Lindon.[6]

Dressed in burgundy pajamas and described as "grabbing chunks of air" as he danced, Lindon caused a small sensation in Bradley's "Marihuana." Only four years earlier, as an uncredited male dancer, he briefly flirted with fame when pulled out of the chorus to partner Claire Luce in *Gay Deceivers*, then fell back into obscurity dancing in middling nightclubs—until he connected with Bradley. In 1939, Lindon introduced "The Shag," the latest jive dance from South Carolina, at the Empire in 1939 (on a bill with Fats Waller, no less), then danced the "Marihuana" number in *Lights Up!* Coached by Bradley, Lindon's fluid body, rippling hands, and skull-like face mesmerized audiences. The next year he followed up his newfound notoriety with a spot in George Black's *Black Vanities*, where he garnered attention, not surprisingly, for a slinky dance wearing little more than a coat of gold paint.[7]

After five collaborations, Bradley and his orchestrator, Ben Frankel, who had written dance music "note by step" with Bradley for the *Swing Song* radio series, barely needed to exchange a word as they set the dances for 1941's *Orchids and Onions*. While Buddy danced a few steps, hummed a few bars, and established his desired rhythms, Frankel stood by the footlights in the Comedy Theatre, cigarette holder in hand, and made marks on a music sheet. Then the dancers would come onstage to work on a number like "Aggravating Rhythm," and Frankel would attentively make more notations as Buddy set the dance, then hand the marked score to conductor Lew Stone.[8]

Despite effervescent satires such as "Pepper Podgers and Fascinating Fred" and "Ballet Ptomaine Poisoning," a send-up of lunchtime ballets (a new development in response to the blacked-out evenings), war cast its shadow over *Orchids and Onions*, where nerves were frayed and raw. Four of Bradley's chorus girls were shaken refugees from the Café de Paris, which weeks earlier had sustained the hit that killed Ken "Snakehips" Johnson. Composer Jayne Ogden had written the show in a flat with the windows blown out from bombings. On opening night, *Orchids and Onions*, still running long in its shakedown period, was cut short by the arrival of London bobbies, enforcing the blackout regulation that theaters must be closed by 8:15 p.m. The Blitz left no room for negotiation.[9]

Bradley's personal refuge from the high alerts and chronic stress was now a mews house in Tyburnia, a leafy enclave north of Hyde Park. In contrast to the humble mews courtyard with craftsmen's workshops, a stable, and a pub, the Mitre, Bradley's five-room house was glamorous, kitted out with blue damask, cream strié walls, a custom lighting plan, an up-to-date tiled bath, an eight-valve Philco radio, the famous collection of gifted cigarette cases, and—somewhat incongruously—a patchwork quilt on his bed. While Bradley's investment in decoration suggests the mews house was intended as a permanent home, not a waystation, 8 Somerset Mews was not destined for eternity. A casualty of the Blitz, it did not survive the war.[10]

Like the resolute East Enders, Bradley was a survivor. Though bereft of furnishings and personal effects, he was soon living nearby in Radnor Lodge, an Italianate nineteenth-century terrace house on the corner of Radnor Place and Sussex Gardens. Also living at Radnor Lodge was former Mr. Cochran Young Lady, singer, dancer, and actress Patricia Burke. Tongues wagged.

Bradley and Burke had worked together on the disastrous 1937 *Take It Easy*, where Burke had nevertheless received promising reviews ("Applause goes to Patricia Burke who is worthy of something good," wrote *The Daily Herald*), and Bradley's dances passed unscathed. They reconnected in 1938 in *Happy Returns*, where Burke distinguished herself via her personality and professionalism. That same year, she married Michael William Kimpton, an RAF officer. Now she appeared everywhere, often connected with Bradley. She was photographed in *The Sketch* taking a class at the Bradley studio with ballet mistress Mary Skeaping and hoofing with Jean Gillie while Bradley, debonaire in pleated trousers with sweater tucked at the waist, smilingly led a rehearsal. She was photographed in a bombed-out dressing room of a Bradley revue, looking leggy and wistful. In July 1940, the twenty-three-year-old was captured exiting the columned portico of Radnor Lodge laden with household items destined for a wartime collection of aluminum to be repurposed for fighter planes.[11]

In 1942, *Picture Post* ran a photo of Bradley rehearsing Burke for her role as Colin, the Principal Boy—a plum role her mother, an actress, had once played—in the pantomime *Mother Goose*. Bradley and Burke are looking into each other's eyes and smiling, matching their stance and rhythm, similarly attired in Cary Grant–style trousers, shirts, sweaters, and ties. In theory, Barbara Aitken was responsible for the dances of the panto, but all of Burke's dances were arranged by Bradley and the chorus was trained by Bradley, with the assistance of Burke. The private coaching paid off: Burke, displaying a swagger as manful as Rosalind's, was deemed reason alone to see the show.[12]

That Bradley and a married actress were having an affair raised few eyebrows in the theater, especially during wartime, when loneliness and amorous entanglements abounded. The scandal was the reaction of Burke's mother, the outspoken actress Marie Burke, who was said to be a communist. Mama stood on the sidewalk outside of Radnor Lodge in the wee hours of the night and screamed at her daughter to get out of Bradley's bed, so vociferous and disruptive that the police were called to restore peace in the genteel neighborhood. Of course, her daughter had a promising career ahead of her that would be derailed by a pregnancy, which may have been a legitimate concern of any mother. But one can't help but wonder, as surely Bradley did, if the color of his skin was at the heart of her objections. Wasn't pregnancy, after all, just as much a risk in her daughter's married life as in her liaison with Bradley?

Bradley couldn't invest much time pondering injustice as he rushed off to register for the US draft, contribute choreography to two war-specific plays—an Anglo-Polish production, *Wednesday After the War*, and the treacly *Room V*, by Peter Wendy, a nom de plume for a writer believed to be a member of General Wavell's staff—then slip into the stalls of the Palace Theatre with Cochran to select a new crop of Young Ladies for *Big Top*. (They also selected the Buddy Bradley Boys, but this was nearly a fait accompli, as Bradley had four agile teens from his school, including the brash Johnny Brandon, that Cochran readily approved.)

After a two-year hiatus, Charles B. Cochran had come roaring back to produce *Big Top*, his last revue, pairing Bradley and Ben Frankel with Herbert Farjeon's wicked book. Bradley's new crop of Young Ladies was very young—one was only fourteen—and anticipated the postwar world. Like the boogie-woogie dance Bradley had created for *Wednesday After the War* and Robert Lindon's Shag at the Empire, vitality and freshness were gradually replacing the grace and sophistication of the 1930s.[13]

But not all of Bradley's dancers were young sprigs—yet. Amid the madcap antics of Jack Hulbert in *Full Swing*, the reality of war marched into the theater, echoing the grim photos from the Russian and Burmese fronts that sat alongside the play's review in the London *Times*. The *Full Swing* chorus line included veterans of ENSA shows, dancers whose overseas careers had been curtailed by war, and wives and widows of RAF men. And, just as a frothy plot mixing spies, psychoanalysis, and South American adventure was a surefire antidote to war, Bradley's choreography raised morale. Dances included the Letter Ballet, with flying jetés and dancers en pointe; a tango for Gerald Fitzgerald; and a spoof on the worshipping of eurythmics by an earnest aesthete, but it was Bradley's renewed focus on rhythm, with his chorus executing a drum routine, that made the biggest splash.[14]

Elsewhere, Bradley pulsed American-style swing into *Green for Piccadilly*, where a bevy of athletic beauties "swung" their barracks drill. In the same revue, he choreographed a samba, backed by a well-drilled team of dancers who provided rhythmic background, for Evelyn Dall, the vocalist for the Bert Ambrose Orchestra described by *The Times* as "vivacity in a bandbox." He worked with Dall again in the film *King Arthur Was a Gentleman*, creating a jazzy shimmy number in "Bee in My Bonnet" and the even more memorable "Actions Speak Louder than Words," in which Dall dances in a Quonset hut, music and dance shaping her entire body from swinging hips, polyrhythmic head bobs, shaking shoulders, emphatic stamps, easy knees, and stylized hands as she moves up and down the aisle among her bunkmates.[15]

There was another reason Bradley swung. In 1943, Pete Nugent came to London with the US Army's all-soldier benefit revue *This Is the Army* by Irving Berlin, for which he was performer, dance captain, and choreographer for the African American dancers. Soloing in "Putting on the Ritz," retitled and reworked as "What the Well-Dressed Man in Harlem Will Wear" (an Army uniform), Nugent brought Bradley's focus squarely back on African American tap.

After years as a dance pioneer in London, Bradley welcomed kindred company, particularly when it was Nugent, a friend since his Hoofers' Club days. Admiring Nugent as a Class Act dancer,

Bradley invited him to guest teach at his school, recently relocated to 12 Denman Street. Nugent accepted, bringing with him his colorful vocabulary and delicate riffs, but at the time he couldn't break down steps or routines, so Bradley acted as his co-teacher. Reminiscing with Marshall Stearns twenty years later, Nugent, by then a seasoned teacher himself, having run the celebrated Dance Craft studio with Honi Coles in New York, ranked Bradley as the greatest teacher of all time.[16]

Long glamorously associated with African American jazz, subtle American tap acquired further cachet from Yank vitality currently seeping into London. One of the many now flocking to Bradley's new studio near Piccadilly Circus was future television personality Bruce Forsyth. At first, he found Bradley's teaching frustrating. He had already been teaching tap dance in his garage and thought himself an accomplished dancer; now Bradley insisted that Forsyth return to the basics, methodically learning to "feel the floor," before advancing to his Number One and Number Two dance routines.

For young Forsyth, the immediate thrill of air raids—when dancers would race from the top floor to the basement, then rush back to the studio after the all-clear signal to not miss a single minute of class—counterbalanced the painstaking process of recrafting tap skills to Bradley's standards. (Finding his idol Jack Buchanan, one of the rare British dancers who danced in the relaxed American style, rehearsing his *Top Hat and Tails* routines with Bradley, provided another high.) And though he never advanced to Bradley's most advanced routines, Forsyth became a lifelong proselytizer of American tap dance in Britain, routinely inviting Sammy Davis Jr. to guest on his popular television program, *Sunday Night at the London Palladium*.[17]

Since arriving at Bradley's studio, Johnny Brandon had graduated from kiddie star to juvenile lead. With Bradley's help, he won both the Gene Kelly role in the West End production of William Saroyan's *The Time of Your Life* and a tap spot in *Big Top*, as a leering boss of Patricia Burke in "Office Rhythm." Bradley now brought Brandon with him to watch tennis at Wimbledon, the Roland Petit ballet, *Deep Are the Roots* at the theater, and on his monthly visit to Keith Prowse on Regent Street, where he would stock up on the latest recordings by Dizzy Gillespie and Chick Webb. He also introduced Brandon to pot. "It's just an herb," Bradley told him. "You'll hear every beat more clearly."[18]

Fifteen-year-old Sheila Mathews was also thrilled to be studying with Bradley—so excited, in fact, that after climbing over wreckage and avoiding unexploded bombs en route, she flew up the dusty stairs to Bradley's studio, eager to begin dancing. Fatigued by sleepless nights in air raid shelters, dancing every day from 10 to 5—tap with Bradley in the morning, ballet with Mary Skeaping in the afternoon—became her salvation.

At first, as the youngest in the studio, Mathews deferentially hung in the back of tap class, awed by the first-row stars such as Jean Gillie and Patricia Burke, and modestly danced Bradley's upbeat routines—including the World War II anthem "Boogie Woogie Bugle Boy"—as well as what she describes as his lovely legato choreography. Within a year, however, Bradley asked her to come to the front of the class and entrusted her with his coveted "In the Mood" routine. She adored dancing it, marveling every time how perfectly each Bradley step fit the Glen Miller arrangement.

She also worked hard at ballet, for ballet was a serious undertaking at the Bradley studio, far removed from "expressive" dancing in soft slippers. Bradley wanted his dancers to have the same supple arms, flexible backs, and fine-tuned awareness of shoulder and head placement that he found in the movement of Ashton, Ada May, and Jessie Matthews. In the 1940s, he hired Mary Skeaping as his ballet mistress. An adherent of the Cecchetti method, Skeaping still used an old-fashioned stick to teach ballet and had her women dancers work in pointe shoes. Later, she became the director of the Royal Swedish Ballet and staged a historical recreation of *Giselle* for the English National Ballet that is performed to this day.

En route to a continuous career in the West End and on Broadway and her own television program, *Friday's Girl*, in the 1950s, Sheila Mathews found Bradley a constant, if somewhat formal, champion. Understanding her need to dance, Bradley gave her the keys to the studio, allowing her to stay after hours with her favorite partner, Donald Reed, dancing until the sweat poured off their bodies. He noticed disapprovingly when she plucked her eyebrows à la Marlene Dietrich, and he carefully monitored her progress with auditions. (She was invariably singled out for her Bradley style, the suppleness of her back, and how dance flowed through her entire body.) One of her first engagements was in an RAF-Army revue starring Frances Day, choreographed by Bradley and coached by his assistant in the 1940s, Dot Bachelor. And while Bradley packed her off for each audition with advice tailored for each show, Mathews soon found such tips hardly mattered; once it was known she had been trained by Bradley, she was usually hired without an audition.

With the victory at Stalingrad in February 1943 representing a turning point to the war, a lightness, unforced and disarming, returned to the theater. Jack Hulbert's *Something in the Air* (a.k.a. *Sorry, Darling*) swept into the Palace Theatre with a premise that forecasted the social changes after the war: the grand owner of a requisitioned house, an enlisted man in the RAF, now deferentially serves drinks to officers billeted in his own house. Bradley provided the dances, orchestrated by Ben Frankel, selecting a chorus that *The Times* said could be called, without presumption, the prettiest in town. Peggy Watson, Sabina Gordon, and Eunice Crowther danced the clever "Housemaids Dance" with bowed caps and feather dusters, then produced the aforementioned rhythm exercise with xylophones.[19]

In June 1944, Sheila Mathews was beyond excited to be performing at the illustrious London Palladium, when she received a telegram instructing her to retrieve her top hat, tails, and cane from the costume mistress and plan on a trip out of town. Dutifully, she collected her costume and climbed into a van with comedian Tommy Trinder and singer Elisabeth Welch. When she walked onto the stage, she was overwhelmed by the size of the audience, even bigger than the Palladium, London's largest live theater. She found herself alone, facing an entire football (i.e., soccer) stadium, with ground forces filling the stands and the field. She performed her number, "Lit Up," and was pleased it went well, then, as mysteriously as they arrived, the three were bundled back into the van and returned to London. The next morning, she shuddered when she learned about the Normandy landings. She had performed for the departing forces on the eve of D-Day. Many in the audience would never return.

The long war was at last coming to an end. Weeks after the Japanese surrender, *Fine Feathers* opened at the Prince of Wales Theatre. Featuring Jack Buchanan and choreographed by Buddy Bradley and Joan Davis, its humor, wit, and gaiety matched the public's celebratory mood, earning it an enthusiastic reception. Though the playbill was still of the skimpy variety—it would take Britain years to recover from the privations of war—the very excesses of fabric, at their loveliest in shades of purple, mauve, and gray for "Ladies of the Evening," made the very idea of rationing coupons seem silly. Buchanan sang poignantly about finding one's way back to a richer life, one with color, choice, and nuance. The dancers, as in any Bradley production, were praised. Once such results were a matter of course; during the war they were nearly miraculous.[20]

But *Fine Feathers* now felt faintly quaint. Its fuss about old school ties, colonial outposts, and top hats and tails no longer aligned with the mood of the day. Only "Question Time," with a refrain referencing current politics ("Why don't they liberate [Prime Minister] Attlee from his friend [Marxist] Harold J. Laski?,") bore any relevance to the issues of the day. Britain now faced the dilemma of how to replace wartime austerity with a new vision to redistribute wealth and improve housing, nutrition, employment, and education for all. Buchanan, of the ageless charm, as well as Mr. Cochran's Young Ladies and fantastical art deco sets, had little place in this brave new world.[21]

Though new challenges lay ahead, it was time for a victory lap. Time and time again, the British entertainment world, from Bradley, Cochran, Frankel, and Buchanan down to the last fourteen-year-old chorus girl, had reached deep into their personal reserves and produced, through sheer will, work that instilled hope in a dark moment, work that spoke, even in the most blithe and irreverent terms, of civilization and a future. After six long years, Bradley was no longer a visitor in London. He was a defender of all it represented.

Conversely, his work became more American. For twenty years, Bradley's dance intertwined with time and place. His origins as a tap dancer during the Harlem Renaissance had born him aloft to Broadway. Over the past decade in London his fluid, exploratory work dovetailed with a cosmopolitan city and the end of an empire. Throughout, his leitmotif was musicality, refined technique, and adherence to jazz music. Now he brought these elements to renew his focus on tap, rhythm, and percussion. In the new world order, this core would become his north star.

CHAPTER 20

ALL THAT JAZZ

Jazz is about being in the moment.

—HERBIE HANCOCK

Churchill's V-E Day address from a Whitehall balcony spoke volumes. With the simple words "My dear friends, this is your victory," he credited the British people—those who had stood alert on rooftops, slept in bomb shelters, sacrificed household necessities, sent their children to live with strangers, survived on unpalatable food, and kept munitions factories running—with the peace. It was astounding, really. He, the great hero of World War II, born in Blenheim Palace, now humbly recognized the contribution of the people to the well-being of Britain, their work as essential as that of toffs in Parliament, titans in the City, or even the valiant armed forces. The recognition flipped institutional power and tradition on its head. A rising Labour government, a country in tatters, the transformative effect of television, and the increasing cultural influence of America were changing the landscape of British politics, society, and entertainment.

So began the postwar era, one of both exhilaration and uncertainty for Bradley. The joy of walking in a newly illuminated London, of resuming old performing schedules, and the return of Jessie Matthews, Adelaide Hall, and Noël Coward from ENSA tours alternated with qualms and a new catalyst. On one hand, Bradley watched musical theater shift from sassy, jazz-based Rodgers and Hart to sentimental, lyrical Rodgers and Hammerstein. On the other, he reveled in the arrival and innovations of the African American dancers now flooding London, from Johnny Worthy, Mable Lee, L. D. Jackson, and Carnell (a.k.a Cornell) Lyons, to Katherine Dunham.

More than ever, his school was a magnet for the entertainment industry, with chairs permanently lined up in the front of the studio to receive distinguished visitors from Duke Ellington to international film directors. At the same time, the democratization of society, accompanied by the growing tendency to stay home and find entertainment on the emerging medium of television, new music, and a hobbled economy, meant navigating new taste and entertainment structures.

Nightclubs would linger on life support a bit longer—Bradley was commissioned to create "The Churchill Hop" for the opening of the Churchill's Club on Bond Street—but the new bebop music coming from America now called into question the fundamental connection of dance and music. Drummer Art Blakey articulated the attitude of bebop musicians, shrugging off dancers with a gruff "We don't need them" after nonchalantly disrupting Pete Nugent, mid-solo, with a spontaneous barrage of syncopated accents, otherwise known as "bombs."[1]

Though Bradley accepted the new music, writing an article on bebop for *Musical Express*, he recognized the ground was shifting beneath him. Bebop, with its irregular phrases, perplexed dancers accustomed to the regular beat of the big bands. Former Whitey's Lindy Hopper Frankie Manning, just released from the Army, stopped at Minton's in Harlem to check out the new sound. The new jazz was cool music, he realized, intended for listening, not dancing, and emphasized musicians as artists, not entertainers. Small stages dictated intimate clubs and smaller movement; large dramatic movement was for vast dance floors like the Savoy Ballroom and passé musicals.[2]

While Busby Berkeley sulked and attempted suicide in Hollywood, Bradley adapted constructively in London. One of his first peacetime projects, *Here Come the Boys*, was another timely satire on role reversals, spoofing the interaction of a man and his very spiffy butler, who had far outranked him in the army. It also represented a role reversal for Bradley. In the past, he occasionally shared dance responsibility with another choreographer, usually a ballet choreographer who would contribute a piece or two, such as George Balanchine in *Cochran's 1931 Revue* or Antony Tudor in *Lights Up!*, but, as the preeminent dance director in the West End, he always had overall responsibility for the show. Now choreography was democratically distributed between Bradley; star Jack Hulbert, Bradley's longtime tap student; and Lydia Sokolova (née Hilda Munnings), formerly of the Ballets Russes.

If Bradley was a bit rattled by this new development, his rhythm dances nevertheless flourished. While Sokolova's daughter, Natasha, floated in and out of the numbers, Hulbert executed a little tap and included a sand dance. Eunice Crowther, whom Buddy had used so effectively in the drumming routine in *Full Swing*, now danced syncopated routines with the Rhythm Brothers. Marie Sellar, who had made her name on the ENSA circuit, was applauded for her "modern" tap dance. Precisely what was meant by "modern" tap is not clear, but contemporaneous cultural currents in London provide a clue.[3]

Though postwar Britain was gray and hollowed out—rationing continued for ten more years and was even more stringent than during the war—it had become a mecca for African American dancers. America's cabaret tax, a wartime fundraising measure, was not repealed, exiling soubrettes and John Bubbles alike from nightclubs and dance halls while inadvertently encouraging bebop and concert dance. As restraints on travel lifted, many fled both the dismal entertainment scene and racial tension, which, despite a war for freedom and the contributions of servicemen of color, continued more or less as before.

With African American dancers now streaming onto British soil, Bradley found both companionship and further opportunities to revisit his jazz roots. New Jersey–born Johnny Worthy, who had partnered with Louise Madison (a teacher of Honi Coles) before coming to England, was one new friend.[4] During and after the war, Worthy was so busy in England entertaining armed forces, touring the provinces, and performing at the Swing Spot, a nightclub in the West End catering to African American servicemen, that he had proposed that Honi Coles come join him for a double act.

Like Bradley's younger brother, Aurelius, Worthy needed a little management, something the grounded Bradley readily supplied. An inveterate ladies' man, Worthy was married in England for a nanosecond to dancer Betty Jackson, whose father was Ellis Jackson of the illustrious Southern Syncopated Orchestra, who now ran a dance school in London. All the while, Worthy, described by his son as a "bit of a rogue," had plenty of fun on the side and was soon living in Paris under the aegis of a female benefactor and tangling with French authorities. After returning to London, Worthy bunked for a while at Bradley's Radnor Lodge flat. Worthy's other weakness was heroin.

Despite his issues, Worthy was multitalented and hyperproductive. He conceived, cowrote, contributed songs, and starred with his stage partner Bertie Jarrett in *Walking on Air*, a film choreographed by Bradley about a group of musicians of color in an English nightclub. Worthy's charismatic presence prompted one reviewer to marvel that he "display[ed] exceptional versatility as himself," judiciously adding that tight footage and plenty of good dance turns elevated a sketchy story to well-balanced variety entertainment. Among the assembled all-Black cast were jazz drummers Ray Ellington and Freddie Crump (who continued the drumming antics of *King Arthur Was a Gentleman*), bassist Coleridge Goode, and guitarist Lauderic Caton.[5]

The Bradley–Worthy dance partnership, like their friendship, was one of contrasts and complements. Shot in close-up, Worthy's footwork is quick and clean as he dances the title song (which he also wrote) but differs in its textbook visibility from Bradley's rapid, close-to-the-floor style. As Worthy tosses off air steps, spectacular trenches, and wings, and glides in a version of Bill Bailey's signature exit, the forerunner of Michael Jackson's moonwalk, he radiates the kind of showmanship Bradley could rarely extract from his West End dancers. In turn, by repeating the moody dancing effect he'd introduced in 1934's *Why Not Tonight?*, Bradley elevates Worthy to the otherworldly: with his silhouette in shadow, Worthy's feet appear to float off the floor as if literally walking on air.

Walking on Air, a Black-driven project with a white director, most likely operating on a shoestring budget, received spotty distribution and quickly disappeared, conferring on it a cult-like mystique. Worthy also disappeared, checking into rehab at Maudsley Hospital. For the holidays, he obtained a pass to spend a weekend with Bradley, with all proceeding calmly until Christmas Eve, when Bradley dropped his guest at Lancaster Gate to catch a bus for the hospital. On exiting the car, Worthy was hit by an oncoming driver and died two days later, on Boxing Day.[6]

The friendship, marked by creativity and mutual understanding, was so rare for Bradley, its loss was nearly unbearable. As with his childhood in Birmingham and the history of his family, Bradley distanced himself from pain with silence. He now consigned Johnny Worthy to silence, too.

Despite the loss, life inevitably danced forward. A brief visit to the US in 1947 led to a chance encounter with Frankie Manning, who had had the good fortune to book his new Lindy Hop dance group, the Congaroos, at one of the few clubs that had not succumbed to the dance tax. Looking to diversify his program, Manning hired Bradley for a snazzy tap routine. Since the music was yet to be selected, Bradley relied on percussive footwork for the beat as he created a routine for the dancers; later, the choreography was set to Artie Shaw's "Begin the Beguine." The number remained part of the Congaroos' act until 1952, when Teddy Hale preceded them on a bill and tore up the stage tap dancing to a bebop version of "Begin the Beguine." It was challenging enough to follow a crowd-pleaser like Hale, let alone to dance to the same music, so Manning prudently switched to Tommy Dorsey's "Swanee River" and altered Bradley's choreography. When Bradley later saw his barely recognizable number, he smiled at the irony. Bebop now trumped all.[7]

Back in London, major stage flirt in heels Mable Lee flaunted her own brand of panache at the Palladium, where she sang, danced, and conquered London with a repertoire of shrugging shoulders, pointing fingers, smiling eyes, and knowing winks in Tommy Trinder's *Here, There, and Everywhere*. When the show closed in 1948, she followed Pete Nugent as a guest teacher at Bradley's school, where she taught Harlem jive, the Suzy Q, and her own razzle dazzle to English dancers. In tribute to her unique style, Bradley supplemented his routine-based curriculum with a dedicated "Mable Lee" routine.[8]

Of all the infusions of energy from America, that of tap dancer Carnell Lyons and his dance partner, L. D. Jackson, childhood friends of Charlie Parker's in Kansas City, was among the most artistically consequential. Bradley first met Lyons and Jackson in 1947, when their act, Two Businessmen of Rhythm, performed in the "Negro Music from Africa to Harlem" episode of BBC's *Variety in Sepia*, alongside Bradley, Mable Lee, Bertie Jarrett, Adelaide Hall, Winifred Atwell, and Evelyn Dove. Soon, Lyons was teaching at Bradley's school and using the studio to practice and perfect his future signature act, the spectacular tap dancing and tray spinning number he memorialized in the 1955 German film *Liebe, Tanz und 1000 Schlager*, which also featured John Bubbles.[9]

Twelve years younger than Bradley and part of the new generation of tappers, Lyons introduced Bradley to the double paddle, a step he claims to have invented in 1942 when on tour with Baby Laurence. Baby often danced a single paddle step (in tap-speak a dig, then brush back, then step and heel), alternating back and forth with his feet, creating a rolling drum effect; Lyons then inserted an additional dig and brush back before the step and heel to create what is now known as the "double paddle step." With its quick and minimal movement, the double paddle, as well as the paddle and roll style of tapping, particularly suited the new bebop jazz and would be central to Bradley's repertoire going forward.[10]

Bradley's new explorations included an unlikely romantic interest. Joan Heal had trained at the Old Vic before arriving at the Buddy Bradley School of Stage Dancing, bringing with her masses of mercurial talent that could switch from glamorous to ridiculous, from revue to Chekhov. It was the sort of talent that would catch the eye of Noël Coward, land her the role of Katherina in *The*

Taming of the Shrew at the Bristol Old Vic, and earn her the sobriquet Queen of Revue. Clearly, some of the excitement for Bradley was drawing out nascent talent. But there was also the eternal appeal of opposing forces: whereas Bradley operated with poise, Heal worked with abandon, took endless risks, and never hesitated to go all out, even at the risk of appearing silly. A photo of the two rehearsing, with Bradley striking a hammy pose, shows that he was far from immune to her zany optimism. In fact, he was smitten. Customarily, the cool Bradley was pursued by women, but now he was in active pursuit—traveling as far as Edinburgh to see Heal in shows and arranging cozy postshow suppers with Heal, Johnny Brandon, and drummer Ray Ellington.[11]

Under the spell of Heal, the reserved Bradley briefly became an extrovert, hosting a party at Cavanaugh's, surrounding himself with his new American pals in London, including actor Gordon Heath and fellow cast members of *Deep Are The Roots*, the acclaimed play about the return of a decorated African American solider to the Deep South; actress-dancer Bessie Love, credited with introducing the Charleston on film, now playing in the London transfer of *Born Yesterday*; and old flame Patricia Burke.[12]

Yet there were moments when London in 1948 echoed New York in 1927. After helping Johnny Brandon secure his first stint as cowriter and performer for a revue, Bradley arrived with Mable Lee at Brandon's opening night celebration at the Coconut Grove and was refused admission. Like the night on Broadway when he couldn't get a plate of eggs with the band members of *A Connecticut Yankee*, the incident brought a stinging realization: after redefining English stage dancing, making international stars of English talent, supporting Britain's six-year war effort, and even losing his home in the Blitz, he was still not an equal.[13]

Bradley's response is unexpected yet revealing: he took out his anger on Brandon. Bradley was used to maneuvering his way through white London and had never been refused admission before. He understood that a quiet word in advance to the maître d', a step the privileged Brandon had neglected, could head off such issues. That such procedures were required at all was humiliating, but Bradley, perhaps so grateful for what Britain had provided him, could not allow himself to acknowledge the prejudice at the heart of the incident.

In the world of entertainment, such matters might be masked. Everyone from friends and overseas visitors to producers, directors, and casting agents now converged on Bradley's studio, a clearinghouse of ideas, talent, and innovation. Bernard Delfont might pick a dancer on the spot and practically carry her directly to a rehearsal at his Prince of Wales Theatre to teach Bradley's steps; others, like Frith Banbury, took lessons, while their chauffeur-driven cars clogged Denman Street. Bradley's old friend John Huston found Rupie Johns at the studio, then cast him (uncredited) as "Chocolate" in *Moulin Rouge*.

Propelled by artistic curiosity, generosity, and a wish to introduce his students to a broad spectrum of dance, Bradley opened his doors wide to visiting dancers. There was the period when the studio echoed with the vibrations of Spanish heelwork as a series of Spanish troupes passed through town. Then there was the time when Katherine Dunham toured London in 1948. Student Annette Battams remembers Afro-Caribbean music sailing out the windows over Denman Street and drum beats flooding the studio and stairwell as the troupe's practice sessions overtook Bradley's studio.

Bradley admired Dunham, not only for her choreography, which erased the demarcation between concert dance and theatrical entertainment, but also for her instinctive flair for promotion. While he had arrived in London self-effacingly, with just a few tattered articles from *The Dance* for credentials, Dunham came fully prepared to make a splash. For her opening night at the Prince of Wales Theatre in London, she took six curtain calls—and changed her dress each time. While on tour, she drew on her bona fides in anthropology to address an audience at the Royal Anthropological Institute. A stunning beauty with a university education, Dunham actively used access that Bradley had never had, even posing for a full-page glamour shot in *The Tatler*. It was understandable. People of color had to find ways to be recognized, command respect, and survive.[14]

But such ambition cut two ways. While in London that summer, the media-savvy Dunham threw a much-publicized party for Alicia

Markova and Anton Dolin, with a midnight supper flown in from New York and a star-studded guest list that included Duke Ellington and Hilda Simms. These were dancers and musicians Bradley knew and with whom, in the case of Markova, had a particular bond. Yet Dunham seems to have intentionally omitted the low-key Bradley, who had so graciously hosted her and her dancers in his studio, from her high-powered party.[15]

While others might be affronted by such slights, Bradley took such things coolly. He seemed serene in his self-knowledge, never altering his personality, even as famous names swirled about him. He was not flash at all; he saved his emotion for music. But his preference to stand outside the spotlight, similar to his preference to choreograph and coach rather than perform, whether motivated by a quiet confidence or a desire to protect himself, could materially disadvantage him—witness the dismissiveness of Dunham.

After teaming for a second time with director Thornton Freeland (*Flying Down to Rio*, *Brewster's Millions*) on the art-theft thriller *The Brass Monkey*, Bradley turned his attention to Cecil Landeau's *Sauce Tartare* at the Cambridge Theatre. Irreverently mixing high art and satire, the revue drew on a range of talents from Jamaican rocker "Cuddly Dudley" Heslop to American mezzo-soprano Muriel Smith (who had attended Curtis Institute with Leonard Bernstein, then bedazzled in the title role of *Carmen Jones*) singing "Sailor Boy" from the upcoming Langston Hughes–Jan Meyerowitz opera *The Mulatto*. *Sauce Tartare* would become a hit, featured on BBC television, then later transferred to Ciro's as a nightclub show. Everyone in the company can do something and has the chance to do it, rhapsodized the London *Times* of a cast that included Claude Hulbert, Ronald Frankau, Jean Bayless, Zoë Gail (later replaced by Jessie Matthews), Joan Heal, and a young Audrey Hepburn.[16]

Hepburn, who had just had her dreams of a ballet career dashed by Marie Rambert, had come to Bradley to repurpose her skills for the theater. Bradley, with his keen eye for that indefinable something that transfixed a house, quickly placed her in the cast of *Sauce Tartare*, where she sparkled in its mixed metaphors and send-ups, poking fun with Joan Heal at Westerners adopting Eastern spirituality in "Boogie Woogie Yogi," then turning her playful malice on Broadway with the "Oklahokum" sketch. (One longs to know exactly what Bradley did to the de Mille choreography here.)[17]

Sauce Tartare was like Hepburn: intimate and sophisticated, devoid of pretentiousness and long on charm, superbly whimsical and infectiously youthful—the accolades were endless and consistent. Bradley's choreography framed Hepburn well; critics quickly singled her out "for an important revue career," and when the revue spawned a sequel, 1950's *Sauce Piquante*, he promoted Hepburn to a featured role. With her heightened visibility, Hepburn went on to a few parts in small movies, then the title role of *Gigi* on Broadway in 1951, then to stardom in *Roman Holiday*.[18]

The *Sauce* revues were also a career booster for Bradley. In addition to his position as choreographer, he assumed the role of assistant producer and acquired management savvy.[19] It was a well-timed move. That year, Bill Robinson died of a heart attack and, whether coincidentally or not, tap dance, like theatrical dance, went into free fall.

CHAPTER 21

JAZZ MAESTRO

Practice means to perform . . .
some act of vision, of faith, of desire.

—MARTHA GRAHAM

The fluidity came from within. One student recalled Bradley moved like silk. Another, that he did not walk, he glided like a god. When he danced, so supremely stylish, light, and precise, one dancer could only pray, "Oh, let me do that, please."

In the postwar years, as Bradley spent more time in the studio, his reputation as a teacher ascended ever higher. Even nondancers were captured by his spell. Teenager Annette Battams, her heart set on studying dance, had dragged her French mother, a translator for General de Gaulle, to Bradley's school. Climbing the stairs at 12 Denman Street, past after-hours clubs emanating stale alcohol and sex, intellectual Maman was more skeptical with every flight—until she arrived on the top floor and glimpsed Bradley through the door. Jazz flowed through Bradley's body, animating every gesture, turn, and step, its very purity and otherworldliness moving the Frenchwoman to tears. Tap dancing, that morning a battleground between mother and daughter, ascended to art in a single glance.

What had filled Madame Battams with wonder animates a series of photos from 1950: Bradley midair in his light-filled studio, vital, poised, and laughing. Bradley leaning forward, beating a djembe, long-fingered and engaged. Bradley encircled by dancers in a riff walk, keeping time with his feet, transferring his rhythm into their bodies. Bradley intently watching a leaping Billy Petch, willing his line and lift into the future choreographer. He filled the space with possibility and energy that now took him in a new direction.

An ad in the London *Times* in 1947 heralded the switch: Bradley was introducing a new training system. Dance and dancers were at a turning point. Much of the performative aspects of jazz dance had disappeared; the stages were smaller, the music less extroverted, and the venues different. Some, like Bradley scholarship student Billy Dainty, realizing that in the age of *Oklahoma!* and *Annie Get Your Gun* there would be little call for tap dancing, now pursued comedy and acting to earn a living. With tastes and trends changing in the theater, Bradley's answer was to double down on rhythm tap.[1]

By 1950, Bradley had dropped the reference to stage dancing in his school's name, and his students thought of him as a jazz man, not a musical theater choreographer. The rechristened Buddy Bradley School of Dancing, while continuing as a training ground for dancers, now became a destination for American musicians, dancers, and choreographers, a pilgrimage site for accomplished dancers and, for all, a temple to the melding of music and movement.[2]

With its new identity and its wartime relocation to Denman Street, the school acquired a louche glamour. The block, bookended by the Piccadilly and Lyric theaters, was down-at-the-heels, populated with the spillover of Soho and theater district businesses. A stone's throw away was the Caribbean Club, the meeting place of West Indians where Lena Horne picked up cockney rhyming slang, and, more importantly, where Lauderic Caton and Coleridge Goode, Bradley's pals from *Walking on Air*, developed a reputation as experimentalist jazz men. Across the street was a shoddy restaurant where dancers grabbed a bargain lunch for 1 shilling, 6 d (such were the outlandish-sounding prices prior to the decimalization of the shilling in 1971 and inflation) for steak, peas, and chips.[3]

If the distempered walls needed a coat of paint, and the changing room was microscopic, the five-hundred-plus students who sought out Bradley in the 1950s barely noticed. What mattered was moving to music. At Bradley's, future choreographers Billy Petch, Lionel Blair, Ralph Tobert, and Jan Lynton first worked out the connection of percussive dancing. Tobert was so elated he invariably sailed out of class, bounded down the stairs, and leapt over the last four steps, pretending he was a Nicholas Brother.[4]

Classes were two shillings sixpence—the going rate for professional dance classes—but the money hardly mattered. One dancer, who sold American cigarettes on the street to pay for class, and often came up short, found that Bradley didn't much care if you paid or not; time and again Bradley waived the fee and signaled him to the back of the studio. Bradley prized dancing over money. He loved his steps, his dance, the people who danced, and the energy of the room.

Despite the energy, the drifts of jazz, and the sounds of taps, the studio was oddly hushed, almost like a church. Was it that dance was a sacred mission or was it Bradley's presence that gave the room its aura? Rarely speaking, slightly distant, Bradley presided with austere devotion yet always got results. And, while Frank Coda and Ralph Tobert marvel that he never lost his temper or became angry, Annette Battams begs to differ, citing a tense moment when a dancer made a thoughtless racial comment. Bradley *could* be hurt or angry and then would become so intensely quiet (that silence quelling pain, again) that it was only apparent to the most observant.

As there usually were about twenty in a class, the studio could get quite busy. But, even if there were significantly fewer dancers, Bradley wanted to be in that room. Sometimes other commitments pulled him away—rehearsing his own dance troupe, helping Mona Inglesby develop a modern dance curriculum for the International Ballet School, coaching singers Shirley Bassey and Alma Cogan in the art of presenting a song onstage, or choreographing for the theater or *The Benny Hill Show*—and one of his assistants would take over class. Red-haired Liz Shelley, technical and an experienced performer, gave a solid class, but the even more inspiring teacher was a woman named Grace (last name, sadly, lost to history) who was a brilliant tap dancer, but, given her diminutive size, relegated to a career in the classroom. Later, Ann Emery, a fluent translator of complex movement into accessible steps, was indispensable to Bradley's class.[5]

The lessons in the alley behind Connie's Inn regained life in that studio in London. Bradley taught tap as he had first learned it, Harlem dancing that responded to sound, not a syllabus. He never laboriously instructed step by step, preferring to teach in musical phrases with swinging accents. His goal was to imprint in his dancers the rhythms and atmosphere of music. His musicianship and his ability to convey it so keen that Annette Battams, who, after hanging up her tap shoes, studied voice with Elisabeth Schwarzkopf and sang with Maria Callas, recalls she learned more about music from Buddy Bradley than any music coach.[6]

Of course, Bradley had always purveyed American tap dance, distinct from the clogging-influenced English variety of tap, but now Bradley was zeroing back to its jazz origins. Since meeting Carnell Lyons, he had embraced the paddle and roll style, with its potential to capture sophisticated jazz rhythms, and made it the centerpiece of his own practice. (The single paddle, as well as the double paddle, both of which Bradley wanted fast, subtle, and sounding like a drum roll, were near-proprietary steps at the Bradley studio and so central to his aesthetic that he told any student standing idle to make good use of the time by practicing paddle steps.) Steps were now notably more transitional and brief, sometimes even fragmented, to keep up with the complex new jazz. Bradley made virtually no distinction between jazz and tap dancing, between music, movement, and percussion as a trinity. Those dances made by young Bob Fosse, Jerome Robbins, and Michael Kidd, however striking, had nothing to do with jazz dance as Bradley defined it.[7]

The holy grail was to veer away from the obvious melody and emphasize the rhythmic line. Bradley particularly liked to follow the lines of an improvised solo, and he looked down on regular time steps as "ricky ticky." Only after close listening had produced a rhythmic figure in his mind would he begin to choreograph. For "Flying Home," for instance, he choreographed a routine on guitarist Charlie Christian's solo, employing in his characteristic fashion all parts of the body: arms, legs, and torso.[8]

Class was accompanied by American jazz recordings or, even better, a drum. Bradley might play a djembe; other times Jimmy Scott, who had learned the talking drums in his native Nigeria, set the rhythms. The record player spun Benny Goodman and Lionel Hampton's jump blues number "Flying Home," Gershwin's "I Got Rhythm," and Goodman's recording of "How High the Moon," among others. But music was not just for accompaniment; it was also for intent listening. Sheila Mathews recalls that Bradley required she replicate the music of a pianist with her feet, while Annette Battams remembers having to match her dance phrasing to "Smoochie" by R&B jazz singer Nellie Lutcher, whose precise diction influenced Nina Simone. Sometimes, Bradley even had his students spend an entire class listening to music without dancing a single step.[9]

The emphasis on musicality demanded definite, clean tap sounds, which meant that tightly affixed taps were the studio norm. While students such as Johnny Brandon experimented with loosening their taps to produce a deep and satisfying—if imprecise—sound, Bradley, a purist and perfectionist when it came to technique, was opposed to shortcuts and gimmicks for his pupils. There were exceptions, however. Ann Emery, a highly skilled dancer, was allowed to wear loose taps, and Bradley himself slightly loosened his own taps, adding a little brightness to his sound, in the manner of contemporaries like Pete Nugent and Honi Coles.

By the 1950s, only stars at the studio wore the heeled tap shoes that Bradley had once preferred; most of the women now wore oxford-style dance shoes with their little tie-tops and tiny shorts or the lower portion of a two-piece bathing suit (stretchy leotards didn't come into widespread use until the 1960s). Nine-year-old Jan Lynton, a special exception to Bradley's policy of not teaching children, remembers first wearing the classic child's shoe with a bow across the vamp, then proudly graduating to top-of-the-line kidskin shoes from Freed, a gift from her hardworking grandfather.

Class began with minimal chatter and a collective warm-up to loosen ankles and engage the hip with springs, heel pickups, and shuffle pull backs, all very low to the ground. Bradley, often smoking, provided no verbal instruction, demonstrated in phrases, and did not give counts, preferring that his students let swing shape their rhythms. Call-and-response exercises were typical. Dancers simply attempted to copy his example, at first tentatively and, with repetition, more confidently.

Riffs, practiced in a circle and revealing in their intricately changing beats their origins in African American culture, were always part of class. Though the basic movement was simple, how Bradley did them—changing the rhythm, hardly lifting the foot from the floor, building from four beats to many, sometimes even reaching an outlandish thirteen counts—was intensely stylish and supremely tricky. It, too, was novel in the West End, so novel, in fact, that, to her surprise, Jan Lynton, when later working as a choreographer, found that even dance professionals in Eastbourne, a seaside town with a long tradition of entertainment, had no knowledge of a riff as late as the 1980s.

In the world of London dance studios, the Shim Sham was probably unique to Bradley's school and reason alone to take class on Denman Street. Lynton recalls often dancing it to "I Got Rhythm," which Bradley would gradually speed up in the course of study. Mathews remembers how Bradley himself danced it, with no tension in the body and beautiful flow.

"Effortless" is the one word dancers consistently use to describe Bradley's dancing. Finesse, lightness, and feeling the floor were recurring themes in a Bradley class. Lynton recalls Bradley's footwork, rapid and light as a butterfly. Lionel Blair remembers how Bradley taught him how to *control* movement; tap, via Bradley, came from the hips, and, though the emphasis was always down, there was no wild flailing and undisciplined stamping. With Bradley, it wasn't a question of pounding sound *into* the floor; a dancer worked like a drummer, connecting to his instrument, then letting the floor speak back.[10]

Bradley's gift of making tap float was in part an illusion, built on technical mastery as much as on his innate grace. As such, he did not choreograph extemporaneously for his students; he taught intentionally, via carefully considered routines. No one now can state the exact number of Bradley's famous routines with confidence—memories vary from five to twelve, with six the most often cited number—but there is unanimous consent that the fifth routine was danced to Lionel Hampton's "Flying Home."

Like the Shim Sham, paddle, and riff, the crafted routines stressed speed, but there was *never* any sense of freneticism—at least in Bradley's demonstrations. The goal was to be natural and mirror the music. Building in difficulty, the routines showed off a dancer's progress. Once a dancer mastered all routines, he or she was deemed capable of performing as a solo act. By the 1980s, the routines were famous; tap teachers placed ads in *The Stage* flouting their knowledge of Buddy Bradley routines; others sought other teachers with knowledge of the routines to band together and create (and monetize) a Buddy Bradley training method.[11]

Dancers watched as Bradley demonstrated a routine, section by section, each opening slowly and subtly, then building to a crescendo. Though he avoided verbal instruction, he was always happy to dance the routine again upon request. When he did speak, he didn't count, dictate, or break down steps; he focused on the stylistic—"No, Sheila, don't use your shoulders like that, move them like this"—or offered recurring admonishments to relax, get into the floor, and get down, get down, get down. Jan Lynton recalls his constant refrain "If you are up here, you're not going to feel the floor," while he gently directed her shoulders downward and shifted her weight, letting gravity prevail so that she, too, could feel the floor. (He was fixated on relaxed shoulders, encouraging one dancer to let them drop as if she were just about to nod off.)

Depending on the class, multiple routines could be taking place, with different subgroups working with different studio assistants, the more advanced dancers progressing to the harder routines. If certain aspects escaped a dancer, Liz, Grace, or Ann was available to help in a corner. One time-honored ploy of Grace was to have a dancer teach the routine to another, thereby fostering confidence and reinforcing the routine. Frank Coda remembers frequently helping, with some frustration, an older (that is to say, mid-forties) nonprofessional student who always left class early. One day he happened to look out the window and saw the man exit the building and climb into a waiting Rolls Royce with driver. He cringed remembering his peevishness. It was the director, Paddy Carstairs.

Toward the end of class, Bradley would assemble all the sections into a routine, then stand back and watch. Occasionally he would add a spectacular four- or eight-bar break at the end that baffled many dancers, and the more intrepid would attempt to imitate. Tobert, the future choreographer who would sail out of Bradley's classes like a Nicholas Brother, remembers standing aghast and muttering, "What did you just do, you bastard!"

It was the absolute stylishness that left Ralph Tobert speechless. Even with minimal movement, the music was visible throughout his entire body. Shoulders loose, limbs without tension, every step a subtle masterpiece, Bradley's dancing gave credence to his dictum that tap dance was not difficult if one simply relaxed. As for Bradley, he was so relaxed he was known to dance with his hands in his pockets.

His clothes were as casual as his dancing. In the studio, Bradley affected everyday trousers and a nondescript shirt, adding in the winter months one of two sweaters, each with a contrasting band of color around the neck and shoulder. (Young Frank Coda so idolized Bradley—his cool, his artistry, and everything he represented—that he had the sweaters copied and the temerity to wear them to class. The preternaturally unflappable Bradley never batted an eye.) And while the dapper movie-star getups were evidently reserved for production meetings, photo sessions, or trips back to the States, Bradley always retained a note of elegance on his feet. His size-seven tap shoes at the time were natty blue suede, with a not-so-thick sole, to which he affixed his perfectly calibrated taps.

Perhaps his remoteness let him observe his students more acutely. He was infinitely patient, as kind to the hard workers as to the gifted dancers. If a dancer struggled, he held off and let him or her work through the combination but was quick to offer affirmation when a dancer finally had the movement flowing through his or her body, as happy for himself as the dancer. For his youngest student, a precociously gifted nine-year-old, Bradley would gently take her hand and dance with her (cue Bojangles and Shirley Temple) to help her get the rhythm in her body.

Despite the school's name change, Bradley was indelibly part of the West End. In the era of Rodgers and Hammerstein and their habitual choreographer Agnes de Mille, musical theater minimized tap and magnified interpretive "jazz" and ballet. Bradley followed suit, with his ads often highlighting ballet instruction. But ballet wasn't simply a sop to trends in musical theater. Even as he emphasized rhythm and footwork, Bradley still adored a supple back. His tap dancers knew he would have been disappointed if they didn't study with Hilda Lumley, his ballet instructor in the 1950s.

The quirky Lumley, trained by Judith Espinosa (and a close friend of Quentin Crisp, who called her "Miss Lumley Who Can Do No Wrong"), followed Mary Skeaping as ballet mistress. Described as an extravagant woman with beautiful arm and hand gestures, Lumley was definitely old-school ("Come along, my dears"), a stickler for turnout, and known to fix an icy stare on any dancer whose attention wandered.[12]

New techniques and teachers now filled Bradley's second studio, making the school a vital hub for innovative dance from America. Most of the new teachers were modern concert dancers, beginning in 1950 with Bertram Ross, a principal dancer at the Martha Graham Company, who was in temporary revolt against Graham's autocratic style—she had just summarily canceled her company's London engagement at the Piccadilly Theatre and ordered her dancers to return to New York at the height of the summer doldrums, despite no scheduled performances.[13]

Richardena Jackson, a dramatic performer from the Katherine Dunham Company taught at Bradley's too. (When the company performed in London, she had captivated audiences with an arrow-straight penché she held for what seemed an eternity.) While she ultimately chose to spend her life in Europe, like Ross, she may have first turned to teaching at Bradley's in rebellion against her company's imperious founder. Bradley was both sympathetic and an admirer—he, too, had experienced the stuff Dunham was made of and had chosen to leave America. Jackson's classes, keyed to professional dancers, stressing African-derived movement and influenced by Dunham technique, engaged muscles rarely used for tap. Bradley students remember hobbling out of the studio, stoically trying to disguise their soreness from one another after Jackson's classes; one dancer—a Tiller girl—had to slide down the stairs on her fanny.

If Jackson, fun and dynamic, was the modern dance counterpart to Bradley, Bert Stimmel, fresh from the MFA program at Yale, was Bradley's otherworldly complement. A refined dancer with a pure vision, Stimmel eschewed showbiz flash and would later establish the Caracalla Dance Company in Beirut. The high-minded Stimmel apparently found similarities between his and Bradley's approach to dance; when he took a troupe on tour to Cairo in 1955, he hired some of Bradley's dancers.[14]

With the energies shifting and cascading, dances informing dances, the Buddy Bradley School of Dancing was the place to go in the 1950s. There simply were no rivals if you wanted to study rhythm and jazz tap, nor equals if you were curious about modern dance in America. In the 1940s former *Blackbirds* star Johnny Nit had tried hanging up his shingle on Newport Street, but he was not a teacher or a choreographer.[15] There was also Ellis Jackson's studio in Brixton, where Betty Jackson, Johnny Worthy's ex-wife, taught, but it was far removed from the action in the center of town. The Clark Brothers had also tried to open a studio, but it was short-lived. (Plus, they were considered a bit heavy-footed and unimaginative compared with Bradley.) Max Rivers, with his cat-filled studio and cigar, was an Englishman doing his best to approximate American tap.

Marie Rambert not only referred Audrey Hepburn; she sent her own daughters to Bradley. Gene Kelly came in search of dancers for *An American in Paris*. When Liz Shelley auditioned for the part of Lise, she held out her hand and said, "I'm Liz Shelley," to which Kelly replied, "Well, then, I am Percy Bysshe," a bon mot that ricocheted around the West End. Shelley did not get the role, but Jamaican dancer Rupie John was cast for the cameo in the entr'acte. Rupie brought a friend from Jamaica, the dancer Charlie Meade, who, in turn, brought the wife of a friend, Dorothy Pitchford Edghill, a "layperson" keen on jazz who was now curious to observe jazz dance. Seasoned professionals like ex-girlfriend Joan Heal and her husband, Jeremy Hawk, often dropped in to polish up their technique—they were jolly and fun, much admired by the class, and added a layer of glamour. Other dancers who passed through Bradley's hands in the 1950s included Ben Aris, Dickie Henderson, Roy Castle, and Richard Lyon.

Bradley had created a collegial environment that reflected his own ethos, where dance as an expression of music was its own reward. Except for some friendly jockeying to position oneself in the front of class, there was no sense of rivalry, even among professionals. All the dancers wanted to do was exactly what Bradley was doing in front of the room. Nobody could dance like him, vowed Lionel Blair.[16]

But it went beyond teaching, tapping, and technique. Bradley emanated a force field based on his dedication to craft, his absorption of music, his life choices, and his personal wisdom. He opened doors to new visions and new ways of being for many. It was a force field that lured Ralph Tobert to break into the studio at night (as his father was a cabinetmaker, he knew how to pick a lock), borrow Bradley's own tap shoes from his office, and practice in solitude, vaguely hoping that the blue suede tap shoes, like Dorothy's ruby red slippers, would convey him to a higher universe. Frank Coda believed Bradley immortal, the one person who would live forever. Even children sensed they were in a higher presence. Impressed by how Bradley engaged with others, young Roy Sone mimicked Bradley in his own interactions. Nine-year-old Jan Lynton didn't simply want to dance like her mentor; she wanted to *be* Bradley.

CHAPTER 22

TROUPES, TOURS, AND BABY LAURENCE

Dance histories are chronicles of people
moving beyond what they think they know.

—THOMAS DEFRANTZ

All the while Buddy Bradley reigned in his universe on Denman Street, new dance ventures steered him onto unfamiliar terrain. Now directing his own two dance companies, Bradley experimented with dance removed from the context of a play. Such undertakings also cast him against type, requiring that he act as protagonist, producer, and publicist as well as choreographer. Along the way, new friendships with American tap dancers Teddy Hale and Baby Laurence reinforced Bradley's connection to rhythm tap and prompted reflections on his own life and career.

While Cochran's death in 1951, changes in the West End, and the fading of the prewar nightclub scene collectively encouraged the formation of Bradley's dance troupes, it was individual dancers, as usual, that inspired him to act. Dancer Liz Shelley first floated the idea of a dance company. A few years later, Jamaican street dancer Charlie Meade gave rise to Bradley's idea for a second troupe, one that contrasted improvised and choreographed dance.

The very idea of a dance troupe was almost inconceivable to Bradley. Though he might well act on opportunity, as he had done since the moment he took a train out of Harrisburg, he never dared ask for anything, even when deserved. Making do with less than perfect circumstances, not temerity, was his birthright. Whether by social conditioning or for emotional protection, he let people and opportunities come to him—fortunately, due to his talent, there had been many. For years, Bradley had existed as the Other, fitting in rather than intentionally trying to stand out; it was alien to place himself directly in the spotlight. As for risk, his entire life had been fraught with it—why assume more voluntarily?

The idea of a dance company, albeit logical, could only have come from someone else. And that someone was Liz Shelley, his studio right hand and protégée. Born Mavis Price in Staffordshire, the granddaughter of Charles Price of McVitie & Price, Ltd. (holders of a royal warrant, makers of internationally renowned shortbread and digestive biscuits, and suppliers of the wedding cake for George V and Queen Mary in 1893), she had been singled out at age seven, in ballet examinations adjudicated by M. Espinosa, of the prominent ballet dynasty, as a budding Pavlova. Dreaming of a life not circumscribed by the haute bourgeoisie but elevated by art, Mavis arrived in London during the war and continued her dance studies with Bradley.[1]

Though she upgraded her prosaic name to Liz Shelley and dyed her pale hair Titian red, Mavis Price never quite discarded the persona of an English head girl. Smart, hardworking, responsible, and quick to pick up routines, the refashioned Liz Shelley was soon helping run the school, assisting Bradley with class, and even teaching in his absence. At one point the only full-time instructor at the school, Liz was invariably the handy body whenever Bradley wanted to work out some choreography. A photo of Liz working with Bradley on a routine, her face radiant, suggests the excitement she found in proximity to the creative process.[2]

But, if dependability was the stuff of which Liz Shelley was made, glamour was the stuff of which she dreamed. She learned to use her sharp features, elongated limbs, and newly acquired red hair to craft a mystique. She was fond of making an entrance, casually dropping her fur coat on the floor as she arrived for class. While younger dancers idolized her, Liz's peers remember that her diligent dancing lacked poetry. If only she made an occasional mistake, Annette Battams sighed, she might have been more pleasing to watch.

Bradley and Liz Shelley's differences were many. He was fluid and creative; she, analytical and determined. He was down to earth; she, aspiring. He was reserved; she, a drama queen. In one way, however, they were perfect complements—Bradley had talent; she had means. Bradley should have his own dancers and artistic autonomy, Liz reasoned, and she would be at the beating heart of creation.

Liz's vision of financing a troupe, the Buddy Bradley Company, was as seductive as it was outlandish to Bradley. Of course, there had been the "Buddy Bradley Dancers"—chorus dancers to fill in some film footage, a revue, or a nightclub act—but what Liz offered was different. Funding meant autonomy. Bradley would be able to work consistently with dancers whose bodies, talents, and temperaments he knew. He would be able to operate with high production values, pay dancers regularly, cover travel expenses, and hire top costume designers, realizing, in effect, his own Gesamtkunstwerk.

Of course, there were strings attached. Liz craved distinction as a dancer, and the troupe would be the vehicle for her own dance ambitions, too. As such, one can assume Bradley used his connection with Marie Rambert to have Liz cast in an experimental ballet with Walter Gore at the Mercury Theatre in 1952. Soon, too, Bradley was dutifully proclaiming her the best all-round dancer in Europe. Nor did Liz's dreams stop at stardom; she, too, wanted her own real-life Gesamtkunstwerk. By 1952, Liz was living with Bradley at Radnor Lodge. Much like Liz's dancing, however, the relationship never sparkled. It was a means to an end.[3]

The demands seemed to weigh on Bradley. Shortly after the troupe formed, they performed alongside Elisabeth Welch, Margot Fonteyn, and Leslie Henson in *Merely Players*, a benefit produced by John Varley at the Drury Lane Theatre. In the course of rehearsals, Varley remarked that though Bradley was a brilliant dancer, a superb maker of steps, and a deft creator of solo routines, he could not fill a stage with arresting movement. It is hard to make sense of this comment. Over the years, Bradley had produced dances of complexity and imagination. Witness Noël Coward's *Words and Music*, the pas de deux in *Sailing Along*, and his collaborations with Frederick Ashton. Perhaps Bradley's choreography for *Merely Players* was one of those unfortunate misses that could happen to any artist, but, just as possibly, was it that working around Liz Shelley and her objectives was an artistic impediment?[4]

While Bradley distanced himself from Liz, smoking more marijuana and communicating even less, he continued to connect with children. When twelve-year-old dancer Roy Sone's plans to make his West End debut in *Merely Players* were dashed by a burst appendix, Bradley, though monopolized by rehearsals, devised a plan to cheer him up. He arranged for bandleader and composer Fletcher Henderson to pay a surprise visit to Roy in the hospital. Fletcher obliged out of affection for his old friend Bradley—their long history included revels together in Harlem and using Henderson's arrangements for Bradley's dance classes on Broadway—but, once at the hospital, he found he had little small talk to entertain an adolescent. For his part, Sone, a schoolboy from the East End with little knowledge of the world, had no idea who Henderson was. After several well-intended but awkward moments, the visit ended as improbably as it had begun, and Fletcher, now walking with a cane after a stroke, hobbled out.

Despite Varley's qualms, the new Bradley troupe was a hit. Vivacity, youth, and exuberance—the rising values of postwar society—were on full display at the Embassy Club, where Bradley's staging of *Accents on Rhythm* filled the Bond Street nightspot to capacity, luring repeat visits from Princess Margaret. *Variety* hailed the program as a vital uplift for postwar Britain, noting with approval its rare, all-British dance cast.[5]

If the cast was British, the zest was African American. Over the past few years Bradley had taught all of his performers American jazz and tap dance; now they displayed it against a backdrop of percussion provided by drummers Jimmy Scott and Ole Shelanki. Also categorically un-English was Bradley's choreography for Jamaican

Rupert Johns (performing as Duke Diamond): he had a trick of picking up a table by the mouth, then adding a handful of splits for extra dash.

Of course, the fact that Bradley could produce shows at the glossiest clubs in town, the kind that demanded the highest production values, where dancers had to arrive in proper frocks and hats for rehearsals, was thanks to subsidies from the Price family. Hiring directors Lew and Leslie Grade—future moguls of the West End, television, and film—was also a shrewd (and expensive) choice, as the Grades' network led to further engagements, both at home and on the Continent. The esteemed Ronald Cobb, many of whose costume sketches now reside in the Victoria and Albert Museum (V&A), was called in for witty costumes, though they were frugally produced in-house; dancer Daphne Selfe recalls hours bent over a sewing machine. Bradley now also had the amenity of assistants. In fact, for *Accents on Rhythm*, he had two: Richardena Jackson and Liz Shelley, one's modernist élan balancing the other's methodical discipline.[6] Dancers, too, were well compensated; besides being able to turn themselves out smartly, they could afford to unwind after performances at actor Gerry Campion's chic club in Soho, a hangout for the acting community.

After several months at the Embassy Club, *Accents on Rhythm* moved to the Coconut Grove on Regent Street, the Embassy's smartest rival. If this second booking affirmed the success of the Bradley troupe, it was also a bitter pill: it was the Coconut Grove that had denied Bradley admission to Johnny Brandon's party. As usual, Bradley subjugated emotion to practicality, arguably with good reason: between 1953 and 1956, *The Evening Standard* listed eight-five appearances of Bradley's dancers at the Coconut Grove. Working with the club's bandleader Edmundo Ros, with whom he had previously collaborated on several BBC programs, Bradley deftly laced his choreography with Cuban, Caribbean and South American rhythms.

Bradley's twenty dancers were versatile, as capable of Afro-Hispanic dance as tap and jazz. Ben Aris, Patsy Parnham, and Charles Yates went on to illustrious careers in the West End. Billy Petch had a knack for visualizing stage geometries and, like Bradley, the ability to whittle individuality from his dancers. With fellow Bradley dancer Bob Chandler, Petch would go on to choreograph at the Talk of the Town, where big American acts like Eartha Kitt, Judy Garland, and Lena Horne headlined. Ann Emery, born in the proverbial actor's trunk, and the most incandescent of dancers, transfixed every audience—as late as 2005 at age seventy-five she brought the house down dancing the grandmother in *Billy Elliot the Musical*. Brenda Harper, mysterious, serious, and elegant, danced with the troupe until it folded and for a while was Bradley's girlfriend. Flamboyant Rupie Johns, a frequent guest artist, beguiled nearly every woman dancer with his charm, much to Bradley's amusement. Annette Battams, whose mother had been a tango champion in Paris during the 1920s, inherited the family gene for Latin and percussive dances. As for stage appeal, when Bradley spotted Daphne Selfe in a revue at the Cumberland Hotel in 1951, he immediately invited her to study at his school, then integrated her into the troupe. As a beauty—she modeled for *Vogue* at age seventy and continues to model in her nineties—it was Daphne, with fellow dancer Christine Carter, whom Bradley dispatched to the BBC nightclub variety show *Café Continental* as the sensational door-openers.[7]

The work flowed in. The troupe performed in 1953's Royal Command Performance, a gala night that capped Queen Elizabeth's coronation season. Though highly prestigious, the industry considered it a nerve-wracking gig; most of the audience preferred opera to variety, and then, of course, there was the additional pressure of performing for royals Queen Elizabeth, Prince Philip, and Princess Margaret. Setting the stakes even higher, the first-half closer—Bradley's assignment—was rechoreographing Michael Kidd's Tony Award–winning number "Take Back Your Mink" from *Guys and Dolls*, considered too racy for the royal presence.[8]

If Bradley had hoped for the legitimacy of the concert stage, he had to settle for royal engagements and nightclubs on the Continent, playing a three-week engagement at Ancienne Belgique in Brussels, then an additional week in Antwerp. (The program cover showed eleven dancers in leopard bustiers posed in a pyramid, with

Liz Shelley prominently standing out in a white costume and identified as lead dancer.) During fiesta season of 1954, the troupe performed blues, boogie, bebop, and spiritual numbers to full houses at the Casablanca Club on the Plaza del Rey in Madrid. On the final evening, Bradley daringly had his dancers perform Spanish dances for the discerning Madrileño audience and met with acclaim.[9]

Stagy photos in *Ebony*—Freda De Knight, the editor, probably knew Buddy via her husband, the jazz musician René De Knight—offered a romantic view of the Continental tour. Troupe members practiced with lipstick on and every hair in place. Duke Diamond rehearsed a split midair in an immaculate shirt and tie. The group relaxed idyllically over drinks on the Plaza de Cibeles in Madrid. The reality was somewhat different from the idealized story. Lodgings were modest; Bradley's rules were strict (no third helpings, no fraternizing with the audience); and traveling to Rome in the summer, in a train reeking of garlic, was ghastly. Once in Rome, the dancers tossed coins in the Trevi; performed at the Belvedere del Rosa, where King Farouk refused to let the show begin until he'd finished his pasta; then performed at the Rupe Tarpea on the via Veneto, a destination for the Cinecittà set, intellectuals, and playboys (the Aga Khan turned up). The club's renowned rhythm section, much admired by Django Reinhardt and Stéphane Grappelli, inspired high-level performances from the dancers.[10]

A year later, the troupe was off to Portugal, where Liz was described—whether in error or by design—on the program as a North American film and television star. Then they headed off to the Italian Riviera in 1956 with a program of modern jazz dances, winding up in Milan at the Cinema Smeraldo, with Liz Shelley always prominently featured. Bradley rarely toured. Liz acted as tour manager and dance captain; whatever her limitations, she was not a diva and did not pull rank. Don Tasker or Gerald Fitzgerald, capable and kind men who also lent their talents to teaching dance to deaf children and championing dancers' equity, managed the organizational details.[11]

When it came to work, Liz and Bradley were a crack team. Photos in Spain show Liz intently listening to Bradley during a rehearsal, taking her role as dance captain seriously. For creating magic for one another, however, their body language while exploring Spain tells a different story. Liz is scowling while Bradley holds himself standoffishly erect. Annette Battams noted this dynamic, too, at a party that Mr. and Mrs. Price hosted for the troupe. It was a gracious, celebratory evening: guests floated in and out of the garden, flowers and foie gras were abundant, and the prospects of an upcoming tour buoyed the dancers. Bradley, the guest of honor and raison d'être for the party, remained oddly aloof and apart, retreating to the drawing room to listen to Battams play Bach rather than mingle with the guests. Battams suspected that he had been smoking pot—he was smoking a lot then, she recalls, a clear indication of a lack of ardor.

By 1957, the group began to unravel. Some dancers—Billy Petch, Daphne Selfe, Annette Battams, and Frank Coda—had moved on to new chapters in their lives and careers. A filmed appearance of the Buddy Bradley dancers in the *Edmundo Ros Half Hour* was described by *Kinematograph Weekly* as a floor show without a flaw, but Bradley knew better. Liz was uncompelling and overselling, and the other dancers were lackluster, as if Bradley was distracted. With touring at an end, Don Tasker moved on to a job in television. The coup de grâce was the unexpected (and intestate) death of the generous Wilfred Price, which brought the underwriting to an end.[12]

There was virtually no drama—and perhaps some relief on Bradley's part—as the troupe wound down. More bittersweet was the nearly simultaneous closing of the twenty-five-year-old Buddy Bradley School of Dancing, the pulsing heart of London's jazz dance world and an extension of Bradley's own persona. He now taught modestly at the Farr Studio in Marylebone, sometimes even at a nightclub where he was currently engaged and used his home address and telephone for inquiries. As for Liz, she resumed life as Mavis Price and eventually married someone with a double-barreled name and "disappeared into Surrey or Sussex, or someplace like that," recalls Daphne Selfe.[13]

Perhaps Bradley's relative calm at the troupe's demise was because he had been running another dance company in parallel.

Rupie Johns had provided the catalyst when he introduced Charlie Meade from Jamaica. As a child in Kingston, Meade had danced barefoot with bottle caps affixed to his feet, coaxing rhythm out of anything from opera arias to Doris Day tunes. Seeing little future in Jamaica and in search of broader horizons, teenage Meade made his way to England. In 1953, after sustaining a near-fatal accident at work, he vowed to follow his passion and live a life of dance.

Bradley received Meade in his sitting room at Radnor Lodge (after the war known as 105 Sussex Gardens), then played one jazz record after another as the twenty-two-year-old danced. Whenever Bradley fastened on a particular step and asked to see it again, a peculiar thing happened: Meade created a new step to the same music. His spontaneity and invention inspired Bradley to conceive of a troupe that would draw the through line from street to stage dancing.

African American jazz had been infiltrating London clubs since the war, but jazz dance, discouraged by the new jazz musicians, had lagged on the stage. The new jazz troupe, the Buddy Bradley Jazz Dancers, would give Britain a glimpse of modern African American jazz dance accompanied by jazz music. Along with the self-taught Meade, Bradley assembled four trained but unconventional dancers: Sarita Fonseca and Chris Parry, both trained in ballet; Bennet Bennison, with a background in mime; and Ann Emery, the unacknowledged star of the troupe. Meade would improvise, while the others would dance choreography by Bradley in counterpoint. Costumes underlined the contrast: one photo shows Meade wearing a zoot suit and Ann Emery a jaunty little sailor middy.[14]

The dances flowed in three dimensions, with the dancers backbending, twisting, kicking, and even lying on the floor. Bradley tailored dances for specific bodies, giving fluid dancers soft movements and edgy dancers more forceful choreography. He highlighted individuality, often introducing his dancers by name and having them perform a signature step, and preserved Meade's innate style, suggesting only minimal performance tips. He tested out foot slapping, touching a hand to a raised foot, a move still found in house and hip-hop dance today. Curious about crossover, he tried adapting the tricky one-legged figure turns of ice skating to jazz movement. Inspired by his coaching of young singer Shirley Bassey, fashioning what would become her famously eloquent hands, Bradley translated baroque hand movements for Ann Emery. The dancers followed Bradley's cue, juxtaposing improvised and crafted dance and experimenting with each other's specialties, often copying Meade's inventions. Music was typically live, even in practice sessions; sometimes Jimmy Scott would drum. When he did work with recorded music, Bradley's choreography focused on trumpet or bass solos rather than melodic line.[15]

Unlike his other troupe, with its generous funding, the Buddy Bradley Jazz Dancers was self-sustaining. Bradley diplomatically downplayed his Jazz Dancers so as not to jeopardize the Prices' funding, as they may have understandably viewed a second troupe as a conflict of interest. As such, the new jazz troupe rehearsed not in the studio at Denman Street (the space may have been largely monopolized by classes, anyway) but in a church hall near Marble Arch. The self-funding model also impacted the production values, venues, and choice of bookings.

The group debuted with a month-long booking at the sophisticated Pigalle supper club in Piccadilly, then moved to the Panama Club on Windmill Street. Though the Panama Club had a reputation for discovering talent, it was far removed from the glossy reaches of the Embassy Club. However, it offered distinct advantages for a troupe that depended on cash flow. It coupled the troupe with other acts, who then went out on the road together, and, even more importantly, it invited the troupe to become its resident dance company—a novelty in the nightclub world, where turnover of acts draws audiences—thereby providing the troupe with the financial security of a home base.

As for tours, they were often to Germany, whose audiences enthusiastically embraced jazz and jazz dancing, associating it with America, freedom, and the future. In 1959 Gisela Gunther, the powerful German booking agent with whom every tap dancer in America longed to work, came up with a plum assignment: a six-week tour on NATO bases. At the time, the US Army operated clubs for the armed forces, with gambling and three Las Vegas-style shows a day, one for the generals, another for officers, and a final show for the troops. Once settled into the German tour, Charlie marveled at his discovery of American pancakes but found German drummers the bane of his existence. They got carried away and played too fast, wreaking havoc on their "How High the Moon" number. It was only when the troupe got to NATO headquarters in Paris that they found easygoing American musicians who played the right tempos.

When at home in London, Jamaican dancers Rupert Johns, Charlie Meade, and Balti (whose last name has disappeared from record) formed a clique around Bradley, spending evenings at the flat in Sussex Gardens, trading steps and stories and addressing him as "Mr. B." Now in his early fifties, Bradley perhaps found a reflection of himself in Charlie Meade, whose passion for dance and curiosity about life were so similar to his own. The two bonded over the significant and the insignificant, sharing a mutual admiration for Fred Astaire and Eddie Rochester, whose satiric comedy came as close to modern humor as was then possible for Black actors. Bradley was also a font of information. If Charlie asked a question for which Bradley did not have an answer, he would do some research, then share his findings a few days later. He frequently offered avuncular advice, too, cautioning his young friends to avoid drugs and suggesting that they keep their distance from certain people.

At the same time, Meade observed Bradley. He noticed how Bradley drew people toward him yet he never put himself forward; how he eschewed nightlife but was happy to preside from his big chair in his living room, listening with a wry smile, drawing on English cigarettes and weed (smoked in a pipe), and rarely touching alcohol. There was also an impenetrable wall about Bradley. "You had to come to him and couldn't get things out of him until he felt comfortable with you," Meade recalled, adding that, even then, Bradley could be secretive. There was no point in asking questions. He would only reveal what he wanted.

Yet despite, or because of, the mystery, American dancers looked up to Bradley, calling on him when they came to London. They respected his talent, considered him a genius. What is more, they were curious. Perhaps they would find answers for themselves in his life lived apart. Teddy Hale arrived in 1954, tapping the most complicated and well-thought-out syncopated solos London had ever seen. He came to Bradley, bringing his wide smile, prodigious talent, and voracious heroin habit. Charlie Meade remembers being delegated by Bradley to show Hale about Soho, the dancer in disgracefully dirty clothes, wearing his tap shoes on the street, and high as a kite. While in London, Hale was arrested and fined for obtaining government-issued heroin under a fake alias—one can imagine who helped bail him out. Five scant years later, Hale died in Washington, DC, just shy of his thirty-third birthday. The combination of his brilliance, his addiction, and his truncated life was a sober reminder of what could happen to men of color in America. Maybe Bradley did have the answer.[16]

Baby Laurence came via Henry Le Tang, displaying all the politeness of a younger African American man addressing a respected elder. Bradley was fifty-four, Baby Laurence not yet forty. Mutual connections, however, brought an easy camaraderie—Baby Laurence was performing on a TV variety show that spring, alongside the Delta Rhythm Boys, whose pianist was René De Knight, and their friend Norma Miller was also in town, performing at the Pigalle—and soon Baby Laurence was in the habit of stopping by Sussex Gardens before or after a performance. As they talked, age differences fell away. Bradley and Baby Laurence talked about the dancers who had gone before them and the Jim Crow days, when they had to enter clubs through the back door. In the presence of the gentle Laurence, whose experiences often paralleled his own, Bradley let his guard down slightly. He shared some memories of growing up in the Deep South, voiced his resentment of his treatment in America, and swore he could never return to the States. Meade and the others listened silently, in awe.[17]

Talking, no matter the depth of the revelations, was but a preliminary; dancing was always the main event for Bradley and Baby Laurence. Though another might have happily traded steps in Bradley's spacious salon-cum-studio, Baby went directly to rehearsals in the church hall with the Buddy Bradley Jazz Dancers. Naturally, the dancer who was considered the dance equivalent of jazz great Charlie Parker was the cynosure, everyone hoping to grasp, up close, aspects of his magic. There was a bit of a contretemps when Baby discovered that Bradley's current girlfriend, Ann Emery, could duplicate his steps with just a glance; spooked by such facility, he pulled Balti and Meade aside and told them he would teach them any step they wanted to know but didn't want to give *her* any more steps. As the dancing continued, Baby Laurence's steps melted into Bradley's dancers and, by extension, into Bradley's choreography. Four decades of tap dance came full circle.

Oddly, what appeared to be dance differences were a bridge. Bradley had spent decades infusing dance throughout the body, placing it on multiple planes, and projecting it in space, but his musicality had kept him in the vanguard of rhythm tap. (To make his point, he suggested that jazz historian Marshall Stearns ask other dancers if his protégé Roland Holder had been rhythm tapping before John Bubbles.) Baby Laurence, on the other hand, had tight-focused on the acoustics of tap. Bradley viewed Laurence's acoustic approach as the continuation of what he had initiated in the 1920s, the linking of movement and music. While he drew rhythm through the entire body, Baby did it exclusively with his feet.[18]

In that studio, Bradley, the best chorus boy of his time, beheld Baby Laurence, a dancer for the ages. They were similar, both orphaned as adolescents, both forging lives as teenagers in Harlem, and both intensely musical. Different times and circumstances, however, had sent them on divergent trajectories. Bradley had been mentored by Leonard Harper when Flo Ziegfeld reigned on Broadway. Baby Laurence had been under the wing of former tap dancer turned Harlem club owner Dickie Wells and had come of age with bebop. Bradley had ridden the vogue of tap to a storied career as a choreographer. Baby Laurence stood at the pinnacle of his art as tap dance entered its dark age. Bradley could only dream of seeing his work on a concert stage. Baby Laurence had been consecrated by Whitney Balliett, music critic of the *New Yorker* as art itself, likened to a great drummer.[19] Bradley's deep admiration for Baby Laurence could only have been accompanied by a touch of sadness and regret, a wistfulness of what might have been.

Ann Emery and Charlie Meade experienced no such complexities with Baby Laurence; they found in him a fellow enthusiastic club-goer. After performances at the Panama Club, Meade and Emery often commandeered the Bradley troupe van and took off for shebeens (after-hours and unlicensed dance clubs) in Ladbroke Grove. Frequented by Caribbean people and Africans, the clubs welcomed Ann and Charlie like celebrities, waiving their entrance fees because they brought a different dance style to the clubs. Now Meade and Emery gathered up Baby Laurence to show him the underground scene. Baby reveled in it, danced in rubber soled shoes—the club they most liked had a carpeted floor—and was, naturally, the center of attention. As for Bradley's admonishment about drugs, if Teddy Hale wasn't already a deterrent, Meade recalled, a glimpse of Baby Laurence's track-strewn leg was a cautionary tale itself. Baby, the immortal, had his vulnerabilities, too.

Circumstances and opportunities led to the demise of the Bradley Jazz Dancers. In 1961, choreographer Hermes Pan hired Meade as a dancer for the film *Cleopatra*. The Jazz Dancers were on a break, and Meade planned on working at Cinecittà in Rome for four weeks, then returning to the troupe. But the film, plagued by numerous rewrites, directorial changes, and Elizabeth Taylor's emerging romance with Richard Burton, famously exceeded its production schedule, and by the time reshoots wound up around 1963, the Jazz Dancers had scattered.

Tensions had arisen with Ann Emery, Bradley's star and live-in girlfriend. It wasn't that she wanted to get married; she was dedicated to dance, not domesticity. But Bradley was *so* casual, so reticent. When a doctor began paying ardent court, Bradley feigned indifference, even though annoyed by the competition. At about the time Meade left for Rome, Emery had pulled together her own independent group of dancers for the Panama Club and appeared as a single act at the intimate L'Hirondelle, then launched a series of tap-dance performances. Benny Bennison drifted off, then became a director, presenting a well-received *Hamlet* in Holland Park. Sarita Fonseca moved to Australia. Chris Parry continued to dance in cabaret and theater, had a baby, then managed American tap dancer Will Gaines.[20]

It is said that choreographers have a fifteen-year life span; after that, it is time for a new generation to bring the pulse of a new era to dance. With thirty-five years onstage, onscreen, and in the studio, Bradley exceeded the allotted run. His dance troupes in the 1950s had provided unique opportunities to experiment and present his own vision, but had also camouflaged that the dance and entertainment worlds had significantly changed. He had just witnessed Baby Laurence. Alvin Ailey had made a sensation in New York with his landmark *Revelations* the previous year. Ann Emery was managing without him. All those years of innovation and experiment, of working collaboratively and making things happen for producers, of congeniality and colleagues, seemed irrelevant. His long reliable path, of finding his identity in dance, was now fading.

Bradley was fifty-five and had less of a road map than ever. He was still creating dancers, envisioning dance, and generating ideas. The question now was how to link his steps.

PART 6

RESOLUTION, 1961–1972

CHAPTER 23

THE SWERVING SIXTIES

There is no agony like bearing
an untold story inside you.

—ZORA NEALE HURSTON

He glided onto the set, easy, poised, and smiling. His suit, with jacket unbuttoned, is elegant and unstudied. When she realizes that Buddy Bradley is joining her, Jessie Matthews's eyes sparkle, her hands flutter in delight, and she rises spontaneously from her chair. Introduced as the great choreographer of Eleanor Powell, Alicia Markova, Anton Dolin, Fred Astaire, and Jessie Matthews, Buddy doesn't bother with the fine points, lightly arranges his trousers, then settles back in his chair and dives into why Jessie Matthews was the greatest. It is the 1961 tape of *This Is Your Life*, a BBC program that springs on an unsuspecting celebrity a cavalcade of his or her life.[1] Elsewhere, in a tribute to Charles B. Cochran, Bradley is equally engaging.

These real-time captures of Bradley—the only two we have—are revealing. He could have regaled the audience with stories of grand first nights and glamorous movie-making, but instead he focused on character, values, and human experience. Particularly noteworthy about Bradley's poise in these appearances is that it occurs in a time of fragility. By now, Bradley's dance troupes had disbanded, and calls for choreography were sporadic. Even teaching dance had contracted. New trends were taking over musical theater. Soon dance music would mean the Beatles (accompanied by Black-derived dances like the Twist and the Frug). In an era marked by an occasional choreographic project, declining health, and recalibration, two elements stand out: a last West End musical, *Divorce Me, Darling!*, and grace.

Bradley is both cool and vital, punctuating sentences with a gesture, a raised eyebrow. His smile is disarming. His generosity of spirit is apparent. He is authentic, and he glows. In a mid-Atlantic accent with just a hint of his childhood in the South, Bradley praises Jessie, citing her prodigious concentration, her ability to memorize a routine in minutes that would take another dancer hours, her tendency to rehearse until she dropped. He alludes to her breakdowns, which they navigated together, then voices his admiration for a woman who made it completely on her own, despite her vulnerability, relying on wit and sensibility to create greatness from bits of instruction and experience gleaned along the way. Once so shy that he tried to duck out of teaching at Billy Pierce's studio, Bradley now displays complete self-assurance.

He brings the same charisma to the BBC celebration of the late Charles B. Cochran.[2] Again, he is a vivid presence, elongating an occasional word, making statements clearly and decisively, and not hesitating to use drama to deliver a point. He dissects how Cochran selected his famous Young Ladies—"wonderful looking creatures," in Bradley's colorful parlance, and with exceptional talent.

But what Bradley dwells on are Cochran's standards, how he insisted on professionalism; how he had no patience with temperament (if a star pulled rank, she was out of the show the following day); how he required that every Young Lady dress well, speak well, and conduct herself with integrity. What truly set Cockie apart from all the great producers he had worked with, Bradley concludes, was his understanding of human nature.

Off camera, Bradley now taught in a faded church hall and choreographed the odd project.[3] Roy Sone, long recuperated from appendicitis and now an established West End dancer and actor, choreographed for nightclubs on the side, subcontracting Buddy for routines at the Establishment and Embassy Clubs. Sone paid handsomely for his services—it was Buddy Bradley choreography, after all, he reasoned. Bradley also contributed to *Exotica*, a revue by Ivor Megiddo at Churchill's Club.

Staging fantasy dances for geishas in Japan, Incas in Peru, and a Trio Capricho Español, Bradley was on familiar territory with *Exotica*, but working with Ivor Megiddo was perplexing. Megiddo had recently danced the "Steam Heat" number in the West End production of Bob Fosse's *The Pajama Game* and now peppered his dances with trendy isolations, shoulder shrugs, and the broken doll walk. Such moves, perceived as novel, came from the Black and burlesque dancing vocabulary that Bradley had known for decades, but it was people like Fosse and Megiddo who were developing it into a new lingua franca of dance. Now, as with rhythm tap with Baby Laurence, Bradley was viewing, once again, the road not taken.[4]

Though Bradley may have been reassessing his career, dance insiders continued to be drawn to his aura. Marie Rambert–trained Betty Dale Fox, who had met Bradley through Ann Emery, wanted something new for her small dance troupe and held her breath that the great Buddy Bradley—everybody looked up to him, she would recall—would deign to choreograph for the Fox Miller Dancers. She was flattered that he accepted. Watching the master create was all she expected; Bradley literally felt the music, he focused the atmosphere, and the work simply flowed out of him. What she hadn't anticipated was the effect of his personality—he could get the best out of every dancer in the studio and instill confidence even when asking her dancers for something outside their comfort zone.

Bradley's willingness to delegate was another surprise. The man who had once been a stickler in rehearsals, famous for his incessant and gentle refrain "Let's try that again," now blithely turned to Fox after blocking out his work, announced she could polish it on her dancers, and made his exit. Perhaps, like Martha Graham, who conserved her creative energy by entrusting rehearsals to Louis Horst, Bradley now saved himself for creation. But perhaps it foreshadowed something else.

How was it, too, that Bradley, once so jealously protective of his solitude, now opened himself to new friendships? Betty Fox's husband, an engineer, wasn't in the least starstruck by Bradley the dance legend but found Bradley had many interesting things to say on a variety of subjects. Wishing to know him better, he invited the choreographer for Sunday lunch, and Bradley, surprisingly, accepted. Betty Fox, busy preparing lunch and keeping an eye on a toddler, retains a hazy recollection of the afternoon but remembers two men deeply engrossed in conversation and an additional surprise: the disciplined Bradley, it turned out, was a bon vivant, who savored second servings of lemon meringue pie.

Only weeks later, Betty found herself hastening to the Chest Hospital (now Victoria Park Hospital) in Bethnal Green. Bradley had been admitted there. She assumed Bradley was ill with tuberculosis—he had a bad cough from time to time, and the Chest Hospital specialized in lung and heart diseases—but delicately refrained from asking. The word spread, drawing others back to Bradley.

Frank Coda heard the news by chance in an actor's café, then jumped into his car, bringing his wife, Debbie, a former Tiller Girl. Though now an actor, Coda considered Bradley his spiritual beacon, once upon a time going so far as to copy his sweaters reverentially. To his surprise, Bradley, so aloof in the studio, even remembered Debbie by name, all these years later. Charlie Meade's friend Dee (Dorothy) Edghill made herself available, too. Though not a part of the inner circle of professional dancers who congregated about Bradley, with stalwarts like Meade and Brandon now a continent away in America, it was Dee who filled the gap and helped Bradley convalesce. She had a nurturing temperament; in the future, she would also take care of Chuck Green and Baby Laurence.[5]

Within months, however, Bradley appeared to have made a full recovery. "Fit and agile, going a touch grey but still a very smooth cool customer," is David Essex's description of Bradley in 1963. At the time, the future singer-actor (Che in *Evita*) and composer (of a musical based on *Mutiny on the Bounty)* studied with Bradley in the parish hall of Christ Church in Lisson Grove, a Victorian pile past its best days but with a good wood floor, where Essex showed up for private tap lessons at the behest of his manager, who intended to make him an all-around performer.[6] Essex, then a drummer with a blues band, was resistant to the idea—he was a musician, not a dancer—but was quickly charmed by Bradley, who put him at ease chatting about blues and percussion. Bradley, quick to size up aptitudes and tailor his teaching, lost no time leveraging Essex's drumming experience to get him up to speed with tap's percussive steps.

But, despite Essex's chipper description, Bradley may not have bounced back. Jazz historian Marshall Stearns came to London that July to interview Bradley for his groundbreaking book *Jazz Dance*. A camaraderie ensued, with letters flying back and forth across the Atlantic. Much of the correspondence was mundane—here's a headshot for the book and a copy of the *Ever Green* program; reminders to send a promised book on jazz—but wistfulness lingers between the lines. Bradley hopes that Stearns, one of the founders of the Newport Jazz Festival, can arrange to bring him to the festival, just as he had featured Pete Nugent, Baby Laurence, Honi Coles, and Bunny Briggs to great acclaim the previous summer. He also wished to share his story; would Stearns help him write it? Bradley's words are dignified and reticent but suggest an encroaching awareness of mortality, of wondering what he has contributed of lasting value. The haunting question remained: Would he become invisible, then vanish, like Billy Pierce, Leonard Harper, and so many others?[7]

New projects offset existential concerns. That summer, in Edinburgh, Bradley directed *Blackbirds of 1964*, a contemporary African diasporic take on the Lew Leslie revues for which he assembled the Manhattan Brothers ("South Africa's Kings of Harmony"), limbo dancers, a Caribbean steel band, and Ena Babb, a "bombshell singer with a wiggle," in settings that ranged from smoky shebeens in Johannesburg to Carnival in Trinidad. All the while, Bradley kept an eye on London and channeled the Côte d'Azur. He was beginning to map out the dances for *Divorce Me, Darling*, Sandy Wilson's musical spoof of Noël Coward's *Private Lives*.[8]

Working on the show cast a rosy glow. Bradley, the quintessential choreographer of the 1930s, was lauded as the perfect fit for

Wilson's musical. *The Tatler* described him and his dances as "more precisely and cleverly 1930ish than anything else in the show." The *Financial Times* raved that his dances were so expressive that he could declaim "To be or not to be" in taps. If Wilson's new play had anything close to the five-year run of his previous hit, the 1920s parody *The Boy Friend*, it could reinvigorate Bradley's career and launch a renaissance for tap dance.[9]

The dances were sublime. Male lead Cy Young and teenage Shaun Warner, playing a bellboy, opened the show with a rapid-fire tap challenge dance. The choreography in which Young dances in and out of bedrooms on a hotel terrace was equally clever. Vicky Clayton, cast as one of the wives, remembers feeling like Ginger Rogers (though Bradley well may have been channeling Jessie Matthews) as she danced with Young, her arms wide, her back arched, a cigarette holder poised in one hand. In another scene, she and two others danced on suitcases, using them like steps, as they chatted about finding the hotel bar. The elaborate grand finale brought the entire cast onstage, the star dancers brought forward with the principals.[10]

Having recently worked with Bob Fosse and Michael Kidd on Broadway, Cy Young, imported from America, was looking forward to dusting off his tap shoes and mastering Bradley's combination of fast footwork and expressive upper body. Also, refreshingly unlike the high-strung Broadway choreographers with whom he'd worked, he found Bradley had the seasoned confidence to *listen* to his dancers and incorporate their suggestions when appropriate. Felled by a car accident shortly after his arrival in London, Young missed the first month of rehearsals, lying flat on his back in his hotel room. When he finally returned to the theater, he was grateful to be working with Bradley, who calmly offered to work with him at whatever level was comfortable, gently easing him back into dance and slowly building routines, never exerting any time pressure. The aggressive Fosse, Young noted, would never have supported him like that.

And, indeed, there was pressure. The skittish playwright didn't trust the director; the actors split into factions; there were endless whispered conversations in the wings; and stage directions were continually changed, then reversed. Patricia Michael, the twenty-three-year-old lead, remembers Bradley as a constant, calm presence in the orchestra stalls while others carried on and screamed.

On opening night, director Steven Vinaver gifted Bradley with an enormous bag of marijuana. Bradley, touched and close to tears, responded, "I don't know what I've done to deserve this." To everyone else, however, it was obvious: Bradley had been the show's peacemaker, diplomat, and nurse as well as choreographer. Despite his current vulnerability, he made everyone feel important and valued. Vicky Clayton, a legitimate actress who was new to musicals, found that whenever she was caught in the cross hairs of director's reversals and high-handed fellow dancers, Bradley noticed. He would gently smile at her quizzical looks, then later take her aside to explain and encourage her. Youngsters like Patricia Michael were astonished to learn, only later, that he was an august theatrical presence, for he presented himself so modestly.

Yet there were occasional chinks in that very charming, kind demeanor. Clayton noticed moments when he wasn't quite so open, friendly, or patient, as if a different person had entered the room. She could never quite work out what it was, but he was definitely preoccupied. At the end of the run, Bradley implored Cy Young to take him to New York, to help him find work on Broadway. Young had adored his experience with Bradley and would happily have worked with him on any show, but, frankly, there wasn't much happening on Broadway at the time that seemed right for him.

With references to Claire Luce, Fred Astaire, and Jack Buchanan, Joan Heal offering a whiplash-precise impersonation of Marlene Dietrich, Roy Sone hoofing as Marcel de la Falaise, and Noël Coward in attendance on opening night, expectations ran high for *Divorce Me, Darling*. But, with a feuding director and playwright, the musical was doomed; the necessary cutting and shaping never happened. Reviews lauded Bradley's choreography but criticized the fossilized dialogue and poor construction. Even more fundamentally, they pointed to the difficulty of sending up the 1930s. For all its merits, the 1930s were over. It was now the age of Fosse.[11]

That spring, Bradley was subdued as he resumed teaching in the vast hall at Christ Church. He had stopped running ads at the end of 1964; now his students came privately, by word of mouth. Vicky Clayton studied with him, often with only Shaun Warner, the scene-stealing bellhop from *Divorce Me, Darling*, in attendance. They danced American-style tap, low to the ground, with light, subtle feet, sometimes to Irving Berlin's "Isn't This a Lovely Day." Occasionally bits of Jerome Robbins's *West Side Story*–type jazz dance crept into routines. When the lesson ended, Clayton would slip out, but Bradley and Warner continued, with Bradley picking up the pace. Pouring himself into this young, new talent reanimated Bradley. It connected him to the future.

Though sixty and slightly fraying, Bradley lived graciously in London. Ensconced in his book-filled flat on Sussex Gardens, he was an esteemed eminence of the theater and dance, no longer a hot young choreographer but universally admired and respected. Unlike so many of his professional colleagues in America, occasional projects still came his way—a dream ballet in the television series, *Blackmail*, and a nostalgic musical hall program on the Isle of Wight. After a long, accomplished career, many would have welcomed the leisure. But Bradley was restless. He who had continually sought to differentiate himself still reached for the indefinable.[12]

CHAPTER 24

BACK TO THE FUTURE

Healing begins where the wound was made.

—ALICE WALKER

In 1967 Bradley's former protégé Johnny Brandon, now living in New York, had the wild idea of creating a musical based on P. G. Wodehouse's Jeeves stories. Wodehouse didn't want to release the rights to Jeeves but suggested that Brandon consider a musical adaptation of his 1934 West End hit with Guy Bolton, *Who's Who?* The far-fetched idea produced a fantastical result: Buddy Bradley would return to New York to choreograph and direct the project.[1]

Who's Who, Baby? (as the new property was titled) transposed the original story of a prince and barber exchanged at birth to a jet-setting earl and cockney rock 'n' roller with a score of rock, ballads, calypso, and jazz and required a versatile director. When Brandon proposed Bradley, Guy Bolton, who was rewriting the book, waxed enthusiastic: he had worked with Bradley in the past, on *Rio Rita* on Broadway, on the English production of *Anything Goes,* and on *Top Hat and Tails* with Jack Buchanan. The suggestion was genius.

It wasn't easy, however, to ferret out Bradley in London in 1967. While Brandon moved to New York to pursue his career as a songwriter, his mentor had closed his school and receded from view.

When Brandon finally found Bradley, now living on Prince's Square near Notting Hill, the choreographer was keen. After years of providing dance that enhanced storylines, he had accumulated his own ideas about directing. Now he had an opportunity to both choreograph and direct—and not just a revue like *Blackbirds of 1964* but a bona-fide musical with characters and a plot. Within days, all parties had come to an agreement.[2]

If excited about his new prospects, Bradley remained characteristically low affect. He arrived in New York without fanfare, stayed temporarily with Charlie Meade, now settled in Manhattan, and roasted a turkey for Thanksgiving. He took his time to contact Johnny Brandon. Though long familiar with Bradley's coolness, Brandon now detected an extra aloofness. He ascribed it to a combination of hurt that Brandon had distanced himself as he pursued his ambitions in New York and Bradley's defensive pride as his career waned. A cozy dinner at Brandon's apartment, catching up and listening to Lena Horne LPs, did much to close the gap.[3]

But when Bradley mentioned casually that his new wife was arriving, the garrulous Brandon was speechless. In all their back-and-forth planning for New York, there had never been any mention of a wife. Furthermore, though Brandon had known Bradley over the course of quite a few girlfriends, he considered him essentially solitary. Meade, too, was bewildered. It was he who introduced Dee Pitchford Edghill to the studio—and while he knew her to be attractive, warm, and friendly, he had never detected any chemistry between his friends. Perhaps Bradley's recent illness had fostered a bond, he mused. Perhaps, prompted by the prospect of coming to America, they had decided to become a team. They married in London on August 4, 1967, Dee using her maiden name, Pitchford, and listing her profession as a singer.[4]

Theater, unlike marriage, was familiar stomping ground for Bradley. He knew how to talk to producers, and they were duly impressed. More importantly, the dancers were smitten. Although they were told he had come from London, they were too young to know Bradley's history but immediately responded to his gentle authority. He was very quiet but endearing; one had an impulse to hug him. Actress and dancer Glory Van Scott was struck by his distinctive way of walking, smooth and deliberate, as if he were thinking as he moved. When he walked down the studio during a barre, it was clear that music was playing in his head, and he was thinking of the next step.

He was organized and decisive, and he knew what he wanted as a director. He had listened to the music and knew what the scenes needed to be, and where the dances were going to occur. As a choreographer he worked out his dances in rehearsal, demonstrating by dancing, then finishing with a little smile. He'd then run his dancers through the work, watching thoughtfully as he smoked a cigarette. He used the whole body. It wasn't just footwork; it was *choreography*, Van Scott thought.

The dancers loved coming to rehearsals. The principals, Jackie Mayro (who had originated the role of Baby June in *Gypsy*) and Van Scott (an accomplished veteran who had danced with Katherine Dunham, Agnes de Mille, and George Balanchine), were the kind of dancers who could tear up anything. If there were any little roadblocks to overcome, Bradley's assistant, Ural Wilson, formerly of Katherine Dunham, was available to translate any steps. Bradley's movements, so smooth and easy, translated into dances that were natural, unified, and coherent. The cast, Van Scott recalls, was not having any problem with Bradley.[5]

Van Scott could also see that Bradley was lifted by working with the dancers of *Who's Who, Baby?* "He is back in America now," Van Scott thought, working with dancers from his culture who could understand and do as he wished. He didn't have to sift through different dance acculturations; he could draw his dance right out of these dancers' bodies. You could see the nostalgia as he sat and watched, she would remember.

In the quiet of the late afternoons, Bradley and Van Scott would chat, standing on the sidewalk in front of the Players Theater on MacDougal Street. Bradley would smoke his cigarette and people watch as their conversation meandered from his school to New York and everything in between. She understood exactly why he left America. He had always been the creator, yet time and again his work was taken away from him, whether by Busby Berkeley, Clifton

Webb, or John Boyle. All of a sudden, his work became theirs—ripped away from him, she mused.

The fact that there was always someone grabbing his ideas and using them, telling him, in effect, that he was always to play second fiddle, had limited his scope. Only the lucky ones could be trained and set out to accomplish their dreams, limited only by their talent and fate; Bradley didn't have that freedom. In moving to London, he had escaped what so many of his colleagues had faced in America: appropriation of work, misplaced credit, prescribed roles, restricted venues, limited visibility, and rare, if nonexistent, opportunities for unfettered creativity. Given the roadblocks, tap dancer and writer Brenda Bufalino thought he had been smart to seize the opportunity to work in London. Van Scott thought so, too, but she also felt his pain. "I wouldn't have liked to go through that," she thought, contemplating a life of loneliness and sadness, of being deracinated, cut off from family, culture, ritual, and the pulsating energy of New York. She sensed, even after all those years, the underlying pain of an orphan, too, of being so alone and unsupported as he pursued an unexplored path.

Soon, however, the privileged intimacy of rehearsals, of getting to know new colleagues, and musings, was to rupture. The show was underfunded, a situation that became apparent when previews began on January 9, 1968. Suddenly the producers needed more money—a lot more money—for advertising and a reserve fund. New producers with deeper pockets were hurriedly brought on and became the dominant partners. It was odd that Charlotte Schiff had bothered to back the show, for she did not like Guy Bolton's storyline, the music, the production, or the director, and demanded wholesale changes. The show became a chessboard, with each move eliminating another player. Guy Bolton, disgruntled with the changes to his book, removed his name from the show. Bradley was the next casualty, fired for ostensibly not having a handle on the project. Brandon then resigned. Marvin Gordon was brought in as director, but his disjointed work was light-years away from the suave approach of Buddy Bradley. With the changes, the show was doomed. *Who's Who, Baby?* wrote *The New York Times*, was nowhere, man.[6]

Bradley was phlegmatic. These things happened, he reassured Brandon. It was surprising, however, that the man who had vowed he could never live in America again did not catch the next flight back to London. Typically, theater transplants stayed in long-term hotels or sublet apartments. An off-Broadway play, even one with aspirations to move to Broadway, didn't necessitate repatriation. But with the offer to direct *Who's Who, Baby?* Bradley had jettisoned his life in London, his cocoon of accomplishment, his reputation, his stature, his flat filled with books, and his fine new car, and had committed to begin life anew in New York.

Perhaps the idea of returning had been planted the night Bradley had been refused entry at the Coconut Grove on Regent Street. Perhaps seeing the subtlety that Baby Laurence brought to tap dance or hearing Cy Young's stories about the new crop of choreographers on Broadway convinced Bradley that he wanted to access New York's energy. Little did it matter that Cy Young had also warned him Broadway currently offered him little. Something larger than directing, even larger than dance, compelled him to come home.

Despite his professed renunciation, Bradley had never fully let go of America, staying up-to-date via subscriptions to *The Chicago Defender* and *The Crisis* and reading the latest African American literature. America and its past, from his family's strivings, his childhood in the South, his formative years in the North, to jazz music, and jazz dance, were central to the man he had become. Bradley's reason to return to America was at once simple and profound: he needed to come to peace with his homeland. With the Civil Rights Act signed in 1964, it seemed a propitious moment.

After thirty-eight years away, however, the theater world knew little about Bradley, and Bradley knew little about how New York worked. Perhaps if he had stayed, been nurtured by a community, and observed the rising generation, he may have learned to bring the light to himself, as Katherine Dunham did so superbly. He would most certainly have benefited from a network of connections.

As it was, there were few. Leonard Harper, Billy Pierce, Thaddeus Drayton, and Eddie Rector were gone. Ralph Cooper, with whom Bradley had worked up a vaudeville act in 1925, was now engrossed with his work in the New York State Department of Human Rights. The Billy Pierce Studio crowd had long dispersed. Of his former juniors at the Pierce Studio, Henry Le Tang stayed busy with commercial work out West and creating routines for a family act called Hines, Hines, and Dad. Herbert Harper, who had replaced Bradley as head instructor at the Pierce Studio and assisted Balanchine with the tap choreography for *On Your Toes*, had retired upstate. Aaron Gates, after staging a few numbers for *Show Boat*, opened a short-lived dance studio, staged a circus, then orbited out of New York. His name last appears in print in *The Billboard* in 1941, as a producer of an "all-colored musical" premiering in Nashville.[7]

Others had struggled dearly. Exquisite Roland Holder, full of youthful promise in *The Exile* and prone to plagiarizing Buddy's dances (who could blame him?), had spiraled downward, addicted to heroin, bounced in and out of Sing Sing, and intermittently worked as a messenger, until he disappeared without a trace. Frank Harrington, who had so brilliantly transposed jazz scores for Bradley, ended up unemployed and living with his grandmother in Port Chester. Eddie "Pee Wee" Williams returned to New York full of hope after his appearance in *Cochran's 1931 Revue* in London, but few opportunities materialized. While his sister, Ruth Williams, went on to establish an influential ballet school in Harlem, Williams appears to have never danced professionally again, settling for a few amateur modeling gigs for the Obisny fraternity in Harlem. His dance partner, Joey Shields, once described as having the face of Apollo and the voice of an angel, ended up as a page in a hotel. They had all tried so hard. Bradley was one of the lucky ones.[8]

For a young generation, however, it was an electrifying moment. Van Scott and her friends Arthur Mitchell, Talley Beatty, Alvin Ailey, and Jean-Léon Destiné were all busy, running from rehearsals to recording studios, participating in workshops, attending performances at night, sometimes working for nothing, but growing and thriving in the burst of creativity. Busy building her career, tucking a sandwich into her bag as she dashed out of her apartment for a long day of rehearsals, Van Scott was young and did not realize that Bradley was at a loss. She could have brought him into the field, to theaters, to dance studios, to workshops, to rehearsals, to the 92nd Street Y, if only she had known.

As always, Bradley's dignity, his protective reserve, was a double-edged sword. He didn't have the brazen self-confidence to push himself forward or ask for help. At parties, he was the observer, not the raconteur. Low and humble does not work in America, states Van Scott emphatically—but that was precisely what Bradley, born in 1905 in the Deep South and coming of age in the 1920s on Broadway, had been taught to be in America.

Other factors added force to the undertow. Tap was all but dead, awaiting its messiah in the form of Gregory Hines. It was associated with people like Bojangles, servilely entertaining Massa, and relegated to TV shows for the middle-aged and middlebrow. A few, like Sammy Davis Jr. and Bunny Briggs, just managed to hold on. The great Baby Laurence now worked in construction, with just an occasional gig. The hip and street-smart, the snazzy and stylish, ran in the opposite direction.

Long gone were the heady days when tap—novel, sexy, and alluring—held sway. Only three years earlier, in 1965, Van Scott was working with Agnes de Mille at American Ballet Theater with Carmen de Lavallade, Judith Jamison, and Cleo Quitman on *The Four Marys*. De Mille's choreography included a time step that dumbfounded her four dancers. "We don't do tap," the four African American dancers haughtily announced—they had studied ballet, modern dance, and jazz. It fell to De Mille's English assistant, ironically, to teach the American dancers the time step. De Mille, Van Scott recalls, was about to fall off her chair.

America itself was collapsing. The assassination of Martin Luther King Jr. on April 4, 1968, sent a chilling message: Blacks, as individuals with agency, were not welcome in the US. Bradley had returned seeking reconciliation. But there could be no closure now, only painful disillusion.

Today, Bradley would be lionized, invited to guest teach at universities, heaped with honorary degrees, and perhaps bestowed with a National Medal of Arts. His story would be prominent in anthologies and encyclopedias of twentieth-century dance, theater, and the

Harlem Renaissance. But, in the 1960s, for those who worked in commercial theater and in popular dance, this was far from the case. After a forty-year career virtually recreating theatrical dance, Bradley was as exposed as the day he checked into a boardinghouse in Harlem. He was running out of money and lived in a walkup at 47 West Eighth Street in Greenwich Village. With no doorman, no graceful architecture, and stripped of his books, it was a comedown from his London flat, and he did not like to receive friends. He would speak to Charlie Meade on the phone, but did not invite him to visit, nor did he go out, attend dance, jazz performances, or the theater.

Possibly old friends like Norma Miller or Henry Le Tang helped when they could, but to get by Bradley had to take a job developing film for Kodak. The chemicals burnt into his hands, those elegant hands that had gestured dramatically in *The Dance*, created the famous Jessie Matthews pushing-against-air backbend, and modeled Shirley Bassey into a world-class performer. The delicate hands with the long fingers that were the first thing former Buddy Bradley Jazz Dancers inquired about when Meade returned to London. After all his work and accomplishments, he was ashamed of this job, of what was happening to his life, and hurt once again by America. He did not want his friends to see him in this state and retreated from the world.

By 1972, rumors crossed the Atlantic that Buddy Bradley had fallen on hard times. Someone in London heard that he was begging on the street—the very idea that such a story circulated would have mortified him. Another mentioned tuberculosis. But nobody really knew. Bradley had withdrawn into silence, and Dorothy Bradley, isolated and in an unfamiliar milieu, was secretive, not even reaching out to trusted friends like Charlie Meade. In March, Bradley rallied to host a panel at Carnegie Hall on Kansas City jazz. It turned out to be his farewell performance; shortly afterward he was in a nursing home.[9]

Four months later, Buddy Bradley died, on July 17, 1972, an exile in America. According to Meade, he died of a broken heart.

EPILOGUE

We are mere journeymen, planting seeds
for someone else to harvest.

—WALLACE THURMAN

Buddy Bradley's funeral took place three days later, on Thursday, July 20, 1972, at the "Jazz Church," St. Peter's Lutheran Church on Lexington Avenue at Fifty-Fourth Street, where Duke Ellington, Thelonious Monk, and Dizzy Gillespie worshipped, and Billy Strayhorn's Steinway held pride of place. Someone—perhaps old friends Pete Nugent and Henry Le Tang working in double time as a double act—had made fitting arrangements for a farewell to a prince of jazz dance.

Glowing tributes flowed. Obituaries described Bradley as a choreographer whose ideas were ahead of his time, an international catalyst for tap and jazz in musical theater, and universally beloved. In New York, his death was noted in *The Daily News*, *The New York Times*, *Variety*, and *Dance Magazine*. In London, there were stories in *The Daily Telegraph*, *Dancing Times*, and *The Stage*. These bouquets were only natural. Buddy Bradley had disseminated African American tap dance to stages worldwide, reconceived theatrical dance for the twentieth century, and bequeathed jazz movement to neoclassical ballet.[1]

Slowly, the news spread through the Bradley diaspora. In New York, the gentle Charlie Meade was pained to learn of Bradley's death only after the funeral. Dee dropped by and sobbed in his arms as she relayed the news. Henry Le Tang fell silent, regretting that Bradley had never had the recognition he deserved. In London, Betty Dale Fox mourned; Bradley, of the magnanimous spirit and quick-as-lightning choreography, would always be in a class of his own. Annette Battams became lost in reflection, remembering not only Bradley's legendary cool and consummate musicality, but also how his face lit up when a dancer brought something original to his choreography.

In Brighton some years later, former dancer now actor Frank Coda was browsing in a secondhand book stall with his wife and young daughter when, while flipping through old issues of *Theatre World*, the name of Buddy Bradley caught his eye. It was in the obituary column. Coda's eyes welled up as the memories sprang forth. He was once again in the studio on Denman Street, with the tap-battered floor, the frumpy sweaters, the constant paddle steps, the grime, the concentration, and, yes, the elation. In that room, Buddy had created glamour. Not the tinseled flash-in-the-pan glamour of a Folies Bergère costume, but the substantive glamour of making art, of rising above the mundane to reach for the transcendent. It was not about any show, any role, any review, or any competition; it was about that hour in the studio, that moment, when breath, dance, music, and individuality embraced.

Time stopped in that studio, as it did that day for Coda in the book stall. Buddy Bradley had cast a spell that would endure forever.

ACKNOWLEDGMENTS

This book, like Buddy Bradley, crossed oceans and genres. Finding Bradley in both remote and cosmopolitan quarters, in written archives and spoken reminiscences, in films and reviews, became a journey that depended on guidance from many. I am grateful to everyone who directed and advised me on this path, and if I have overlooked anyone in these acknowledgments, I hope you'll accept my sincere apologies. This book is a tribute to your collective knowledge, expertise, and contributions.

Theresa Ruth Howard planted the seed that became the genesis of a biography. Linda Murray, the Anne Bass Curator of the Jerome Robbins Dance Division and associate director for the Library of Performing Arts, New York Public Library, helped map out the context and territory of Buddy Bradley. Dr. Thomas DeFrantz gave me the courage to pursue what became a life-changing path. My agent extraordinaire, Rob McQuilkin, believed in this project from the beginning and helped identify the beating heart of this book. Buddy and I were particularly blessed to have the very thoughtful as well as tap-savvy editor Amy Caldwell, editorial director, and Gayatri Patnaik, publisher, at Beacon Press, to help us turn an idea into a book. Also at Beacon, I wish to thank Alison Rodriguez, Beth Collins, Marcy Barnes, Thea Smith, and, particularly, Carol Chu for her inspired jacket design, as well as Susan Lumenello, and Emily Shelton for sensitive copyediting.

My deepest thanks to all those who knew, loved, worked with, and studied with Bradley—and shared him so generously with me.

The firsthand insights, stories, memories, and experiences of Annette Battams, the late Vicky Clayton, Frank and Debbie Coda and Michelle Coda Rentell, Angela Easterling, David Essex, Betty Dale Fox, Pepi Lemer, Jan Lynton, Sheila Mathews and Sally Reading, Charlie Meade and Lynn Ringhaver, Patricia Michael, Daphne Selfe, Roy Sone, Ralph Tobert, Glory Van Scott, Johnny Worthy Jr., and Cy Young transformed a personage into a man. We, the Buddy Bradley tribe, are now bound as a family.

So much of this book, like Bradley's character, was profoundly shaped by his family. Evelyn Davis Harmon, Bradley's second-cousin-once-removed and family genealogist, illuminated the maternal side of Bradley's family and became my companion-in-arms, reading each chapter as I drafted it. Bradley's niece, Pamela Epps—Aurelius's daughter—shared memories of her father and provided keen perspective on Buddy's relationship with his closest sibling.

Dancers, historians, and theater experts lent their expertise to clarify Bradley's story. My list includes Dali Adekunle, the late Hinton Battle, Leah Bass-Baylis, Betsy Baytos (big shoutout for the interview quotes pulled from your upcoming documentary on eccentric dance!), Ninotchka Bennahum, Andrew Black, Brenda Bufalino, Duke Dang, Juliana Ariel De Vaan, Moncell Durden, Bill Egan, Silas Farley, Eric Foner, Caseen Gaines, Amy Hall Garner, Jane Goldberg, Jreena Green, Ray Hesselink, Constance Valis Hill, Angelina Hoffman, Jennifer Homans, Laura Jacobs, the late Dexter Jones, Tanisha R. Jones, Lauren King, Jill Kenney, Ed Ku, Sean Mayes, Patricia Mears, Margaret Morrison, Andrew Nemr, Norton Owen, Max Pollack, Allana Radecki, Claudia Rahardjanoto, Howard Rye, Suki Schorer, Brian Seibert, Lenwood Sloan, Terence Spivey, Shea Sullivan, Tony Waag, Dianne Walker, Annette Walker (whose own PhD explores Buddy Bradley's tap influence in Britain), William Whitener, and Chazz Young. Librarians deserve extra special thanks, including several at the Jerome Robbins Dance Division at the Library of Performing Arts, New York Public Library: Erik Stolarski, reference librarian, who took ownership of the book as much as I, and the unfailingly available Joshua Persaud, oral history project assistant; and Phillip Cosgrove, supervising librarian, who was crucial in locating the best and most obscure photos. Doug Reside, curator of the Billy Rose Theatre Division at the Library of Performing Arts, New York Public Library, and his tireless staff were invaluable in helping me reconstruct the 1920s Broadway in which Bradley first emerged as a choreographer.

In Alabama, I leaned on the guidance of Ethel Alexander and Wanda Looney of the Birmingham African American Genealogy Group; Mary Beth Newbill, librarian, Southern History Department, Birmingham Public Library; James L. Baggett, Department of Archives, Birmingham Public Library; and Germaul Barnes, Alabama School of Fine Arts. For exploring the history of Sumter County, Sheila Limerick, curator of the Alabama Room at the Julia Tutwiler Library, University of West Alabama; Christin Loeher, also of the Tutwiler Library; and Shari Williams and Debra Love, both of the Black Belt African American Genealogy Group, helped assemble local history and provided suggestions for tracing the Epps family story. Margaret Winston McGough was invaluable, giving me a sweeping tour of the county, introducing me to the best truck stop food in the South, cracking the mystery of where Bradley's grandfather was buried, and showing me the ropes for locating critical and unanticipated information in the Sumter County courthouse.

The Walker family of Habersham County, Georgia, came to life through records assembled by Evelyn Davis Harmon and, thanks to her introduction, by local historians and preservationists E. Lane Gresham and Ivy Hall, and by the very thoughtful Will Lockwood, who grew up with Bradley's family. In Harrisburg, Pennsylvania, Calobe Jackson Jr.; Chef Joseph G. Randall; Dave Morrison, and Jeb Stuart, Historic Harrisburg Society; Ken Frew, Dauphin County Historical Library; and Jesse Stowell made critical years of Bradley's formation come alive.

Bradley's Broadway and New York years were captured by hours in the Schomburg Center for Research in Black Culture, New York Public Library, cared for by Joy Bivins, director, and her resourceful staff, especially Auburn Nelson, AJ Muhammad, Musa Jatta, Rhonda Evans, and Sonia Richards. Further records were sourced at the Milstein Division of Genealogical Records of the New York

Public Library. Insight into Bradley's context and colleagues came from the rich records of Rutgers University's Institute of Jazz Studies with the assistance of archivist Angela Lawrence and Adriana Cuervo. Timely advice and fellowship were supplied at key moments by Dr. Leslie Camhi, Debra Martin Chase, Stephanie French, Elizabeth Howard, Peter Kayafas, Cynthia Millman, John Reddick, Deborah Roberts, Meryl Rosofsky, Eric K. Washington, Hal Witt, and Bill Wright. Grant Harper Reid's research and generous sharing of the story of his grandfather Leonard Harper was a gift for entering Bradley's story during the Harlem Renaissance.

London, where the body of Bradley's professional life unfolded, was initially unlocked by Jane Pritchard, curator of dance, Victoria and Albert Museum, then unfolded in front of my very eyes by Robert Hazle and Julie Gambling, Noël Coward Foundation and Archive; Tom McErlain, Gloucester Square Community; Josephine Botting and Steve Tolevey of the British Film Institute; Georgina Colbeck, Westminster Archives; Robyn Armour of the News Reference Team at the British Library; Daniel Albon, senior archivist, Rambert; Rob Mortimer, Chapman-Petrie Co.; Philip Watson, Thames & Hudson; Jill Sullivan, Theatre Division, Bristol University; Karin Lowen and Hester Colley, genealogists; Dame Shirley Bassey; Lance Ellington; Alastair Macaulay; Geraldine Morris; Andrew Pepper; Justine Picardie; Hugo Vickers; Martin Williams; and Jay Cartwright and Peter Torley, private investigators. Stephen Bourne, your work, sharing, and advice were instrumental and generous. Durrant's Hotel, a stone's throw from most of Bradley's London addresses, became my home away from home.

I am grateful to Lynn Garafola, biographer of Arthur Mitchell, for Saturday morning chats about the biographer's process and especially for her invitation to present my work on Bradley to the Columbia University Studies in Dance Seminar. The insights gleaned from the many dance perspectives of the seminarians sharpened my understanding considerably and helped further focus my narrative.

Those who read my work, whether partially or in its entirety, gave me untold confidence in this project, not only by confirming my research and validating its conclusions but by your encouraging comments: Alex Gleason, Adrian Wright, and Margo Jefferson, enormous thanks to you. Kurt Adler and De Witt Fleming, thank you for the long conversations and sharing so generously your professional insights into the practice of tap dancing. Elizabeth Kendall, my eternal gratitude for your belief in this project, for your vital introductions, and, above all, for so generously helping me shape reams of raw research into a human story as you simultaneously shepherded your own work into publication. This book would well be a lesser one without you. Thomas DeFrantz, you are the alpha and omega of this project!

I was privileged to tell Bradley's story and doubly privileged to have worked with all of you. Thank you.

CHRONOLOGY

BUDDY BRADLEY (1905–1972)

Note: It is impossible to account absolutely for every work that Buddy Bradley contributed to or choreographed. The following list, therefore, is but a partial summary. All works listed are choreographed solely by Bradley unless otherwise noted.

STAGED WORKS

(Opening night dates are supplied when available.)

Broadway

1926

Greenwich Village Follies (reworked by Bradley)

- Lyrics and music by Harold Levey and Owen Murphy
- Shubert Theatre, Mar. 15, 1926 (reopened)

George White's Scandals of 1926 (partial choreography by Bradley)

- Book by William K. Wells and George White; lyrics by B. G. De Sylva and Lew Brown; music by Ray Henderson
- Apollo Theatre, June 14, 1926

Broadway (coaching actors cast as chorus dancers in mannerisms, movement, and rituals of dancers)

- By Philip Dunning
- Broadhurst Theatre, and George Abbott, Sept. 16, 1926

1927

Showboat (dance coach for ingenue role, Magnolia, originated by Norma Terris)

- Book and lyrics by Oscar Hammerstein II; music by Jerome Kern
- Ziegfeld Theater, Dec. 27, 1927

Rio Rita (choreography by Sammy Lee and Albertina Rasch; Bradley, brought in to doctor the show, created the "Kinkajou" dance.)

- Book by Guy Bolton and Fred Thompson; music and lyrics

by Harry Tierney and Joseph McCarthy
- Lyric Theatre, Feb. 2, 1927

Half a Widow (choreographing under the name of Billy Pierce)

- Book and lyrics by Frank Dupree and Harry B. Smith; music by Shep Camp
- Waldorf Theatre, Sept. 12, 1927

A Connecticut Yankee (Bradley called in to doctor choreography of Busby Berkeley)

- Book by Herbert Fields; music by Richard Rodgers; lyrics by Lorenz Hart
- Vanderbilt Theatre, Nov. 3, 1927

1928

Hello, Daddy! (co-choreographed, without credit, with Busby Berkeley)

- Book by Herbert Fields, music and lyrics by Dorothy Fields and Jimmy McHugh
- Mansfield Theatre, Dec. 26, 1928

1929

The Little Show (Bradley choreographs "Moanin' Low" for Clifton Webb and Libby Holman)

- Music by Arthur Schwartz, Ralph Rainger, and others; lyrics by Howard Dietz and others
- Music Box Theatre, Apr. 30, 1929

Other

Frankie Manning and the Congaroos Act

- Club 845 (the Bronx), 1947

Who's Who, Baby? (Off-Broadway)

- Book by Guy Bolton, based on play by Bolton and P. J. Wodehouse (reworked by Gerold Frank); music and lyrics by Johnny Brandon
- Players Theater, Jan. 29, 1968

"Contrast and Confrontations in Black Music: Up from Kansas City"

- Hosted by Buddy Bradley and Chris White in conjunction with the Rutgers Institute of Jazz Studies
- Carnegie Hall, Mar. 23, 1972

West End and Europe

1930

Ever Green (choreography by Billy Pierce and Buddy Bradley)

- Book by Benn Levy; lyrics by Lorenz Hart; music by Richard Rodgers
- Adelphi Theatre, Dec. 10, 1930

1931

Cochran's 1931 Revue (choreography by Billy Pierce, Buddy Bradley, and George Balanchine)

- Music by Noël Coward and others
- Pavilion Theatre, Mar. 19, 1931

Creation Cabaret (choreography by Billy Pierce and Buddy Bradley)

- Trocadero Grillroom, Apr. 1931

Fifty Million Frenchmen

- Book by Herbert Fields (adaptation by Arthur Wimperis); music and lyrics by Cole Porter
- King's Theatre (Glasgow), Sept. 1, 1931

Hold My Hand

- Book by Stanley Lupino; music by Noël Gay; lyrics by Desmond Carter
- Gaiety Theatre, Dec. 23, 1931

1932

The Cat and the Fiddle (choreography by Buddy Bradley; act I finale by Frederick Ashton)

- Book by Otto Harbach; music by Jerome Kern
- Palace Theatre, Mar. 16, 1932

Ciro's (floor show), Mar. 1932

Magic Nights Cabaret (choreography by Buddy Bradley and Frederick Ashton)

- Trocadero Grillroom, Apr. 4, 1932

High Yellow, presented at the Camargo Society (choreography by Buddy Bradley; groupings arranged by Frederick Ashton)

- Music by Spike Hughes
- Savoy Theatre, June 6, 1932

Words and Music

- Book, music, and lyrics by Noël Coward
- Adelphi Theatre, Sept. 16, 1932

Desperate Blues

- Music by Jerome Kern; danced by William Chappell
- Ballet Club, Mercury Theatre, Nov. 27, 1932

Cinderella

- Royal Theatre (Glasgow), Dec. 10, 1932

Ballyhoo (dances and ensembles by Buddy Bradley; ballets by Frederick Ashton)

- Music by William Walker; lyrics by Robert Nesbitt
- Comedy Theatre, Dec. 22, 1932

1933

Mother of Pearl

- Book and lyrics by A. P. Herbert; music by Oscar Strauss
- Gaiety Theatre, Jan. 27, 1933

Revels in Rhythm

- Music and lyrics by Annette Mills
- Trocadero Grillroom, Apr. 3, 1933

After Dark (dances and ensembles by Buddy Bradley; ballets by Frederick Ashton)

- Written by Ronald Jeans; music by Kenneth Duffield and Kenneth Leslie-Smith
- Vaudeville Theatre, July 6, 1933

Nice Goings On

- Douglas Furber; music by Arthur Schwartz; lyrics by Douglas Furber and Frank Eyton
- Strand Theatre, Sept. 13, 1933

Slow Water Blues

- Music by Raie de Costa; danced by Anton Dolin and Vera Zorina
- Ciro's, Nov. 6(?), 1933

Folies en Folie

- Produced by Paul Derval featuring Mistinguett and Henri Wessels
- Folies Bergère (Paris), Nov. 1933

1934

Yours Sincerely

- Devised by Rita John
- Daly's Theatre, Feb. 19, 1934

Why Not Tonight? (dances and ensembles by Buddy Bradley; ballets by Agnes de Mille)

- Book and lyrics by Herbert Farjeon; music by Ord Hamilton; additional numbers by Harry Woods, Walford Hyden, and others
- Palace Theatre, Apr. 24, 1934

Happy Weekend

- By Dion Titheradge (based on the Hungarian play *Katz im Sack* by Ladislaus Szilagzi); lyrics by Arthur Stanley; music by Michael Eisemann
- Duke of York Theatre, Mar. 30, 1934

Lucky Break

- By Douglas Furber; lyrics by Douglas Furber and Harlen Thompson; music by Harry Archer
- Strand Theatre, Oct. 2, 1934

1935

Let's Go Gay

- Written by Cecil Landeau and George Frank Rubens
- Embassy Theatre, Mar. 27, 1935

Jubilation (dances and ensembles by Buddy Bradley; ballet by Daniel T. Dolinoff)

- Music and lyrics by Annette Mills
- Trocadero Grillroom, Apr. 4(?) 1935

Charlot's Char-a-Bang (choreography by Hedley Briggs; one number staged by Buddy Bradley)

- Sketches and lyrics by Arthur Macrae and Robert Nesbitt; music by Dennis Van Thal, Arthur Macrae, and Geoffrey Wright
- Vaudeville Theatre, Apr. 10, 1935

The Flying Trapeze (Choreography by Frederick Ashton; Jack Buchanan's dances by Buddy Bradley)

- Book by Douglas Furber (based on a play by Hans Muller); lyrics by Douglas Furber, Desmond Carter, and Frank Eyton; music by Ralph Benatzky and Mabel Wayne
- Alhambra Theatre, May 4, 1935

Anything Goes

- Book by Guy Bolton and P. G. Wodehouse; music and lyrics by Cole Porter
- Palace Theatre, June 14, 1935

Tulip Time

- Worton David and Alfred Parker; lyrics by Bruce Sievier; music by Colin Wark and Hubert W. David
- The Alhambra, Aug. 14, 1935

1936

Follow the Sun (dances and ensembles by Buddy Bradley and Frederick Ashton)

- Dialogue by Ronald Jeans and John Hustings Turner; lyrics by Howard Dietz and Desmond Carter; music by Arthur Schwartz
- Adelphi Theatre, Feb. 4, 1936

Round and Round

- Trocadero Grillroom, Apr. 6, 1936

Blackbirds of 1936

- Conceived by Lew Leslie; lyrics by John Mercer; music by Rube Bloom

- Gaiety Theatre (later moved to the Lyceum Theatre, then the Adelphi Theatre), July 9, 1936

This'll Make You Whistle

- Book by Guy Bolton and Fred Thompson; music and lyrics by Sigler, Goodhart, and Hoffman
- Palace Theatre, Sept. 15, 1936

1937

Floodlight (dances arranged by Buddy Bradley; ballets by Frederick Ashton)

- Written and composed by Beverley Nichols
- Saville Theatre, June 23, 1937

Take It Easy

- Music and lyrics by Herman Timberg, Barbara Blair, and Sammy Timberg
- Palace Theatre, Sept. 23, 1937

1938

Going to Town

- Trocadero Grillroom, Apr. 4, 1938

Happy Returns

- Lyrics and music by Ian Grant, Arthur Johnston, Lorenz Hart, Richard Rodgers, Ira Gershwin, Harold Arlen, Howard Deitz, Arthur Schwartz, and others
- Adelphi Theatre, May 19, 1938

All the Best

- Opera House (Blackpool), June 24, 1938

Aloma and Nutane

- Book by John B. Hyman and LeRoy Clemons; music and lyrics by Hastings Mann
- Opera House (Manchester), Sept. 27, 1938

1939

Night Lights (choreography by Buddy Bradley and Antony Tudor)

- Music selected, arranged, and composed by Elsie April; new lyrics by Lorraine
- Trocadero Grillroom, Apr. 3, 1939

I Can Take It

- Book by Lesser Samuels; music and lyrics by Harry Woods; musical arrangements by Ben Frankel
- Palace Theatre (Manchester), Apr. 1 (?), 1939

All Clear

- Lyrics by Noel Coward, Lorenz Hart, Arthur Macrae, and others; music by Noël Coward, Richard Rodgers, Arthur Schwartz, and others
- Queen's Theatre, Dec. 20, 1939

1940

Lights Up!

- By Ronald Jeans; lyrics by Ian Grant, Frank Eyton, Arthur Wimperis, and Reginald Arkell; music by Noël Gay
- Savoy Theatre, Feb. 9, 1940

Come Out to Play

- Book by Eddie Pola and Peter Watson; music and lyrics by Eddie Pola, Harry Parr-Davies, Roma Campbell Hunter, Freddy Grant, and Ben Frankel
- Phoenix Theatre, Mar. 19, 1940

Top Hat and Tails

- Book by Guy Bolton
- The Palace Theatre (Manchester), Apr. 22, 1940

1941

Orchids and Onions

- Book by Ian Grant; music and lyrics by Jayne Ogden
- Comedy Theatre, Apr. 1, 1941

Wednesday After the War

- Book by J. Walter, J. Olivier, and P. Tracy; lyrics by Val Guest, music by Stefan Craig and G. S. Mathis
- New Theatre, Apr. 5, 1941

Room V

- By Peter Wendy
- Garrick Theatre, Sept. 8, 1941

1942

Big Top

- A revue by Herbert Farjeon
- His Majesty's Theatre, May 8, 1942

Full Swing

- A musical comedy by Arthur Macrae, Archie Menzies, Jack Hulbert
- Palace Theatre, Apr. 16, 1942

Green for Piccadilly

- A revue by Ronald Jeans; music by Kenneth Leslie-Smith; lyrics by Max Kester
- Royal Court, Liverpool, Dec. 15, 1942

Mother Goose (dances for Principal Boy, Patricia Burke, by Buddy Bradley)

- Adapted from the book by J. Hickory Wood by Francis Laidler
- Coliseum, Dec. 24, 1942

1943

La-Di-Da-Di-Da

- Written by Stanley Lupino; music by Noël Gay
- Victoria Palace Theatre, Mar. 30, 1943

It's Foolish but It's Fun

- Revue devised by Douglas Furber; music by Vivian Ellis, John Ridley, Marc Anthony, Fred Prisker and Ralph Reader
- London Coliseum, Mar. 12, 1943

Magic Carpet, a.k.a. *Spick and Span* (Buddy Bradley performing)

- Dialogue scenes by Douglas Furber and Austin Melford; music by Manning Sherwin; lyrics by Ann Coventry
- Prince's Theatre, May 27,1943

It's Time to Dance

- Book by Douglas Furber and Arthur Rose; music by Kenneth Leslie-Smith, Harry Roy, Gaby Rogers, and Harry Phillips; lyrics by Roy, Rogers, and Phillips and James Dyrenforth
- Winter Garden, July 22, 1943

Something in the Air, a.k.a. *Sorry, Darling*

- Arthur Macrae, Archie Menzies, Jack Hulbert; music by Manning Sherwin; lyrics by Harold Purcell and Max Kester
- Palace Theatre, Sept. 23, 1943

Fine Feathers (ensembles and dances by Buddy Bradley and Joan Davis)

- Devised and staged by Robert Nesbitt
- Prince of Wales Theatre, Oct. 11, 1945

1946

Here Come the Boys (choreography by Buddy Bradley, Jack Hulbert, and Lydia Sokolova)

- By Eric Maschwitz
- Saville Theater, Apr. 11, 1946

1949

Sauce Tartare

- Sketches by Matt Brooks; lyrics by Geoffrey Parsons; music by Berkeley Fase
- Cambridge Theatre, May 18, 1949

Christmas Party (choreography by Buddy Bradley and Andrée Howard)

- Devised by Cecil Landeau
- Cambridge Theatre, Dec. 12(?), 1949

1950

Sauce Piquante (choreography by Buddy Bradley and Andrée Howard)

- Lyrics by Geoffrey Parsons; music by Berkeley Fase and others
- Cambridge Theatre, Apr. 27, 1950

1952

Merely Players, a performance to benefit theatrical charities

- Theatre Royal, Drury Lane, Mar. 30, 1952
- Act 1 finale: "Three Sisters" from Hammerstein and Kern

1953

Royal Command Performance

- The finale, "Take Back Your Mink," choreographed by Buddy Bradley
- Coliseum, Nov. 2, 1953

1961

Exotica with Ivor Meggido

- Churchill's Club, Bond Street, July 27, 1961

1964

Blackbirds 1964

- Multiple contributors
- Palladium (Edinburgh), May 18, 1964

Divorce Me, Darling!

- By Sandy Wilson
- Players Theatre (London), Dec. 15, 1964
- Globe Theatre, Feb. 1, 1965

1966

Old Time Music Hall (produced by Buddy Bradley)

- Esplanade Pavilion (Isle of Wight), July–Aug. 1966

THE BUDDY BRADLEY DANCERS

"Rhapsody in Rhythm"

- Embassy Club, Bond Street, London
- Mar. 1953 (exact date unspecified)

"Rhapsody in Rhythm"

- Coconut Grove, Regent Street, London
- Nov. 3, 1953

"Accent on Rhythm"

- Ancienne Belgique, Brussels
- Opened Dec. 19, 1953, for a three-week engagement, followed by one week in Antwerp

Casablanca Club, Madrid

- Summer 1954

Belvedere del Rosa, Rome

- Summer 1954

Rupe Tarea, Rome

- Summer 1954

Portugal—details unknown

- Summer 1955

Italian Riviera tour—details unknown

- Fall 1956

Cinema Smeraldo, Milan

- Oct. 1956

THE BUDDY BRADLEY JAZZ DANCERS

Pigalle Club, Piccadilly

- 1955–56

The Panama Club, Windmill Street

- Resident Dancers, 1956–61

NATO tour

- Beginning approximately Jan. 1959

FILMS

The Little Damozel

- Director: Herbert Wilcox (British and Dominion)
- Released Feb. 1933

Bitter Sweet

- By Noël Coward
- Director: Herbert Wilcox (British and Dominion)
- Released July 1933

On the Air

- Director: Herbert Smith (British Lion)
- Released Jan. 17, 1934

Two Hearts in Waltz Time

- Director: Carmine Gallone (Nettlefold Fogwell Studios)
- Released Aug. 6, 1934

Radio Parade of 1935

- Director: Arthur Woods (British International Pictures)
- Released Dec. 12, 1934

Evergreen

- Director: Victor Saville (Gaumont-British)
- Released June 7, 1934

Oh, Daddy!

- Directors: Graham Cutts and Austin Melford (Gaumont-British)
- Released Feb. 7, 1935

Brewster's Millions

- Director: Thornton Freeland (British and Dominion)
- Released Feb. 19, 1935

Abdul the Damned (a.k.a. *Abdul Hamid*)

- Director: Karl Grune (British International Pictures)
- Released Mar. 16, 1935

A Fire Has Been Arranged

- Director: Leslie S. Hiscott (Twickenham)
- Released Oct. 14, 1935

First a Girl (Ralph Reader, dance director; solo dances for Jessie Matthews by Buddy Bradley)

- Director: Victor Saville (Gaumont-British)
- Released Nov. 7, 1935

Joy Ride (with the Buddy Bradley Rhythm Girls)

- Director: Harry Hughes (City Film Corporation)
- Released Dec. 16, 1935

The Amazing Quest of Ernest Bliss (with the Buddy Bradley Dancing Girls)

- Director: Arthur Zeisler (Garrett-Klement Pictures)
- Released July 28, 1936

This'll Make You Whistle

- Director: Herbert Wilcox (General Film Distributors)
- Released Oct. 1936

It's Love Again

- Director: Victor Saville (Gaumont-British)
- Released Nov. 6, 1936

Stardust (a.k.a. *Mad About Money* and *He Loved an Actress*)—Larry Ceballos, dance director of record

- Director: Melville Brown (British Lion)
- Released Dec. 1937

Head Over Heels

- Director: Sonnie Hale (Gaumont-British)
- Released Mar. 29, 1937

Gangway

- Director: Sonnie Hale (Gaumont-British)
- Released Oct. 1, 1937

Sailing Along

- Director: Sonnie Hale (Gaumont-British)
- Released Apr. 17, 1938

The Spider

- Director: Maurice Elvey (General Film Distributors—Admiral Film Victor M. Green production)
- Released Jan. 23, 1940

King Arthur Was a Gentleman

- Director: Marcel Varnel (Gainsborough Pictures)
- Released Dec. 28, 1942

It's That Man Again (a.k.a. ITMA)

- Director: Walter Forde (Gainsborough Pictures)
- Released Feb. 22, 1943

Flight from Folly

- Director: Herbert Mason (Warner Brothers–British)
- Released May 21, 1945

Walking on Air

- Director: Aveling Ginever (Piccadilly Cinematograph Film Productions)
- Completed in 1946 and released in 1947(?)

The Brass Monkey a.k.a. *Lucky Mascot*

- Director: Thornton Freeland (Alliance Film Studios)
- Released 1948

Edmundo Ros Half Hour

- Released 1957

TELEVISION AND RADIO

Oliver Wakefield, "The Voice of Inexperience" cabaret (BBC TV)

- Dec. 15, 1936

Burnt Sepia Cabaret (BBC TV)

- With Mabel Scott, Garland Wilson, Eunice Wilson, and Buddy Bradley's Sepia Chorines
- Aired Dec. 11, 1936; Dec. 15, 1936; Jan. 2, 1937; Jan. 6, 1937; Jan. 8, 1937

Starlight (BBC TV)

- First aired Nov. 3, 1936
- Records unavailable; information supplied by Dorothy Bradley to Stephen Bourne

Swing Song (BBC Radio)

- Feb. 22, 1939–Mar. 31, 1939

Tuesday Radiogram (BBC Radio Forces Program)

- Sept. 21 and 28, Oct. 12 and 19, 1943

Café Continental (BBC TV)

- Nov. 8, 1947

Just for Fun (BBC TV)—Bradley in cast

- July 5, 1947

Variety in Sepia (BBC TV)

- Oct. 9, 1947

Paging You (BBC TV)—Bradley appears as a dancer

- Feb. 28, 1948

Kentucky Minstrels (BBC TV)

- June 19, 1948

Black Magic (BBC TV)—Bradley contributes as choreographer, dancer, and actor

- July 13, 1949–Jan. 30, 1950

Saturday Night Revue (BBC TV)—choreography by Buddy Bradley and Andrée Howard

- July 2, 1950

Kaleidoscope (BBC TV)–Bradley contributes as choreographer and dancer

- Dec. 1, 1950–May 4, 1951

Shop Window (BBC TV)

- Feb. 23, 1953–Oct. 12, 1953

Thursday Spectacular (ATV/ITV)

- Records unavailable; information provided by Frank Coda

The Benny Hill Show (BBC TV)

- Mar. 1, 1958

Blackmail (ITV)

- Dec. 2, 1965

Ragtime Revue (Rediffusion-ITV)

- Dec. 26, 1965

NOTES

ABBREVIATIONS

IJS: Institute of Jazz Studies, Rutgers University, Marshall Stearns Archives, box 20, folder 6, transcripts of interviews with Buddy Bradley, July 21 and 23, 1963 (unless otherwise attributed)

JRDD: Jerome Robbins Dance Division, New York Public Library

INTERVIEWS

Many quotes and insights on Buddy Bradley and his work are from my interviews and exchanges, some that extended over months and years. Following is a list with date of initial conversation or correspondence: Kurt Adler, Sept. 29, 2024; Hinton Battle, Feb. 12, 2022; Brenda Bufalino, Sept. 19, 2024; Vicky Clayton, July 25, 2023; Frank Coda, Feb. 13, 2023, ff; Thomas DeFrantz, Sept. 14, 2021; Angela Easterling, Nov. 21, 2023; Pamela Epps, July 12, 2022; David Essex, Nov. 27, 2024; De Witt Fleming, Mar. 12, 2025; Betty Dale Fox, July 18, 2023; Lynn Garafola, Apr. 24, 2023; Alex Gleason, Mar. 7, 2025; Jane Goldberg, Apr. 15, 2022; Evelyn Davis Harmon, Aug. 17, 2023; Calobe Jackson Jr., Dec. 13, 2023; Dexter Jones, Mar. 2, 2022; Pepi Lemer, June 14, 2024; Will Lockwood, Aug. 18, 2023; Jan Lynton, June 5, 2023; Sheila Mathews, Apr. 21, 2023, and June 21, 2023; Margaret Winston McGough, Mar. 14, 2023; Charlie Meade and Lynn Ringhaver, July 17, 2022; Patricia Michael, Apr. 26, 2023; Dr. Geraldine Morris, Apr. 12, 2023; Linda

Murray, June 1, 2021; Andrew Nemr, Jan. 27, 2022; Jane Pritchard, Feb. 13, 2022; Allana Radecki, June 6, 2023; Chef Joseph G. Randall, Dec. 13, 2023; Brian Seibert, Mar. 5, 2025; Daphne Selfe, Mar. 21, 2023; Roy Sone, Mar. 11, 2025; Terence Spivey, July 26, 2025; Shea Sullivan, July 23, 2025; Ralph Tobert, Feb. 14, 2023; Dr. Glory Van Scott, Sept. 19, 2023; Tony Waag, July 14, 2022; Annette Walker, Feb. 12, 2023; Dianne Walker, Feb. 19, 2022; Eric K. Washington, June 30, 2022; Johnny Worthy Jr., July 28, 2023; Adrian Wright, Apr. 21, 2025; Cy Young, Apr. 27, 2023.

FURTHER RESEARCH SUPPORT PROVIDED BY:

NEW YORK: Erik Stolarski and Linda Murray of the Jerome Robbins Dance Division, New York Public Library; Auburn Nelson and all reference staff, Schomburg Center for Black Culture, NYPL; Angela Lawrence, Marshall Stearns Jazz Institute, Rutgers University; Leslie Camhi, De Witt Fleming, Elizabeth Kendall, Cynthia Millman, and Grant Harper Reed. HABERSHAM COUNTY, GA: E. Lane Gresham, Ivy Hall. BIRMINGHAM, AL: Ethel Alexander and Wanda Looney, Birmingham African American Genealogy Group; Mary Beth Newbill, Birmingham Public Library. SUMTER COUNTY, AL: Sheila Limerick, University of West Alabama; Shari Williams and Debra Love, Black Belt African American Genealogy Group. HARRISBURG, PA: Dave Morrison and Jeb Stuart, Historic Harrisburg Society; Ken Frew, Dauphin County Historical Library. LONDON and UNITED KINGDOM: Robert Hazle, Noël Coward Office; Tom McErlain, Gloucester Square Community; Josephine Botting and Steve Tolevey, British Film Institute; Georgina Colbeck, Westminster Archives; Philip Watson, Thames and Hudson; Jill Sullivan, Theatre Division, Bristol University; Karin Lowen, Hester Colley, genealogists; Jay Cartwright, Peter Torley, private investigators; Rob Mortimer, Chapman-Petrie Co.; Martin Williams; Justine Picardie; Hugo Vickers; Alastair Macaulay. AUSTRALIA: Bill Egan.

CHAPTER 1: ANCESTRAL WHISPERS

1. Harmon, "With Roots in Habersham."
2. Harmon, "With Roots in Habersham," 20.
3. Du Bois, *Black Reconstruction in America*, 239.
4. Milteer, *Beyond Slavery's Shadow*, 87.
5. Milteer, *Beyond Slavery's Shadow*, 162.
6. Christopher J. Bryant, "Without Representation, No Taxation: Free Blacks, Taxes, and Tax Exemptions Between the Revolutionary and Civil Wars," *Michigan Journal of Race and Law* 21 (2015): 92, 103.
7. Milteer, *Beyond Slavery's Shadow*, 87.
8. Petition to Habersham County Inferior Court, July 1845, by Harriet Allen.
9. Georgia County Deed Book T–U, 609, Habersham County Courthouse.

CHAPTER 2: FATHERS AND SONS IN THE BLACK BELT OF ALABAMA

1. Sumter County Heritage Book Committee, *The Heritage of Sumter County, Alabama* (Clanton, AL: Heritage Publications Consultants, 2005), 2.
2. Jenkins, *Pioneer Families of Sumter County*, 2; Cathal Smith, "Second Slavery, Second Landlordism, and Modernity: A Comparison of Antebellum Mississippi and Nineteenth-Century Ireland," *Journal of the Civil War Era* 5, no. 2 (June 2015): 204–30.
3. Jenkins, *Pioneer Families*, 40; obituary of Dr. J. W. Epes, *Our Southern Home* (Livingston, AL: July 7, 1915).
4. Oral history of John Estes in the Alabama Room archives of the Julia Tutwiler Library, University of West Alabama, Livingston, AL.
5. 1855 Alabama State Census; Smith, *A History of Sumter County, Alabama*, 92.
6. 1855 Alabama State Census; 1860 US Federal Census–Slave Schedules, Alabama Room, Tutwiler Library, University of West Alabama.
7. Jenkins, *Pioneer Families*, 2; Sumter County Heritage Book Committee, *The Heritage of Sumter County, Alabama*, 40.
8. Will of Richard Junius Epes, Dec. 23, 1865, Sumter County Courthouse, Wills, vols. 1–2, 1833–72; Smith, *A History of Sumter County*, 155.
9. Smith, *A History of Sumter County, Alabama*, 157; Peter Kolchin, *First Freedom; The Responses of Alabama's Blacks to Emancipation and Reconstruction* (Tuscaloosa: University of Alabama Press, 2008), 4–7.
10. Du Bois, *Black Reconstruction*, 232.
11. Gwendolyn Lynette Hester, *Freedmen and Colored Marriage Records, 1865—1890, Sumter County, Alabama* (Bowie, MD: Heritage, 1996); *Gainesville* (Alabama) *Messenger*, Feb. 26, 1886.
12. *Livingston* (Alabama) *Journal*, June 9, 1871; *Our Southern Home* (Livingston, AL), May 2, 1901.
13. Alabama Room, Tutwiler Library, University of West Alabama; article in Arrington Gainesville Folder SF2D3, folder 6; *Our Southern Home* (Livingston, AL), Oct. 18, 1900.

14. Alan Brown and David Taylor, eds., *Gabr'l Blow Sof': Sumter Co, Alabama, Slave Narratives* (Livingston: Livingston Press, University of West Alabama, 1997), 39.
15. *Livingston* (Alabama) *Journal*, Apr. 4, 1873.

CHAPTER 3: POST-RECONSTRUCTION

1. Assistant Commissioners Report for Sumter County for Feb. and Mar. 1868, filed by A. J. Burnett; Du Bois, *Black Reconstruction in America*, 493; Smith, *A History of Sumter County*, 200.
2. Robert Rhodes et al. "A Black Worker and the Bricklayers and Masons' Union, 1903," *Journal of Negro History* 54, no. 4 (1969): 398–404; *Commercial Appeal* (Memphis), July 12, 1903; Herman D. Bloch, "Labor and the Negro," *Journal of Negro History* 50, no. 3 (1965): 163–84.

CHAPTER 4: AN OBSERVANT CHILD IN BIRMINGHAM

1. Feldman, *A Sense of Place*, 6.
2. Feldman, *A Sense of Place*, 10–11; John Sparks, "American Negro Reaction to Disfranchisement, 1901–1904" (master's thesis, Samford University, 1973), 86–92.
3. Birmingham Chamber of Commerce Report of 1911, Linn–Henley Research Library, Birmingham Public Library.
4. US passport of Aurelius Lainer Epps; Wilson, *Uplifting the People*, xi–xii.
5. Feldman, *A Sense of Place*, 7, 40.
6. Birmingham City directory, 1909, 1911, and 1912; Sanborn Map, 1911, vol. 3, 364; Charles E. Connerly, *The Most Segregated City in America: City Planning and Civil Rights in Birmingham, 1920–1980* (Charlottesville: University of Virginia Press, 2010), 24; Feldman, *A Sense of Place*, 71.
7. Feldman, *A Sense of Place*, 2–3, 73; Tarry, *The Third Door*, 75.
8. Feldman, *A Sense of Place*, 15, 51.
9. James L. Baggett, "Miss Fancy, Queen of the Avondale Zoo," *Alabama Heritage* (Fall 2012): 56–58; Tarry, *The Third Door*, 19–20.
10. IJS, 1.
11. Herchel V. Cashin et al., *Under Fire with the Tenth U.S. Cavalry* (New York: Arno, 1969).
12. *Birmingham Times*, Aug. 12, 2021; Hollis, *Memories of Downtown Birmingham*, 83–84.
13. "Leonard Harper Brings Harlem Culture to Local Cafes," *Chicago Defender*, Apr. 21, 1934, 8; Hollis, *Memories of Downtown*, 83–84; IJS, transcript of interview with Buddy Bradley, July 21 and 23, 1963, 4; Beth Genné, "Glorifying the American Woman: Josephine Baker and George Balanchine," *Discourses from Dance* 3, no. 1 (2005): 5; IJS, 4.
14. Feldman, *A Sense of Place*, 7; Carl V. Harris, *Political Power in Birmingham 1897–1921* (Knoxville: University of Tennessee, 1977), 167; *Birmingham Age Herald*, Oct. 21, 1918.
15. Lamonte, *Politics and Welfare in Birmingham*, ix, 15; W. David Lewis, *Sloss Furnaces and the Rise of Birmingham District: An Industrial Epic* (Tuscaloosa: University of Alabama Press, 1995), 293–95.

16. Feldman, *A Sense of Place*, 118.
17. Lamonte, *Politics and Welfare in Birmingham*, 10–11; Wilson, *Uplifting the People*, 127; *The Common School and the Negro American*, Atlanta University Publication 16 (Atlanta: Atlanta University Press, 1911), 7.
18. "Thought Negro Had Been Slain," *The Tennessean* (Nashville), May 10, 1913, 1.
19. Feldman, *A Sense of Place*, 10; "Tuberculosis 'Cures' Will Be Denounced from the Pulpit," *Birmingham News*, Oct. 6, 1912; Julia Truitt Bishop, "Fighting Great White Plague in Birmingham," *Birmingham News*, Aug. 10, 1913, 1.
20. Clarification on Birmingham Street names provided by Mary Beth Newbill, Linn–Henley Library, Birmingham Public Library; 1915 Birmingham city directory.
21. "Marriages," *Voice of the People* (Birmingham, AL), Jan. 6, 1917.
22. 1918 Birmingham city directory; WWI Draft Registration Cards (1917–18) for Thomas Patterson, Sept. 12, 1918; WWI Soldiers' Draftees, by County (1918–19), Alabama Department of Archives and History.
23. Kenneth T. Jackson, *The Ku Klux Klan in the City, 1915–1930* (New York: Oxford University Press, 1967), 82; Feldman, *A Sense of Place*, 22; Michael Newton, *Ku Klux Klan Terror: Birmingham, Alabama from 1868–Present* (Atglen, PA: Schiffer, 2013), 20, 23; Dorothy Autrey, "The National Association for the Advancement of Colored People in Alabama, 1913–1952" (PhD diss., University of Notre Dame, 1985), 59; WWI Draft Registration Cards (1917–18) for Robert Epps, Sept. 12, 1918; *Birmingham Truth*, Apr. 20 and June 15, 1928.
24. Feldman, *A Sense of Place*, 123; Tarry, *The Third Door*, 25.
25. Tarry, *The Third Door*, 25; Feldman, *A Sense of Place*, 4, 126; August Meir, "Vogue of Industrial Education," *Mid-West Journal* 7 (Fall 1955): 246; Arthur Harold Parker, *A Dream That Came True: Autobiography of Arthur Harold Parker* (Birmingham, AL: Industrial High School Printing Department, 1932–33), 48.
26. Tarry, *The Third Door*, 25; Parker, *A Dream That Came True*, 70.
27. Feldman, *A Sense of Place*, 133.
28. Lamonte, *Politics and Welfare in Birmingham*, 8, 13; Feldman, *A Sense of Place*, 13, 160.
29. "Alabama, U.S., Deaths and Burials Index, 1881–1974," https://www.ancestry.com/search/collections/2543/.

CHAPTER 5: CROSSING THE MASON-DIXON LINE TO HARRISBURG

1. US Bureau of Census 1920; Sanborn map for 1929–29, vol. 2, sheet 20, 6.
2. US Bureau of Census 1920; Census Place: Harrisburg Ward 11, Dauphin, PA; Roll: T625_1559; Page: 3A; Enumeration District: 10; Sanborn map for 1929–29, vol. 2, sheet 20, 6.
3. Beers, *City Contented, City Discontented*, 25, 50.
4. Beers, *City Contented*, 128; "Horace Payne 5th out of 100 at Central High," *Harrisburg Telegraph*, Sept. 16, 1914.

5. Beers, *City Contented*, 128, 190; "Educators from Philadelphia Refused a Seat," *Philadelphia Inquirer*, Mar. 23, 1937.
6. IJS, 1.

CHAPTER 6: HARLEM CHORUS BOY

1. Smith, "How One American Fares Abroad"; IJS, 1.
2. Eslanda Goode Robeson, *Paul Robeson, Negro* (New York: Harper Brothers, 1930), 56.
3. Lewis, *When Harlem Was in Vogue*, 103.
4. Douglas, *Terrible Honesty*, 13.
5. Johnson, *Black Manhattan*, 188–89; Woll, *Black Musical Theatre*, 60, 69–70; Hughes, *The Big Sea*, 223–24; Langston Hughes, "When Harlem Was in Vogue," *Town and Country*, July 1940, 49, 64–65.
6. Seibert, *What the Eye Hears*, 100, 138; Lewis, *When Harlem Was in Vogue*, 32, 105–6; Johnson, *Black Manhattan*, 225.
7. Woll, *Black Musical Theatre*, 60; Jim Haskins and N. R. Mitgang, *Mr. Bojangles: The Biography of Bill Robinson* (New York: Welcome Rain, 2000).
8. Gilbert Osofsky, *Harlem: The Making of a Ghetto, Negro New York 1890–1930* (New York: Harper & Row, 1971), 4, 139, 141; Lewis, *When Harlem Was in Vogue*, 25–27.
9. Smith, "How One American Fares Abroad."
10. "Performing with James P. Johnson," *Variety*, Jan. 21, 1925, 61; "Flips on Phone Book," *Billboard*, July 2, 1921, 40.
11. IJS, 1; "Colored Society Changes Title After Official Visit," *Variety*, Oct. 7, 1925, 8; IJS, Pete Nugent file, "Miscellaneous Comments from Peter Nugent"; "Runnin' Wild," *Baltimore Afro-American*, May 29, 1926, 4.
12. Stearns and Stearns, *Jazz Dance*, 163, 293–96; Reid, *Rhythm for Sale*, 80–81.
13. Reid, *Rhythm for Sale*, 17; Barry Singer to Grant Harper Reid, Mar. 23, 1998, 81, 107, 100, 50, 86, 52.
14. Stearns and Stearns, *Jazz Dance*, 163.
15. IJS, 1; Maurice Dancer, "Harlem Night by Night," *Pittsburgh Courier*, Mar. 4, 1933, A6.
16. "Broadway at Its Best Has Nothing on Connie's Inn," *Amsterdam News* (New York), July 25, 1923, 7.
17. "Leroy Smith's Orchestra to Be at Connie's Inn," *Amsterdam News* (New York), Sept. 12, 1923, 5; Lewis, *When Harlem Was in Vogue*, 210.
18. Reid, *Rhythm for Sale*, 108.
19. Reid, *Rhythm for Sale*, 55, 108; "Harper as Stager," *Variety*, July 2, 1924, 40; IJS, 2; "Watched Dancers at Night Club; Now Teaches Steps on Broadway," *Pittsburgh Courier*, Jan. 15, 1927, 3.
20. Reid, *Rhythm for Sale*, 50.
21. IJS, 2–3; Nick Castle to Marshall Stearns, 1965.
22. Stearns and Stearns, *Jazz Dance*, 289.
23. Stearns and Stearns, *Jazz Dance*, 127, 289; "A Footloose Aristocrat," *New York Times*, May 27, 1932.

24. IJS, 2.
25. Stearns and Stearns, *Jazz Dance*, 163; *Variety*, Oct. 22, 1924, 10; Smith, "How One American Fares Abroad"; Connie's Inn (advertisement), *Variety*, Sept. 17, 1924, 40.

CHAPTER 7: CELEBRITY DANCE INSTRUCTOR ON BROADWAY

1. "Charleston 'Strutt' and Black Bottom" (advertisement), *Variety*, May 20, 1925, 60; "Vaudeville News," *Variety*, May 20, 1925, 28.
2. Johnson, *Black Manhattan*, 174.
3. Douglas, *Terrible Honesty*, 336; Hughes, *The Big Sea*, 228.
4. Seibert, *What the Eye Hears*, 142.
5. Danielle Robinson, "Oh, You Black Bottom! Jazz Dance Teaching in New York in 1920s," *UC Riverside Dance Research Journal* 38 (Summer–Winter 2006): 19–21, 26, 27; Douglas, *Terrible Honesty*, 359; IJS, 4–5.
6. Reid, *Rhythm for Sale*, 82; A. H. Lawrence, *Duke Ellington and His World: A Biography* (New York: Routledge, 2001), 108; "If It's Dancing You Want, We Have It" (advertisement), *Billboard*, Aug. 23, 1924, 49.
7. "Brokers Kept Busy for Business Spaces," *New York Tribune*, Dec. 17, 1926, 41; "If It's Dancing You Want, We Have It," *Billboard*.
8. Stearns and Stearns, *Jazz Dance*, 163; *Variety*, Aug. 9, 1924, 34; "If It's Dancing You Want, We Have It," *Billboard*; "Can Always Place First Class People," *Chicago Defender*, Aug. 30, 1924, 2.
9. *Dance Magazine*, Nov. 1926 and Jan. 1927, entire issues.
10. Reid, *Rhythm for Sale*, 108; Ries, "Sammy Lee," 1–95; "Leonard Harper Stages Bee Palmer," *Variety*, Aug. 3, 1924, 47; "New York Society Notes," *Chicago Defender*, Aug. 16, 1924, A8.
11. Pierce, *Billy Pierce*, 12; "Cabarets: Harper Rehearsing New All Colored Revue for Connie's Inn," *Variety*, Sept. 3, 1924, 39; Reid, *Rhythm for Sale*, 111; "Picked Up by the Page," *Billboard*, Dec. 20, 1924, 48; Carter Elmer, "He Smashed the Color Line," *Opportunity: The Journal of Negro History* (May 1930): 149.
12. Something of a Victorian and keenly aware of public perception, Pierce stipulated that only "clean cut girls—appearance wise and morally" should apply for his jobs. "Calls for Browns for New Berlin Revue," *Baltimore Afro-American*, Nov. 15, 1924, 6; "Crossing the Briny," *Chicago Defender*, Nov. 22, 1924, 8; "A Country Judge," *Billboard*, Jan. 10, 1925, 51; "The Palace New York," *Billboard*, Feb. 7, 1925, 14; "Bert Williams' Contract Presented to Billy Pierce," *Pittsburgh Courier*, July 10, 1926, 9; "The William Pierces Hold Baby's First Shower," *Variety*, Apr. 18, 1928, 28; Lewis, *When Harlem Was in Vogue*, 31; "Billboard Callers," *Billboard*, Dec. 29, 1923, 116; "A Country Judge," *Billboard*, Jan. 10, 1925, 51; Pierce, *Billy Pierce*, 14; "A Program from Paris," *Billboard*, Mar. 21, 1925, 82; "Pierce's Brownskin Vamps," *Baltimore Afro-American*, Feb. 21, 1925, A5.
13. "Picked Up by the Page," *Billboard*, Dec. 20, 1924, 48; "Tap Dancing Negro . . . Once Ran Elevator," *New York Tribune*, Jan. 5, 1930, 4.
14. "Note," *New English Weekly*, Aug. 11, 1932, 234.

15. "Pierce Dance Studio Largest of Its Kind," *Baltimore Afro-American*, Jan. 12, 1929, 7; Stearns and Stearns, *Jazz Dance*, 162; "Billy Pierce, General Manager," *Billboard*, May 17, 1924, 48; Pierce, *Billy Pierce*, 12; IJS, Herbert Harper interview with Marshall Stearns, Apr. 19, 1964.
16. Caspary, *The Secrets of Grown-Ups*, 90.
17. Hughes, *Big Sea*, 225; Tarry, *The Third Door*, 202.
18. IJS, 8.
19. Wilkinson, "He Gives the Stars Their Legs"; ISJ, 2.
20. ISJ, 6; Wilkinson, "He Gives the Stars Their Legs"; Stearns and Stearns, *Jazz Dance*, 215;.
21. IJS, 5–6, 8; Margo Jefferson, "'Noise' Taps a Historic Route to Joy," in *The Jazz Cadence of American Culture*, ed. Robert G. O'Meally (New York: Columbia University Press, 1998), 381.
22. "The Billy Pierce School" (advertisement), *Variety*, May 20, 1925, 60; "Teaching Children," *Variety*, Feb. 10, 1926, 5; "Round the Square," *Variety*, Apr. 14, 1926, 14; "The Best School of Tap Dancing in the World," *The Dance Magazine*, Dec. 1927, 6; IJS, 1 and 4.
23. Stearns and Stearns, *Jazz Dance*, 223; Barbara Stratyner, "Ned Wayburn and the Dance Routine: From Vaudeville to the Ziegfeld Follies," *Studies in Dance History* 13 (1966): 55; Ries, "Sammy Lee," 7.
24. IJS, Herbert Harper interview.
25. "Pierce Dance School Largest of Its Kind," *Baltimore Afro-American*, Jan. 12, 1929, 7; "Dance Magazine Awards," *The Dance*, Jan. 1930, 18.
26. Reid, *Rhythm for Sale*, 108; Beaton, *The Wandering Years*, 215–16; Chuck Green interview with George Nierenberg, Rutgers University, part 1, 19; Paula Broussard and Lisa Royère, *Eleanor Powell: Born to Dance* (Lexington: University Press of Kentucky, 2023), 38; "Did You Know That?" *Variety*, Feb. 5, 1930, 48.
27. "Opera Artists Get It," *Variety*, Dec. 30, 1925, 7; "Inside Stuff," *Variety*, Nov. 16, 1927, 30; ISJ, Herbert Harper interview.
28. "Ethel Barrymore Hoofing in Blackface Character," *Variety*, June 19, 1929, 1; ISJ, 4; "White's 1924 'Scandals' Praised on West Coast," *Billboard*, Apr. 24, 1926, 26; *Sunday Mirror*, Sept. 17, 1933; "The King on Main Street," *Theatre Magazine*, Jan. 1926, n.p. Other noted Bradley students include Peggy Gilligan, a favorite of columnist and vaudeville MC Ed Sullivan, and Peggy O'Neil often booked at the Palace, the premiere vaudeville house in New York. *Opportunity* magazine adds Ed Wynn, Bobby Agnew, Ruth Fallows, Mary Eaton, Barbara Newberry (the Ziegfeld Girl known to have the most beautiful legs in America), Paula Stone, and Dorothy Stone (who could reliably replace stars Ruby Keeler and Marilyn Miller) to the list of Billy Pierce Studio students. Marshall Stearns named Gilda Gray, Lily Damita, Dorothy Knapp, Will Mahoney, Jack Donahue, Fred Allen, Eddie Foy Jr., Jack Oakie, Carter and Gloria De Haven, as Bradley students. "Colored Revue Broke," *Variety*, May 26, 1926, 31; "Dimpled Darlings," *Variety*, Dec. 1, 1926, 181; "Vaudeville Reviews," *Variety*, October 6, 1926, 58; Carter Elmer, "He Smashed the Color Line," *Opportunity: The Journal of Negro History* (May 1930): 149; ISJ, 6, 8.

29. IJS, 3, 6; Stearns and Stearns, *Jazz Dance*, 186.
30. Chuck Green interview, part 1.
31. "The Best School of Tap Dancing in the World," *The Dance Magazine*, Dec. 1927, 6; "Low Down Dancing," *The Dance Magazine*, Sept. 1927, 38; "Mess Around's Late New York Arrival," *Baltimore Afro-American*, July 10, 1926, 6; "The Black Bottom," *Dance Magazine*, Mar. 1927, 15.
32. "Buddy's Sugar Foot Strut on New $2,100 Floor," *Variety*, Oct 26, 1927, 30; Hill, *Brotherhood in Rhythm*, 14.
33. "Hippodrome, New York," *Billboard*, Oct. 9, 1926, 14; "Palace," *Variety*, Oct. 6, 1926, 58; "Watched Dancers at Night Clubs, Now Teaching Steps on Broadway," *Pittsburgh Courier*, Jan. 15, 1927, 3.
34. Saxon could be as ungracious as she was ungraceful: after Bradley covered her taps when she was late for a radio appearance, she took full credit, without any mention of Bradley. It mattered to him: it was reported that he didn't recover his breath for two days. Such incidents were not isolated. Without prior arrangement, Joe Laurie, a well-known monologist, dragged a ruffled Bradley onstage during an appearance at the Palace, proud to show off his association with the celebrity dance instructor and oblivious to any imposition he caused; "Bradley's Doubling," *Variety*, Feb 2, 1927, 24; "Joe Laurie, Jr.," *Billboard*, Mar. 24, 1928, 11.
35. "Ill and Injured," *Variety*, Nov. 18, 1925, 6; "Obituary," *Variety*, Jan. 11, 1928, 57; "Buddy's Sugar Foot Strut on New $2,100 Dance Floor," *Variety*, Oct. 26, 1927, 30; "Watched Dancers at Night Club, Now Teaches Steps on Broadway," *Pittsburgh Courier*, Jan. 15, 1927, 3.
36. "Low Down Dancing," *Dance Magazine*, Sept. 1927, 38; "More Low-Down Dancing," *Dance Magazine*, Jan. 1928, 41.
37. "Inside Stuff on Legit," *Variety*, June 16, 1926, 36.
38. "Wanted! Peppy Brown Skin Girls" (advertisement), *Amsterdam News*, Dec. 29, 1926, 12, and *Inter-State Tattler*, Jan. 2, 1927, 9; "Colored Beautifier Prefers Dancing," *Variety*, Jan. 15, 1930, 68; "The 9:15 Revue Closes Suddenly," *New York Times*, Feb. 18, 1930; Pierce, *Billy Pierce*, 14.
39. "Brokers Kept Busy for Business Space in Many Zones," *New York Tribune*, Dec. 17, 1926, 41; Carter Elmer, "He Smashed the Color Line," *Opportunity: The Journal of Negro History* (May 1930): 149; IJS, 2.
40. "Billy Pierce Op'ns Elaborate Dance Studio," *Baltimore Afro-American*, May 28, 1927, 8; "On the Pan," *Chicago Defender*, July 7, 1928, 7; "Billy Pierce Plays Host to Celebrities," *Amsterdam News*, Mar. 15, 1933; "St. Paul's Youthful Artists," *Pittsburgh Courier*, Dec. 24, 1927, 4.
41. "Pierce Dance Studio Largest of Its Kind," *Baltimore Afro-American*, Jan. 12, 1929, 7.
42. Billy Jones, "Stars That Shine," *Chicago Defender*, Dec. 15, 1928, 6.
43. "Billy Pierce Op'ns Elaborate Dance Studio," *Baltimore Afro-American*, May 28, 1927, 8; IJS, 2; "Cochran Wants Colored Stagers from New York, and Likely Getting 'Em," *Variety*, July 23, 1930, 53.
44. "Billy Pierce Op'ns Elaborate Dance Studio," *Baltimore Afro-American*, May 28, 1927, 8; "Post Writer Thinks Well of Billy Pierce," *Amsterdam News*, Aug. 26, 1927, 7; Seibert, *What the Eye Hears*, 284, 286.

45. "Ernest Carlos: Karin Baker's Memories & Remembered Choreography," YouTube video, 21:42, May 23, 2023, https://www.youtube.com/watch?v=EiCdLPXCxd4; Mayes and Whitfield, *An Inconvenient Black History of British Musical Theatre*, 152; "John Burk Attending Dance Congress in New York," *Binghamton Press*, Oct. 1, 1934, 8; Jennifer Dunning, "Before Dancers, There Must Be Dance Teachers," *New York Times*, Apr. 28, 2002, section 2, 12; Stearns and Stearns, *Jazz Dance*, 167; IJS, Herbert Harper interview; Mason, *I Remember Balanchine*, 210. IJS, Pete Nugent interview; Reid, *Rhythm for Sale*, 164. "Billy Pierce Op'ns Elaborate Dance Studio," *Baltimore Afro-American*, May 28, 1927, 8; "Bottomland," *New York Times*, June 28, 2002.
46. Stearns and Stearns, *Jazz Dance*, 167; IJS, Herbert Harper interview; Mason, *I Remember Balanchine*, 210.
47. IJS, Pete Nugent interview with Marshal Stearns, Feb. 23, 1960; Reid, *Rhythm for Sale*, 164.
48. "Billy Pierce Op'ns Elaborate Dance Studio," *Baltimore Afro-American*, May 28, 1927, 8; "Bottomland," *New York Times* June 28, 1927; Decker, *Show Boat*, 108; "Aaron Gates Studio," *Chicago Defender*, Apr. 21, 1928, 6.
49. IJS, Herbert Harper interview.
50. "Detroit Delineations," *Billboard*, Apr. 21, 1928, 29.
51. New York State Census, 1925.
52. Allison Hughes, "Meet the Neighbors of 409 Edgecombe, One of Harlem's Most Fashionable Addresses," Schomburg Center for Research in Black Culture, New York Public Library, July 27, 2022, https://www.nypl.org/blog/2022/07/27/409-edgecombe-harlem-fashionable-address; US Bureau of Census, 1930.
53. "The High Hatters," *Inter-State Tattler*, June 8, 1928, 10; Lewis, *When Harlem Was in Vogue*, 212; "Backstage with Stagestruck," *Inter-State Tattler*, Sept. 13, 1929, 5; Hughes, *The Big Sea*, 258.
54. Caspary, *The Secrets of Grown-Ups*, 90; "Side Lights on Society," *Amsterdam News*, Dec. 15, 1926; "Revue at Big Fashion Show," *Amsterdam News*, Apr. 27, 1927, 10; "Fashion Show to Be Dazzling," *Amsterdam News*, Apr. 11, 1928, 12; Bessye J. Bearden, "Tid-Bits of NY Society," *Chicago Defender*, May 5, 1928, A5; Richard L. Baltimore, "Radio News and Programs," *Amsterdam News*, Nov. 27, 1929, 11.
55. Pierce, *Billy Pierce*, 15, 148; Henry Louis Gates et al., eds., *Harlem Renaissance Lives: From the African American National Biography* (New York: Oxford University Press, 2009), 396; "Billy Pierce Plays Host to Celebrities," *Amsterdam News*, Mar. 5, 1930, 4.
56. "The Talk of the Town," *New Yorker*, June 14, 1969, 32–33.
57. "The Columbia, New York, Brings Forth a New Producer," *Variety*, July 2, 1924, 40; *The Dance Magazine*, Jan 1930, Jan. 1931, entire issues.

CHAPTER 8: A BLACK CHOREOGRAPHER ON THE GREAT WHITE WAY

1. Mordden, *Make Believe*, 94–97; McDonagh, *Martha Graham*, 33; Baral, *Revue*, 285.

2. *Billboard*, June 13, 1925, 32; *Greenwich Village Follies*, program, 1926; "Unleavened and Unrehearsed," *Boston Transcript*, Dec. 1, 1925.
3. "Unleavened and Unrehearsed," *Boston Transcript*, Dec. 1, 1925; "The New GV Follies Beautiful Though a Bit Dumb," *New York Herald Tribune*, Dec. 28, 1925, 14; *Boston Globe*, Dec. 1, 1925; Ries, "Sammy Lee," 1–95; IJS, 4.
4. "Irene Delroy Found Ladder to Fame," *New York Herald Tribune*, Feb. 14, 1926, D4; *Ziegfeld Follies*, program, 1927.
5. IJS, 1.
6. "Short Run Cost $50,000 over GVF," *Variety*, Apr. 21, 1926, 19; IJS, 1; Smith, "How One American Fares Abroad."
7. "Short Run Cost $50,000 over GVF," *Variety*, Apr. 21, 1926, 19; Gordon M. Leland, "New Faces, Fresh Dances," *Billboard*, Mar. 27, 1926, 10; IJS, 4.
8. "GV Follies Opens Garbed for Spring," *American*, Mar. 16, 1926, from GV Follies clipping file, JRDD, n.p.; "Gossip of the Rialto," *New York Times*, Mar. 14, 1926; Leland, "New Faces, Fresh Dances," *Billboard*, March 17, 1926, 10; IJS, 3; "Legitimate: B'way in Hock," *Variety*, Mar. 24, 1926, 23; "Shows in New York and Comment," *Variety*, Mar. 31, 1926, 27; " G.V. Follies Booked Early for Atlantic City Showing," *Billboard*, June 26, 1926, 26.
9. Woll, *Black Musical Theatre*, 115; Johnson, *Black Manhattan*, 209; Ries, "Sammy Lee," 59.
10. Mordden, *Make Believe*, 6, 89; *New York Age*, Nov. 17, 1923; Steyn, *Broadway Babies Say Goodnight*, 24.
11. *George White's Scandals*, program, 1926; "Everybody's Welcome," *Variety*, Sept. 29, 1931, 54; IJS, 4.
12. Mordden, *Make Believe*, 90.
13. IJS, 4, 6; *George White's Scandals*, program, 1924.
14. "Buddy Bradley, Master of Tap . . ." *Inter-State Tattler* (New York), July 13, 1928; IJS, 4; Woll, *Black Musical Theatre*, 51; James Weldon Johnson, *Along This Way: The Autobiography of James Weldon Johnson* (New York: Da Capo, 2000), 200–201.
15. "Broadway Show Has Negro Dance Instructors," *Baltimore Afro-American*, July 7, 1926, 10; "*Bright Lights* Has Race Dance Instructors," *Pittsburgh Courier*, Aug. 28, 1926; "Rialto Gossip," *New York Times*, May 30, 1926, x1.
16. "Jed Harris, Broadway Producer and Director for 30 Years, Dead," *New York Times*, Nov. 16, 1979.
17. "Rialto Gossip," *New York Times*, May 30, 1926, x 1; *Broadway*, souvenir program; "And Now Mr. Tracy," *New York Times*, Sept. 26, 1926, x 1.
18. "As Co-Author of *Broadway* I Give All of You My Humble Thanks," *Variety*, Nov. 24, 1926, 47.
19. Stearns and Stearns, *Jazz Dance*, 53; Seibert, *What the Eye Hears* 146; IJS, Thaddeus Drayton interview; "Broadway," *Variety*, Sept. 22, 1926, 40.
20. Steyn, *Broadway Babies*, 66–67; Carol Oja, *Bernstein Meets Broadway: Collaborative Art in a Time of War* (New York: Oxford University Press, 2014), 155; "60 Negroes in Show Boat," *Variety*, Oct. 5, 1927, 30;

Decker, *Show Boat*, 110; "Hi Yaller Girls No Longer Wanted," *Variety*, Jan. 19, 1927, 1, 3.

21. Decker, *Show Boat*, 108, 119; "Dances in Show Boat," *Variety*, Dec. 8, 1926, 45; "Paul Robeson for *Show Boat*," *Billboard*, Dec. 18, 1926, 26.
22. Ries, "Sammy Lee," 70; "Show Boat Here with Cargo of Song and Color," *New York Tribune*, Dec. 28, 1927, 13; Decker, *Show Boat*, 80; IJS, 2; "Show Boat," *New York Times*, Dec. 28, 1927, 26.
23. Reynolds and McCormick, *No Fixed Points*, 687; "Fewer Long Run Musicals in Past Season Than 1927," *Billboard*, Sept. 15, 1928, 11.
24. Ries, "Albertina Rasch," 102; *Rio Rita*, program, week of Jan. 2, 1928; Ries, "Sammy Lee," 60, 61.
25. IJS, 7; *Rio Rita*, program, Jan. 2, 1928; "Plays on Broadway," *Variety*, Feb. 9, 1927, 40.
26. "Plays on Broadway," *Variety*, Feb. 9, 1927, 40; "Ada May to Aid Charity," *New York Herald Tribune*, Apr. 8, 1927, 23.
27. "Dancing Derby Prize," *New York Herald Tribune*, Aug. 23, 1927, 7; *Hartford Courant*, Feb. 19, 1928, D6; *Boston Daily Globe*, Nov. 4, 1927, 4; *Manchester Guardian*, Apr. 11, 1928, 17; *Los Angeles Times*, Sept. 18, 1927, 17; *New York Times*, Nov. 9, 1927, 29; *New York Herald Tribune*, Aug. 10, 1928, 18.
28. *Chicago Defender*, Sept 1, 1934, 11; *The Dance Magazine*, Mar. 1927, 22.
29. "Billy Pearce [*sic*] Who Makes Stars," *Pittsburgh Courier*, Apr. 25, 1931, 7; Smith, "How One American Fares Abroad."
30. "Half a Widow Full of Good Humour," *New York Herald Tribune*, Sept. 13, 1927, F4.
31. "Constance Carpenter," *New York Herald Tribune*, June 15, 1928, F4; "In the Limelight—and Pertinent Facts About Miss Carpenter," *New York Times*, Nov. 20, 1927, 2.
32. *Theater Magazine* 49 (Feb. 2, 1928): 41.
33. Spivak, *Buzz*, 33, 34, 303–5; John Martin, "The Dance: New Musical Comedy Talent," *New York Times*, June 22, 1928.
34. IJS, 5.
35. Mark Barron, "Rialto Fame Comes Suddenly to Young Director of Dances," *New York Herald Tribune*, Nov. 20, 1927, E2.
36. Spivak, *Buzz*, 35.
37. Robeson, *Paul Robeson, Negro*, 56; IJS, 5.
38. "The Theatre," *New Yorker*, Nov. 12, 1927, 33.
39. "Colored Dance Stagers Buddy Bradley and Billy Pierce on Lew Fields' New Show," *Variety*, Nov. 14, 1928, 51; "Theater News," *New York Herald Tribune*, Dec. 14, 1928, 26.
40. Spivak, *Buzz*, 40; *Hello, Daddy!*, program, Apr. 15, 1929.
41. "This Week on Broadway," *Billboard*, Dec. 15, 1928, 46; "Future Plays," *Variety*, Nov. 28, 1928, 53; "Cast Changes," *Variety*, Dec. 19, 1928, 54; "Dancing Generates Creative Power," *Herald Tribune*, May 2, 1926, E5; "Picture Possibilities," *Variety*, Jan. 16, 1929, 6.
42. "Lew Field's Denials," *Variety*, Jan. 30, 1929, 54; "Daddy's New Chorus," *Variety*, Mar. 6, 1929, 51.

43. J. Brooks Atkinson, "The Play," *New York Times*, Dec. 27, 1928.
44. "Hello, Daddy," *Billboard*, Jan. 5, 1929, 47.
45. IJS, 3.
46. James Baldwin, *Go Tell It on the Mountain* (New York: Penguin Random House, 2013), 211; Danielle Robinson, "Oh, You Black Bottom! Appropriation, Authenticity, and Opportunity," *Dance Research Journal* 38, nos. 1–2 (Summer 2006): 27, 39n17.
47. Wilfred J. Riley, "The New Plays on Broadway," *Billboard*, May 11, 1929, 35; "Rialto Gossip," *New York Times*, May 5, 1929; John Martin, "The Dance: When Jazz Becomes Art: A Number in 'The Little Show,'" *New York Times*, July 14, 1929, X7.
48. Reynolds and McCormick, *No Fixed Points*, 685; Stearns and Stearns, *Jazz Dance*, 161.
49. Langston Hughes, "When Harlem Was in Vogue," *Town and Country*, July 1940, 49, 65; Clifton Webb interview by Mary Morris, Nov. 11, 1945, newspaper unknown (from *Little Show* clipping file, JRDD); "Plays on Broadway," *Variety*, May 8, 1929, 68.
50. Reid, *Rhythm for Sale*, 53; Stearns and Stearns, *Jazz Dance*, 12; IJS, 4; Clifton Webb interview by Mary Morris, Nov. 11, 1945, newspaper unknown (from *Little Show* clipping file, JRDD).
51. IJS, 4; "The Little Show," *Variety*, May 8, 1929, 68; Whitney Bolton, *Telegraph*, May 2, 1929 (from *Little Show* clipping file, JRDD); Eudora Garrett, *Telegram*, May 1, 1929 (from *Little Show* clipping file, JRDD); Wilfred J. Riley, "The New Plays on Broadway," *Billboard*, May 11, 1929, 35; "The Blues Number from the Little Show," *Dance Magazine*, Oct. 1929, 30–31; Stearns and Stearns, *Jazz Dance*, 236.
52. John Martin, "The Dance: When Jazz Becomes Art: A Number in 'The-Little Show,'" *New York Times*, July 14, 1929. X7.
53. IJS, 4.
54. "Footlight Fashions," *Billboard*, May 18, 1929, 40; "NAACP Benefit," *Baltimore Afro-American*, Dec. 21, 1929, 40.
55. IJS, 3.

CHAPTER 9: *EVER GREEN* AND AFFIRMATION

1. Mordden, *Make Believe*, 136.
2. Frank E. Franks (advertisement), *Stage*, Aug. 29, 1929, 10; Ivan H. Browning, "Shows in London," *Amsterdam News*, Jan. 1, 1930, 8 (also in *Chicago Defender*, Jan. 11, 1930, 6); Smith, "How One American Fares Abroad," 11.
3. Mordden, *Make Believe*, 129; "Cochran's 1931 Revue," *Theatre World*, Apr. 1931, 155; Matthews, *Over My Shoulder*, 109–11; Smith, "How One American Fares Abroad," 11; "Looking at Life," *Daily Mail*, Aug. 2, 1930, 6; Charles B. Cochran, *I Had Almost Forgotten* (London: Hutchinson, 1932), 217–18.
4. Pierce, *Billy Pierce*, 20; "Cochran Wants Colored Stagers," *Variety*, July 23, 1930, 53; "Looking at Life," *Daily Mail*, Oct. 2, 1930, 8.
5. "Pierce Victim of Pneumonia," *Chicago Defender*, Aug. 16, 1930, 5; "Sailings," *Variety*, Aug. 13, 1930, 2; "Footlights by the Tattlin' Twins,"

Chicago Defender Oct. 11, 1930, 5; "Cochran Wants Colored Stagers," *Variety*, July 23, 1930, 53.

6. Jane Stevenson, *Baroque Between the Wars: Alternative Style in the Arts, 1918–1939* (New York: Oxford University Press, 2018), 3, 34; "Chit Chat: Evergreen," *Stage*, Aug. 14, 1930, 12.
7. Matthews, *Over My Shoulder*, 26, 111; A. C. Astor, "Just Jottings," *Stage*, Feb. 5, 1931, 5; Gary Marmorstein, *A Ship Without a Sail: The Life of Lorenz Hart* (New York: Simon & Schuster, 2012), 184.
8. "Modern Stagecraft," *Yorkshire Post*, Aug. 24, 1931, 8; "Ever Green," *Era*, Oct. 15, 1930, 1; "London by Cockaigne," *Billboard*, Dec. 6, 1930, 56; "London Fashions," *The Times* (London), Dec. 3, 1930, 17; "This Week's Premieres," *Sunday Times* (London), Nov. 9, 1930, 4; *Evergreen*, program, Apr. 27, 1931.
9. Harding, *Cochran*, 201; Carol Eason, *No Intermissions: The Life of Agnes de Mille* (New York: Da Capo, 1996), 103–4.
10. IJS, 5; "This Week's Premieres," *Sunday Times*, Nov. 9, 1930, 4; Marmorstein, *A Ship Without a Sail*, 185; *Evergreen*, program, Apr. 27, 1931; Hill, "Buddy Bradley," 77–84.
11. www.AlastairMacaulay, Feb. 23, 2021.
12. "Evergreen," *Era*, Sept 3, 1930, 6; Cockaigne, "Letter from London," *Billboard*, Sept. 13, 1930, 40; "Jewels of the Empire," *Daily Mirror* (London), Nov. 11, 1930, 11.
13. "Looking at Life," *Daily Mail* (London), Oct. 2, 1930, 8; *Evergreen*, program, Apr. 27, 1930; Ross Adler, "Buddy Bradley Puts the Wiggle into Show Business," *John Bull*, Dec. 5, 1953, 19; "Mr. Cochran's Revue of Revues," *Times*, Mar. 3, 1931, 12.
14. Cockaigne, "Letter from London," *Billboard*, Dec. 6, 1930, 56, and Sept. 20, 1930, 42; Harding, *Cochran*, 156; "*Ever Green* in Glasgow," *Stage*, Sept. 4, 1930, 12; "*Ever Green* in Rehearsals," *Stage*, Sept. 25, 1930, 14; "*Ever Green* in Preparation," *Era*, Sept. 24, 1930, 6.
15. Buddy Bradley, *Tribute to C. B. Cochran*, BBC, Mar. 7, 1961; "Looking for the Stars of the Future," *Evening Telegraph* (Dundee), Aug. 7, 1933, 2.
16. Smith, "How One American Fares Abroad," 11.
17. "Yesterday's Weather," *Daily Mail*, Oct. 9, 1930, 9; "Dazzling Spectacle of *Ever Green*," *Dundee Courier*, Oct. 14, 1930, 7; "Plays and Players," *Sunday Times*, Oct. 12, 1930, 5; "This Week's Premieres," *Sunday Times*, Nov. 9, 1930, 4.
18. Cockaigne, "Letter from London," *Billboard*, Jan. 3, 1931, 40; Mike Kilburn, *London's Theatres* (London: New Holland, 2002), 16; A. C. Astor, "Just Jottings," *Stage*, Dec. 11, 1930, 8; "Splendours of *Ever Green*, Newest Cochran Show," *Sheffield Daily Telegraph*, Dec. 5, 1930, 2.
19. "*Ever Green* at the Adelphi," *Country Life*, Dec. 20, 1930, 800; "Straight Shows Need Oddities," *Variety*, Apr. 22, 1931, 55; "Cochran in Vienna," *Era*, May 20, 1931, 13.
20. "Apron Strings," *Times*, July 9, 1931, 12; "Sailings," *Variety*, Dec. 17, 1930, 2; "New Band at Ciro's," *Daily Mirror* (London), Nov. 18, 1930, 2; ship manifest, CGT Paris, departing Plymouth, England, Dec. 16, 1930.

21. IJS, 5; "Inside Stuff-Pictures," *Variety*, Jan. 22, 1935, 6; "Ever-Grinning," *Stage*, June 30, 1931, 46; Maurice Dancer, "Harlem Night by Night," *Pittsburgh Courier*, July 23, 1932, A6.
22. Howard Rye and Jeffrey Green, "Black Music Internationalism in England in the 1920s," *Black Music Research Journal* 15, no. 1 (Spring 1995): 93–107.
23. Gardiner, *The Thirties*, 631; D. J. Taylor, *Bright Young People: The Rise and Fall of a Generation, 1918–1940* (New York: Farrar, Straus & Giroux, 2007), 130; Breese, *Hutch*, 54; "England Laughs at America," *Baltimore Afro-American*, June 11, 1932, 16; "Billy Pierce Shaved by White Barber," *Variety*, Nov. 19, 1930, 40.
24. Buddy Bradley, *Tribute to C. B. Cochran*, BBC, March 7, 1961.

CHAPTER 10: APPRAISING LONDON

1. Beaton, *The Wandering Years*, 215–16; "Cochran's 1931 Revue," *Era*, Feb. 18, 1931, 1; "Creation Cabaret," *Daily News/London News Chronicle*, March 21, 1931, 3; "Sailings," *Stage*, Jan. 7, 1931, 2.
2. Gardiner, *The Thirties*, 26; "Roundtrip," *Variety*, Dec. 31, 1930, 40.
3. Harding, *Cochran*, 52–52, 89, 101.
4. "When Cabaret Held Sway," *Stage*, Nov. 13, 1980, 12; Stevenson, *Baroque Between the Wars*, 110.
5. "Colored Boys Sent for in London's New Revue," *Variety*, Jan. 28, 1931, 48; *Cochran's 1931 Revue*, program; "About John Mills," *Picturegoer*, June 12, 1943, 7–8.
6. Mayes and Whitfield, *An Inconvenient Black History*, 131; *Cochran's 1931 Revue*, program (Palace Theatre, Manchester); Hughes, *Second Movement*, 104.
7. Harding, *Cochran*, 69.
8. There is much conjecture in dance circles, but no conclusive findings, about George Balanchine's working with Josephine Baker prior to 1931. It is likely he had seen Baker perform in Paris in the 1920s and, according to former New York City Ballet dancer Robert Maiarano, visited Baker at her home in Le Vesinet. Phyllis Rose in *Jazz Venus* and Jean-Claude Baker in *The Hungry Heart* record only that Balanchine worked with Baker in 1936 in the Ziegfeld Revue while dance historian Beth Genné, of the University of Michigan, speculates that, in 1932, Balanchine *possibly* staged some of her act at the Casino de Paris; both of these work interactions were post his collaboration with Bradley and his jazz-trained dancers in *Cochran's 1931 Revue*. Further, others, such as Patrick O'Connor, speculate in hindsight that Balanchine taught her ballet. However, Baker herself records in her memoirs, coauthored by Bouillon, that a Russian ballerina named Madame Vromska taught her ballet prior to the 1932 Casino de Paris appearance.
9. *Cochran's 1930 Revue*, program; *Cochran's 1931 Revue*, program.
10. Mason, *I Remember Balanchine*, 210; Homans, *Mr. B.*, 231; *City Ballet: The Podcast*, episode 23.1, May 4, 2020.
11. "Cochran's 1931 Revue," *Montrose Standard and Mearns Register*, Apr. 24, 1931, 6.

12. "Charles B. Cochran's 1931 Revue," *Era*, Mar. 25, 1931, 12; "End of 1931 Revue," *Daily News* (London), Apr. 10, 1931, 9; "Chit Chat," *Stage*, Mar. 26, 1931, 14.
13. "Cochran's 1931 Revue," *Theatre World*, Apr. 1931, 155; *Daily Telegraph* (London), Mar. 20, 1931 (retrieved from the Popular Balanchine dossiers of the Balanchine Foundation); "The London Pavilion: Cochran's 1931 Revue," *Stage*, Mar. 26, 1931, 14; "Charles B. Cochran's 1931 Revue," *Era*, Mar. 25, 1931, 12; "Double Helping of Showmanship," *Era*, Apr. 4, 1931, 14.
14. "The Passing Shows," *Tatler*, Apr. 8, 1931, 62; "The Variety Stage," *Stage*, Apr. 30, 1931, 3; "Variety Theatres," *Daily Herald* (London), Apr. 20, 1931, 8; IJS, 7.
15. "The Variety Stage," *Stage*, Apr. 30, 1931, 3; Matera, *Black London*, 166.
16. "New Cochran Cabaret," *The People* (London), Apr. 5, 1931, 13; "A Cabaret Show: Cochran's 'Creation,'" *Daily Mirror*, Apr. 1, 1931, 4; "Creation at the Trocadero," *Bystander*, Apr. 15, 1931, 113; Ivan Patrick Gore, "Cabaret," *Stage*, Apr. 2, 1931, 4.
17. Philip Page, "The Play's the Thing," *Sphere*, Apr. 11, 1931, 66.
18. Gore, "Cabaret."
19. "Notes from Here and There," *Tatler*, Apr. 15, 1931, 88; Vaughan, *Frederick Ashton and His Ballets*, 74.
20. Seibert, *What the Eye Hears*, 180; Gore, "Cabaret," *Stage*, Mar. 26, 1931, 5.
21. Ivan Patrick Gore, "Cabaret," *Stage*, Aug. 20, 1931, 6, and Apr. 2, 1931, 4.
22. "Harris and Van Star at Lafayette," *New York Amsterdam News*, May 30, 1928,10; Hughes, *Second Movement*, 116; "Bradford and Mr. Cochran," *Yorkshire Post and Leeds Intelligencer*, Mar. 27, 193, 8; "A Trocadero Cabaret," *Sunday Times*, Mar. 22, 193, 17; Gore, "Cabaret: The Trocadero 'Creation,'" *Stage*, Apr. 2, 1931, 4; Page, "The Play's the Thing."
23. Harding, *Cochran*, 108; "Billy Pierce, Once Unable to Pay Rent," *Baltimore Afro-American*, Apr. 25, 1931, 12; "The Return of Sir William Pierce," *Amsterdam News*, Dec. 31, 1930,8.
24. Audition call for *50MM*, *Stage*, June 25, 1931, 15.
25. Steyn, *Broadway Babies*, 77.
26. "American Musical Comedy," *Scotsman*, Sept. 2, 1931, 7.
27. J. Brooks Atkinson, "Tourist Philosophy to Tunes," *New York Times*, Nov. 28, 1929, 34; "Provincial Productions," *Stage*, Sept. 3, 1931, 13; "A Page of Theatres and Amusements," *Manchester Evening News*, Sept. 26, 1931, 2 "American Musical Comedy," *Scotsman*, Sept. 2, 1931, 7; Steyn, *Broadway Babies*, 125.
28. "Manchester," *Stage*, Oct. 1, 1931, 2; "Plays with Medicine," *Daily News* (London) Aug. 26, 1931, 9.
29. "Big Scale Shows for Autumn," *Daily News* (London), July 22, 1931, 9; "50 Million Frenchmen Being Cleaned for London," *Weekly Dispatch* (London), July 26, 1931, 15; "Death of Mr. Daniel Mayer," *Daily Mail* (Hull), Aug. 24, 1928, 11; "Edinburgh," *Stage*, Sept. 24, 1931, 4; "American Musical Comedy," *Scotsman*, Sept. 2, 1931, 7; "Glasgow," *Stage*, Sept. 10, 1931, 2.

30. Beaton, *The Wandering Years*, 215–16; Eddleston, *Zelia Raye and the Development of Modern Theatre Dance*, 19–20.
31. IJS, 6.
32. "To Revive the Glories of the Gaiety," *Bystander*, Dec. 16, 1931, 556; "Grammophone Notes," *Nottingham and Midland Catholic News*, Jan. 2, 1932, 12.
33. "A Gaiety Winner," *Sheffield Daily Telegraph*, Dec. 24, 1931, 8; Vernon Woodhouse, "Gaiety Nights Past and Present," *Bystander*, Jan. 20, 1932, 117.
34. "Gaiety Bound," *Bystander*, Dec. 9, 1931, 486; "Theatre Chat," *Bayswater Paddington News*, Dec. 5, 1931, 5; J. T. Grein, "The World of Theatre," *Illustrated London News*, Jan. 9, 1932, 62; "The Passing Shows," *Tatler*, Feb. 3, 1932, 186–87; "Provincial Productions," *Stage*, Dec. 3, 1931, 19.
35. Vernon Woodhouse, "Gaiety Nights Past and Present," *Bystander*, Jan. 20, 1932, 117; Philip Page, "The Play's The Thing," *Sphere*, Jan. 9, 1931, 55.
36. Stephen Bourne, "Uncrowned King of Dance," *Stage*, Dec. 3, 1998, 11; "Theatre Chat," *Bayswater and Paddington News*, Jan. 23, 1932, 556; "The Passing Shows," *Tatler*, Feb. 3, 1932, 187.
37. "The Leading Lady," *Sketch*, Dec. 2, 1931, 393.
38. Photos, *Bystander* Dec 16, 1931, 556.
39. Matthews, *Over My Shoulder*, 118.
40. "Chatter: London," *Variety*, Aug. 2, 1932, 40.

CHAPTER 11: EXPATRIATION

1. Ries, "Albertina Rasch," 285.
2. "Shop Talk," *Era*, Mar. 2, 1932, 2; "News of the Theatres," *Daily News* (London), Feb. 24, 1932, 6; "Theatre Chat," *Bayswater Chronicle*, Mar. 19, 1932, 7; Philip Page, "Plays," *Sphere*, Mar. 19, 1932, 442.
3. E. A. Baughan, "This Hi-Diddle Diddle Stuff," *Era*, Mar. 9, 1932, 9; Trinculo, "The Cow Has Jumped over the Moon," *Tatler*, Mar. 23, 1932, 486–87; J. T. Grein, "Criticisms in Cameo," *Sketch*, Mar. 16, 1932, 476.
4. Ries, "Albertina Rasch," 118; "Bubble and Squeak," *Tatler*, Mar. 23, 1932, 498; "Old and New Stagecraft," *Reynolds Illustrated News*, Mar. 6. 1932, 18 ; Philip Page, "Plays," *Sphere*, Mar. 19, 1932, 443.
5. "Gramophone Notes," *Gloucestershire Echo*, Apr. 1, 1932, 3; Vaughan, *Frederick Ashton*, 72, 474–78, 483.
6. Angela Lambert, *1939: The Last Season of Peace* (New York: Grove, 1989), 152–55; "The Lindy Hop: Startling Cabaret by English Girls," *Daily Mail* (London), Mar. 8, 1932, 9; "England Laughs at America," *Baltimore Afro-American*, June 11, 1932, 16.
7. "Items," *Era*, Apr. 13, 1932, 17; "Magic Nights," *Daily News* (London), Apr. 5, 1932, 3; "Big Ben in Cabaret," *Weekly Dispatch* (London) Apr. 3, 1932, 18; "A Wireless Cabaret," *Era*, Apr. 6, 1932, 3; *Magic Nights*, British Pathé, May 16, 1932, https://www.britishpathe.com/asset/64721.
8. "A Wireless Cabaret," *Era*, Apr. 6, 1932, 3; photo caption, *Bystander*, Apr. 13, 1932, 84; "Magic Nights," *Times*, June 24, 1932.
9. Conversation with Professor Lynn Garafola, June 19, 2024, regarding training of English chorus dancers in the 1930s.

10. Vaughan, *Frederick Ashton*, 75.
11. Vaughan, *Frederick Ashton,* 28–29; "Magic Nights," *Daily News* (London), Apr. 5, 1932, 3.
12. "Cleethorpe's Girl's Success," *Skegness News*, Apr. 13, 1932, 3; IJS, 7.
13. Vaughan, *Frederick Ashton*, 75; *Magic Nights*, program, 1932; Kavanaugh, *Secret Muses*, 143; IJS, 3.
14. "Ballet in Cabaret," *Daily Mirror* (London), Apr. 6, 1932, 11.
15. "Dramatic News," *Nottingham Midland Catholic News*, Jan. 16, 1932, 12.
16. Kavanagh, *Secret Muses*, 143; "Employment Agency of Training School Licenses," *Era*, June 8, 1932, 22.
17. 1921 Census of England & Wales shows Coleman Goodman, 40, as a cinema proprietor.
18. "Frank Looks at the News," *Era*, Mar. 6, 1935, 7; "Frank Looks at the News," *Era*, Mar. 13, 1935, 16; Buddy Bradley School of Stage Dancing (advertisement), *Stage*, Apr. 11, 1935, 3, Jan. 30, 1936, 3, and Dec. 3, 1936, 2; Wilkinson, "He Gives the Stars Their Legs."
19. Photo, *Picturegoer*, Mar. 7, 1936, 15; Kelly's London Directories, Reel 150 (1936), Westminster Archives.
20. Gardiner, *The Thirties*, 630; Matera, *Black London*, 149.
21. Wilkinson, "He Gives the Stars Their Legs"; De Mille, *Dance to the Piper*, 18; Smith, "How One American Fares Abroad."
22. "Looking for the Stars of the Future," *Evening Telegraph* (Dundee), Aug. 7, 1933, 2; *Magic Nights*, two undated programs, courtesy Jane Pritchard, Victoria & Albert Museum; "The Theatres," *Truth*, Jan. 4, 1933, 18.
23. Smith, "How One American Fares Abroad"; Wilkinson, "He Gives the Stars Their Legs"; "The Trade Shows," *Era*, May 13, 1936, 12; Matera, *Black London*, 154.
24. "Looking for the Stars of the Future," *Evening Telegraph* (Dundee), Aug. 7, 1933, 2; IJS, 5.

CHAPTER 12: ON POINTE WITH FREDERICK ASHTON AND NOËL COWARD

1. Sir Frederick Ashton, interview by Don McDonagh, May 29, 1970, JRDD archives; Frederic Franklin, interview by Betsy Baytos, for her upcoming documentary on eccentric dancing; "Frederic Franklin, Inventive Ballet Star," *New York Times*, May 5, 2013, section B, 10; Tina Sutton, *The Making of Markova: Diaghilev's Baby Ballerina to Groundbreaking Icon* (New York: Pegasus, 2013), 210.
2. Kavanagh, *Secret Muses*, 143; "Shop Talk," *Era*, Mar. 2, 1932, 2; Sutton, *The Making of Markova*, 211.
3. Hughes, *Second Movement*, 104.
4. Hughes, *Second Movement*, 106.
5. Kavanagh, *Secret Muses*, 143.
6. Hughes, *Second Movement*, 168.
7. Spike Hughes, "Dancing Master," *Daily Herald* (London), Dec. 20, 1935, 16; Hughes, *Second Movement*, 106–7; Kavanagh, *Secret Muses*, 143.
8. Vaughan, *Frederick Ashton*, 78; Sutton, *The Making of Markova*, 197, 210; Ross Adler, "Buddy Bradley Puts the Wiggle into Show Business," *John Bull*,

Dec. 5, 1953, 18; "England Laughs at America," *Baltimore Afro-American*, June 11, 1932, 16; Sutton, *The Making of Markova*, 60, 162, 199, 211.

9. "A Remarkable Ballet," *Northern Whig*, June 4, 1932, 6; Hughes, *Second Movement*, 106–7; Arnold L. Haskell, *The Ballet in England* (London: New English Weekly, 1932), 25.
10. Vaughan, *Frederick Ashton*, 44.
11. Hughes, *Second Movement*, 175, 177.
12. Vaughan, *Frederick Ashton*, 44; Kavanagh, *Secret Muses*, 144; Katherine Sorley Walker, "The Camargo Society," *Dance Chronicle* 18, no. 1 (1995): 48; "Camargo Society," *Sunday Times*, June 12, 1932, 7.
13. "Ballet Is Coming Back," *Era*, June 29, 1932, 3; Arnold L. Haskell, *The Ballet in England* (London: New English Weekly, 1932), 24; "Camargo Ballet," *Manchester Guardian*, June 7, 1932, 8; *Morning Post*, June 7, 1932 (found in clipping files, JRDD); Buddy Bradley Puts the Wiggle into Show Business," *John Bull*, Dec. 5, 1953, 19; "Rio Grande and High Yellow," *Harper's Bazaar*, July 1932, 22–23.
14. Beryl de Zoete, "The Camargo Ballet Season," *Monthly Musical Record*, July–Aug. 1932, 133; Vaughan, *Frederick Ashton*, 78.
15. Morris, *Frederick Ashton's Ballets*, 65; Frederick Ashton, *Les Masques*, film, revived by Franklin White, 1994, call no. MGZIA4-2165, JRDD; Vaughan, *Frederick Ashton*, 145.
16. Maurice Leonard, *Markova, the Legend: The Authorised Biography* (London: Hodder & Stoughton, 1995), 117; "The Camargo Society," *Observer*, June 12, 1932, 13.
17. Maurice Dancer, "Harlem Night by Night," *Pittsburgh Courier*, July 23, 1932, A6.
18. "The Genius of Noël Coward," *Northern Whig*, July 18, 1932, 6; "Noël Again," *Sunday Dispatch* (London), July 17, 1932, 15; "Mr. Coward's Revue," *Times*, Sept. 17, 1932, 8; "Mr. Cochran Getting Ready," *Manchester Guardian*, Aug. 18, 1932, 8.
19. "Shavian Wit and Immaculate Coward-ice," *Bystander*, Sept. 28, 1932, 591; "Dancing Thro Life," *Reynold's Illustrated News*, Mar. 3, 1935, 23; Max Rivers (advertisement), *Stage*, Feb. 21, 1929, 17; obituary, Graham Payn, *Independent*, Nov. 29, 2005; "Chit Chat," *Stage*, Sept. 29, 1932, 10; Harding, *Cochran*, 147.
20. Noël Coward, *Excerpts from Words and Music*, film, v1932, Noël Coward Foundation; "Mr. Coward's Revue," *Times*, Sept. 17, 1932, 8; "Low Down Dances," *Dance Magazine*, Sept. 1927, 38; Ivor Brown, "This Week's Theatre," *Observer*, Sept. 18, 1932, 15.
21. "Shavian Wit and Immaculate Coward-ice," *Bystander*, Sept. 28, 1932, 591; "Plays of the Week," *Sphere*, Sept. 24, 1932, 474.
22. Alan Bott, "Entertainments a la Carte, " *Tatler*, Oct. 5, 1932, 22–23.
23. Vaughan, *Frederick Ashton*, 40, 62.
24. "Low Down Dances," *The Dance Magazine*, Sept. 1927, 38.
25. "Theatre Great," *Bayswater Chronicle*, Nov. 5, 1932, 7; "Shavian Wit and Immaculate Coward-ice," *Bystander*, Sept. 28, 1932, 591; "Hollywood Snaps Up Steffi Duna," *Picturegoer Weekly*, Oct. 21, 1933, 7.

CHAPTER 13: BALLYHOO TO THE FOLIES BERGÈRE

1. Eddleston, *Zelia Raye*, 23.
2. "The Theatres," *Bystander*, Feb. 8, 1933, 238; "Dance and Theatre Clubs," *Times*, Nov. 6, 1933, 1; IJS, 7B; "London Theatre," *Stage*, Feb. 22, 1934, 10.
3. Pierce, *Billy Pierce*, 22; IJS, Herbert Harper transcript.
4. Classified advertisement, *Evening Standard*, Apr. 28, 1933, 20. Kavanagh, *Secret Muses*, 78; The Ballet Club, "A Special Programme," program, presented Nov. 27, 1932.
5. Alan Bott, "Entertainment a la Carte," *Tatler*, Apr. 5, 1933, 22; "Ballyhoo Revue at the Comedy," *Manchester Guardian*, Dec. 23, 1932, 8.
6. "London Theatres," *Stage*, Dec. 30, 1932, 18; *Ballyhoo*, program, Comedy Theatre, London; "Meet *Ballyhoo*," *Sketch*, Jan. 11, 1933, 73.
7. "Ballyhoo at the May Fair" (advertisement), *Sunday Times*, May 29, 1933, 19; Ivan H. Browning, "Across the Pond," *Chicago Defender*, Feb. 4, 1933, 5.
8. "Yours Sincerely," *Stage*, Feb. 22, 1934, 10; "Grace and Acrobatics," *Manchester Evening News* Jan. 16, 1934, 9.
9. "The Bronte Sisters in Revue," *Yorkshire Post*, July 8, 1933, 16.
10. "Second Thoughts on First Nights," *Bystander*, July 19, 1933, 110, 111; "London Theatres," *Stage*, July 13, 1933, 10; Alan Bott, "Entertainment a la Carte," *Tatler*, Aug. 2, 1933, 210-211; Frederic Franklin, interview by Betsy Baytos, for her upcoming documentary on eccentric dancing.
11. Kavanagh, *Secret Muses*, 90, 97, 150; Lewis, *When Harlem Was in Vogue*, 169; "Stein Opera is Elegant Performance," *Hartford Courant*, Feb. 9, 1934, 1.
12. "Peter Burnup's Parade," *Era*, Apr. 5, 1933, 2.
13. "Trocabaret," *Gloucestershire Echo*, Apr. 7, 1933, 4; "London Clubs and Cabarets—Trocadero Restaurant, 1933," British Pathé, May 15, 1933, https:www.britishpathe.com/asset/65011/.
14. "Revels in Rhythm," *Era*, Apr. 5, 1933, 18.
15. Photo caption, *Bystander*, June 7, 1933, 440.
16. "A Waterside Road House, Stage Version," *Sketch*, Sept. 27, 1933, 29; *Nice Goings On*, program, Strand Theatre.
17. "Provincial Productions," *Stage*, Aug. 31, 1933, 10; "Nice Goings On," *Leeds Mercury*, Sept. 15, 1933, 4; "Nice Goings On," *Era*, Aug. 30, 1933, 6; Harold Conway, "New Fashions in Musical Shows," *Daily Mail*, Sept. 26, 1933, 21; "Nice Goings On," *Sunday Mirror*, Sept. 17, 1933, 26.
18. "The Town by Autolycus," *Sunday Times*, Sept. 3, 1933, 13; Eason, *No Intermissions*, 102; "Volunteers for Charity," *Times*, Dec. 6, 1932, 17; "Kit Kat Club," *Daily Telegraph*, Oct. 28, 1932, 15; "Debutantes in Cabaret," *Daily Mail*, Dec. 6, 1933, 11.
19. "Backstage Folies en Folie," *Eve and Britannia*, June 1, 1934, 83; Baral, *Revue*, 243; Perry, *Bluebell*, 61.
20. Patrick O'Connor, *Josephine Baker* (London: Jonathan Cape, 1988), 41.
21. "Dark Doings," *Era*, June 28, 1933, 16; "Appearing in Public and Private—Photographs of Henri Wessels," *Gods and Foolish Grandeur* blog, Oct. 7, 2022, https://godsandfoolishgrandeur.blogspot.com/2022/10

/appearing-in-public-appearing-in.html; *Folies en Folie*, program, Folies Bergère, 1933–34.

22. *Folies en Folie*, program, Folies Bergère, 1933–34 (Thérèse Clément created the masks for Messel).
23. Stearns and Stearns, *Jazz Dance*, 277.
24. Castle, *The Folies Bergère*, 122; "Legend Leads Blue Bell Girls," *Liverpool Echo*, Jan. 10, 1986.

CHAPTER 14: SEDUCTION AND THE CAMERA'S EYE

1. "Dancers on the Spot: Buddy Bradley," *Film Weekly*, Apr. 4, 1936, 8–9; Ries, "Albertina Rasch," 287; Spivak, *Buzz*, 48.
2. "Pulse of the Studios," *Kinematograph Weekly*, Sept. 29, 1932, 46; "News and Gossip," *Film Weekly*, Feb. 10, 1933, 5.
3. "Films for Christmas," *Times*, Dec. 24, 1934, 8; Wright, *Cheer Up!*, 4; "Britain's First Color Film," *Daily Herald*, Oct. 20, 1934, 3.
4. "B.I.P. Completes Three," *Kinematograph*, Nov. 22, 1934, 47.
5. "Colour in British Film," *Picturegoer*, Nov. 3, 1934, 8; Bourne, *Black in the British Frame*, 71; Mayes and Whitfield, *An Inconvenient Black History*, 109.
6. "B.I. Pictures First with Colors," *Derry Journal*, Nov. 12, 1934, 9; "Paris Fantasie" (advertisement), *Daily News* (London), Sept. 15, 1933, 5.
7. *Dance Magazine*, Oct. 1971, 35.
8. Josephine Botting, curator, 20th Century Films, British Film Institute, Aug. 27, 2024.
9. Letter Dorothy Bradley to Stephen Bourne, Jan. 12, 1991.
10. Matera, *Black London*, 154–58.
11. James Agate, "Oh, Daddy!" *Tatler*, Apr. 3, 1935, 8.
12. C. A. Lejeune, "Films of the Week," *Observer*, Dec. 8, 1935, 14.
13. "Twickenham," *Era*, June 26, 1935, 6.
14. "Flanagan and Allen," *Era*, Oct. 16, 1935, 14.

CHAPTER 15: THE GAUGUIN OF THE DANCE

1. "Entertainment a la Carte," *Tatler*, Aug. 28, 1935, 396–97.
2. Advertisement for Bradley's school, *Era*, Aug. 7, 1935, 6.
3. "A Polished Spectacle," *Manchester Guardian*, Mar. 22, 1934, 11.
4. "Farjeon's Saucy Review," *Era*, Mar. 29, 1934, 20; "London Theatres," *Stage*, Apr. 26, 1934, 10; "When Marriage Is Boring," *Daily Mail*, Apr. 25, 1934, 8.
5. Eason, *No Intermissions*, 102, 104; "London Theatres," *Stage*, Apr. 26, 1934, 10.
6. Program, *Lucky Break*; J. T. Grein, "Criticisms in Cameo," *Sketch*, Oct. 17, 1934, 136.
7. "Provincial Productions," *Stage*, Sept. 20, 1934, 11; "Henson and Heather," *Sketch*, Oct. 10, 1934, 92; "Second Thoughts on First Nights," *Bystander*, Oct. 16, 1934, 10; "Lucky Break," *Times*, Oct. 3, 1934, 10; "At the Theatre," *Country Life*, Oct. 13, 1934, 54; program, *Lucky Break*, Strand Theatre.

8. "John Burk Attending Dance Congress," *Binghamton Press*, Oct. 1, 1934, 8; passenger list, CGT "Paris," arriving Dec. 21, 1934.
9. "Round the Show World," *Era*, Jan. 30, 1935, 16.
10. "Char-a-Bang," *Stage*, Apr. 4, 1935, 7.
11. "Let's Go Gay," *Stage*, Apr. 25, 1935, 10; "The Embassy," *Stage*, Apr. 4, 1935, 10; "Plays Abroad," *Variety*, May 15, 1935, 56.
12. Ethan Mordden, *Sing for Your Supper: The Broadway Musical in the 1930s* (New York: Palgrave Macmillan, 2005), 2, 6, 71, 73.
13. De Mille, *Dance to the Piper*, 184.
14. J. T. Grein, "World of the Theatre," *Illustrated London News*, June 22, 1935, 1128; "Shows Worth Seeing," *Illustrated Sporting and Dramatic News*, Dec. 27, 1935, 676; "Anything Goes," *Illustrated Sporting and Dramatic News*, Aug. 16, 1935, 343; "You're the Top," *Bystander*, Nov. 6, 1935, 225; "Anything Goes," *Stage*, June 20, 1935, 10.
15. Mordden, *Sing for Your Supper*, 72–73.

CHAPTER 16: DANCING ON THE CEILING

1. "He Gives the Stars Their Legs," *Picturegoer*, Mar. 7, 1936, 15; Matthews, *Over My Shoulder*, 118; Low, *Film Making in 1930s Britain*, 143; "Uncrowned King of Dance," *Stage*, Dec. 3, 1998, 11; "Dancers on the Spot," *Film Weekly*, Apr. 4, 1936, 8–9.
2. Kobal, *Gotta Sing, Gotta Dance*, 95.
3. "On the Screen," *Hendon and Finchley Times*, Sept. 28, 1934, 18 ; Matthews, *Over My Shoulder*, 139, 142.
4. Advertisement for the Buddy Bradley school, *Stage*, Jan. 30, 1936, 2; Low, *Film Making in 1930s Britain*, 137.
5. Kobal, *Gotta Sing, Gotta Dance*, 95, 100.
6. "Dancers on the Spot," *Film Weekly*, Apr. 4, 1936, 8–9; Spike Hughes, "Dancing Master," *Daily Herald*, Dec. 20, 1935, 16; Matthews, *Over My Shoulder*, 26, 139.
7. "Summing up Film Fashion," *Daily News* (London), May 12, 1936, 4; "It's Love Again," *Shields News* (Northumberland), Jan. 26, 1936, 6.
8. "Love Again Has a Staircase Complex," *Sydenham, Forest Hill, and Penge Gazette*, Jan. 31, 1936, 10.
9. Croce, *The Fred Astaire & Ginger Rogers Book*, 57–59; Brian Seibert, email exchange, Mar. 5, 2025.
10. IJS, 5.
11. "Jessie Matthews' Best Film," *Era*, Jan. 27, 1938, 11.
12. "A Mile of Dance," *Kinematograph Weekly*, Nov. 18, 1937, 44; Thornton, *Jessie Matthews*, 143.
13. "Sailing Along," *Monthly Film Bulletin*, Jan. 1938, 11.
14. *This Is Your Life*, episode on Jessie Matthews, BBC, Mar. 4, 1961.

CHAPTER 17: TOP HAT AND TAILS

1. Michael Marshall, *Top Hat and Tails: The Story of Jack Buchanan* (London: Elm Tree, 1978), 30, 36, 44, 45.

2. "Jack Buchanan and June, 1925," British Pathé, April 16, 1925, https://www.britishpathe.colm/asset/63216/.
3. Marshall, *Top Hat and Tails*, 11.
4. Low, *Film Making in 1930s Britain*, 247; "Brewsters' Millions," *Worthing Gazette*, July 31, 1935, 3; "Reeling Around London," *Hollywood Reporter*, June 6, 1934, 7.
5. Marshall, *Top Hat and Tails*, 77.
6. R. J. Whitley, "Plane Holds Up Britain's: Shock for Hollywood Director—Brewster's Millions Secrets," *Daily Mirror*, Oct. 5, 1934, 22–23; "On with the Dance," *Era*, Sept. 26, 1934, 6; "Film Topic by Globe," *Picturegoer*, Nov. 3, 1934, 32.
7. "Corsican Roll and Side-Walk," *Daily Mirror* (London), Feb. 20, 1935, 12; "What Is the Caranga?" *New York Times*, Mar. 31, 1935, x4; Herbert Harris, "Our Busby Berkeley," *Film Weekly*, Jan. 25, 1935, 12; "British and Proud of It," *Picturegoer*, Jan. 25, 1935, 23.

CHAPTER 18: FOLLOW THE SUN TO HAPPY RETURNS

1. "Pleasures in Advance," *Sunday Times*, May 8, 1938, 6; "Gaumont ADS," *Era*, May 9, 1934, 16; "BIP's 5th Annual Ball," *Kinematograph*, Nov. 8, 1934, 55; Brandon, *One More Step!*, 14, 21, 153.
2. "Answers to Correspondents," *Era*, Aug. 29, 1934, 15; "Times Square: Chatter—London," *Variety*, Sept. 25, 1935, 76; Edgar Wiggins, "Across the Pond," *Chicago Defender*, Nov. 30, 1935, 8, and Feb. 22, 1936, 8.
3. Ad for Billy Pierce Studio, *The Dance Magazine*, Dec. 1927, 6; Riley, *The Astaires*, footnote 17; Luce papers, JRDD.
4. "Follow the Sun," *Stage*, Jan. 2, 1936, 19; "The Lady with the Tap," *Theatre World*, Mar. 1936, 118; "Follow the Sun," *Era*, Jan. 1, 1936, 14; Claire Luce papers, JRDD; "Spends $8K to Decorate," *Pittsburgh Courier*, Mar. 20, 1937, 2.
5. Rusty M. Frank, *Tap!* (New York: William Morrow, 1990), 122, 123; Seibert, *What the Eye Hears*, 250, 270; Allan McMillan, "Theater Chat," *Baltimore Afro-American*, Dec. 28, 1935, 8.
6. Frank, *Tap!*, 124; "Follow the Sun," *Era*, Jan. 1, 1936, 14; Jeni Le Gon, interview by Betsy Baytos for her upcoming documentary on eccentric dance.
7. "Provincial Productions," *Stage*, June 25, 1936, 10; "How High Can a Little Bird Fly?" *Illustrated Sporting and Dramatic News*, July 17, 1936, 137; "Blackbirds at the Gaiety," *Era*, July 15, 1936, 6; IJS, 8.
8. Stearns and Stearns, *Jazz Dance*, 167.
9. *Blackbirds of 1936*, program, Lyceum Theatre; "At the Theatre," *Country Life*, July 18, 1936, 69.
10. "Provincial Productions," *Stage*, June 25, 1936, 10; Hill, *Brotherhood in Rhythm*, 119.
11. Stephen Bourne, *Black in the British Time Frame*, 80; Ross Adler, "Buddy Bradley Puts the Wiggle into Show Business," *John Bull*, Dec. 5, 1953, 19.
12. "Television," *Daily News* (London), Jan. 6, 1937, 9; "London Television Programmes," *Liverpool Daily Post*, Jan. 8, 1937, 4.

13. "Swing Song, " *Radio Times*, Feb. 22, 1939, 48; Leonard G. Feather, "Signature Tune," *Radio Times*, Feb. 17, 1939, 6; "Blackpool Revue," *Lancashire Daily*, May 27, 1938, 7; "Blackpool Walk Fascinates Dance Teachers," *Era*, July 28, 1938, 10.
14. Beatrice Lillie, photo caption, *Bystander*, Aug. 3, 1938, 175; *Happy Returns*, program; Harold Conway, "Mr. Cochran Brings Us a New Dance," *Daily Mail*, May 17, 1938, 4; Ivor Brown, "Happy Returns," *Observer*, May 22, 1938, 15; "Happy Returns," *Times*, May 20, 1938, 14; Richard Clowes, "Plays and Players," *Sunday Times*, May 8, 1938, 6.

CHAPTER 19: DANCING IN THE BLITZ

1. Matthews, *Over My Shoulder*, 162.
2. "Reviews for Showmen," *Kinematograph Weekly*, Feb. 15, 1945, 39.
3. Panter-Downes, *London War Notes*, 68; "London Clamps Down on Italians," *Variety*, July 3, 1940, 38; "London," *Variety*, Aug. 27, 1941, 53; "All Clear at Aldershot," *Times*, Jan. 25, 1940, 4; London Theatres," *Stage*, Dec. 28, 1939, 13; "It's Time to Dance," *Variety*, Aug. 11, 1943, 44.
4. "Palace Theatre," *Times*, Apr. 17, 1942, 6; "Full Swing," *Sketch*, July 14, 1942, 42; "Victoria Palace," *Stage*, Apr. 1, 1943, 5.
5. "Tuesday Radiogram," *Radio Times*, Sept. 24, 1943, 5; "CBC Management Reorg," *Variety*, Nov. 10, 1943, 51.
6. Baral, *Revue*, 231.
7. Herbert Farjeon, "The Theatre," *Bystander*, Feb. 21, 1940, 229; "Lights Up! at the Savoy," *Sketch*, May 1, 1940, 140; Alan Bott, "Lights Up!" *Tatler*, Feb. 21, 1940, 244; "On the Stage," *Leicester Mercury*, June 13, 1939, 5; "Black Vanities," *Guardian*, Apr. 26, 1941, 8.
8. "Theatre Notes," *Evening Standard*, Mar. 24, 1941, 8.
9. "Revue in the Making," *Tatler*, May 28, 1941, 219; "New Revue Cut by Police," *Daily Telegraph*, Apr. 2, 1941, 6.
10. "Spends $8K to Decorate," *Pittsburgh Courier*, Mar. 20, 1937, 2.
11. "Last Night's Shows," *Daily Herald*, Sept. 24, 1937; "Theatre," *Truth*, May 25, 1938, 710; "Principal Boys Go into Training," *Sketch*, Dec. 11, 1940, 353.
12. *Mother Goose*, program, Coliseum; "A Principal Boy Gets Ready," *Picture Post*, Dec. 26, 1942, 19; "Christmas Plays," *Observer*, Dec. 27, 1942.
13. "Britain's No. 1 Showman," *Tatler*, Nov. 19, 1941, 20; "The Opera House," *Manchester Guardian*, Apr. 2, 1942, 6; Philip Page, "New Plays in London," *Sketch*, June 6, 1942, 30.
14. "Palace Theatre," *Times*, Apr. 17, 1942, 6; "Full Swing," *Sketch*, July 14, 1942, 42; *Full Swing*, program, Palace Theatre.
15. "Follow the Girls," *Times*, Oct. 26, 1945; Adrian Wright, *West End Broadway*, 24.
16. Kurt Albert and Klaus Bleis (Tap & Tray), "Pete Nugent—Public Tapper No. 1," *German Tap Magazine*, Jan.–Apr. 2023, 5; IJS, 7; Stearns and Stearns, *Jazz Dance*, 161.
17. Bruce Forsyth, *Strictly Bruce: Stories of My Life* (London: Penguin Random House, 2015), 14; Forsyth, *Bruce*, 22, 23, 132.

18. Brandon, *One More Step!*, 21–22, 24–26.
19. "The Palace Theatre," *Stage*, Sept. 30, 1943, 5; "Something in the Air," *Sketch*, Nov. 17, 1943, 270, 271; "Palace Theatre," *Times*, Sept. 24, 1943, 6.
20. "Fine Feathers," *Stage*, Sept. 12, 1945, 4, and Oct. 18, 1945, 1.
21. "Fine Feathers," *Manchester Evening News*, Sept. 26, 1945, 3; "Prince of Wales Theatre," *Times*, Oct. 12, 1945, 6; "The Theatre," *Tatler*, Oct. 31, 1945, 134.

CHAPTER 20: ALL THAT JAZZ

1. "Left or Right?" *Sunday People*, Nov. 13, 1949, 5; Seibert, *What the Eye Hears*, 311.
2. Manning and Millman, *Frankie Manning*, 203; Ray Ellington and Buddy Bradley, "The Truth About Bebop!" *Musical Express*, Sept. 10, 1948, 4.
3. *Here Come the Boys*, program, Savile Theatre; "Spectacle, Fun, and Satire in New Musical," *Aberdeen Press and Journal*, Feb. 4, 1946, 4.
4. Seibert, *What the Eye Hears*, 205.
5. "Walking on Air," *Kinematograph Weekly*, Nov. 7, 1946, 25; "Walking on Air," *Picturegoer*, Jan. 4, 1947, 15.
6. "Evidence at the Inquest on John Worthy," n.d., courtesy of Johnny Worthy, Jr.
7. Manning and Millman, *Frankie Manning*, 204–7.
8. "Tough on Trinder," *Birmingham Gazette*, Apr. 7, 1947, 2; recorded interview with Mabel Lee, Nov. 16, 2017, JRDD.
9. Kurt Albert and Klaus Bleis, "A Tribute to Carnell Lyons," *ITA Magazine*, Mar. 2002, n.p.
10. Albert and Bleis, "A Tribute to Carnell Lyons."
11. Brandon, *One More Step!*, 60.
12. "Show Talk," *What's On in London*, Aug. 1, 1947, 157; Brandon, *One More Step!*, 14.
13. Brandon, *One More Step!*, 57, 61–62.
14. IJS, 8; "Caribbean Rhapsody," *Stage*, June 10, 1948, 8; "Renowned Scholar," *Sphere*, Oct. 16, 1948, 23; "Ballet Circle: Katherine Dunham," *Stage*, Feb. 21, 1952, 10.
15. "Variety Gossip: Katherine Dunham Party," *Stage*, July 8, 1948, 3.
16. "Sauce Tartare," *Times*, May 19, 1949, 3.
17. "Keen Dancer," *Stage*, June 23, 1955, 4; *Sauce Tartare*, program, Cambridge Theatre.
18. "BBC Television Service," *Radio Times*, Sept. 2, 1949, 42; "Variety Stage," *Stage*, Oct. 27, 1949, 3; "Producer for Everyone," *Stage*, May 4, 1950, 1.
19. *Sauce Piquante*, program, Cambridge Theatre.

CHAPTER 21: JAZZ MAESTRO

1. "Dainty Feet," *Guardian*, Dec. 26, 1974, 10.
2. "Dancing," *Daily Telegraph*, Aug. 5, 1950, 8.
3. Matera, *Black London*, 177–78.
4. "Buddy Bradley," *Ebony*, July 1, 1950, 61.

5. "International Ballet School," *Stage*, June 17, 1954, 8, 13; "Television Programmes," *Radio Times*, Feb. 21, 1958, 23.
6. IJS, 3.
7. IJS, 8; Stearns and Stearns, *Jazz Dance*, 340.
8. IJS, 3, 8.
9. "Buddy Bradley Tours Europe," *Ebony*, Nov. 1, 1954, 136; Will Gaines, Frank Holder, and Chris Parry, "Rhythm Tap, Jazz Improvisation, and Buddy Bradley in 1950s and 60s London," in Monaghan and Feeney, *Dancing at the Crossroads*, 17–20.
10. "Angela Rippon Meets the Hoofers," BBC, Sept. 8, 1981.
11. Wilkinson, "He Gives the Stars Their Legs"; advertisements, *Stage*, Nov. 18, 1982, 24, and Oct. 17, 1985, 16.
12. Andrew Barrow, *Quentin and Philip: A Double Portrait* (London: Pan Macmillan, 2002), 101, 104.
13. Stuart Hodes, *Onstage with Martha Graham* (Gainesville: University of Florida Press, 2021), 129.
14. "Bert Stimmel Auditions," *Stage*, Mar. 24, 1955, 14.
15. "Dalton Murray's World Famous Dancing Academy," *Stage*, Dec. 28, 1945, 5.
16. "Angela Rippon Meets the Hoofers," BBC, Sept. 8, 1981.

CHAPTER 22: TROUPES, TOURS, AND BABY LAURENCE

1. "A Budding Pavlova," *Stapleford News*, Dec. 22, 1934, 6; "Expert Dances," *Beeston Gazette*, Apr. 23, 1937, 2.
2. "Buddy Bradley," *Ebony*, July 1, 1950, 61.
3. "Ballet Workshop," *Stage*, Jan. 17, 1952, 8; "Buddy Bradley," *Ebony*, July 1, 1950, 61.
4. *Merely Players*, program, Theatre Royal, Drury Lane.
5. "Night Club Reviews," *Variety*, Mar. 25, 1953, 66.
6. *Accent on Rhythm*, program, Embassy Club.
7. "News Digest," *Stage*, Mar. 10, 2005, 1; "The Oldest Model in Town," *Sunday Telegraph*, Jan. 10, 1999, 37.
8. "British Queen at Command Vaud Show Prior to Empire Tour," *Variety*, Oct. 21, 1953, 2, and 65; "Royal Variety Supplement," *Stage*, Nov. 5, 1953, 9.
9. *Ancienne Belgique*, program, Dec. 19, 1953; "Buddy Bradley Tours Europe," *Ebony*, Nov. 1, 1954, 136.
10. IJS, 8: "Buddy Bradley Tours Europe," *Ebony*, Nov. 1, 1954, 136.
11. Gina Carlo, "Milan," *Variety*, Oct. 3, 1956, 86, and Oct. 17, 1956, 77; "Among the Dancers," *Stage*, Dec. 19, 1968, 17; "Obituaries," *Stage*, Oct. 5, 1995, 36.
12. "The Edmundo Ros Half-Hour," *Kinematograph Weekly*, June 13, 1957, 18; "BBC Children's Caravan," *Stage*, Sept. 20, 1956, 12; "£97,585 Man Left No Will," *Sunday Express* (London), Dec. 15, 1957, 7.
13. Buddy Bradley, advertisement, *Stage*, Oct. 3, 1957, 2; Buddy Bradley, advertisement, *Stage*, Jan. 5, 1961, 5.
14. "Ballet Program," *Stage*, May 21, 1953, 10; "Distinctive Ballets," *Bristol Evening Post*, June 21, 1953, 10; Monaghan and Feeney, *Dancing at the Crossroads*, 17–20.

15. Monaghan and Feeney, *Dancing at the Crossroads*, 17–20; "Nightbeat: Rhapsody in Rhythm," *Stage*, July 21, 1960, 7.
16. "Rhythm? Ah, Now," *Daily Express*, May 8, 1954, 6; "Norman Wisdom at Palladium," *Manchester Guardian*, May 7, 1954, 7; "Cabaret Man Got Heroin by a Trick," *Evening Standard*, Aug. 20, 1954; "Cabaret Man Fined," *Daily Express*, Aug. 21, 1954, 5; "The Grim Reaper," *New Pittsburgh Courier*, May 23, 1959, 22.
17. "Something to Make Spines Tingle," *Nottingham Evening News*, Apr. 21, 1960, 7; "Diary," *Television Mail*, Apr. 8, 1960, 2.
18. IJS, 3.
19. "Something Else," *New Yorker*, Apr. 9, 1960, 34.
20. "Cabaret," *Stage*, May 11, 1961, 21; "Going West," *Stage*, Aug. 10, 1961, 7; "Nightbeat," *Stage*, Nov. 2, 1961, 7; "Gaytime," *Stage*, Aug. 2, 1962, 32; "Holland Park Hamlet," *Stage*, Aug. 20, 1992, 33; "Calls for Next Week," *Stage*, Sept. 25, 1969, and Feb. 3, 1972, 2; Monaghan and Feeney, *Dancing at the Crossroads*, 17–20.

CHAPTER 23: THE SWERVING SIXTIES

1. *This Is Your Life*, segment on Jessie Matthews, BBC, Apr. 3, 1961.
2. *Tribute to Charles B. Cochran*, BBC Home Service, Mar. 7, 1961.
3. Buddy Bradley classes, advertisement, *Stage*, Apr. 25, 1963, 18.
4. Reg Barlow, "Two Hour Search for the Most Beautiful Girl," *Stage*, Aug. 17, 1961, 7; "Churchill's London," *Variety*, Aug. 16, 1961, 51–52.
5. Brandon, *One More Step!*, 21, 154.
6. Buddy Bradley classes, advertisement, *Stage*, Apr. 25, 1963, 18.
7. Buddy Bradley to Marshall Stearns, Dec. 10, 1963; 1962 Newport Jazz Festival flyer.
8. "Blackbirds of 1964," *Dalkeith Advertiser*, May 14, 1964, 7; "South African Harmony Kings," *Stage*, May 21, 1964, 7.
9. Pat Wallace, "On Plays," *Tatler*, Feb. 17, 1965, 43; B. A. Young, "Divorce Me, Darling!" *Financial Times*, Feb. 3, 1965, 22.
10. Pat Wallace, "On Plays," *Tatler*, Feb. 17, 1965, 43; C. J. Trewin, "The Arts Last Night," *Birmingham Post*, Feb. 2, 1965.
11. "A Pastiche of the Thirties," *Times*, Feb. 25, 1965.
12. Jack Bell, "Tonight's View," *Daily Mirror*, Dec. 2, 1965, 18; Esplanade Pavilion, advertisement, *Isle of Wight County Press*, July 2, 1966.

CHAPTER 24: BACK TO THE FUTURE

1. Brandon, *One More Step!*, 150.
2. Brandon, *One More Step!*, 152.
3. Brandon, *One More Step!*, 153.
4. General Register Office, application no. 13643832-1, Clarence Bradley Epps and Dorothy Pitchford Edghill, Registration District of Paddington.
5. "Who's Who, Baby?" (advertisement), *New York Times*, Jan. 8, 1968.
6. Dan Sullivan, "Cradle Mix-Up," *New York Times*, Jan. 30, 1968, 36; Brandon, *One More Step!*, 155–56.

7. "New Acts," *Variety*, Oct. 7, 1925, 6; Brenda Dixon Gottschild, *Waltzing in the Dark: African American Vaudeville and Race Politics in the Swing Era* (New York: St. Martin's, 2000), 19; "Mandy Green Gets Going in Nashville," *Billboard*, May 24, 1948, 26.
8. "Arrest," *Amsterdam News*, June 1, 1940, 2; Sing-Sing Prison, record, June 27, 1940; "New York Society," *Chicago Defender*, Sept. 29, 1934, 7; Howard Rye, "A Loud Voice and a Great Jazz Feeling," *Vintage Jazz Mart*, n.d., 170-joey-shields-2.pdf, 4.
9. "Black on Black: Up from Kansas City" (advertisement), *New York Times*, Mar. 23, 1972, 51.

EPILOGUE

1. Obituaries: *Variety*, July 26, 1972, 63; *Dance Magazine*, Sept. 1972, 14; *Daily News* (New York), July 20, 1972; *New York Times*, July 25, 1972; *Daily Telegraph*, Aug. 1, 1972; *Dancing Times*, Sept. 1972, 641; *Stage*, Aug. 3, 1972, 19.

BIBLIOGRAPHY

Baldwin, James, with an introduction by Edward P. Jones. *Notes of a Native Son*. Boston: Beacon, 2012.

Banes, Sally. *Writing Dancing in the Age of Postmodernism*. Hanover, NH: Wesleyan University Press, 1994.

Baral, Robert. *Revue: A Nostalgic Reprise of the Great Broadway Period*. New York: Fleet, 1962.

Beaton, Cecil. *The Wandering Years: Diaries, 1922–1939*. Boston: Little, Brown, 1961.

Beers, Paul. *City Contented, City Discontented: A History of Modern Harrisburg*. Harrisburg, PA: Midtown Scholar Press, 2011.

Bourne, Stephen. *Black in the British Frame: Black People in British Film and Television 1896–1996*. London: Cassell, 1998.

———. *Deep Are the Roots: Trailblazers Who Changed Black British Theatre*. Cheltenham: History Press, 2021.

Brandon, Johnny. *One More Step!* Brighton: Book Guild, 2008.

Breese, Charlotte. *Hutch*. London: Bloomsbury, 1999.

Bret, David. *The Mistinguett Legend*. New York: St. Martin's, 1990.

"Buddy Bradley: Nimble Ex-Harlemite Runs Most Successful Dance School in England with 500 Students." *Ebony*, July 1, 1950, 61–62.

"Buddy Bradley Tours Europe." *Ebony*, November 1, 1954, 136.

Caspary, Vera. *The Secrets of Grown-Ups: An Autobiography*. 1979. New York: McGraw-Hill, 2013.

Castle, Charles. *The Folies Bergère*. New York: Franklin Watts, 1985.

Clark, Stephen. *Living with Legends: The Story of the World Famous Clark Brothers*. Luton: Bartham, n.d.

Cochran, Charles B. *Showman Looks On*. London: J. M. Dent & Sons, 1945.

Coward, Noël. *Future Indefinite with the Unfinished Past Conditional*. London: Methuen Drama, 2004.

Croce, Arlene. *The Fred Astaire & Ginger Rogers Book*. New York: Galahad, 1972.

Decker, Todd. *Show Boat: Performing Race in an American Musical*. Oxford: Oxford University Press, 2013.

DeFrantz, Thomas F., ed. *Dancing Many Drums: Excavations in African American Dance*. Madison: University of Wisconsin Press, 2002.
DeMille, Agnes. *Dance to the Piper.* Boston: Little, Brown, 1952.
Douglas, Ann. *Terrible Honesty: Mongrel Manhattan in the 1920s*. New York: Farrar, Straus & Giroux, 1995.
Du Bois, W. E. B. With an introduction by David Levering Lewis. *Black Reconstruction in America: 1860–1880*. New York: Free Press, 1998.
———. With an introduction by Ibram X. Kendi. *The Souls of Black Folk*. New York: Penguin Random House, 2018.
Eddleston, Pamela. *Zelia Raye and the Development of Modern Theatre Dance*. London: Imperial Society of Teachers of Dancing, 2002.
Emery, Lynne Fauley. *Black Dance in the United States from 1619 to 1970*. Palo Alto, CA: National Press Books, 1972.
Federal Writers' Project. *Alabama Slave Narratives: A Folk History of Slavery in Alabama from Interviews with Former Slaves*. Bedford, MA: Applewood Books/Library of Congress, n.d.
Feldman, Lynne B. *A Sense of Place: Birmingham's Black Middle-Class Community, 1890–1930*. Tuscaloosa: University of Alabama Press, 1999.
Forsyth, Bruce. *Bruce: The Autobiography.* London: Sidgwick & Jackson, 2001.
Frank, Rusty E. *Tap! The Greatest Tap Dance Stars and Their Stories, 1900–1955*. New York: William Morrow, 1990.
Gaines, Caseen. *When Broadway Was Black: The Triumphant Story of the All-Black Musical That Changed the World.* Naperville, IL: Sourcebooks, 2023.
Gardiner, Juliet. *The Thirties: An Intimate History*. London: Harper, 2010.
———. *Wartime: Britain 1939–1945*. London: Hodder Headline, 2004.
Genovese, Eugene D. *Roll, Jordan, Roll: The World the Slaves Made*. New York: Pantheon, 1974.
Gomez, Michael. *Exchanging Our Country Marks: The Transformation of African Identities in the Colonial and Antebellum South*. Chapel Hill: University of North Carolina Press, 1998.
Gottschild, Brenda Dixon. *Digging the Africanist Presence in American Performance: Dance and Other Contexts*. Westport, CT: Praeger, 1998.
Graves, Robert, and Alan Hodge. *The Long Week End: A Social History of Great Britain, 1918–1939*. New York: Macmillan, 1941.
Harding, James. *Cochran*. London: Methuen, 1988.
Harmon, Evelyn Davis. "With Roots in Habersham." *Georgia Backroads* (Spring 2022): 19–21.
Hill, Constance Valis. *Brotherhood in Rhythm: The Jazz Tap Dancing of the Nicholas Brothers*. New York: Oxford University Press, 2000.
———. "Buddy Bradley: The Invisible Man of Broadway Brings Jazz Tap to London." *c2AM*, Society of Dance History Scholars, 15th US Conference, University of California, Riverside, 1992.
———. *Tap Dancing America: A Cultural History.* New York: Oxford University Press, 2010.

Hollis, Tim. *Memories of Downtown Birmingham: Where All the Lights Were Bright*. Charleston, SC: History Press, 2014.

Homans, Jennifer. *Mr. B*. New York: Random House, 2022.

Hughes, Langston. *The Big Sea*. New York: Alfred A. Knopf, 1940.

Hughes, Spike. *Second Movement: Continuing the Autobiography of Spike Hughes*. London: Museum Press, 1951.

Jenkins, Nelle Morris. *Pioneer Families of Sumter County*. Livingston, AL: Livingston, 1961.

Johnson, James Weldon. *Black Manhattan*. New York: Alfred A. Knopf, 1930.

Kavanagh, Julie. *Secret Muses: The Life of Frederick Ashton*. New York: Random House, 1996.

Kobal, John. *Gotta Sing, Gotta Dance: A Pictorial History of Film Musicals*. London: Hamlyn, 1971.

Lamonte, Edward Shannon. *Politics and Welfare in Birmingham, 1900–1975*. Tuscaloosa: University of Alabama Press, 1977.

Lewis, David Levering. *When Harlem Was in Vogue*. New York: Alfred A. Knopf, 1981.

———. *W. E. B. Du Bois: Biography of a Race, 1868–1919*. New York: Henry Holt, 1993.

Low, Rachael. *Film Making in 1930s Britain*. London: George Allen & Unwin, 1985.

Malone, Jacqui. *Steppin' on the Blues: The Visible Rhythms of African American Dance*. Urbana: University of Illinois Press, 1996.

Manning, Frankie, and Cynthia R. Millman. *Frankie Manning: Ambassador of Lindy Hop*. Philadelphia: Temple University Press, 2007.

Mason, Francis. *I Remember Balanchine: Recollections of the Ballet Master by Those Who Knew Him*. New York: Doubleday, 1991

Marshall, Michael. *Top Hat & Tails: The Story of Jack Buchanan*. London: Elm Tree, 1978.

Matera, Marc. *Black London: The Imperial Metropolis and Decolonization in the Twentieth Century*. Oakland: University of California Press, 2015.

Matthews, Jessie, with Muriel Burgess. *Over My Shoulder: An Autobiography*. New Rochelle, NY: Arlington House, 1974.

Mayes, Sean, and Sarah K. Whitfield. *An Inconvenient Black History of British Musical Theatre, 1900–1950*. London: Methuen Drama, 2022.

McDonagh, Don. *Martha Graham: A Biography*. New York: Praeger, 1973.

McGruder, Kevin. *Philip Payton: The Father of Black Harlem*. New York: Columbia University Press, 2021.

Milteer, Warren Eugene, Jr. *Beyond Slavery's Shadow: Free People of Color in the South*. Chapel Hill: University of North Carolina Press, 2021.

Monaghan, Terry, and Eileen Feeney, eds. *Dancing at the Crossroads: African Diasporic Dances in Britain*. London: Metropolitan University, 2002.

Mordden, Ethan. *Make Believe: The Broadway Musical in the 1920s*. New York: Oxford University Press, 1997.

Morris, Geraldine. *Frederick Ashton's Ballets: Style, Performance, Choreography*. Blinsted, Hampshire: Dance Books, 2012.

Panter-Downes, Mollie. *London War Notes, 1939–1945*. New York: Farrar, Straus & Giroux, 1971.
Perry, George. *Bluebell: The Authorized Biography of Margaret Kelly, Founder of the Legendary Bluebell Girls*. London: Pavilion, 1987.
Pierce, Lemoine De Leaver. *Billy Pierce: Dance Master, Son of Purcellville*. Leesburg, VA: Friends of the Thomas Balch Library, 2007.
Randel, Don M., Matthew Shaftel, and Susan F. Weiss, eds. *A Cole Porter Companion*. Urbana: University of Illinois Press, 2016.
Reid, Grant Harper. *Rhythm for Sale*. New York: self-published, 2012.
Raye, Zelia. *American Tap Dancing*. Rev. ed. London: Imperial Society of Teachers of Dancing, 1955.
Reynolds, Nancy, and Malcolm McCormick. *No Fixed Points: Dance in the Twentieth Century*. New Haven, CT: Yale University Press, 2003.
Ries, Frank W. D. "Sammy Lee: The Broadway Career." *Dance Chronicle* 9, no. 1 (1986), 141–218.
———. "Albertina Rasch: The Broadway Career." *Dance Chronicle* 6, no. 2 (1983), 95–137.
Riley, Kathleen. *The Astaires: Fred and Adele*. New York: Oxford University Press, 2012.
Rose, Phyllis. *Jazz Cleopatra: Josephine Baker in Her Time*. New York: Doubleday, 1989.
Sawyer, Gordon. *Northeast Georgia: A History*. Charleston, SC: Arcadia, 2001.
Seibert, Brian. *What the Eye Hears: A History of Tap Dancing*. New York: Farrar, Straus & Giroux, 2015.
Smith, J. Murray. "How One American Fares Abroad." *Chicago Defender*, Sept. 1, 1934, 11.
Smith, Louis Roycroft. *A History of Sumter County, Alabama, Through 1886*. Tuscaloosa: University of Alabama Press, 1988.
Spivak, Jeffrey. *Buzz: The Life and Art of Busby Berkeley*. Lexington: University Press of Kentucky, 2011.
Stearns, Marshall, and Jean Stearns. *Jazz Dance: The Story of American Vernacular Dance*. New York: Macmillan, 1968.
Steyn, Mark. *Broadway Babies Say Goodnight: Musicals Then and Now*. New York: Routledge, 1999.
Tarry, Ellen. *The Third Door: The Autobiography of an American Negro Woman*. Tuscaloosa: University of Alabama Press, 1992.
Taylor, Frank C., and Gerald Cook. *Alberta Hunter: A Celebration in Blues*. New York: McGraw-Hill, 1988.
Thornton, Michael. *Jessie Matthews: A Biography*. London: Granada, 1974.
Vaughan, David. *Frederick Ashton and His Ballets*. London: Dance Books, 1999.
Wilkinson, Charles. "He Gives the Stars Their Legs." *Picturegoer*, Mar. 7, 1936, 15.
Wilson, Fallin, Jr. *Uplifting the People: Three Centuries of Black Baptists in Alabama*. Tuscaloosa: University of Alabama Press, 2008.

Woll, Allen. *Black Musical Theatre: From Coontown to Dreamgirls*. Baton Rouge: Louisiana State University Press, 1989.

Wright, Adrian. *Cheer Up! British Musical Films, 1929–1945*. Woodbridge: Boydell, 2020.

———. *West End Broadway: The Golden Age of the American Musical in London*. Woodbridge: Boydell, 2012.

IMAGE CREDITS

Thaddeus Drayton and Rufus Greenlee: Billy Rose Theatre Division, New York Public Library for the Performing Arts
Connie's Inn: Photographs and Prints Division, Schomburg Center for Research in Black Culture, New York Public Library
Ad for the Billy Pierce Studio: © 1925, Penske Media Corporation
U. S. Thompson: Rutgers University Marshall Stearns Jazz Collection
Henry Le Tang with Gregory Hines: Frederick M. Brown/Getty Images Entertainment via Getty Images
Betty Compton: Keystone-France/Gamma Keystone via Getty Images
"Low Down Dancing": Jerome Robbins Dance Division, New York Public Library for Performing Arts
Pete, Peaches and Duke: Apeda, NY, Gary Lambert "Pete" Nugent Papers, Jerome Robbins Dance Division, New York Public Library for the Performing Arts
Clifton Webb: George Hoyningen-Huene/Condé Nast Collection via Getty Images
Eddie Rector: Rutgers University Marshall Stearns Jazz Collection
Bradley with Charles B. Cochran: © Illustrated London News Ltd./Mary Evans
Frederick Ashton: Hulton Deutsch/Corbis Historical via Getty Images
Alicia Markova: From the Alicia Markova Collection, Boston University Libraries, Howard Gotlieb Archival Research Center
Noël Coward: United Archives GmbH/Alamy Stock Photo
Male chorus line from *Words and Music*: Sasha/Hulton Archive via Getty Images
"Club Ballet": Billy Rose Theatre Division, New York Public Library for the Performing Arts
Ken "Snakehips" Johnson: Courtesy of the BFI National Archive. Licensed by Shutterstock.
George Balanchine with Arthur Mitchell: Photo by Martha Swope, © Billy Rose Theatre Division, New York Public Library for the Performing Arts
Jessie Matthews and Cyril Wells: Courtesy of the BFI National Archive. Licensed by Shutterstock.

Evergreen: Hulton Archive/Moviepix via Getty Images
"Book Worms": © Illustrated London News Ltd./Mary Evans
Nina Mae McKinney: De Carvalho Collection/Moviepix via Getty Images
Jeni LeGon: © Illustrated London News Ltd./Mary Evans
Florence Mills: National Portrait Gallery, Smithsonian Institution, © Condé Nast
Jessie Matthews: Courtesy of the BFI National Archive. Licensed by Shutterstock.
Bradley with Jack Buchanan: © Illustrated London News Ltd./Mary Evans
Patricia Burke at Radnor Lodge: William A. Atkins/Hulton Archive via Getty Images
Ballet at the Bradley studio: George Dallison/ Hulton Archive via Getty Images
Bradley rehearses Patricia Burke: Kurt Hutton/Picture Post Collection via Getty Images
Ebony: © 1950, EBONY. All rights reserved.
Ebony: © 1950, EBONY. All rights reserved.
Baby Laurence: © Raymond Ross Archives/CTSIMAGES
Carnell Lyons: Photo: Fradel Nogrady
Shirley Bassey: David Sim/Arena PAL
Glory Van Scott: Photo © AGIP/Bridgeman Images

INDEX